Murder, Mayhem, Pillage, and Plunder:
The History of the Lebanon
in the 18th and 19th Centuries

Mikhāyil Mishāqa.

Murder, Mayhem, Pillage, and Plunder

The History of the Lebanon
in the 18th and 19th Centuries
by
Mikhāyil Mishāqa

Translated from the Arabic by
W. M. Thackston, Jr.

State University of New York Press

Published by
State University of New York Press, Albany

Printed in the United States of America

For information, address State University of New York
Press, State University Plaza, Albany, N.Y., 12246

Photographs reproduced with permission from the
Harvard Semitic Museum.

Library of Congress Cataloging-in-Publication Data

Mishāqah, Mikhā'īl, 1799-1888.
Murder, mayhem, pillage and plunder.

Translation of: al-Jawāb 'alā iqtirāḥ al-aḥbāb.
Bibliography: p.
Includes index.
1. Lebanon—History—1516-1918. I. Thackston.
Wheeler M. (Wheeler McIntosh), 1944- . II. Title.
DS84.M5613 1988 956.92 87-18034
ISBN 0-88706-712-3
ISBN 0-88706-714-X (pbk.)

10 9 8 7 6 5 4 3 2 1

In Memoriam

Anne Royal

who conceived and initiated
the translation of this work.

Abbreviated Contents

Complete Contents

Part II: 1804-1820

Part III: 1820-1830

Part IV: 1831-1840

Part V: 1840-1873

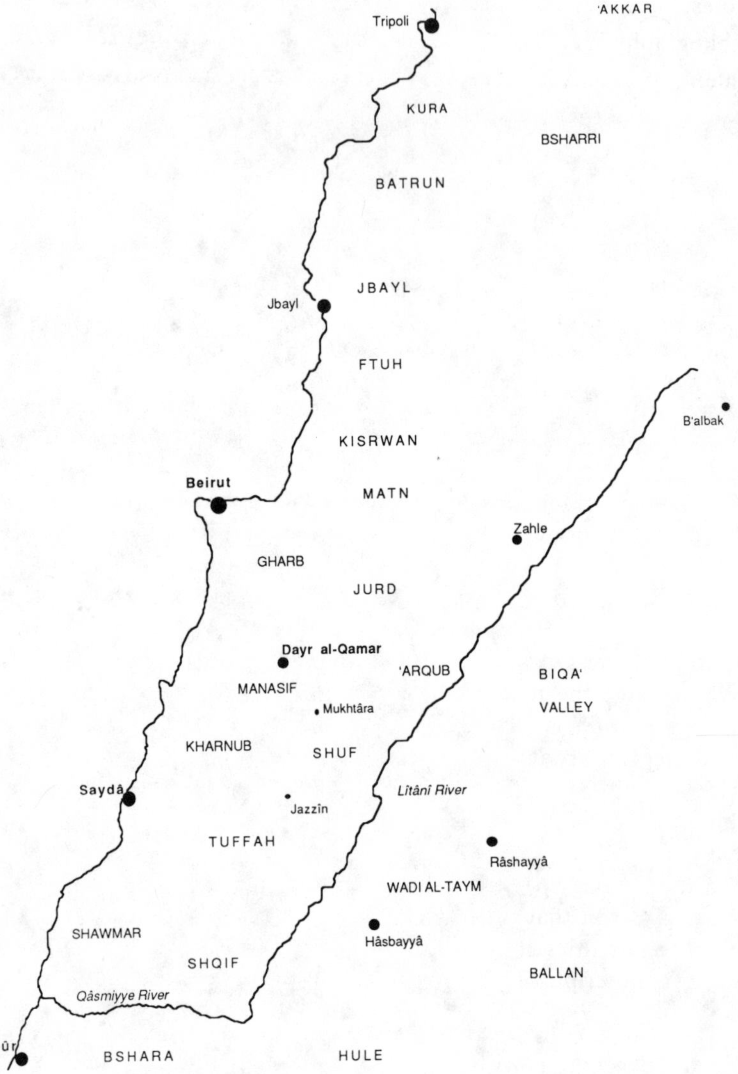
'AKKAR
Tripoli
KURA
BSHARRI
BATRUN
JBAYL
Jbayl
FTUH
B'albak
KISRWAN
Beirut
MATN
Zahle
GHARB
JURD
Dayr al-Qamar
'ARQUB
BIQA'
VALLEY
MANASIF
Mukhtâra
KHARNUB
SHUF
Saydâ
Lîtânî River
Jazzîn
TUFFAH
Râshayyâ
WADI AL-TAYM
Hâsbayyâ
SHAWMAR
SHQIF
BALLAN
Qâsmiyye River
Sûr
BSHARA
HULE

Preface

Mikhāyil Mishāqa's memoirs, entitled *al-Jawāb 'alā iqtirāḥ al-aḥbāb* ("response to a suggestion by beloved ones"), were edited by Assad Rustom and Soubhi Abou Chacra and published in an abbreviated from as *Muntakhabāt min al-Jawāb* &c. by the Lebanese Ministère de l'Éducation Nationale et des Beaux-Arts, Direction des Antiquités (Textes et Documents Historiques, 2. Beirut: Catholic Press, 1955). The Beirut edition was based upon a manuscript version in the possession of the Greek Orthodox Patriarchate in Damascus and believed by the editors to be in Mishāqa's own hand.[1] However, suppressed from publication were all portions of the text that might have caused offense to any religious community in the Lebanon. Since these portions are by and large the most interesting and of the greatest historical value, this translation is based on the manuscript of the work contained in the Jaffet Library at the American University of Beirut (MS 956.9 M39jA), which Rustom and Abou Chacra believe to have been made by the Ṣarrūf family, well-known copyists in Damascus at the end of the nineteenth century.[2] The few significant differences between the printed version and the manuscript are noted in the translation, and the portions from the manuscript that were not included in the printed text are signaled.

Section titles have been taken from the table of contents of the AUB manuscript. The division into five roughly equal parts was made by the translator. Page numbers from the Beirut edition are included in the translated text in square brackets for easy reference. The material covered from page 228 to the end of the translation is lacking in the Beirut edition: page references in brackets therein refer to the page numbers of the AUB manuscript.

The rendering of Arabic names into English is a perennial problem, and it was decided to write personal names as Mishāqa spells them in Arabic. Mishāqa's own given name, Mikhāyil (Michael), is a good case in point: in all but one or two places he writes his name as it was generally pronounced, "Mikhāyil," not the classical form Mīkhā'īl. "Sid-Aḥmad" and some typically Lebanese family names like Ḥbaysh and Frayj have been written as pronounced and not classicized to "Sayyid-Aḥmad," "Ḥubaysh" or "Furayj." The spelling and pronunciation of the majority of personal names, classical and medieval, are identical, and they have been so written in English. Ecclesiastical names adopted by the clergy, such as Euthymius and Ignatius, are given in their more familiar Latinized forms and not transliterated from Arabic as "Afthīmiyūs" and "Ighnāṭiyūs." Toponyms without generally accepted English equivalents, many of which are of Aramaic origin anyway, are written in a compromise between transcription and transliteration from the Arabic spelling to render the local pronunciation as recorded in Anīs Frayḥa's *Mu'jam asmā' al-mudun wa'l-qurā al-lubnāniyya* (Beirut: Maktabat Lubnān, 1972) and Stefan Wild's *Libanesische Ortsnamen: Typologie und Deutung* (Beirut, 1973)—thus "Hlāliyye" and "Bshāra," not "Hilāliyya" or "Bishāra."

Ottoman Turkish words and titles are transliterated as spelled in the Arabic script; modern Turkish spelling is given for these in Appendix A.

Appendix B is a genealogical chart of the Shihāb emirs of Mount Lebanon who are mentioned in Mishāqa's memoirs. It has been constructed from information given by Ṭannūs al-Shidyāq in his *Akhbār al-a'yān fī jabal lubnān*, edited by Fouad E. Boustany (Beirut: Librairie Orientale, 1970), pp. 47ff., and by Iliya F. Harik, *Politics and Change in a Traditional Society: Lebanon, 1711-1845* (Princeton: Princeton University Press, 1968), p. 56f.

Appendix C consists of genealogical charts for the branches of the House of Shihāb in Ḥāṣbayyā and Rāshayyā and the shaykhs of the House of Jumblāṭ who figure in this work. The chart for the Ḥāṣbayyā emirs has been constructed based on information given by Mishāqa in the present work and on information scattered throughout Ḥaydar Aḥmad's *al-Ghurar al-ḥisān fī tawārīkh ḥawādith al-azmān*, edited by Asad Rustum and Fouad E. Boustany (Beirut: Imprimerie Catholique, 1933). The chart for the Rāshayyā emirs has been constructed from information based on a manuscript by Sayyid Aḥmad al-Bizrī, Mufti of Ṣaydā, that was found among the effects of A. Catafago, Austrian consul in Acre, and translated by Heinrich Fleischer, "Über das syrische Fürstenhaus der Benū-Schihāb," *ZDMG* 5 (1851): 46-59, and corroborated by information gleaned from Ḥaydar Aḥmad's *al-Ghurar al-ḥisān.*

Finally, it is with sadness that I acknowledge the initiator of this translation, Dr. Anne Royal, who had done much of the comparison between manuscript and printed text and, just before her untimely death in 1985, had begun the translation under the auspices of the National Endowment for the Humanities. It is to her memory that this work is dedicated.

Introduction

Mikhāyil Mishāqa was born in Rishmayyā, a small village in Mount Lebanon, on March 20, 1800, was raised in Dayr al-Qamar, then the seat of the ruling emirs of Mount Lebanon, and died in Damascus in 1888. His father Jirjis was a treasury official for Emir Bashīr II Shihāb of Mount Lebanon. Mikhāyil, following in his father's footsteps, was appointed fiscal manager to the emirs of the House of Shihāb in Ḥāṣbayyā. After the demise of the Shihāb emirs in 1841, he practiced medicine in Damascus and held the post of vice-consul for the United States of America, his conversion from Greek Catholicism to Protestantism undoubtedly responsible to some degree for this appointment.

Largely self-educated and raised, as he says, in a town where multiplication and division were unknown, while still quite young he sought out teachers and texts in astronomy, mathematics, music and medicine, in all of which fields, in addition to the trades to which he was unwillingly apprenticed by his father, he gained some proficiency. A forerunner of the religious and educational modernists of the late nineteenth century in the Levant, he has been described by Jurjī Zaydān as follows:

> Among the most extraordinary and commendable aspects of his character was that he saw and heard nothing without curiosity for its own sake, and he had such complete confidence in his intellectual capabilities that he believed he could learn anything he wanted to.[1]

In these memoirs, composed at the age of 73 at the request of a relative, Mishāqa follows the historical development of the region from the time of his grandfather, Ibrāhīm Mishāqa, a tax-farmer under the notorious Aḥmad Pasha al-Jazzār, down to the massacres known as the

"1860 Incident" in Damascus and the Lebanon. Much of the time he centers on the internal policies and intrigues of the ruling House of Shihāb, with whom both he and his father were closely connected, and the Shihābs' rocky relations with their Ottoman suzerains. During this period, in which an entity recognizable as the Lebanon of today can be seen emerging, Mount Lebanon, along with its neighboring regions, the Beirut coast, Ṣaydā, Acre, Tripoli and the Province of Damascus, suffered the upheavals of successive Ottoman pashas, not all of whom were benevolent in their administration, was invaded by Egypt, and saw the increasing influence and intervention of the Concert of Europe in the region.

Against the backdrop of historical events, Mishāqa includes in his narrative sketches and anecdotes that allow the reader a rare glimpse into the everyday life of the period: Mūsā Rizq's discovery of buried treasure (pp. 26-28); how Shaḥāda Fārḥī outwits a fraudulent *shaykh* and a clever Jewish bursar thwarts the Shaykh al-Islam's enemy (pp. 65-67); Sulaymān al-Ḥakīm's assassination attempts on Shaykh Bashīr Jumblāṭ and Emir Bashīr (pp. 78-85); the gruesome exploits of Zakhkhūr al-Sham'ūnī (pp. 88-92); the conscription of Ghālib Abī-'Ikr to strangulate prisoners (pp. 114-16); and the investigation of the murder of the Capuchin Padre Toma (pp. 193-200), an international *cause célèbre.* All these stories reflect something of intercommunal personal relations, the relationship between lord and peasant, ruler and subject—microcosmic views into society that are only rarely found in chronicles. Mishāqa's own narrow escape from death during the Damascus Massacre of 1860, still the only first-hand account of the incident in Arabic, is as valuable as a historical document as it is fascinating to read.

The language of the text is an unreformed, late medieval Arabic, construed with typical Middle Arabic syntax, often highly colloquialized and, as might be expected, replete with Ottomanisms. The late 19th-century "reclassicization" of literary Arabic came too late to influence Mishāqa's style, which is more reminiscent of the style used by 18th-century chroniclers of Damascus like Aḥmad al-Budayrī and Mīkhā'īl Burayk and the early 19th-century chronicler of the Lebanon, Ḥaydar Aḥmad al-Shihābī.[2]

Mishāqa by no means attempts an impartial analytical history of the area. An unabashed partisan of Emir Bashīr II (r. 1788-1840), whom he knew from childhood, he seldom misses an opportunity to justify the emir's political actions, in the deliberations behind which he often took part and in the thick of which he usually found himself. On the other hand, he is not a blind adherent of the Shihābs and reports dispassionately their foibles and weaknesses as well as their successes and strengths. The reports he gives of conversations and the attribution of motive he supplies must simply be taken at face value and assessed as the chronicling of an era seen through the eyes of an individual who was well acquainted with the personalities and intimately involved in the movements he describes. If his analysis of historical forces is not that of a modern person, he had the advantage of being an eyewitness to the events of his own lifetime. Yet, quite unlike a medieval chronicler, Mishāqa attempts to view the changes and upheavals in society with a new eye and prides himself on being an enlightened, "modern" man of the nineteenth century who has broken free of the shackles of the past. He does not simply list events in chronological order but gives relevant background information for his analysis of the topic at hand. Also, unlike earlier chroniclers, he is not concerned with his own community to the exclusion of all others.[3] Even if the history of his family was intimately connected with the history of the Greek Catholic community as a whole,[4] he and his contemporary Greek Catholic historians[5]

> were not trying to write a religious or an exclusive history of their community but perceived it as part of a more general development. They were especially interested in the immediate context in which the development of their community unfolded. For this purpose they recorded the rivalries between the Greek Catholic community and other minorities, . . . they discussed the relations of the Greek Catholics to the local rulers and their interaction with the Muslim environment, and they reflected upon the economic and political role the Greek Catholics played.[6]

The larger society into which Mishāqa was born was provincial, a remote backwater of a far-flung empire in decline. Mount Lebanon had been under nominal Ottoman control for centuries, but in practice the princes of the mountain, confirmed in their seats by the Ottoman governors of Ṣaydā, had enjoyed almost total autonomy so long as they remitted their taxes in full and on time. Damascus, the capital of the vast province of Syria, was of much more importance to the Ottomans, but even it was far from the splendors of court in Constantinople and a provincial capital at best. Left almost entirely to its own devices, the social order of the Lebanon was feudal, hierarchical, fixed and largely, if not entirely in practice, immutable: prince ruled clan chief, and clan chief alone was responsible to the prince for his clansmen. At the top of the social order were the princely houses with the status of emir (*amīr*), first among whom was the House of Shihāb. Next in rank were those who held the title *muqaddam*, followed by those who held the rank of *shaykh*, the lowest rank of the nobility. All below them were commoners (*'āmmiyya*), consisting of burghers and peasants. The great families held in fief tracts of land (*muqāṭa'a*) of varying size, for the administration and tax-collection of which they were responsible to the ruling emir. Unlike most areas in the Islamic world, where the temporary nature of the fief had prevented hereditary nobility from forming, among the predominantly Druze lords of the mountain the Druze chief "headed a feudal system based on hereditary land tenure, and was the overlord of a number of feudal families who controlled the various Druze districts."[7] When the Ma'n emirs spread their influence into the northern Lebanon, they introduced the Druze type of hereditary tenure throughout the country, and this system was maintained by the Shihābs. In his history of the Lebanon Emir Ḥaydar Aḥmad, a cousin of Emir Bashīr II, writes describing the appointment of the great houses to their fiefs:

> We have mentioned in this history of ours that Emir Ḥaydar, [our] ancestor, was the first of the emirs of the House of Shihāb to rule Mount Lebanon, and that he appointed deputies under himself over the fiefs of the mountain for the imperial (*mīrī*) taxes collected for the Ottoman Empire. The fief of the Matn was administered by the [emirs] of the House of Abullam', the fief of the Jurd by the shaykhs of the House of 'Abdul-Malik, the Upper Gharb by the shaykhs of the House of Talḥūq, the Lower Gharb by the emirs of the House of Arslān, and the Kisrwān mountain by the shaykhs of the House of Khāzin. This arrangement has lasted until now: the command and power are in the hands of the emirs of the House of Shihāb, under whose rule the fiefholders are. If any of them does anything displeasing to the ruler, he relieves him of control of his fief and puts another in his place to collect the imperial taxes.[8]

As the ruling emir enjoyed a large measure of autonomy from his Ottoman overlords, so too did the feudal lords enjoy a great deal of autonomy in their fiefs, where the ruling emir could not intervene unless asked. For instance, the ruling emir's seat was Bayt al-Dīn Palace (commonly known as Bteddīn) at Dayr al-Qamar, but the town itself was the territory of the House of Abū-Nakad. If a Nakadī liegeman committed a misdemeanor within the palace area and managed to get across the Shālūṭ River without being caught by one of the emir's men, he was safe from retribution.[9] A similar instance is given when Mishāqa tells the story of Zakhkhūr al-Sham'ūnī, whom Emir Yūsuf could not chastize directly but had to deal with through his liegelord, Shaykh Kulayb Abī-Nakad.[10] On the other hand, the lords could not inflict the death penalty without the express consent of the ruling emir.[11]

Although clan membership was generally drawn along religious, or confessional, lines—Druze Jumblāṭīs, Maronite Khāzinites, e.g.—members of other confessional groups were attached to a clan, house or even an individual as "followers" or liegemen, as Mishāqa says of the Shi'ite clansmen who served his Greek Catholic grandfather Ibrāhīm Mishāqa:

> These four [Shi'ites] promoted Ibrāhīm's interests the most energetically of all of his followers, who exceeded forty mounted men, Shi'ites and Christians, for it is the custom among clansmen to distinguish followers not with regard to sect (*madhhab*), but rather with regard to allegiance and loyalty (*ṣidq al-widād*).[12]

In the small, pluralistic society of the Lebanon, localism, kinship and clan loyalties were the primary societal bonds. Confessional adherence to the sect into which one was born was inevitable, for no one could exist without such a tie;[13] but religious affiliation appears to have been of less importance overall and certainly less a factor than liege loyalty. Many of the ruling House of Shihāb converted from Islam to Maronite Christianity without sacrificing the allegiance of their vassals.[14] When the Druze Shaykh Bashīr Jumblāṭ made a show of being Muslim to impress the Ottomans, he seems to have run little risk of alienating his liegemen. When regional, clan and sectarian lines coincided, as they sometimes did in the northern part of the mountain populated almost exclusively by Maronites, concerted action may appear to have been religiously motivated; but it is a dangerous conclusion to draw for the earlier period, as purely sectarian motives would have been secondary, if present at all. Later, however, as the feudal structure and its network of traditional loyalties collapsed when the rule of the nobility was replaced with bureaucratic administration, the situation changed rapidly, and Mishāqa expresses his contempt and regret for the redefining of loyalty along confessional lines. He argues passionately for a geographical unity based on mutual respect among the various groups so that the Lebanon might stand as one against the outside world that had so easily manipulated the area by playing on its divided state.

* * *

Since much of Mishāqa's history of the region is the history of the House of Shihāb, the various branches of which ruled Mount Lebanon and Wādī al-Taym, it may be useful here to trace briefly how and when this princely house came to dominate the political scene.

The House of Ma'n, who preceded the Shihābs, had been in Mount Lebanon since the time of the Crusades.[15] In 1515 the most famous of the Ma'n emirs, Fakhr al-Dīn I, sided with the Ottoman Sultan Selim against his nominal Mameluk overlord, Qānṣawh al-Ghūrī; and when the Ottomans won the area from the Mameluks, the sultan rewarded him with the rulership of the Lebanon,[16] eclipsing the Tanūkh emirs who had ruled previously. In 1697 Emir Aḥmad, the last scion of the House of Ma'n, died without issue, and the electors of the seven Druze fiefs of the Lebanon (the Shūf, Manāṣif, 'Arqūb, Jurd, Matn, Shaḥḥār and Gharb) met and chose to the rulership of the mountain Emir Bashīr of the House of Shihāb, son of Emir Ḥusayn of Rāshayyā by Emir Aḥmad Ma'n's sister. No sooner was Emir Bashīr elected than Constantinople sent word that Emir Bashīr's cousin in Ḥāṣbayyā, Emir Ḥaydar, should succeed the Ma'ns, but the pasha of Ṣaydā objected, and eventually a compromise was worked out whereby Emir Bashīr would stand as regent until the twelve-year-old Emir Ḥaydar reached his majority. In 1707 Emir Bashīr died, poisoned by his Ḥāṣbayyā cousins,[17] and Emir Ḥaydar succeeded as ruler of the mountain, leaving other branches of the family to rule in Ḥāṣbayyā and Rāshayyā in Wādī al-Taym.

Emir Ḥaydar ruled until 1729 and was succeeded by his son Emir Mulḥim, who abdicated the rulership in 1754 in favor of his brother Emir Manṣūr. After Emir Mulḥim's death in 1761, another brother, Emir Aḥmad, contested Manṣūr's rule. Emir Aḥmad died in 1770, and that same year Emir Manṣūr abdicated in favor of Mulḥim's son, Emir Yūsuf, who ruled until 1788, when he abdicated in favor of his young cousin, Emir Bashīr II—at which point Mishāqa's narrative begins. By the 19th century Emir Ḥaydar's descendants had become so interwoven in the political fabric of the mountain that it was unthinkable that any other family should rule. There were, of course, innumerable revolts against the ruling emir, but they were always in the name of another Shihāb: "it was an established custom in the land of the Druze that no one would raise a weapon against a Shihābī emir unless he had another emir with him"[18] to legitimize the attack. The rule of the Shihābs over the mountain remained until 1842, when the emirate was abolished by the Ottomans and replaced by a dual administration of the mountain known as the "Double Kaymakamate."

When Emir Ḥaydar began his reign, there were two other princely houses, Arslān and 'Alam al-Dīn, the older Tanūkh House having been exterminated by the 'Alam al-Dīns in 1633. At the Battle of 'Ayn Dāra in 1711, when the ancient feud between the "Qaysī" and "Yamanī" factions was finally resolved by the utter defeat of the Yamanīs, the 'Alam al-Dīns, who led the Yamanī faction, were slaughtered to the last, and the remaining Yamanī supporters were exiled to the Ḥawrān in Syria. The only Yamanīs allowed to remain were the princely House of Arslān, whose holdings in the Gharb were so reduced that they ceased to play an important role in the political machinations of the mountain. For their assistance at 'Ayn Dāra the House of Abullam' was raised from the status of muqaddam and given the fief of the Matn. They subsequently intermarried with the Shihābs to such an extent that they become all but indistinguishable from them.[19] Below the emirs in rank came the muqaddams, but the elevation of Abullam' left only one house of muqaddams, that of Muzhir, whose holdings were limited to the village of Ḥammānā in the Matn, and they were not rich or powerful enough to play a major role. Next in rank came the shaykhs, of whom there were Jumblāṭ in the Shūf, 'Imād in the 'Arqūb, and Abū-Nakad in the Manāṣif (Dayr al-Qamar) and the Shaḥḥār regions. In addition to these three, Emir Ḥaydar raised the houses of Talḥūq and 'Abdul-Malik to the status of shaykh, giving to Talḥūq the Upper Gharb to balance the Arslān emirs in the Lower Gharb, and to 'Abdul-Malik the Jurd region. These five were the "great Druze shaykhs." The three important Maronite noble houses were the Khāzin shaykhs in Kisrwān, Ḥbaysh in Ghazīr and Daḥdāḥ in the Ftūḥ.

No sooner had the Qaysī-Yamanī split been resolved than a new division among the Druze houses, Jumblāṭī-Yazbakī, arose in its place and quickly involved the whole of the Lebanon, regardless of religion. The Ottomans, especially the wily Aḥmad Pasha al-Jazzār, were not slow to make use of this new division to fan the flames of resentment and rebellion. The Jumblāṭ faction consisted of the Jumblāṭs themselves and their powerful allies in Kisrwān, the Khāzins. The Yazbakī faction was headed by the House of 'Imād, and to it belonged Talḥūq, 'Abdul-Malik, Ḥbaysh and Daḥdāḥ. The Abū-Nakads generally maintained neutrality but on occasion lent their support to one camp or the other when they saw their interests furthered by joining the fray. "Our land," the saying went, "is a balance between Jumblāṭ and Yazbak, while Nakad is a single weight. If it is added to one of the two, it will counterbalance the other."[20] The Yazbakī faction was more numerous, but the Jumblāṭ faction, which usually enjoyed the support of the Shihābs, was far richer and more powerful. Beginning with the massacre of the Abū-Nakads in 1797, Emir Bashīr II systematically eliminated or reduced the Yazbakīs to insignificance, leaving the House of Jumblāṭ as the only clan chiefs with any real power. Emir Bashīr and Shaykh Bashīr Jumblāṭ worked in close alliance to eliminate their rivals; however, eliminating the others left Shaykh Bashīr himself as the only powerful noble, and therefore the only possible focal point of all opposition to Emir Bashīr. When opposition crystalized around Shaykh Bashīr, it was his turn to suffer the emir's wrath. This factionalism and the friction it generated pervade Mishāqa's history.

The areas outside of Mount Lebanon that figure in Mishāqa's work are as follows: Wādī al-Taym (Ḥāṣbayyā and Rāshayyā), now part of the Republic of the Lebanon, was then a dependency of the Province of Damascus, to which the Biqā' Valley also belonged. The older regions forming Jabal al-'Āmil (now south Lebanon), the Tuffāḥ, Jazzīn, Jabal al-Rīḥān, Bshāra and Shqīf, were severed from the emirate of the Shūf (Mount Lebanon) in 1705 and made administrative dependencies of the pashalik of Ṣaydā, the Ottoman province to which the mountain proper also belonged.[21] Egypt, where Mishāqa lived for a few years among the Levantine mercantile community in Damietta, had been under nominal Ottoman control since the early 16th century, though the 18th-century rulers of Egypt to whom Mishāqa refers, the "neo-Mameluk" Janissaries, reigned in virtual autonomy until the French invasion in 1798. In 1805 Muḥammad-'Alī Pasha became Ottoman viceroy of Egypt, and he and his son Ibrāhīm Pasha played an important role in Syria, which Ibrāhīm Pasha occupied in 1832 and held until he was forced by the Concert of Europe to withdraw in 1840. For the political developments and reorganizations that were effected in the area from 1840 until the aftermath of the 1860 "incidents," Mishāqa's own account should suffice.

It has not been our intention to give an exhaustive account of the Lebanon during the 18th and 19th centuries, but it was felt necessary, before letting Mikhāyil Mishāqa tell the story of his family, to "set the stage" for readers unfamiliar with the area, particularly for the 18th century, which still remains one of the least known periods, even to historians of the Near East.

Part One

1750-1804

*In the Name of God, the One, the Eternal,
the Being without Beginning, the Everlasting and Eternal Living One:
Praise, Glory, Power and Might to Him for Ever and Ever.*

This humble writer, Mikhāyil son of Jirjis Mishāqa, having dwelt for forty years in Damascus and, well advanced in years, having reached the age of infirmity and confined to his home away from all work, says:

Some of my beloved brethren have asked me for a historical account containing what I know of the origin of our family and how it acquired the surname Mishāqa, what has occurred to [the family] in general and to me in particular from the beginning until this date, and what I know of the events in the Lebanon and Syria[1]—be it handed down by my forebears or what has occured in my [own] days, whether I learned of it [by hearsay] or witnessed it [myself]. I acceded to the request to the best of [my] abilities, asking God's help.

THE HISTORY OF THE AUTHOR, MIKHĀYIL MISHĀQA.

[The author] is Mikhāyil, son of Jirjis, son of Ibrāhīm, son of Yoseph Petraki, who was given the surname Mishāqa. Yoseph was from Corfu, which was under Venetian rule. He owned his own ship and sailed by himself to Egypt and the coast of Syria to trade. He had a special liking for the seaport of Tripoli in Syria and married a girl of the Qalafāṭ family from the village of Anfe. He used to buy the floss (*mushāqa*[2]) from hemp and flax to trade in the shipyards of his country; it was on account of this trade that he was called Khawāja[3] M'shāqa. [2]

Yoseph's wife bore him a single son he named Jirjis. Then he grew old and his wife died, and after a short while he too died. After this, the son Jirjis, not wanting to live in Tripoli, sold his father's ship, consolidated his inheritance and moved to Ṣaydā in the year 1752. It seems that he collected an ample amount of money, for in Ṣaydā he engaged in trade with Egypt in the tobacco known as *tūtūn*,[4] and it was due to this trade that commercial relations were established between him and the Mutawālī shaykhs[5] who ruled Ṣūr[6] and the Bshāra region, which was plentiful in tobacco. Thus began the friendly relations between him and these shaykhs.

At that time the Empire's viziers[7] ruled in name only; real power lay in the hands of clan chieftains. The Mutawālī shaykhs of the House of 'Alī al-Ṣaghīr held the Bshāra region from the borders of the Liṭānī River and the Qāsmiyye Bridge to al-Nāqūra, along with the city of Ṣūr. The area from al-Nāqūra to Carmel and the Ṣafad region, along with the city of Acre, was in the hands of the Zaydānī shaykhs. From the Liṭānī River in the direction of Ṣaydā, i.e. the Shawmar region, and the Shqīf region were in the hands of the Mutawālī Ṣa'bī shaykhs.[8] In the direction of Ṣūr the governor of Ṣaydā held only the distance of one mile to the Sānīq Creek, and similarly one mile north from the sea to the Tuffāḥ region, which belonged to the Lebanon, and in the direction of Beirut a distance of two miles to the al-Awwalī River. From there the coast, with the cities of Beirut, Jbayl and others up to the vicinity of Tripoli, was controlled by the ruler of the Lebanon.

When Jirjis Mishāqa decided to marry, he chose a girl from the Mansī family, who had originally come from Anfe, his mother's village—and there may have been some degree of kinship between them. He asked for her hand, but they replied that they had become Catholics and no longer married Orthodox. When he asked them what Catholics were, they took him to a monastery in the Lebanon, about eight miles from Ṣaydā, named [Dayr] al-Mukhalliṣ [Monastery of the Savior], which had been founded thirty years previously, in 1725, early after the Patriarch Seraphim al-Ṣayfī of Damascus, who was called Cyril V, and five bishops from the Patriarchate of Antioch had united with the followers of the Pope.[9] When Jirjis arrived at the monastery they welcomed him and did their utmost to honor him. Staying a few days with them and attending their services, he found them to be in accordance with the services he had heard in his own church. They used the Greek language, and the monks' robes and hoods were similar to the dress of Orthodox monks. "So then Catholics are Orthodox!" he said. "Why have you changed your name? This is the same as my rite!" [3] He thereupon declared himself a Greek Catholic and married the sister of Ḥājj Mūsā Mansī.

He saw that the Monastery of the Savior was in need of assistance, for the church lacked a cover for its tabernacle, the central altar was without a dome, and there were other things lacking to make it complete. He therefore out of his own pocket provided a dome and marble pillars from Europe for the altar area. Likewise he had covers and doors made for the three tabernacles and bequeathed to the monastery many properties he had purchased, including the village of al-Wardiyye in Jabal al-Rīḥān,

Dervish.

and four houses in Ṣaydā, among others. His donations to the monks were repaid by their establishing a daily mass for his soul in perpetuity and celebrating the mass of the Feast of St. George in his name. In 1757 was inscribed in marble on the right side of the main sanctuary door: "I WILL ENTER THY HOUSE, I WILL WORSHIP TOWARD THY HOLY TEMPLE IN THE FEAR OF THEE."[10] On the left side was written: "JIRJIS MISHĀQA THY SERVANT LOVED THE BEAUTY OF THY GLORY." Indeed, the ties of affection between the Mishāqa family and these monks have remained to this day.

Then the two shaykhs ruling Ṣūr persuaded Jirjis to move to their area on the grounds that Ṣūr was more suitable for his dealings with the people of Bshāra because it was both nearby and plentiful in tobacco, grain, and timber. At that time there was not a single Christian living in Ṣūr, [but] Jirjis went, taking with him his Mansī relatives and others. When a goodly number of families had gathered, Christians from elsewhere began to arrive in increasing numbers, all of them of the Greek Catholic sect.

When the Christians there had grown in number, work was begun on a church in the name of St. Thomas the Apostle. There was [at that time] no mosque for the Muslims in the town, since the local Muslims were of the Shi'ite sect, who can properly assemble for congregational prayer only under conditions that are not found in all places or times—unlike the Sunni rite, which was the rite of the Empire and most of its Muslim subjects. Therefore Jirjis Mishāqa thought it would be a good thing to build a mosque for the Muslims with his own funds, and it was begun simultaneously with the building of the church. When word reached the vizier of Ṣaydā he summoned Jirjis Mishāqa and questioned him. He answered him, saying, "I see Muslims coming to Ṣūr, merchants, transients and wandering dervishes, for whom there is no place of shelter or gathering for prayer. Indeed the lack of a mosque in the city is a matter that attracts criticism of its inhabitants abroad. The Creator [4] does not permit such negligence. Since I have taken up residence in this town, I should do anything I can to contribute to its development or to the comfort of those who come here. This will be counted as a good work during your term of governance." The vizier was delighted with this answer, awarded Jirjis Mishāqa a sable fur and said, "God bless your labor. But you must leave the minaret for me to build with my own money and so have a share in this good work." Thus the construction of both mosque and church was completed.

Jirjis Mishāqa expanded his household buildings in Ṣūr, along with other buildings in the village of Qānā, where he later died and was buried. He also renovated a number of shops and warehouses in Ṣūr. He acquired a great reputation among the people of Bshāra, among their shaykhs and religious leaders.

Jirjis had two sons, Ibrāhīm and Bishāra, the ancestor of the Mishāqas who live today in Alexandria, who are Bishāra and Ilyās, the sons of Yūsuf son of Bishāra, and their children. Ibrāhīm is the ancestor of our family. He was an outstanding person and surpassed his father in skillful management and organization. He was considered an intelligent and prosperous man. He married a girl from Acre of the 'Awaḍ family, who bore him a number of sons and daughters. Three sons survived: the oldest Jirjis, born in 1765, then Anton, born in 1779, and Ayyūb, born in 1782.

AN ACCOUNT OF AHMAD PASHA AL-JAZZĀR; BEIRUT IS DETACHED FROM THE RULERSHIP OF MOUNT LEBANON.

During Ibrāhīm's time, the infamous tyrant Aḥmad Pasha al-Jazzār was appointed governer of Ṣaydā.[11] He was the first vizier in Syria to begin to destroy the clan chiefs, whose power ended entirely in 1860 after the murder of Emir Sa'd al-Dīn al-Shihābī, the last Emir of Ḥāṣbayyā. Aḥmad Pasha al-Jazzār was originally from Bosnia,[12] but he went to Egypt and entered the service of the Ghuzz emirs.[13] He was clever and wily on the one hand, and on the other he was cruel-hearted, pitiless and merciless. At his death poets produced many defamatory chronograms on account of his evil deeds. Among the things composed for the year of his death, 1219 [A.D. 1804], are: "Mankind triumphed, and chronicled it with the words: 'The wretch has perished and departed to Hell.'"[14] Another poet said after reviling him in a chronogram: "I sang out for joy over the arrival of the news that Aḥmad Pasha al-Jazzār had perished."[15] [5] There is an error of 39 in the chronogram; perhaps it is due to a copyist's mistake.

During his stay in Egypt this man gave a banquet in his home to which he invited some of his Ghuzz Mameluk companions. He got them drunk, and when they had fallen into a stupor he slaughtered them all. It is said that there were eighteen of them.[16] Fleeing to Syria, he went to Dayr al-Qamar in Mount Lebanon.[17] Since at that time there were no lodgings for strangers other than the coffeehouses, he stopped in the coffeehouse in the town square, which was overlooked by an arcade in the residence of Emir Yūsuf al-Shihābī, who was then the ruler of the Lebanon. Since he often saw al-Jazzār sitting outside the coffeehouse, he inquired about him and was informed that he was a stranger, a Turk who spoke Arabic in the Egyptian dialect. This went on until one cold day the emir noticed that this man did not have on enough clothing to protect him from the cold. He asked one of the servants about this and was told that the stranger had sold all his belongings and, just the day before, had sold the cloak he had been wearing in order to buy food. The emir said, "He is to be given food from our kitchen as long as he stays."

Next to the emir was his intendant[18] Shaykh Ghandūr al-Khūrī, grandfather of the Ghandūr Bey who now lives in the village of 'Ayn Trāz. (The Greek Catholic Patriarch's school there now, which was bought by the Patriarch Agapeios Maṭar in 1810, was the home of this same Shaykh Ghandūr.) Shaykh Ghandūr said to the emir, "If this stranger had found work on the coast from which he could live, he wouldn't have come to the mountain. With your approval he could be taken into service. He may prove useful for special tasks."

The emir agreed and had him summoned. When he came the emir questioned him about why he was there, and he replied that he had been in the service of a *sanjaq* in Egypt. The Mamluk race who accepted employment, he said, did not like for a lord among them to serve any who was not one of them lest he take precedence of them. He was a freeman, of the Bosnians, and had gone from the service of one to another, yet he had met with opposition from all. He had been forced to leave Egypt and come to Syria, but he had not succeeded in finding employment with the Zaydānīs, the Mutawālīs or the governor of Ṣaydā. The Emir responded, "I accept you into my service. If I find loyalty and talent in you, you will rise to the rank you merit." The emir ordered that a suitable garment, weapons and a mount be given him, and that food for him, fodder for his beast and a place to live be provided.

The emirs of the Lebanon used to spend the summer in Dayr al-Qamar and the winter in the city of Beirut. Aḥmad Āghā al-Jazzār evinced such acumen, courage and energy in serving Emir Yūsuf that he was promoted until he was entrusted with the rule of Beirut, and even the people of Beirut praised him for the fairness of his dealings. Thus the emir's confidence in him increased until Aḥmad Āghā reported to the emir that "the walls of Beirut are mostly falling into ruin, and [6] we have no security from treachery on the part of the Empire, especially during the winter, when you are known to be unprepared for defense. If just one vessel were to take us by surprise on a dark winter night, even if there were only two hundred men aboard, it would have us at its mercy. Therefore we must take precaution against the Empire's treachery. We could easily do this: it does not require more than repairing the walls and putting the gates in order, and we can accomplish most of the work by levying a tax on the people of Beirut and the nearby villages, for it would safeguard the whole area."

The emir was grateful for Aḥmad Āghā's acuity of observation, the cunning that was concealed in the recesses of this Aḥmad's mind never occurring to him, and he authorized the repair of the walls. Aḥmad Āghā carried out the work promptly, expeditiously, and energetically, exerting himself to minimize costs by raising taxes and supervising the work himself. When he finished in a short period of time, the emir was delighted and increased his stipend and the honorifics in his correspondence with him. Similarly Shaykh Ghandūr al-Khūrī reminded [the emir] of his foresight in suggesting that this noble and energetic man be employed. Of course, neither of them realized that herein lay the greatest and worst disaster, not only for them and the people in general in the province of Ṣaydā, but indeed for the whole of Syria.

After Aḥmad Āghā had completed the fortification of Beirut, he began to work clandestinely to find a means for seizing control of the province of Ṣaydā. At that time there was no regular post to carry letters between countries. The Empire and its governors in the provinces arranged to have special men called *tātār*, or *ṭaṭar*, carry communications back and forth between the court and its governors. For important matters the Empire would send reliable high officeholders, such as the Qapūjī Bāshī, the Silāḥshūr or the Bustānjī Bāshī, who might be accompanied by up to forty Tatars.[19] The Tatars' and these [officials'] trips were accomplished by commandeering horses without recompense. When they arrived in a town they would appropriate the steeds required by them, leaving behind the ones they had broken down with harsh treatment. It is said that an energetic Tatar could make his way from Damascus to Constantinople in a week and return in a similar period of time, even though the distance between these two took forty days at the pace of pack animals. From this one can realize the extent of the loss suffered by the owners of these animals.

Since Aḥmad Āghā al-Jazzār was governor of Beirut, he engratiated himself with the Tatars bound for Ṣaydā passing through his territory, provided for their needs and showed them honor, particularly if they were high imperial officials. He pretended to the emir that he was doing this that they might praise [7] the emir to the governor and the Empire, but his underlying purpose was to commend himself. So when his good name with the Empire was established, he spoke confidentially with a wily *qapūjī* who was passing through, saying, "Why is the Empire content for its vizier, governor of this far-flung province, to remain confined to the city of Ṣaydā and not govern any more of the land than the three miles in length from the mouth of the al-Awwalī River to the Sānīq Creek, and one mile in breadth from the shore to the outskirts of the village of Hlāliyye, which belongs to the Lebanon? In the meantime the clan chieftains and their followers enjoy the resources of the whole province."

[The *qapūjī*] replied that to subdue the clans would require wars and much financing, and the result was not worth the effort or the expense. "If the State were to entrust its servant with the governorship of Ṣaydā," al-Jazzār said, "I could accomplish this task without costing [the Empire] anything. My first step would be to sever the city of Beirut from the rulership of the Lebanon. I have already repaired the walls and fortified it well to this end." He then asked the *qapūjī* to petition the Empire for the office of Ṣaydā, and [the *qapūjī*] pledged that upon his arrival he would strive to fulfill his request. The necessary papers were written, and after the *qapūjī*'s return to court he did as he had promised, whereupon a decree of governorship was sent. Thus his [old] master Emir Yūsuf came under his command. When he moved to Ṣaydā he conferred the rulership of the Lebanon on Emir Yūsuf as before, except that Beirut was separated from the Lebanon.

THE EMPIRE'S FLEET ATTACKS ACRE, AND SHAYKH ẒĀHIR AL-'UMAR IS KILLED; HIS SONS ALONG WITH M'ALLIM IBRĀHĪM AL-ṢABBĀGH, ARE ARRESTED.

A little before that, Admiral Ḥasan Pasha al-Jazāyirī moved against Acre, from where Shaykh Ẓāhir al-'Umar al-Zaydānī ruled the Ṣafad region and the coastal area around Acre and Haifa. This shaykh had constructed the inner wall of Acre, fortified it with towers and cannons, built a treasury tower in the seraglio,[20] repaired the old citadel and set up a battalion of Turkish artillerymen. Ḥasan Pasha demanded money from the shaykh in the name of the Empire and expressed his contentment with a sum of fifty thousand piastres, which in the currency of that time was roughly equal to twenty-five thousand French réals. Most of the shaykh's supporters counseled him to pay, but there was an extremely wealthy merchant and physician who supplied the shaykh when he was in need of money, taking in compensation oil, cotton, grain, and "what was not permitted anyone else,"[21] with which goods he dealt in commerce. The shaykh relied on his opinion because of his good understanding and great discernment and learning. This man was the Greek Catholic M'allim[22] Ibrāhīm ibn 'Abbūd al-Ṣabbāgh, paternal grandfather of the Khawāja Ḥabīb al-Ṣabbāgh living today as a respected merchant in Damascus. This Ibrāhīm was opposed to the opinion of the majority, placing his reliance on the Empire's weakness and on the fortification of Acre, not taking into account the possibility of treachery on the part of the Turks who manned the cannons. He advised the shaykh that he should refrain from paying because, as he said, "The Ottoman Empire always demands more and more. If you give in to them now, they will be forever coming back to you demanding more. Once this door is opened it can never be closed again. It is more politic not [8] to open it in the first place and thus nip their ambition in the bud so they won't make more demands on you." The shaykh considered this a good idea and answered with a refusal.

Ḥasan Pasha ordered the cannons to fire on Acre, and from Acre the shaykh ordered the ships to be fired on. However, they fired and missed, because the taboo against opposing the sultan's troops [amounted to] a religion, especially when the artillerymen were Turks. It is said that they spiked the cannons, and the naval troops stormed Acre. When Shaykh Ẓāhir realized the treachery of his soldiers, he fled, but the Sultan's soldiers overtook him outside the town, where they killed and buried him, his grave being well known to this day.[23]

THE DEATH OF MUḤAMMAD BEY ABŪ'L-DHAHAB; IBRĀHĪM AL-ṢABBĀGH IS HANGED IN THE CAPITAL.

Then [Shaykh Ẓāhir's] sons and M'allim Ibrāhīm al-Ṣabbāgh were arrested, and all that could be found of the shaykh's property, along with that of his children and Ibrāhīm al-Ṣabbāgh, was confiscated, of which it was said that eighty-three thousand purses in the currency of that time reached the sultan's coffers. This would be the equivalent of five million liras or twenty-five million francs. This figure does not include what Ḥasan Pasha pilfered for himself or what the officials at his side managed to snatch. It is said that at Ṣabbāgh's was found an emerald inkwell with a diamond lid, said to have been the inkwell of Joseph son of Jacob. He is said to have come into possession of it as follows: Muḥammad Bey[24] Abū'l-Dhahab, a *sanjaq* of Egypt who came to Syria intent on plunder but turned back from Damascus unsuccessfully, died suddenly upon arrival at Carmel. The Christians say that because he had decided to destroy the Monastery of the Prophet Elias there, the prophet strangled him. This occurred in A.H. 1188 [A.D. 1774-75], and the chronogram is "on this date died Abū'l-Dhahab," the numerical values of the letters of which add up to 1188.[25]

At that time Shaykh Ẓāhir was in the house he had built in Haifa Port near Carmel. As soon as news of Abū'l-Dhahab's death reached him, he went with his men to the latter's camp and took possession of the treasury. Among the things he found there was the inkwell, which he gave to Ibrāhīm al-Ṣabbāgh, telling him, "This is your share, since you are one of the masters of the pen."[26]

After confiscating the assets of Shaykh Ẓāhir and his sons and of al-Ṣabbāgh, they took the shaykh's sons and grandsons with al-Ṣabbāgh to Constantinople and for a time put al-Ṣabbāgh in chains in Tarskhāna.[27]

By chance the queen was stricken with an illness for which the physicians could find no cure, and they gave up all hope of saving her. One of the king's confidants proposed to him, "The physicians have lost hope of curing the queen, but we have here imprisoned in Tarskhāna a physician, brought with the sons of Shaykh Ẓāhir al-'Umar, who is said to be extremely skillful. With your approval he could be summoned to examine the queen." He was sent for and treated her, and she recovered under his care. Thereupon the sultan gave him his freedom and bestowed upon him a golden chain to wear. Having thus achieved widespread fame for the practice of medicine among the citizens of the Empire, elite and commoners alike, he was consumed by an ambition to make enough money to gain the Empire's consent to restore Shaykh Ẓāhir's sons to their homeland. [9]

One day Ḥasan Pasha encountered [al-Ṣabbāgh] and reproved him for failing to visit him on board his ship, for which he apologized. Then [Ḥasan Pasha] ordered him to come the next day to share a meal with him. As soon as he arrived, Ḥasan Pasha ordered him hanged, and he was executed on board ship. The real reason for this was that the pasha had concealed from the Empire many of the things he had taken from [Ibrāhīm al-Ṣabbāgh], and when he saw him at large, mingling with the men of the Empire, the pasha feared he would report what he had taken and expose his embezzlement, which would be sufficient, in accordance with the Empire's custom at that time, for him to lose his head. Therefore he sought to conceal his treachery by murdering the innocent [Ṣabbāgh, whom he had] wronged by looting his property and laying waste his homeland. It is suspected that Ṣabbāgh's wealth, the like of which was not known in Syria in those days, was not all from commerce but rather from his having discovered buried treasure from the Crusades, Acre having seen many reversals of fortune in its time.

JAZZĀR PASHA MOVES TO ACRE.

But let us return to Aḥmad Pasha al-Jazzār. He seized the opportunity occasioned by the conquest of Acre to safeguard himself from the not unlikely danger of being removed from the governorship of Ṣaydā by the Empire, which had dismissed other governors in rapid succession, either because it suspected that governors with a prolonged period of governorship would rebel, as it well knew from experience, or because it wished to realize cash for the treasury from bribes from those who aspired to office. Therefore, al-Jazzār removed from Ṣaydā and established his residence in Acre, pretending that his aim was to clear up the region Shaykh Ẓāhir al-'Umar had ruled, where the clans were constantly causing sedition and disturbances. His real motive, however, was to maintain a long tenure as governor by fortifying himself in the Acre citadel. To this end he made every effort to increase its fortification and to stock munitions and war matériel within. For the most part he had foreign soldiers of the Bosnians, his own race, Albanians and cruel Kurds. He appointed as steward a Kurdish shaykh, Shaykh Ṭāhā, whose saintship was believed in as [a kind of] divinity, although the Muslims say that he was a Yazīdī who worshipped the devil. After al-Jazzār's death the [Muslims] revolted against him and killed him as an example. A poet said in the chronicle of that year: "You did not depart, O year, until you had won from me and healed a saddened heart. In you God destroyed the two tyrants and gave [them] no more power to be cruel and oppressive. You slew the Butcher and then sent after him an accursed heretic, the hellish Yazīdī Ṭāhā, and the date was stated: 'and in it Ismā'īl was imprisoned.'" The words of the chronogram total 1203, whereas the correct date is 1219. Perhaps the copyist made a mistake.[28] Ismā'īl Pasha was released from prison and given the governorship until the Empire issued an order for the succession. [10]

SEDITION IS SOWN BETWEEN THE SHI'ITE SHAYKHS AND THE EMIR OF THE LEBANON; AL-JAZZĀR'S TROOPS ARE SENT TO FIGHT, AND SHAYKH NĀSIF AL-NASSĀR IS KILLED; AL-JAZZĀR GAINS CONTROL OF THEIR LAND, WHICH IS GIVEN TO IBRĀHĪM MISHĀQA FOR TAX FARMING.

Let us return to more of Aḥmad Pasha's deeds.[29] After consolidating Acre and the Ṣafad region, he sowed sedition between the shaykhs of Bshāra and the Shqīf on the one hand and the Emir of the Lebanon, Emir Yūsuf al-Shihābī, on the other. However, the shaykhs appeared to be a good deal weaker, so al-Jazzār readied his troops to attack them, and a number of skirmishes took place. Finally the greatest of them, Shaykh Nāṣīf al-Naṣṣār received a bullet wound that killed him on the spot. His men were scattered, and the other shaykhs fled with their followers. The soldiers entered the region and slaughtered many of the men, plundering and outraging women and virgins, as is the usual custom of Turks and Kurds. Then, having been weakened by the loss of its brave young men, some of whom had been killed and others put to flight, the region was brought to its knees before al-Jazzār in defeat.

The internal affairs of these regions, the stipends paid to officials, and the number of levies that could be made on a village were all unknown to provincial governors; instead, they were given a trivial amount of money by the shaykhs, who would then take as much from the people as they could be made to bear. For that reason al-Jazzār thought it would be good to give the Bshāra region to Ibrāhīm Mishāqa as a tax-farm for a fixed annual revenue, for he was well acquainted with the internal affairs and important people of the region, had sufficient administrative ability and was capable of paying what he contracted for. So he summoned him and gave him a tax-farming contract. Along with [him he appointed] a Muslim as *ḥākim* for the sake of appearances, since most of the people of the region were Shi'ite Muslims, but his actions were to be directed by Ibrāhīm Mishāqa, who made his central residence in the fortress of Mārūn. He conducted himself well with the people and with Jazzār Pasha his overlord, who therefore renewed his tax-farming contract at the beginning of each year until his death.

Scattered among the Muslims in the villages of the Bshāra region were numerous Greek Catholic families who had neither priests nor churches for performing their religious duties. [Ibrāhīm] gathered these families together in an "umbrella" village called Naffākhiyye, which, along with a church, he built for them, and provided a priest to oversee their religious needs, as the Maronites had [similarly] congregated in the villages of Rmaysh and 'Ayn Ibl.

The persons left homeless [by al-Jazzār] hid in the vast forests of Bshāra, where they endangered the safety of travellers by plundering and killing, and raided the villages and inhabitants of the region, demanding money [11] and supplies. Al-Jazzār was forced to form a possé of deputies to hunt them down, but [the brigands] often found some of them alone and, getting the better of them, killed them, just as the deputies, if they overcame [the brigands], would kill anyone they could not bring alive to al-Jazzār to collect the bounty. This unrest lasted until after al-Jazzār's death.

Another thing that happened to Ibrāhīm Mishāqa was as follows. During one of his visits to al-Jazzār, the deputies had brought in nearly forty of the displaced who were disturbing the peace of the countryside. Al-Jazzār ordered them executed by the stake outside the Acre gate. They were piercing them with the stake, one through the buttocks, another through the side, another through the shoulder, when Ibrāhīm Mishāqa chanced to pass by. They were just finishing this barbaric deed, with only four youths remaining. He asked the officials to refrain from killing the four youths until he should go in to the vizier and send them word whether to release them or to execute them. As the officials were from Shaykh Ṭāhā's people and knew of Ibrāhīm's frequent visits to their shaykh and of the friendly relations between them, they obeyed him. Fortunately al-Jazzār happened to be present, sitting at the palace entrance near the city gate. [Ibrāhīm] went over to al-Jazzār, who greeted him warmly, and forthwith sought pardon for the four, [promising] to pay a ransom for them to the treasury. He granted his request and issued an order to turn them over. They were sent to him, and he told them of the vizier's compassionate pardon of them, provided they would forswear their former conduct and stay peacefully in their homes. They replied, "We were to be slain, as were our comrades, in a most hideous fashion. Our deliverance was through your intervention. Therefore it is you who have bought us, and we are your slaves for the rest of our lives. We will never leave you, and we will serve you with our very lives. If you drive us away we will sit at your gate. Count us among your followers." He gave them garments [to cover themselves, as they had] been stripped for execution, and on completing his business in Acre he took them to Ṣūr and Bshāra as his escort.

This deed made a good name for Ibrāhīm Mishāqa, not only among the Christians, but more particularly among the Muslims, and especially among the Shi'ites in Bshāra, of whom those who had been rescued from death were. These four promoted Ibrāhīms's interests the most energetically of all of his followers, who exceeded forty mounted men, Shi'ites and Christians, for it is the custom among clansmen to distinguish followers not with regard to sect, but rather with regard to allegiance and loyalty.

SHI'ITES BETRAY IBRĀHĪM MISHĀQA, BUT HE ESCAPES.

It so happened that some of those fanatically eager to resist the authorities thought they could betray first Ibrāhīm Mishāqa and then the official Muslim *ḥākim* who was with him, as a means of returning the rule [12] of their land to the shaykhs. A group of them came and requested an audience with Ibrāhīm. He went out to meet them, and while he was speaking with them one of them rushed at him, wielding a dagger to stab him. However, Raḥḥāl, one of the four persons he had intervened to save from death, threw himself between them and the took the dagger blow in the chest, falling mortally wounded. Before he died he said, "Now have I been able to repay him who delivered me from the stake!" Ibrāhīm's servants surrounded him and he [fought] valiantly, scattering the traitors after several had been killed. But Ibrāhīm suspected that many more would band together against him, and he did not have enough strength to oppose large numbers. Therefore he immediately left his place and went to al-Jazzār to inform him of what had transpired. Not long after his departure news reached him that many villagers and displaced persons were searching for him and had plundered the cash and goods they had found in his dwelling, leaving nothing there. He came to report[30] what had occurred and petition to be discharged from this service in order that he might stay at home and enjoy [al-Jazzār's] benevolent protection.

Al-Jazzār was consumed with rage at this action and refused to accept his resignation. He commanded him to return to his place and ordered soldiers to destroy the insurgents, issuing on the spot orders to the officers of the Bosnian, Albanian and Kurdish troops to accompany Ibrāhīm Mishāqa to the region of Bshāra with a number of troops to seize everyone involved in this outrage. If they encountered resistance, they were to overpower them by force of arms. Within two days the troops were equipped and set forth accompanied by Ibrāhīm Mishāqa. Upon his arrival in the region, the rebels met him with gunfire, so the troops attacked them. After a fierce battle the rebels were routed and put to the sword, and more than three hundred men were slain. A number of them were taken prisoner and sent to Acre, where they were put to the stake as soon as they arrived. Then he took a great deal of money from the land to compensate for the expense of the troops. As a consequence, the revolts in the region itself died down, but there still remained the raids of the shaykhs and their followers, who hid in the forests, made the roads unsafe and forced the people of the region and neighboring areas to supply provisions and money. The government's search for them was unceasing, and those who fell into their hands were immediately put to the stake.

EMIR YŪSUF IS DEPOSED FROM MOUNT LEBANON AND REPLACED BY EMIR BASHĪR "THE GREAT."

When al-Jazzār no longer had to worry about the region of Ṣafad and the region of the Mutawālīs, I mean the regions of Bshāra and the Shqīf, and their strongholds were under his control, and similarly the ports on the coast from Haifa to Beirut, in which the clans had not the slightest power, he turned his attention to the subjugation of the Lebanon, which was ruled by Emir Yūsuf Shihābī, al-Jazzār's benefactor who has been mentioned before. He began to make demands of him with an insatiable obdurancy until he had demanded that he give up control of the Kharnūb,[31] [13] Tuffāḥ, Jabal al-Rīḥān and Jazzīn regions. He acceded to these demands.

There occurred many vicissitudes, and demands were made which the emir was no longer able to meet. So he resolved to abdicate the rulership, but he feared to confer the rule on any of his relatives, who might take revenge on him and his children and close associates, for

Emir Yūsuf had a brutal nature and had killed his younger brother Emir Efendī and put out the eyes of his brother Emir Sīd-Aḥmad, father of Emir Salmān and Emir Fāris, who passed away recently in the village of al-Ḥadath on the Beirut coast. He had also killed his two maternal uncles Emir Ismā'īl and Emir Bashīr. If he dealt in this fashion with his brothers and uncles, the people nearest to him, [imagine] how he treated those farther from him! Therefore all the Shihābī family had left their homes in Dayr al-Qamar to live elsewhere, some on the Beirut coast, and others in Dayr Dūrīt, and later in Majdal M'ūsh, Shimlān and 'Abayh, in anticipation of his treachery.

Among those in his service was a youth, a relative of his, Emir Bashīr, son of Emir Qāsim, son of Emir 'Umar, son of Emir Ḥaydar, the founder of the line of Shihābī emirs in Mount Lebanon and one of the bridge over the Ḥāṣbānī River is inscribed.[32] In [Emir Mūsā] the lineage of the Shihābī Emirs of the Lebanon converges with the lineage of Emir Sa'd al-Dīn, the Emir of Ḥāṣbayyā who was slain in the Incident of 1860. The emirs of the Lebanon were gradually won over by the Maronites to their religion, but the rest of the family in Ḥāṣbayyā and Rāshayyā persisted in the religion of their Muslim forebears in the Ḥanafī rite. Their origin lies with the Banū-Makhzūm Arabs who accompanied Khālid ibn al-Walīd in the conquest of Syria.[33] Amīr Ḥārith, ancestor of the Shihābī emirs, was slain at the siege of Damascus at Bāb Sharqī.

When Emir Yūsuf summoned his maternal uncle Emir Bashīr[34] from Ḥāṣbayyā and treacherously killed him, he deputized the young Emir Bashīr we have just mentioned to sequester the murdered Emir Bashīr's possessions. He went to Ḥāṣbayyā and, while accomplishing his mission, saw the murdered man's widow, who had borne him two daughters, Khaddūj and Nasīm. She was the Lady Shams al-Murīd, sister of the Emir Qa'dān who resided in the village of 'Abayh in the Upper Gharb of the Lebanon. At that time the members of [the Shihāb] family married amongst themselves and were unconcerned with a difference in religion, so the [Ḥāṣbayyā Shihābs] married the daughters of, and gave their own daughters in marriage to, the emirs of the Matn, even though at that time they were Druze and were only gradually converted to Christianity.[35] (The last one of them to die a Druze, which was a few years ago, was Emir Aḥmad, father of Emir Bashīr of Brummānā, who became ruler of North Lebanon.) When Emir Bashīr Shihābī saw this widow's beauty he made up his mind to ask for her as a wife. He married her, and she later bore him three sons, Emir Qāsim, Emir Khalīl, and Emir Amīn.

At last Emir Yūsuf thought it a good idea to let Emir Bashīr, whom he trusted, go to al-Jazzār [14] and promise to pay a sum to the treasury if [al-Jazzār] would give him the rulership of the Lebanon. When he informed him of his plan, [Emir Bashīr] answered saying, "I am poor and possess neither money nor men. Under such conditions al-Jazzār may order me to act against your wishes. Now I am accounted by everyone as your son, but when I serve al-Jazzār I will become like his son, obliged to do as he orders. I can only serve in total fidelity. Perhaps he will send soldiers with me and order me to attack you. What should I do then?"

"If you are ordered to attack me," he replied, "I won't resist. I'll get out of your way. I ask only that you inform me one day in advance that you are coming, and I'll leave before you [come]. I am giving you ten of my best mounted men to be under your command, and ten purses (equivalent at that time to five hundred liras) for your expenses." At once he ordered ten horsemen to serve him, among whom were Ibrāhīm al-Tarābulsī, Yūsuf 'Azīz and eight of his best horsemen. (Ibrāhīm al-Ṭarābulsī was renowned for his equestrian ability and was the grandfather of the Ṭarābulsī family in Dayr al-Qamar.)

THE FIRST CONNECTION BETWEEN THE MISHĀQA FAMILY AND EMIR BASHĪR.

Emir Bashīr set off for Acre. On his way through Ṣūr he was received by Ibrāhīm Mishāqa, who lodged him for the night in his house and did everything he could to honor him. He also sent one of his intelligent followers to Acre in the emir's service and wrote a letter of recommendation for the emir to take to his friend Shaykh Ṭāhā, the chief of the Kurds, and to the Sakrūj brothers, Greek Orthodox who were influential with al-Jazzār and managed the treasury accounts. He entreated the emir to have his retinue [stay at] the Mishāqa house and to stop there himself when travelling to and from Acre, and he promised he would do so. This was the first connection between the Mishāqa family and the Shihābī emirs and was in 1203 [A.D. 1788-89].

EMIR YŪSUF'S TREACHERY TOWARD EMIR BASHĪR AND HIS ESCAPE.

Thus Emir [Bashīr] received orders for the rulership of the Lebanon, and al-Jazzār sent troops with him to deal a blow to Emir Yūsuf and drive him from the borders of the land. Emir Bashīr returned to Ṣūr and sent messengers to the mountain that the rule had been delegated to him, and to Emir Yūsuf he sent word two days beforehand that he was leaving for Dayr al-Qamar. The next day he arrived in Ṣaydā, and the following day he set out for Dayr al-Qamar. The notables of the area nearby met with him and pledged their allegiance, informing him that Emir Yūsuf had fled before him, taking the road to the Matn. He rested for one day, during which he sent word to Emir Yūsuf that he was ordered to follow him and expel him from the borders of Mount Lebanon, and that he would set out after him from Dayr al-Qamar the next day. The second day the emir went to a nearby spot so that Emir Yūsuf would have time to distance himself from the troops. On the third day he set off with the soldiers, confident that Emir Yūsuf was far away and safely out of reach of the soldiers.

As he arrived at a narrow pass in the mountains, bullets poured down on him like rain: it was Emir Yūsuf and his men blocking the road. When he saw this shameless betrayal, his anger waxed over this treacherous treatment. Now he was one of the most valiant cavaliers of his time and so expert in warfare that in [15] none of the battles he directed during his life did he ever meet defeat. So now he ordered the troops to attack, himself in the forefront. The battle raged between them, and only when many of his troops were dead or wounded did Emir Yūsuf withdraw in retreat, pursued by Emir Bashīr and his soldiers to the borders of Lebanon. The emir returned victoriously with his soldiers to Dayr al-Qamar and notified al-Jazzār of what had happened. Immediately he ordered the state revenues from the mountain to be collected and dispatched, and al-Jazzār was pleased by the emir's zeal and fidelity.

AL-JAZZĀR HANGS EMIR YŪSUF, SHAYKH GHANDŪR AL-KHŪRĪ, IBRĀHĪM AL-'AZZĀM AND HIS SON KHALĪL; THE SIEGE OF SĀNŪR CITADEL.

Emir Yūsuf did not give up all hope of al-Jazzār. He went to him along with his steward, Shaykh Ghandūr and al-Khūrī, who had procured for himself the position of French consul at Beirut. Upon their arrival, [al-Jazzār] greeted them and appointed accommodations for them, but then he had them fettered with iron chains and thrown into the criminals' prison, a great dark dungeon over which the Palace of Justice was built. At that time al-Jazzār himself was fighting in the region of Nabulus and had laid siege to Sānūr Citadel. Ibrāhīm 'Azzām, a Greek Catholic, was imprisoned alongside the emir, not for any crime, but until he paid a fine set by al-Jazzār higher than he could pay. His son Khalīl was employed in receiving supplies from Acre and delivering them to the camp at Sānūr.

It happened that al-Jazzār had ordered the citadel mined, but [his men] were not skillful at laying explosives, and when they lit the charges they backfired on the camp, destroying much of it and compromising al-Jazzār's dignity. When Khalīl 'Azzām returned from Sānūr, he wrote this to his imprisoned father in a code they had devised. Since letters to prisoners were forbidden, he placed it inside a loaf of bread with the food, where it was discovered by the jailer and sent to al-Jazzār, who gave it to the scribes to decipher for him. It turned out to be news of the backfire of the explosives on the camp and al-Jazzār's humiliation, along with word that Emir Yūsuf should be informed and that it was hoped this incident would put an end to al-Jazzār and that Emir Yūsuf would rule in Acre after him. When al-Jazzār learned of the contents of the message, he issued an order that Emir Yūsuf, Shaykh Ghandūr, Ibrāhīm 'Azzām and his son Khalīl should be hanged; and all four were executed. The prisoners were totally innocent of anything in this, and such was the reward for the favor Emir Yūsuf and his steward had formerly shown to al-Jazzār!

In his early days al-Jazzār used to drink intoxicants, but his behavior was less evil than what it came to be after he forswore them. Yet even in the worst of his infamy he maintained equal treatment of his subjects of different religions, for he would imprison Muslim ulema, Christian priests, Jewish rabbis [16] and Druze elders[36] alike. Similarly, in applying different types of excruciating torture to them, he made no distinction among them—they who would be guilty of nothing more than not paying fines he levied on them, although they might not possess as much as he demanded. If we were to describe all of al-Jazzār's atrocities, we would have to write a large volume.

MŪSĀ RIZQ STUMBLES UPON BURIED TREASURE AND DIES UNDER TORTURE.

An incident occurred that almost involved Ibrāhīm Mishāqa. During the time of his administration in Bshāra, the Christians began taking up farming because of the incentives he offered for reclamation of the land, which had been much devastated by lawless soldiery during the many wars with the shaykhs and by the reduction of the local population, who had either been killed or run away.

One of the Tyrene Christians who took up farming was a man named Mūsā Rizq. He chanced upon an ancient hoard of buried gold estimated to be of great value. In order to hide it from the eyes of the government, this man took a substantial portion and buried it secretly in various fields. The peasants came and began to find the gold, word spread, and people poured in to dig for it. This Mūsā was among those who were searching. This reached the ears of al-Jazzār, who sent orders to find out the names of all persons who had come to search, where they lived, the day of their arrival and the amount each had found, accompanied by threats for everyone who denied anything. Those who had come to search were still in these fields looking for gold, and the official was easily able to take down their names and places of residence, the day of their arrival and what each had collected. Having confiscated everything he found on them, he asked whether anyone else had come. They told him that Mūsā Rizq had come two days later than the others and searched with them for one day, during which he had a stroke of good luck and found a cache of gold. He had gone to stash it in his house and then return, but days had passed and they had not seen him in the fields. [The official] summoned him, confiscated what he admitted to, wrote down his name and his account, and sent it to al-Jazzār.

[Al-Jazzār] was extraordinarily sharp, and his suspicion fell squarely on Mūsā Rizq, for he reckoned that if he had been in want of gold he would not have been satisfied with searching for only one day. He ordered him brought to Acre and had him interrogated, first with enticements, then with threats; but he persisted in his denial. Envy led many rumormongers to declare that this man was connected with Ibrāhīm Mishāqa, with whom he must have divided the money, for this man was not capable of acting thus in the affair without the guidance of the other.

These things were whispered into al-Jazzār's ear, who said, "I know very well how intelligent and capable Ibrāhīm is. He would not act in this way. Anyway, there is no reason at present to question him. If suspicion should point to him, we will do what is necessary." Then he ordered [17] Mūsā Rizq turned over to the band of Kurds he employed to administer torture like the myrmidons of hell. They began to torture him first with whips, then by hanging him upside down by his hands and feet, then with weights on his back, then by putting a hot iron bowl on his head, then driving spikes under his fingernails, and other types [of torture]. Every day when they finished torturing him, they imprisoned him in a deep, covered well that had a little water in it. After enduring for a few days the harshest and cruelest tortures, he confessed that he had found the treasure intact. He had scattered some of it, taken some to his house and left the rest underground. When asked the location, he said he could not recall. When al-Jazzār was notified of this, he had the gold brought that [Mūsā] said he had taken to his house, and ordered them to cease torturing him for a few days.

Then they brought Mūsā's wife to exhort him to confess in order to save himself from torture and to tell the truth if he had a partner.

They had her speak with him from above the cover to the well while they listened to what she said. "I got permission from al-Jazzār to see you alone to put an end to this incident and save you from the plight you are in," she said. "He allowed me this and promised me that everything will be all right if you tell the truth. Have pity on yourself and on your children, make an effort to save yourself. Don't worry about informing on Ibrāhīm Mishāqa, who everybody says was your partner. How much of the treasure do you think is left? What use is it to you if you have to die under torture if you don't tell the truth?"

"Only God and I know where the treasure is," he replied. "I have no partner in it, not Ibrāhīm Mishāqa or anyone else; and I don't know how much it is exactly, although I can say that there must be hundreds of pounds of gold stored in a vault as wide as a threshing floor. I can't say where it is because it would be a king's ransom. If al-Jazzār got his hands on it he could gain power, and it's not right to help a tyrant. It would be better for me to die under torture. This is my resolve and my last word."

When al-Jazzār was told what Mūsā had said, his rage increased and he ordered them to torture him again, but to guard against his dying under torture, for he hoped that at length he would confess the truth. He was subjected to horrible torture, and one day, while being tormented with smoke, having been tied to a wall and having billows of smoke blown into his face, he suffocated and died. Al-Jazzār sent trusted agents to dig in many of the fields Mūsā Rizq had frequented, but to no avail.

Mīkhāyīl Ḥallāj married [Mūsā Rizq's] widow and had by her Ibrāhīm, who died in Egypt. I learned of this incident from her in Ṣūr in 1814.

AL-JAZZĀR SLAUGHTERS TWO HUNDRED AND THIRTY HUMAN BEINGS FOR NO REASON.

We must mention one of al-Jazzār's deeds that went beyond the bounds of bestiality, not to mention the bounds of humanity, for [beasts] kill to eat, to defend themselves, or to carry out what they have been ordered [18] to do by human beings, who were created in God's image but who have rebelled against Him and are so self-satisfied that they have become more savage than beasts. Indeed it is from humans that animals learn cruelty to their own kind, for we see that lions, tigers and elephants do not attack their own kind unless they have been trained to do so by man. We see that the dog, the most domesticated animal, learns by association with humans how to injure members of its own kind. Humans are not content to have people slaughter one another, but do so with tame animals like rams and cocks when they incite one ram against another and set cocks one upon another to destroy each other.

Another of al-Jazzār's deeds is as follows. One day he ordered the craftsmen and artisans to be gathered together. All traders, merchants, and artisans that could be found were brought to his palace. Al-Jazzār stood in the doorway and ordered them to be presented to him one by one, and he ordered each to uncover his forehead, which he regarded attentively; some he sent on their way and others he detained. Around 230 persons of different religions, classes and occupations he kept. Among them was the grandfather of Khawāja Rūfāyīl Qanawātī and Mīkhāyīl al-Bāshā, a relative of the two al-Bāshās who now live in Beirut. Towards the end of the day he ordered them to be taken outside the city to the seashore, to be butchered by a blow to the back of the neck, and to be left lying prone so that the beasts might eat their fill until the next day, when the remains could be buried. So the "myrmidons of hell" escorted them to the place of martyrdom, killed them as ordered and left them around sunset.

It happened that a pious Muslim peasant had finished a job in Acre and wanted to leave, but the gate was locked until the "myrmidons" had finished their task and was not opened again until sunset, when the butchers returned. Then he went out riding on his donkey, his path leading to the slaughtered men. He saw one of them move, but as he advanced toward him the movement ceased. He called to him: "I saw that you're still alive. Don't be afraid of me, I'm coming to help you, for God's sake!" Thereupon he answered him in a mournful, choked voice: "Yes, I am still alive." The peasant got off his donkey and saw that the man's throat had not been slit to the principal arteries, so he bound the wound as best he could and mounted him on his donkey, supporting him with his arms and walking by his side until he had conveyed him to his village, where he hid him in his house and stitched up his wound to the best of his ability.

The next day he went down to Acre, got some ointment for him and attended him until he had recovered. Then he told him that he feared for him to stay in al-Jazzār's territory because it might cause them both to be killed, and he was not confident that the case could remain secret. [Mikhāyīl] offered him his gratitude, which was all he had to offer, and asked him to get him to Syria, where he would be able to find some means of supporting himself. The peasant was dubious about sending him in the company of anyone else, lest news of the matter leak out, so he mounted him on his beast and left [19] with him by night, proceeding hastily until he was out of al-Jazzār's territory. Only then did he stop to rest and then moved on to Damascus at a more leisurely pace. When they arrived, the peasant rented a place in which he installed the man he had saved, gave him what he would need to live on until he could find means to support himself, bade him farewell and returned to his village. This person whose throat was slit was Mīkhāyīl al-Bāshā.

This case reminds me of what it says in the Holy Gospel about the Samaritan who dressed the wounds of the man who had fallen among thieves, but what this Muslim did for the Christian is greater, because he endangered himself to rescue a stranger he had never seen before. Thus are piety and virtue to be found among Muslims, who practice charity toward perfect strangers. Suffice it as an example to mention the deeds I witnessed with my own eyes of His Excellency Emir 'Abdul-Qādir al-Jazāyirī, the late Ṣāliḥ Āghā al-Mahāyinī, and many other pious Muslims of various classes during the Incident of 1860. From massacre at the swords of raving villains, they preserved sixteen thousand Christian souls, who, for reasons that have remained secret and unacknowledged, were left unprotected by the Damascene authorities. There is evidence to establish it, but it is forbidden to utter it.

To return to al-Jazzār's part in this affair. One of his spies reported to him, "Mīkhāyīl al-Bāshā, who was one of those whose execution you ordered, did not die. It is not known how he was rescued, but it has been established that he is now in Ṣūr working as a builder, and his neck is bent forward. With your approval an order could be issued to have him brought in and an investigation made as to how he was saved, what the name of the person was who saved him, and who was in charge of slaying him but did not discharge his duty faithfully. It's up to you to say what ought to be the punishment of these traitors, along with those who rescued him, for their disloyalty to our efendi's order."

"It appears that this man didn't deserve to die," al-Jazzār replied, "so the Creator provided the means for his rescue and sent you to be a substitute for him." With this he ordered the spy to be slain, and he was beheaded with a blow to the back of the neck. The people were very happy over this.

FORTY INNOCENT PRISONERS ARE KILLED FOR THEIR CHAINS.

Let us mention another of al-Jazzār's evil deeds. There was a Malikī,[37] M'allim Khalīl 'Aṭiyya from Dayr al-Qamar, the engineer who brought water from the al-Bārūk River to Shaykh Bashīr Jumblāṭ's house in the village of al-Mukhtāra, then in 1230 [1815] from the Ṣafā River to the palace of Emir Bashīr the Great in Bayt al-Dīn. This Khalīl had four brothers, two of whom went in 1798 to trade in Egypt. When

Egypt was conquered in 1799 by the French,[38] the English blocaded the sea route and cut off trade. Most of the Levantines there [20] tried to return to their homeland, and among them were the two 'Aṭiyya boys and a Maronite priest of the Qayyāla family of Mount [Lebanon] who was coming home from a Greek Orthodox school. They set sail in a small ship for the harbor of Ṣaydā, but the wind prevented them from reaching it, so they entered the harbor at Acre. Al-Jazzār ordered everything found on the ship confiscated and all the passengers placed in shackles in the prison. It was done as he ordered. There were more than forty persons.

When the news reached Dayr al-Qamar, the 'Aṭiyya family sent the third brother with a sum of money to serve his brothers and procure necessities for them as long as they were in prison. He found them imprisoned in the large dungeon beneath the harem. The gate to the dungeon was at the bottom of the steps leading to [the harem], the treasury and the tower. Once the 'Aṭiyya boy was bringing food to his brothers when al-Jazzār happened to be coming down the steps and saw him. He asked who he was and was told that he was taking food to his two imprisoned brothers; thereupon he ordered him imprisoned alongside them.

One day the warden complained that he had no more iron chains to shackle those he had been ordered to fetter. Al-Jazzār told him to strangle the prisoners who had come from Egypt and throw them into the sea. And should that not suffice, he should take a hundred of the remaining prisoners. At night the Kurds came with porters and palm-leaf baskets. They did not use strangulation, but instead stripped the unfortunate wretches, made them sit in the baskets, broke their backs with an iron sledgehammer, then sewed them up in the baskets and had them thrown into the sea. Thus the operation was carried out. The three young 'Aṭiyya boys along with the Maronite priest we have mentioned were among the group of unfortunates whom this hideous fate befell.

THE SAKRŪJ CLERKS IN THE TREASURY ARE KILLED.

The Sakrūj brothers we have mentioned before were among the foremost of al-Jazzār's [retinue], for the running of the treasury was in their hands. They were friends of Ibrāhīm Mishāqa, trusted him and relied upon his advice. Al-Jazzār turned against them, arrested them and demanded they hand over money to his treasury. Ibrāhīm Mishāqa advised them to pay, and they promised to pay it little by little. Then al-Jazzār restored them to favor and reinstated them to their posts. When they had finished paying what had been demanded of them, he arrested them again. They informed Ibrāhīm Mishāqa of this and [said] they had already given all they owned and were determined not to agree to pay anything [more] lest al-Jazzār come back asking a third and a fourth time. Ibrāhīm Mishāqa sent a written answer to them that they ought to agree to pay what was demanded of them and not risk their lives. If they had no more money, he had enough to pay for them. His reply reached them, but they would not agree and remained defiant, responding that they would not agree to pay a thing. Thereupon al-Jazzār ordered their execution. After they were killed, their papers were collected and brought to al-Jazzār. Among them was the letter [21] from Ibrāhīm Mishāqa, who, as soon as [news of] their refusal of his advice and their subsequent execution reached him, came down with a fever and had to be taken from Bshāra to his home in Ṣūr.

IBRĀHĪM MISHĀQA DIES, AND THE BSHĀRA REGION IS GIVEN TO HIS SON JIRJIS FOR TAX-FARMING, ALONG WITH THE SAKRŪJ [BROTHERS'] FINE.

When al-Jazzār came across Ibrāhīm Mishāqa's reply that he had enough to pay for them, he said, "We haven't lost a thing," and immediately sent to summon him to Acre. However, they found him gravely ill in his house and notified al-Jazzār, who ordered them to wait: if he recovered, they were to bring him; if he died, they should bring his eldest son. A few days later he passed away at the age of forty-two. His eldest son Jirjis was about twenty years old. They took him straightaway to Acre, not even allowing him time to bury his father. There Shaykh Ṭāhā took him into his home, rather than prison, because of his former friendship with his father. He explained to him that fifteen thousand piastres (equivalent to 50,000 liras in today's currency) had been demanded of the ones who had been killed. "In this letter," he said, "your father pledged to pay for them. Our efendi wants you to pay this amount and assume your father's position, with his favor upon you as it was on your father."

"When my father and the ones who were killed were alive, they knew what they were about," he replied, "but I don't know anything more of my father's affairs than an occasional paper he would tell me to write. I don't know whether he possessed such sums in cash that I could pledge to pay an enormous sum like this. True, my father had real estate and shops and many animals, sheep, cows, camels, horses, and other things. I will present them all to our efendi's treasury, but I am not able to offer more than that. It is his decision."

Then he was taken to face al-Jazzār, who was told what answer he had made. When al-Jazzār saw that he was young and delicate and replied modestly, he ordered that only two-thirds of the sum be taken from him in installments over eighteen months and that he be assigned the tax-collection of the Bshāra region like his father. He also ordered him to be dressed in fur as a sign of favor. Jirjis wrote a bond for himself to the treasury for the tax revenue in the aforementioned installments, which he would pay as salary to the troops. Returning home, he found only a small amount of cash left by his father, so he began to sell herd animals and movable property. The camels he sold for thirty piastres and the ewes with their lambs for five piastres. At first he paid the installments on time and avoided selling the immovable property such as houses, warehouses, shops, fields and orchards. This was the cause of his second fall and the total loss of his wealth, as shall be recounted.

In the year in which he died, Ibrāhīm Mishāqa had been thinking of arranging his son Jirjis' marriage. He had a trade partnership in Ṣūr with a Damascene named Jirjis Surūr. He was the father of Mikhāyīl Surūr, who was the French vice-consul in Damietta. Jirjis Surūr approved of Ibrāhīm Mishāqa's idea to betrothe his wife's sister, the daughter of Ḥanna 'Anḥūrī, grandfather of the Ḥanna 'Anḥūrī who is a [22] respected merchant in Damascus, on condition that he bring her for a visit to her sister in Ṣūr, at which time he could decide whether to take her or not. They agreed upon this, he brought her to Ṣūr, and she proved to be a marvel of beauty and intelligence. It so happened that Ibrāhīm was away and did not return to Ṣūr until he was stricken with the illness of which he died. When the period of mourning was over, Jirjis Mishāqa married this girl.

JIRJIS MISHĀQA IS ARRESTED AND HIS WEALTH IS PLUNDERED, BUT HE IS RELEASED.

When Jirjis finished paying the installments on the tax revenues, he hoped that al-Jazzār would be more pleased with him, but this hope was dashed, for he was arrested by a North African officer and taken to Acre. There Shaykh Ṭāhā took charge of him and installed him in one of his offices, not allowing him to be put in prison. He told al-Jazzār that the boy had been raised in luxury and was still young, and that he had paid everything that had been assigned to him and was guilty of nothing deserving punishment. "If the aim is to get money from him," he said, "we will kill him if we put him in the criminals' prison, and we will get nowhere. It would be more fitting to treat him gently." Al-Jazzār agreed.

Now the reason for this treachery was as follows. [Al-Jazzār] had a henchman, a Christian from Ṣūr who made his living spying on people and was greatly feared by wealthy people on account of the mischief he did. (We don't want to publish his name out of consideration for his descendants.) Anyway, people would go to great lengths to curry his favor by paying him enough to satisfy him. To Jirjis Mishāqa, however, having once fallen into al-Jazzār's clutches[39] and been forced to pay enormous sums on installment, and having forthwith sold his possessions to pay them, it never occurred that this evil individual, who, after all, belonged to the same church and was from the same town, would have a hand in doubling his misfortune with no ostensible reason to compel him to do such an atrocious thing. What actually transpired was as follows.

Once in a gathering al-Jazzār was praising the trustworthiness of the Mishāqa family and [saying], "Even though Jirjis is young and hasn't had much experience, he knows how to manage well. He has come through with all we asked of him and paid it in full and on time—even sold his possessions to honor his pledge."

This spy was present and asked permission to speak, saying, "I am from his town and know his financial situation well. What he paid to the treasury is only a fraction of what he has. His father got hold of nearly three hundred villages over a period of eight years, and [Jirjis] has had the running of them for a year and a half now. What he is paying on them to the treasury isn't more than what one of their shaykhs would take from them. This is aside from the wealth of his rich father and grandfather, and not to mention the buried treasure Mūsā Rizq found, in which he was a partner. What has he sold in relation to what he owns? True, he sold a few camels and ewes to make people think he has no money, but what of the houses, warehouses, shops, orchards and fields he owns in Ṣūr, Ṣaydā and the Bshāra region? His mother's jewelry suffices, to say nothing of his tobacco trade with Egypt."

This speech made an impression on al-Jazzār, who never tired of extorting his subjects' money. The greatest sinner in his eyes was one who refused to [23] come up with what he was asked for. If he treated him mercifully and did not kill him outright, he would cut off his nose, then his right ear, then put out his right eye, even if he was one of his most devoted servants. M'allim Ḥannā al-'Awra, grandfather of the Ḥanna Efendi alive today, was a clerk of correspondence in the vizierate, and we know[40] his nose was cut off. Similarly the Jew M'allim Ḥāyīm Fārḥi, a man renowned for his learning and skillful management of affairs and for satisfying his master, as well as for being beloved by the population at large, had his nose and ear cut off and his right eye gouged out.

Anyway, on the spot al-Jazzār asked this spy to make a list for him of the Mishāqa family property everywhere and the names of their trading partners. He confiscated all of this to his treasury and, summoning Jirjis Mishāqa as stated previously, placed him under guard at Shaykh Ṭāhā's. When they demanded of him sums over and above what was registered with the treasury, he answered: "I will give all I own to remain in our efendi's favor." Then he gave them a ledger of all the debts people owed him and said, "I don't own anything but this." The spy did not give up and suggested he be sent to Ṣūr so his mother, wife and relatives could see him as the necessary tortures were being applied. His mother must have many things, [he suggested,] and perhaps he himself had no knowledge or awareness of them. When she saw her son being tortured she would pay whatever she had to lessen his torture, *as the uncritically faithful do in paying sums to the clergy to alleviate the torment of their dead relatives' souls. But there is a difference between the two: the desired result of what the clergy take is not apparent, while the profitable result of what tyrannical rulers take is quite obvious.*[41]

Al-Jazzār, with all his cruelty, was more equitable and merciful than this Christian. True, he issued the order to send Jirjis Mishāqa to Ṣūr, but he charged them not to torture him to death, just to threaten his mother and relatives with torturing him so they would be conciliatory[42] in paying prodigious sums when the torture began. Therefore they took him to Ṣūr as a prisoner and let his mother and family know they would be receiving orders for torturing him. They said an order had arrived to give him 500 lashes of the whip, and his mother sent word she would "buy" them from the treasury for such-and-such an amount, and they took the money from her. After some days they put a rope around his neck and paraded him before the house; his wife heard of this and gave them her jewelry, and they took him away. They "solicited" his pardon from al-Jazzār and took money [for it]. After a while they made him carry a plank and paraded him by the house, saying that an order had been issued to put him to the stake; his mother paid [more] money, and they took him away. They kept varying their threats all the while until they had taken the family's money—from his mother, wife, sisters, uncle's widow and daughters, who sold all the furnishings and carpets he owned. Even his relatives began to pay for him, although he told them he had nothing left to repay them, for he was indebted to his relatives and friends for a sum equivalent to about ten thousand rials.

Only when his complete bankruptcy was confirmed [24] was an order issued for his release, *although his mother, under the guidance of their priests, was not remiss in having numerous masses said along with invocations to the Mother of God and the saints to intercede to save her son. She also made many votive offerings to the monasteries and churches of their community. The only benefit she derived from this was that they too joined with al-Jazzār in pilfering the family's money. If they pray and offer what they call divine sacrifices for their people, it is all done for a price, and in that they are not at all so remiss as were Christ's apostles, who would have lowered the price of breaking bread, which now they call mass, and given prayers on behalf of the people for free. But instead they have fixed prices and special fees that vary according to the station of the officiating [priest] and for whom it is done. For example, the wage of a village priest for a mass is less than that of a city priest, who costs less than a monseigneur, who is surpassed by the bishop, who comes for less than a patriarch, who is outdone by a cardinal, who is less than the pope. The hierarchy among them is by and large fiercer than among Shi'ite shrines.

When Jirjis was released, he possessed nothing to cover the expenses of his large family—his mother, wife, brothers, sisters, his uncle's widow and her sons and daughters. A monk advised him to go to the abbot at the Monastery of the Savior, saying, "Surely he will not fail to assist you with your own money, [if] not the monks' money." He went there, and the abbot and the monks made a display of their grief over what had befallen him, and the abbot gave him five hundred piastres.

"Do you not hold anything of my father's?" he asked.

"I have treated you charitably with the monks' money," [the abbot] replied. "You want to create a ruckus about it that will reach al-Jazzār's hearing and cause it to be taxed away?"

"I'm not going to raise a ruckus," he said. "I'm just asking whether there might possibly be anything of ours with which we can keep the family from starving."

He returned to his family and told the monk what happened. He looked sad and said, "The abbot answered you so boldly?" He said yes. More concerning this case will come later.*[43]

JIRJIS MISHĀQA TRAVELS TO EGYPT AND RETURNS TO MOUNT LEBANON.

Jirjis no longer had enough money to trade with. Since his father had been rich, he had not taught him a trade by which to live. Now no one would employ him as a scribe for fear of al-Jazzār's reprisals. He gave his mother what he had received from the abbot, taking for himself only fifty piastres for travel expenses, and went to Egypt in the hopes of finding work with the help of his wife's brothers there, Mīkhāyīl, Rūfāyīl and Buṭrus 'Anḥūrī, who were wealthy merchants. When he reached them and they learned what he wanted, they answered, "We cannot keep you here or put you to work. Al-Jazzār's spies are many, and they will inevitably tell him that you came to Egypt to claim your monies being held by your wife's brothers; then he will summon us and you to come to him. The Ghuzz *sanjaqs* in this land will immediately grant his request, and we will be ruined. We will give you enough to meet your needs. Go hide in Mount Lebanon until things get better." They gave him a thousand piastres (worth four hundred rials [now]).

After spending the winter in Egypt and Damietta, and sending half of what he then had to his mother, he journeyed to Beirut and went up to Dayr al-Qamar, where he turned his name into Jarjūra,[44] with no surname, informing not even his family where he was. With the exception of two Tyrenes there, Ibrāhīm Dāūd Mansī, a relative of his employed by Emir Bashīr, and Jirjis Buṭrus, who worked as a goldsmith and was the paternal uncle of the valiant Ibrāhīm al-Ṭarābulsī, grandfather of the family now living in Dayr al-Qamar, whom we have already mentioned, no one knew who he was. (Jirjis was originally from Ṣūr and had been raised without a father; his mother had married a Maronite in Tripoli, and he had gone there with her.) "Jarjūra" Mishāqa figured that the rest of the money the 'Anḥūri *khawājas* had given him would soon be eaten up by expenses and he would then be reduced to begging. So he set himself to learn goldsmithing with Jirjis Buṭrus. He learned it in one month because he was good with his hands, and so he worked as a goldsmith and excelled in the craft. There exist to this day some of his products, the workmanship on which cannot be matched by any Syrian goldsmith.

Jirjis' mother feared she would be poverty stricken when the money her son had left for her was used up. She therefore embarked on an enterprise by which the family could live, baking bread for sale. For twenty piastres she bought a sturdy donkey to carry wheat to be milled in Rās al-'Ayn. In charge of this operation she put Yūsuf, son of her brother-in-law Bishāra, who had passed away before her husband. Her son Anton carried the dough to the oven to be baked. Her son Ayyūb and Yūḥannā, the second son of her brother-in-law Bishāra, carried trays of bread on their heads and made the rounds of the markets. She herself, her daughters, sister-in-law and niece washed and sifted the wheat and prepared the dough. By these means they avoided [25] begging.

She had two sons younger than Ayyūb, Nīqūlā and Qusṭanṭīn. They were killed by a smallpox epidemic that left blind their sister[45] Maryam, who survived until 1848, when she died of cholera in Damascus. Extremely bright and skilled with her hands, she was expert at the preparation of all sorts of dishes and other forms of housework. She could even thread a needle and sew her dresses and other necessities and weave straw mats with patterns of different colors; she could also

Bread vendor.

spin linen thread as evenly and correctly as if she could see.

Some time passed in this condition, in which the family suffered the misery of poverty, after having such vast wealth. Jirjis had been parted from his wife after she had borne him, on the 29th of November 1794, his first son, who was named Ibrāhīm after his grandfather.

THE GOVERNORSHIP OF DAMASCUS IS GIVEN TO AL-JAZZĀR, WHO LEAVES FOR THE PILGRIMAGE.

In this year al-Jazzār resolved to discharge his religious obligation of the pilgrimage to Mecca, and what the poet says is true:

A villain made the pilgrimage, but his money was wasted:
His abomination in the sight of people only increased with what he did.
He thinks going on pilgrimage will cause his sins to be forgiven,
But a dog is the vilest thing there is when it is washed.

He asked the Empire for permission, and it appointed him to the governorship of Damascus and the superintendence of the pilgrimage, in addition to the governorship of Ṣaydā. So he set off on the pilgrimage and performed his religious duty.

AL-JAZZĀR RETURNS AND MURDERS THE WOMEN OF HIS HAREM; THE MAMLŪKS REVOLT AGAINST HIM AND PLUNDER ṢŪR.

Upon his return he ordered his troops to attack the Lebanon, appointing Salīm Pasha, one of his *mamlūk*s, as commander. The officer of the Kurdish soldiers was the famous Mullā Ismā'īl, to whose authority all the Kurdish chiefs in Syria yielded. Also accompanying Salīm Pasha was his friend Ibrāhīm [Bū-] Qālūsh, a Greek Catholic of Ṣafad, who had been under the patronage of the Zaydānī shaykhs, a brave and generous man who could, if need be, mount 400 horsemen. He established such a firm friendship with al-Jazzār's *mamlūk*s that they considered him one of them.

After Salīm Pasha had set off with his troops and comrades from al-Jazzār's *mamlūk*s and had arrived at Ḥārat Ṣaydā with his troops, news reached him that, when al-Jazzār returned from the pilgrimage, someone had reported to him that his *mamlūk*s had acted perfidiously and had been having relations with his harem during his absence. "Therefore," [Salīm Pasha was told,] "he has sent you from him in order to do away with you. After your departure from Acre, he murdered everyone in his house, except for a young slavegirl eight years old, by grilling their faces. He locked the door of the house from within, the eunuchs with him, lit a great pile of coal in the courtyard, seized each woman by the hair and held her face down on the coals with his foot until she died. In this horrible operation he killed thirty-seven women."

When Salīm Pasha learned of this, he resolved to kill al-Jazzār and deliver the land from such evil. He made an agreement with Mullā Ismā'īl, the rest of the officers and his friend Ibrāhīm Qālūsh. They retraced their steps to Ṣūr to get the food and fodder the soldiers required for their horses. However, the guards at Ṣūr locked the city gates and would not allow them to enter for fear of [26] al-Jazzār's wrath, even though they were too few to be able to put up a resistance. Ibrāhīm Qālūsh approached them and addressed their chief politely, as they were acquainted, saying: "The troops must have food to eat and barley to feed their mounts. If you wish, we will take the troops and spend the night in Rās al-'Ayn. Just give us what the soldiers need from the government stores, as you did when we came to you from Acre. Don't give the troops a reason to get agitated and attack the city, for incidents may happen that will harm the people."

The [head guard] replied: "You took [supplies] before by al-Jazzār's order. We cannot give you anything now without his permission, for we will be held responsible. It is our duty to resist you to the best of our ability, even if we die."

When the reply reached Salīm Pasha, he ordered the soldiers to attack the city. He entered it by force, ransacking the houses and churches and taking the men's clothing. Even the women were left nothing save the barest covering. They went out to Rās al-'Ayn, where they made a market to sell what they had plundered. Anyone who had money that had not fallen into the hands of the looters could redeem his plundered goods for cash. Those who had nothing left borrowed from those who did, or from elsewhere, and redeemed what possessions they could not do without. The Mishāqa family, who were in worse straits than anyone else, were in a pitiful state, having no one to come to their assistance when everybody was similarly afflicted. With great effort they found someone to lend them the small amount they needed to redeem their most indispensable possessions. The soldiers did not pillage any foodstuffs but left them for the [people], because in the government storehouses there was more than they needed. In this incident only two Shi'ites and a Christian were killed resisting the looters.

After this the troops left and camped outside Acre. The only troops al-Jazzār had left to fire on them were the artillerymen on the walls and a few officers. He mustered them, supplementing them with any he could find in Acre—laborers, donkey drivers, grooms and Egyptian vendors of dried fish and baked beans. He put weapons in their hands, but most of them did not know how to use them. Shaykh Ṭāhā had a messenger sent clandestinely to Mullā Ismā'īl to win him over from Salīm Pasha. The reply came back that he would fight neither for nor against him. And he was the leader of Salīm Pasha's troops! At this point al-Jazzār approached them himself, escorted by the troops he had mustered, and battle began with the *mamlūk*s and Qālūsh's band. Mullā Ismā'īl withdrew from them with his men. The rest of the officers followed him, and no one remained with Salīm Pasha except the *mamlūk*s and Qālūsh, who, seeing what Mullā Ismā'īl and the other officers had done and fearing they would band together with al-Jazzār against them, fled and scattered over the countryside.

IBRĀHĪM QĀLŪSH IS KILLED.

Ibrāhīm Qālūsh headed for Mūsā al-Ḥannā's sons in the Ḥiṣn region, hoping for protection since they were Christian and ruled the area. He was escorted by his sons Ya'qūb, Nāṣir, Ilyās, and As'ad. Al-Jazzār made inquiries [27] until he found out where they were, but they were in the province of Damascus, which was another jurisdiction. He therefore peitioned the Empire for the governorship, and they gave it to him. Immediately he demanded that the sons of Mūsā al-Ḥannā surrender Ibrāhīm Qālūsh. They handed him over and sent him to Hama, where he was informed that al-Jazzār was demanding his head be cut off. He was advised to save himself by converting to Islam, but he would not consent and was beheaded. His sons fled and sought refuge with the beys of the 'Akkār region, who received them and treated them well. Their father had a brother named Abū-Kharmā in the region of Ṣafad. Al-Jazzār seized him and hanged him in Acre. When Sulaymān Pasha, al-Jazzār's *mamlūk*, became governor of Ṣaydā, Qālūsh's sons came to him, received a pension, and settled in Ṣūr.

In March of 1796 Jirjis Mishāqa summoned his family to Dayr al-Qamar; and on the 29th of November 1796, two years to the day after his first son, a second son was born to him. He named him Andreos because he was born on the eve of the feast [of St. Andrew]. [Jirjis'] brother Anton did not want to go to Dayr al-Qamar, so he went to Cairo and lived in the house of a prominent merchant who was a son of the paternal uncle of Khawāja Yūḥannā Frayj, who now resides in Beirut. This man undertook to educate Anton, taught him a good hand, accounting, Turkish and Italian, and took him with him to Europe, dying shortly after their return. Then Anton went to Damietta and spent some time in the establishment of Khawāja Niqūlā Kaḥīl. Then he went into partnership with Khawāja Buṭrus 'Anḥūrī, his sister-in-law's brother. He later married and had three sons, and he died in 1821 at the age of forty-two.

JIRJIS MISHĀQA IS EMPLOYED BY EMIR BASHĪR.

Emir Bashīr happened to come down to Acre. Passing through Ṣūr, he found the ruler residing in the Mishāqa house, which had become government property. He remembered Ibrāhīm Mishāqa and asked about his eldest son. They informed him of what had befallen him and of his being in Dayr al-Qamar with his family, working as a goldsmith. He felt sorry for them and, upon his return from Acre to Dayr al-Qamar, summoned Jirjis Mishāqa for an interview. Jirjis was very afraid, since the emir had been in Acre, and thought that al-Jazzār had demanded him from the emir, who had never asked about him before, even though most days he passed beneath the windows of his councilroom. However, he reconsidered, thinking that perhaps the emir had seen something of his goldwork and wanted something made. Anxious, he went with the messenger, and when he arrived at the emir's, he kissed his hand and was greeted with a smile that relieved his anxiety. Then, when coffee was ordered, he was reassured. [The emir] then dismissed the servants in attendance and asked him to relate what had befallen him. He told the emir everything that had happened, that he had not been spared until all he possessed had been lost and he had gone into debt for such-and-such sums for loans friends had made to save him, that he had gone to Egypt, where they had feared to keep him, and that therefore he had taken refuge under the protection of His Excellency [28] and had learned goldsmithing, which he pursued to provide his family with the necessities of life.

The emir evinced much distress and asked him to show him his handwriting, which he did. "Don't worry," he said, "God willing, you will have peace. For the time being, serve me as my personal scribe until I can find you a more suitable occupation. As of now I assign you a salary of 3000 piastres a year plus 500 piastres every Easter and Shrovetide, and 500 piastres' worth of garments plus three sacks of wheat delivered to your house a year. As for your debts in arrears to your benefactors, these must be paid to whom they are due, for you are unable to pay. Arrange them in installments, and I will pay them for you." And he ordered that he be given a fitting robe and some provisions for his house. With this, [Jirjis] kissed his hand and went out rejoicing, and the next day he joined [the emir's] service.

EMIR BASHĪR IS SEIZED AND IMPRISONED IN ACRE, BUT HE IS RELEASED AND REINSTATED AS RULER OF THE LEBANON.

Jirjis' peace of mind did not last long, and this was due to al-Jazzār's acts to devastate the mountain, change its rulers and impose fines on it. The emir happened once to be cut off from his retinue among al-Jazzār's soldiers on the Beirut coast. They seized him, his brother Emir Ḥasan and Shaykh Bashīr Jumblāṭ, took them to Acre and placed them in prison in chains. After more than twenty months had passed, al-Jazzār restored the emir to favor and released him from prison along with those who were with him. He restored the rulership of the Lebanon to him on condition that he make up all the past payments for the mountain that had fallen due, not only from him but also from the one who had been given the interim rule, and that he leave his son Emir Qāsim as a hostage with him. So he had his son Emir Qāsim brought and went up himself to Dayr al-Qamar; and Shaykh Bashīr went to his place, appointed as ruler of the Shūf along with the Jazzīn, Rīḥān, Kharnūb and Tuffāḥ regions. This shaykh was of the utmost integrity, and the emir relied on him, and they both relied for council on the opinion of Shaykh Najm al-'Uqaylī, who lived in the village of al-Samqāniyye between Dayr al-Qamar and al-Mukhtāra. He was one of the chief elders of the Druze and renowned in the Lebanon for piety, intelligence and sound opinion.

THE DRUZE PLOT AGAINST THE EMIR AND THE CHRISTIANS, BUT THEIR PLAN IS THWARTED BY THE POLICY OF SHAYKH NAJM AL-'UQAYLĪ, WHO WAS KNOWN FOR HIS SAGACITY.

During his time there was a plot among the Druze to attack the emir and the Christians, as occurred again in these recent years. A pact was made among the shaykhs and elders and was brought to Shaykh Najm for his signature and seal. The document was left for him to scrutinize, but he went secretly by night[46] to the emir and asked him what information he had of activity in the region. He answered that he knew of none. Then [the shaykh] said, "There is a great revolt afoot, but amnesty from the punishment they justly deserve must be granted to all those involved, because this is the most politic action. When [you promise this] I will acquaint you with the facts." The emir answered: "I don't doubt your integrity or the soundness of your advice. What you have requested is granted." Then he showed him the document [29] with its signatures and repeated his request that the matter be kept quiet, for if its authors knew that the emir knew about them, they would be forced to raise a revolt in which there would be no amnesty.

Then [Shaykh Najm] said to the envoys [of the Druze], "I have considered the contents of the document and discovered it to be a powerful means of destroying the Druze, not the Christians, because on the mountain alone they are many times our number, not to mention their great number in the Ottoman Empire, of which they make up half, and abroad they have a number of powerful kings. If we could achieve the impossible and kill all the Christians of the Lebanon, would the Sublime Empire maintain silence, even supposing that the Christian kings would ignore such an attack on their coreligionists? How could we defend ourselves? Do you suppose that of the seven thousand of us in the Lebanon more than five thousand are suitable for fighting? What can we do about forty thousand Christians on the mountain, let alone others?

*"Why do we not live in the major cities and dwell instead among rocks in the arid mountains, enduring poverty and hardship? It is in order to safeguard our honor, possessions and lives from attack by the Muslims. The Muhammadan Law requires them to treat us with such harshness. Even if we were to convert to Islam, they would not accept our conversion or tolerate our living in Muslim territory, whether we paid the poll-tax[47] or not. It is not lawful for them to eat meat we have slaughtered or to marry our women; rather it is incumbent on those in authority to wage war on us and shed our blood, even if we recognize the religion of Islam. This is different from their dispensation for Christians and Jews—even for Mazdaeans. When they pay the poll-tax, they treat them like Muslims, protect them from their enemies, and spend money and shed blood in their defense. It is licit for them to eat meat they slaughter and to marry their women, who may retain their own religion. Thus Christians have the utmost peace of mind wherever they live in Muslim territory, especially in that the Koran commends them and their monks and says that they are the people closest in affection to Muslims. However, when any of our community meet with Muslims they are forced to lie and deny their true religion, to pretend to be Muslims in order to preserve themselves from the precepts of the Muhammadan Law. Muslims think it was about us that the Koran says, 'When they meet those who believe, they say, "We do believe," but when they retire privately to their devils, they say, "We really hold with you, and only mock at those people." '[48]

"The presence of Christians among us is to our benefit, for many advantages accrue to us from their being here, such as the fact that there are those who serve our leaders and further their fortunes. Many of them shed their blood for their employers while fighting their enemies or defending them. If they were to leave the land to be rid of your arrogance, could you pay for their property? If you are thinking to rob them, you could not do it, for the Empire would be obligated to render them their rights, and it would love to separate itself from you, and you would be unable to dispute it with your small number. You would not be capable even of gaining your livelihoods. By doing this you would destroy both your nation and your leaders, who now are rulers over the Christians among them, for they would then be placed under Turkish and other rulers appointed by the Empire, who would make every endeavor to humiliate the clans and their leaders. Look around you at those who are Muslims, not outsiders like us: where are the Zaydānī shaykhs, rulers of Acre and the region of Ṣafad? How much degradation have their lords and peasantry been subjected to, especially the Druze living there, who have become the most degraded of all groups. Look at the Bshāra and Shqīf regions. Where are their shaykhs and leaders? What calamities have befallen them by the domination of foreign rulers over them? A rational man learns from the misfortune of others. What has happened to others can happen to you.*[49] It is necessary to guard against falling into the snare into which others like us have fallen. If you do not take heed and be like a single family with the Christians, then I tell you that from now on I am with anyone who says what I say, that we are with the Christians against their adversaries."

Through this wise man's guidance the plans of the leaders of the revolts came to nought. All became like a single family thanks to his act, which preserved the land from destruction. If there had been two like him among the Druze and Christians in our time, they could have preserved their land from the calamities that befell them in the Incidents of 1841 and 1860, which ended, to the everlasting detriment of the Druze, in the loss of the independence every emir and shaykh had in his region. Indeed, the Christian loss was great in property and men, but they were compensated for their property by the government treasury; and as for the men, if they hadn't died in the civil strife, they would have died off gradually anyway and been replaced by others. They gained in that they had been ruled by an emir from amongst themselves who had not the slightest authority over the Druze, who were under the rule of a Druze emir; but then they were consolidated with the Druze under the rulership of a Christian vizier appointed by the sultanate and sanctioned by the great Christian kings. Furthermore, much of the land that was formerly ruled by Druze shaykhs was taken from their hands and permanently assigned to a Christian administrator. Dayr al-Qamar, the capital of the Lebanon, which had belonged to the Abū-Nakad shaykhs and was their seat, came under the control of a Christian administrator, with Druze forbidden to settle there. Their houses, along with the houses of those shaykhs and the shaykhs of the Qāḍī family and the Abū-

Harmūsh family, along with their places of worship, fell into oblivion and were razed. This is the result of acting with ignorant zeal and lack of foresight.

Let us return to Emir Bashīr. He ruled the land, and his intendant for the affairs of the subjects [30] and for issuing orders within the land was Shaykh Abū-Khaṭṭār Sallūm al-Daḥdāḥ, the grandfather of the Metropolitan Ni'mat-Allāh who presently occupies the Maronite archepiscopal throne in Damascus. He was the first shaykh of the Daḥdāḥ family to be addressed by the emir as "my dear brother."[50]

The land, its people and shaykhs, even Christian and Druze emirs, were divided into two parties, one Jumblāṭī, headed by the Jumblāṭ clan,[51] and the other Yazbakī, headed by the 'Imād clan.[52] Emir Yūsuf had sided with the Yazbakīs, while Emir Bashīr sided with the Jumblāṭīs. Although he strove to create harmony between the two parties, he was not able to bring them together with impartiality because the Jumblāṭī leaders were wealthy, while most of the Yazbakīs were unable to maintain a style of living befitting their rank without a helping hand from the ruling emir. Because they had supported Emir Yūsuf, after he was killed they supported his children, minors whose guardian was Shaykh Jirjis ibn Bāz Abū-Shākir from Dayr al-Qamar, the father of Dāūd Bey Bāz, the present administrator. Emir Bashīr was not inclined to be friendly to them and was strongly attached to Shaykh Bashīr Jumblāṭ because of his integrity and wealth.

Now the shaykhs of the House of Abū-Nakad[53] were a party in their own right, sometimes leaning toward Jumblāṭ, who would then have ascendency over the 'Imād, and sometimes siding with the 'Imād, who would then preponderate over the Jumblāṭ. This is the reason they say on the mountain, "Our land is a balance between Jumblāṭ and Yazbak, while Nakad is a single weight. If it is added to one of the two, it will counterbalance the other." For a long time the existence of this division has left the mountain no rest from disturbances, and al-Jazzār always sowed strife among the chieftains in order to bring about the fall of them all. Such is the custom of the Turkish Empire.

ACRE IS BESIEGED BY THE FRENCH TROOPS UNDER THE LEADERSHIP OF BONAPARTE, BUT HE WITHDRAWS; EMIR BASHĪR IS DEPOSED AND HAS AN INTERVIEW WITH THE GRAND VIZIER IN AL-'ARISH FORT, RETURNS TO THE LEBANON AND FIGHTS THE SONS OF EMIR YŪSUF AND AL-JAZZĀR'S TROOPS; A TRUCE IS MADE AMONG THEM.

Let us return to Jirjis Mishāqa. The emir made him fiscal treasurer, and they called him "bursar." In 1799 Bonaparte brought French troops from Egypt and laid siege to Acre for two months, but when English ships cut off supplies, he was forced to withdraw. Although Emir Bashīr had observed strict neutrality to avoid helping the French, al-Jazzār accused him of supplying them with provisions. There is no basis for such an allegation, although there were people from the mountain and other places who sold intoxicants to the soldiers for profit. Al-Jazzār was so enraged with the emir that he forced him to leave the mountain. He left with all his attendants, among them Jirjis Mishāqa, who placed his family in the village of Rishmayyā. Along with [the emir] went also his dedicated companions such as Shaykh Bashīr Jumblāṭ and those Jumblāṭī clan leaders who relied on his protection, headed for the regions of al-Ḥiṣn and 'Akkār, which belonged to the Province of Damascus.

At this time the Grand Vizier Ziyā Pasha al-Ma'danī came with imperial troops to the al-'Arīsh Fort to drive the French from Egypt. Emir Bashīr wrote a letter to Admiral [Sir Sidney] Smith, the leader of the English fleet, and told him of his devotion to the Sublime Empire, [31] of how faithful in service he had been, of what al-Jazzār had unjustly done to him, and he solicited the Empire's compassion for just treatment. The admiral brought his ship near Tripoli and requested an interview with the emir. Accordingly he went with some attendants. After the meeting [the admiral] had him accompany him to meet the grand vizier in the al-'Arīsh Fort. [The vizier] met with him and treated the emir with deference, promising to return him as ruler of his lands as he had been. Then the emir returned to his men in 'Akkār. A few days later orders reached him from al-Jazzār to return to his lands as ruler. That was in 1800, and he returned to take possession of the land.

In this year, on the 20th of March [1800], at midday on Thursday, corresponding to the 23rd day of Shawwāl 1214 of the Hegira, in the village of Rishmayyā, a son was born to Jirjis Mishāqa before his return from 'Akkār. They called his name Mīkhāyīl, and he is the writer of this small piece.

After Emir Bashīr returned to Dayr al-Qamar and things settled down, Jirjis Mishāqa sent his family back there. It was not long, however, before al-Jazzār sowed discord between Emir Bashīr and the sons of Emir Yūsuf, whose guardian was Shaykh Jirjis Bāz, a man renowned for nobility and moral rectitude, as well as for his chivalry and bravery. In battle he was reckoned the equal of any five hundred cavaliers, and the people liked him because of his generosity and good nature. He was supported by the House of 'Imād and the shaykhs who followed them, just as Emir Bashīr was supported by the Jumblāṭ faction. The feud between these two factions was never-ending because the shaykhs of the Nakad family would support sometimes one faction and sometimes the other, and the faction with which they joined would have the upper hand.

When it became apparent to Emir Bashīr that he was hard put to maintain his advantage and that al-Jazzār's troops together with Emir Yūsuf's sons were contending for the Beirut coast with a strength he no longer had the power to resist, he thought the best thing to do would be to make peace. Therefore he secretly sent a message to Shaykh Jirjis Bāz, saying, "How long will this fighting continue in which we lose men and our land is devastated? Let us assume that you gain total victory and enter the land by force with foreign soldiers who make war on us.[54] and consider our blood, property and women fair game—especially of Druze and Christians. Do you think it would be possible for you to stop them from looting the wealth of the land or from outraging the women and shedding the blood of the men? You will be the cause for such calamities befalling your land. Would the people want to look you in the face? You must rather consider the consequences and inform me of your opinion and determination in this serious matter."

The reply to the envoy was as follows: "I detest anything that is bad for my country as much as His Excellency the Emir does. My conscience compels me [to act as I do] on behalf of the children of his uncle, of whom I am guardian. Nonetheless, tell His Excellency the Emir that I will come to him myself tonight under the cover of darkness to discuss this matter. I hope it will be an opportunity to resolve the matter in a manner satisfactory to both parties."

When it was dark, he went alone to the emir and kissed his hand [32] when presented to him. The meeting began with Shaykh Jirjis Bāz saying, "You, House of Shihāb, are the lords of all the inhabitants of the Lebanon, high and low alike. There is no doubt of your zealousness toward us all, Christian and Druze, and we are your subjects. If any of us is employed by you, it behooves him to serve you with all sincerity, to be faithful to you by all he holds holy and to shed his blood for what pleases you. It is well known to Your Excellency that I am a subject [of yours] from Dayr al-Qamar. Emir Yūsuf employed me, I served him faithfully, and he was better to me than I deserved. He was the eldest son of Emir Mulḥim, the eldest son of Emir Ḥaydar al-Shihābī, who gained control of the Lebanon after his cousin Emir Bashīr [I], who died without issue. Emirs [Bashīr and Ḥaydar] became lords of the mountain through the designation of their maternal uncle Emir Aḥmad al-Ma'nī, the last of the emirs of the House of Ma'n. Emir Yūsuf had more right to inherit the rule of the mountain than any of his relatives, but al-Jazzār betrayed him and killed him. He had three sons, minors who were put in my charge, and and I am bound by conscience to make every effort on their behalf and to demand the rights of inheritance due them from their forefathers. Your Excellency has taken possession of what is theirs by right and left them nothing to live on. Can I be blamed for speaking the truth in their service? Yes, this offensive on their behalf will cause harm to our land we do not wish; but if we look to the causes, you will find that it is your own indifference to the well-being of the children of your uncle, who patronized you and chose you over his own brothers and nearer cousins. Your Excellency should praise me for my zeal on behalf of your cousins, who are related to you, not to me. Despite all this, I have come to you alone, trusting in your sagacity, that I may know what you think the best plan is to put an end to these evils and that we may act accordingly."

The emir replied to him, "Your words are good and acceptable to me. What I consider the best thing to keep peace and end the strife is that the territory of Jbayl be given to Emir Yūsuf's sons, and your brother Shaykh 'Abdul-Aḥad be steward to them. Let me retain the rulership of Dayr al-Qamar and its dependencies, and you stay here in Dayr al-Qamar as my steward. Let the Yabak, Jumblāṭ and Nakad district lords remain tenured in the lands they hold by custom."

Shaykh Jirjis Bāz accepted this and asked the emir for an inviolable pledge to that effect. [The emir] swore on the Gospel and the Koran[55] that he would neither break his promise to them nor betray any of them. Shaykh Jirjis then returned to the camp and took Emir Yūsuf's sons and all their entourage to the emir by night. The next morning, when none of the emirs or shaykhs could be found in al-Jazzār's camp and it was realized that they had come to terms with Emir Bashīr, [al-Jazzār's men] left. There was general rejoicing among the people of the mountain over this truce, and each [of the parties] went to the place that had been determined for him and got ready to repel al-Jazzār's troops, [33] but as he made no disturbance, they calmed down.

M'ALLIM ḤĀYĪM FĀRḤĪ IS EMPLOYED AS SUPERINTENDENT OF THE TREASURY OF ACRE.

Let us interject here an event that was al-Jazzār's doing. After killing the two Sakrūj [brothers] who were his treasurers, he summoned from Damascus an intelligent man, a worthy Jew called M'allim Ḥāyīm Fārḥī. The Jews called him Ḥākhām Ḥāyīm because he "read," which word in their parlance means that he knew the Talmud well. This book is enormous and is divided into more than thirty volumes. It took more than four generations of Jewish scholars to compile it, half of this period falling before the Christian era. It contains exegesis of the Old Testament of the Holy Bible, the opinions of their scholars on what it means, both that over which they disagree and that on which they are in agreement, and an exposition of their laws and codes. It is a book to be respected, and even if there are some things in it human nature would find tasteless and sound minds could not accept—which we do not need to go into here—it can only be called a book that merits respect because of the precise[56] discussions contained therein.

Anyway, M'allim Ḥāyīm had few equals in goodnaturedness, moral character and perceptiveness of what was proper conduct and what was not. Al-Jazzār employed him as administrator of his treasury, though occasionally he would get angry with him for no reason and have him imprisoned. Then, when he realized how much he needed him for his good counsel and administrative ability, he would restore him to favor and return him to his position. Once in anger he had his nose cut off, another time his right ear, and another time he had his right eye plucked out, these being, next to outright execution, the worst of his punishments.

Al-Jazzār was late making the payments assigned to him by the sultanate and made excuses for not paying by claiming to need to hire soldiers to bring the mountain into submission. The Empire, however, got tired of his longwinded excuses and wrote to him that [payment] was long overdue and it appeared that he was incapable of managing. The Empire had therefore decided to dispatch a vizier plenipotentiary with enough soldiers to humble the Lebanon to its authority. In answer he wrote: "In a few days, God willing, I will present tidings of conquest, for it is apparent that they are too weak to resist and many of them have fled from battle engagements. We have prevented the arrival of supplies to them from the Biqā' and the coastal lands, and they cannot survive without them because the arable land on the mountain is too little to support the inhabitants."

A short time later he sent false news to the imperial government with a couple of Tatar [couriers] that he had conquered the mountain and found there 120,000 Christian men and 60,000 Druze, in addition to 30,000 Shi'ite Muslims and a like number of Sunnis. He was presented with a jewel-encrusted sword and praised for his diligence. M'allim Ḥāyīm was in prison at the time and knew nothing of al-Jazzār's scheme. After some time they sent him from the capital the usual number of tax[57] bills for the Christians, to which they added 120,000 bills to cover the Christians of the Lebanon. He summoned M'allim Ḥāyīm back to his post and asked what arrangements he thought should be made in this matter. "It will have to be paid now," he said, "from [34] your treasury to lend credence to your report to the Empire that you conquered the Lebanon and to the number of Christians you reported there. Shortly thereafter we will make some arrangement to have the excess cancelled." Therefore he paid the bills, but a few months later he sent news to the Empire that the Christians of the Lebanon had converted to Islam. At the beginning of the next year they again sent him the increased number of tax bills as before, but he returned the extra ones, claiming that he had already reported that the Christians of the Lebanon had converted to Islam and were therefore legally exempt from the poll-tax. Thus did the Empire at that time neglect to investigate the truth of what her agents reported to her.

JUMBLĀṬ AND 'IMĀD ALLY AND TREACHEROUSLY KILL THE NAKAD SHAYKHS.

Let us return to the events of the mountain. The 'Imād and Jumblāṭ shaykhs agreed among themselves to destroy the Nakad faction, the chief cause of contention between Jumblāṭ and 'Imād by uniting sometimes with Jumblāṭ and sometimes with 'Imād and thereby provoking strife between the two. The emir too was constrained in his actions because, although he dwelt in Dayr al-Qamar, the seat of the ruler, nonetheless the real rule was in the hands of the Nakad shaykhs. If a man committed a crime at the palace gate and then ran across the water of the Shālūṭ, which divided the palace from the shaykhs' houses, the emir's men were not permitted to follow him across to apprehend him. The emir therefore gave his consent to what Jumblāṭ and 'Imād had decided to do.

One day the shaykhs met in the emir's presence. Unaware of what had been arranged, six of the most feared leaders of the Nakad faction were seized and put to death. Among them was Shaykh Qāsim and his brother Shaykh Sīd-Aḥmad, both of them grandfathers of Qāsim Bey and Bashīr Bey, who are alive today.[58] This operation led to an increased attachment of the Christians of Dayr al-Qamar to Shaykh Jirjis Bāz. Ignorant youths among them often acted hostilely toward the Druze who came to Dayr al-Qamar for judgment in their affairs, taunting them with curses and obscene words no Druze would dare utter. Those who were so abused would complain to their leaders of what had happened to them, and they would report the complaints to the emir, who would imprison the offender to be punished. [The offender's] people would then apply to Shaykh Jirjis Bāz, who would suspend the sentence. Sometimes he released prisoners without even asking the emir's permission. Jirjis Bāz's presumption went so far that the emir and the Druze shaykhs became annoyed at his highhandedness and secretly agreed to kill on the same day both him and his brother ʻAbdul-Aḥad in Jbayl. Emir Ḥasan, the emir's brother, lived in the village of Ghazīr and had many grudges against ʻAbdul-Aḥad.

The emir exhibited his displeasure with the shayhs of the ʻImād family by putting out a bill against them for an amount of money they were unable to pay. This was part of the secret plan and was intended to provoke them into going to Jbayl to ask Shaykh ʻAbdul-Aḥad to intercede [35] with the emir and smoothe over his displeasure with them, and there they would be treacherously dealt with; and thus they set out. However, Shaykh Bashīr Jumblāṭ had come to the emir as usual with some of his servants and hidden many of his men at the approach to al-Samqāniyye opposite Dayr al-Qamar, fearing an attack by the men of [Dayr al-Qamar] on the emir. He charged them to rush Dayr al-Qamar immediately if they heard gunshots from the palace.

On the day it was calculated that the ʻImād shaykhs would be entering Jbayl in the afternoon, the emir sent one of his followers to invite Shaykh Jirjis Bāz for an interview. The shaykh was asleep, so they woke him up. He customarily carried a dagger in his belt, but at that hour he thought it was too much to carry, since he would be accompanied by his attendants while crossing the square and many of the youthful inhabitants would follow. So that day he took with him only one unarmed servant and went out the secret door at the back of his house and entered the Maronite monks' cloister, where there was a secret door into the emir's reception hall. Entering and finding the emir seated in a room, he went in and sat down as usual. Then the emir got up as though to tend to some business, went through the door and locked it behind him. Inside the room was a hidden alcove in which were ten men of the Zayn al-Dīn family, whose job it was to imprison criminals and administer punishment. As soon as the emir had left, they attacked Shaykh Jirjis, strangled him and threw his body into the monks' cloister. At the same time agents brought the Malikī Yūsuf Āghā al-Turk from his house and killed him because he was a supporter of Jirjis Bāz.

The emir, fearing a failure of the operation in Jbayl, immediately rode out with a number of his retinue and headed for Jbayl. As he entered the place called Qabr Shmūn, he was met by a messenger from Jbayl who informed him that Shaykh ʻAbdul-Aḥad had been killed and Emir Yūsuf's sons had been seized after some resistance, during which several on both sides were killed. When he reached Jbayl he ordered Emir Yūsuf's sons to be blinded, a task undertaken by Qāsim ibn al-ʻArab Ṣāliḥ, a black slave of the emir's father. He put their eyes out in a most cruel fashion by heating iron rods and sticking them in their eyes. This hideous operation he repeated three times in one day. That was in the month of August 1808.

THE DEATH OF AL-JAZZĀR; SULAYMĀN PASHA ASSUMES THE GOVERNORSHIP.

Let us return to al-Jazzār. In 1219, which corresponds to A.D. 1804, he died in his bed at the age of eighty-four; and there was great rejoicing among all the people of the province of Ṣaydā over his death and their deliverance from his oppression. On behalf of the sultanate came Rāghib Efendī, who later became the governor of Aleppo, to record what al-Jazzār had left, for it was the rule of the Empire at that time to take whatever property, assets and effects were left by those it employed. He made a record of the estate and promisory notes [al-Jazzār] used to have the emirs and shaykhs [36] of the country make out, over and above state taxes, when they were given office, after which he would depose them before payment was due. These tyrannical debts were calculated as due to the Empire, but when they discovered how vast they were and realized that it was impossible to collect them, they imposed them in installments over a period of years on the peasantry of those emirs' and shaykhs' lands.

Mount Lebanon used to pay taxes twice, and a single tax amounted to four hundred purses. On the mountain were some state taxes, such as the tax on the number of goats and on state lands, the *jawālī* tax on Christians and the *farīda* tax on Druze,[59] the latter two being distributed among the chieftains instead of the poll-tax. Some places, such as Dayr al-Qamar and others, were exempt from this tax, which would be paid as part of the lump sum due the treasury of the provincial vizier. What was left over would go to provide for the emir and his servants. The portion of al-Jazzār's demands imposed on the Lebanon was equal to six times the state tax and was called a "deduction." The people had to pay two taxes, the state tax plus six times as much for the "deduction," from which no place was exempted except Dayr al-Qamar, because it provided special services for the ruler not imposed on any other town.

When the surplus of the state taxes was not spent, [the emir] used to purchase from the Empire land in the Biqā' called al-Ḥille al-Gharbiyye, near Zaḥle, in the name of his sons with a *mālikāna* lease.[60] If the holder of [a *mālikāna* lease] died before turning it over to his sons or someone else, it reverted free and clear to the Empire, which would sell it again for more; but whatever the price, the sons of the holder had the first option to buy. On this land he built a village called al-M'allaqa. In this same manner he also took from the governor of Damascus an extensive tract of land, called Tall al-Akhḍar, by executive order and judicial ruling from the Court of Damascus to the effect that if he was improving and developing the land, it belonged to him, and if any governor took it from him by aggression, he would have the right to recoup all he had spent on improvement and development. The emir thus acquired several places in the Biqā', the income from which sufficed to cover the difference between his income from the mountain and his expenses. On Tall al-Akhḍar he spent huge sums, draining the bogs, digging ditches to drain the water away, clearing the land of thistles and wild vegetation and building dwellings for the peasants; and thus it became an important village.

After al-Jazzār's death, one of his *mamlūk*s, Sulaymān Pasha, was posted to the governorship of Ṣaydā. He was originally a Georgian Orthodox Christian who had been abducted as a youth and sold to the Muslims, and in the end he came to al-Jazzār. This man was clement by nature, goodhearted and peaceloving; he hated all evil, was humble and detested prideful people. Every action he did was in accordance with the religious law, and he ordered [the agents of] the Sublime Empire to treat all subjects with equality, whether Muslim, Christian, Jew, [37] Druze or Nuṣayrī, and would permit no one, peasant or soldier, to transgress upon another in any matter. He had a friend and companion who was like a brother to him, also one of al-Jazzār's *mamlūk*s and a Georgian by origin, named 'Alī Pasha. For him he obtained the rank of *mīrmīrān* from the Empire and made him his steward.

M'ALLIM ḤĀYĪM IS EMPLOYED; AMNESTY IS GRANTED TO THE DISPLACED MUTAWĀLĪ SHAYKHS.

[Sulaymān Pasha and 'Alī Pasha] summoned M'allim Ḥāyīm Fārḥī the Jew, who has been mentioned before, and said to him, "We want to employ you because we know of your loyalty in serving al-Jazzār."

"Yes," he replied, "I served him in all loyalty, but he repaid me by grilling my face[61] and putting my right eye out, whereas my only fault was to offer advice to put a stop to some of his actions that were wearing him out and ruining the country. If you are determined to conduct yourselves like him, I beg you to excuse me from service and allow me to stay at home or to go to my people in Damascus."

Sulaymān Pasha answered, "From the bottom of my heart I detest every action that harms the people and angers God. I seek peace for the country and the contentment of the Sublime Empire with the payment of regular taxes yearly, along with the amount that was imposed to cover al-Jazzār's legacy. For myself I shall not ask from you more than that a thousand quarter gold *funduqlī*s be put in my pocket on Fridays for me to distribute among the poor when I come out from the prayer. My household and personal expenses shall be turned over to you to deal with, as I shall put you in charge of all works in the province.

Turkish customs official.

I shall issue no order without your sanction, that I promise you; and God is my witness that I will never betray you or go against your opinion in anything. Do your job as you think best."

M'allim Ḥāyīm replied: "The prosperity of the country depends upon having agents who are competent to administer the departments they are put in charge of, who will not covet what the subjects possess and will not be tempted into corruption. The subjects must be secure of their lives and possessions from their rulers, who are bound to maintain and protect them from miscreants. If an official charged with some service or other discharges it faithfully, he should be well rewarded and promoted. However, if misconduct is proven against him in any action, or he takes a bribe against the interests of either ruler or ruled, then he should be punished and never employed again in any governmental capacity for the rest of his life.

"Next, the displaced Mutawālī shaykhs who prey upon the country, now that it has come under the control of the government, constantly disturb the peace by attacking villages and highway banditry, extort wayfarers and kill those who resist them. The government is forced to employ special soldiers to seek them out and destroy those they find, but very often the troops are defeated and killed wholesale. The losses incurred by the government and people because of them are nearly equal to what the treasury derives from the land. These unseemly acts they are obliged to do in order to obtain the wherewithal to live. Therefore it would be best to give them amnesty and a living and have them dwell outside their country to prevent unrest."

Then he added, "The impositions [38] of the governor of Ṣaydā have become too heavy in proportion to what the Empire had established in lieu of al-Jazzār's legacies, none of which were in cash but rather were all things pertaining to the functions of the governorship. The state taxes and duties scarcely suffice for provincial expenses, and the annual payment of taxes assessed goes to the sultanate; therefore, it is incumbent upon us to raise the amount we still owe. If we want to impose it on the subjects however we will, it will be difficult for them to bear, and instead of carrying out our intention of giving them peace, we will bring down upon them numerous hardships. We must then reduce the taxation of our subjects and impose it on the foreigners. That is possible if the sale of grain, oil and cotton to foreigners is limited exclusively to Acre; the people can get what they need directly from the peasants without imposts. Trustworthy agents should be appointed for this purpose, and at the end of every day the surplus of these three commodities taken in, over and above the needs of the [local] people, should be taken from the owners and they should be paid the price at which it was sold during that day. That which is obtained should be deposited in storehouses and sold by the government to the ships of foreign merchants at the highest possible price."

The governor Sulaymān Pasha and his steward 'Alī Pasha replied, "All functions of the province are entrusted to your opinion and arrangement. Do what you deem appropriate. Write the necessary orders, and the governor will sign them." And thus the rulership of the Lebanon was assigned to Emir Bashīr al-Shihābī, and in the matter of courtesy titles in official correspondence [it was established] that the governor would address him as "our son" but would raise his name above the line in deference to him, and that he would not be addressed as a servant by his superior but rather as follows: "Pride of noble princes, authority over great lords, our noble son Emir Bashīr al-Shihābī—may his glory increase. After greetings with all forms of honor and respect, and hoping your noble person is well, may it be known to you that. . . ."

RULERS ARE POSTED TO VARIOUS PARTS OF THE PROVINCE; MUḤAMMAD ĀGHĀ ABĪ-NABŪT IS DRIVEN FROM JAFFA.

Next, the rulership of Tripoli was given to Muṣṭafā Āghā Barbar, who was originally from al-Qalamūn, near Tripoli. At the beginning [of his career] he was in the service of Emir Ḥasan, Emir Bashīr's brother. This man, by virtue of his acumen and bravery, attained high office and acquired standing among the viziers and subjects.

The rulership of the region of Jaffa and Gaza was given to Muḥammad Āghā Abī-Nabūt, one of al-Jazzār's *mamlūks*, and he remained the ruler there until he craved independence. When what he was about was reported to Sulaymān Pasha, he attacked him with some troops, and he fled to Egypt. Later he went to the capital, where he attained promotion to the rank of vizier. To the Bshāra region was appointed the Kurd Ibrāhīm Āghā, a pious man and a rarity among Kurds.

Thus to every region a suitable ruler was sent with the understanding that an honest man would not be removed from his post unless it were to promote him to a higher position; but whoever displayed the slightest deviation from the straight and narrow would, over and above the prescribed punishment, never again be able to obtain a position in the government for the rest of his life. [39]

Then he appointed trustworthy [agents] to purchase grain, cotton and oil in Acre and store it for sale to foreigners at prices sometimes double the amount invested.

THE SHAWMAR REGION IS GIVEN AS A LIVING TO THE MUTAWĀLĪ SHAYKHS.

Next he wrote orders granting amnesty to the displaced Mutawālī shaykhs on condition that they settle down and send to Acre an envoy empowered by them all to parley with him how they might have peace and a living without unrest. When the order reached them, they complied; and directly the leaders themselves came to Acre, excusing themselves for what they had done by saying that al-Jazzār had left them neither property to live on nor security of life and limb. In order to preserve their lives they had been forced to do unseemly things. In answer they were granted amnesty and security, and they and their progeny were granted the Shawmar region, which lies between Ṣūr and Ṣaydā, with all its villages, in perpetuity exempt from taxation and state imposts, in lieu of their property in the Bshāra region. The districts of this region were divided among them, and to that effect ministerial documents were written to be kept safe in their hands. They left Acre pleased with what had transpired, and each of them settled in the village that had been apportioned to him. Thus peace obtained in the Bshāra region, roads became safe, and all the people in the province were as well-off as could be.

There was no longer any necessity for many soldiers, so only about two hundred infantrymen were put under the command of an Albanian officer named Muḥammad Āghā al-Nu'mān who lived in Ṣūr, and about five hundred cavalrymen were put under the command of three Kurdish officers, Shamdīn Āghā, Ni'mat Āghā and Ajalyaqīn Āghā; and two officers, 'Alī Abū-Zayd Āghā and Mūsā al-Ḥāsī Āghā, were put in charge of around four hundred Hawwāra Arab horsemen, while an officer called the *sagbān bāshī* was posted over a few footsoldiers stationed as guards at the palace gate in Acre. [There was also stationed] a group of cannoneers on the city walls, just as there were artillerymen and officers in every city.

There were not many clerks, for the customs offices and bureaux were leased to tax-farmers for fixed amounts; however, in Acre there were the treasury clerks M'allim Jirjis Masadiyya and Ibrāhīm al-Ṣābūnjī and their assistants, who were known for their honesty. The clerk of Arabic correspondence was M'allim Ḥannā al-'Awra, who was one of those inflicted with the most bestial of al-Jazzār's actions by having his nose cut off; with him were his sons Mīkhāyīl and Ibrāhīm, and they were all expert at calligraphy and epistolary style. M'allim Ḥayīm preferred to employ Greek Catholics and had little confidence in the Greek Orthodox because of their partiality for his predecessors, the Sakrūj family. Yet, because of the dispute with his people in Damascus, he mistrusted the sincerity of the Catholics employed in the Damascus treasury administration because they leaned toward the Catholic Baḥrī family who vied with [the Fārḥīs] for the treasury throughout the period of the Kurd Yūsuf Pasha's governorship. What transpired will be mentioned later. [40]

Part Two

1804-1820

SHAYKH 'ALĪ 'IMĀD WITHDRAWS TO EGYPT; WAHHĀBIS SEIZE CONTROL OF THE HEJAZ.

With the development [of the land], security of the roadways, establishment of justice and elimination of tyranny among the local people themselves on the one hand and between them and the government on the other, all the people of the province of Ṣaydā dwelt in peace. In this state of affairs no trouble occurred in the province, except for a few instances of aggression on the part of the 'Imād shaykhs, whose income had been reduced, that occasioned complaint of their conduct. Emir Bashīr did not trust them, because he was known to prefer the Jumblāṭ faction and never sat to make policy without Shaykh Bashīr Jumblāṭ, to the exclusion of [the 'Imād shaykhs]. In this way the hatred of the two factions for each other grew, and the emir was left without a single Yazbakī friend save Shaykh Shiblī 'Abdul-Malik, the *mutawallī* of the Jurd, who was righteous and had an ample income from his properties. The 'Imād shaykhs no longer felt safe from their rival, Shaykh Bashīr Jumblāṭ, because the ruling emir sided with him against them. They themselves had also weakened their party by taking part not only in the plot to kill the Nakad shaykhs, who had been wont to join with them when they saw the Jumblāṭīs overextending themselves, but also in the murder of Shaykh Jirjis Bāz and his brother 'Abdul-Aḥad and the blinding of Emir Yūsuf's sons, who were the greatest mainstay of the Yazbakī faction. No longer having anyone to support them, the leaders of [the 'Imād faction] were forced to quit the country. Shaykh 'Alī al-'Imād, the chief, left with his retainers to remain in Egypt until he could return to his country.

THE PILGRIMAGE IS SUSPENDED; 'ABDULLĀH PASHA AL-'AẒM IS REMOVED FROM DAMASCUS, WHICH IS GIVEN TO YŪSUF PASHA THE KURD; THE WAHHĀBIS APPROACH THE ḤAWRĀN.

With the departure of 'Imād, the country was quiet and incidents subsided until 1225 [1809], when news came of the approach of the Wahhābī army, which had gained control of the Hejaz, to al-Muzayrīb in the Ḥawrān. The governor of Damascus at that time was Kanj Yūsuf Pasha the Kurd, a renowned horseman and officer of a Kurdish battalion under his predecessor 'Abdullāh Pasha al-'Aẓm, during whose governorship the pilgrimage route was closed because the Wahhābīs had seized control of the Hejaz. Therefore Yūsuf implored the Empire to appoint him to Damascus, promising to get the pilgrimage reopened.[1] He was given the rank of vizier and the governorship of Damascus, along with the superintendence of the pilgrimage; and his predecessor went to reside in the city of Hama. However, Yūsuf Pasha was not capable of fulfilling his promise because he could neither send enough soldiers nor supply them with enough ammunition to drive the Wahhābī from the Hejaz, which was a forty-day march away through burning sands without food or water along the way for themselves or their beasts. In addition he had neither the wherewithal to spend on five hundred cavalry on a road like that nor any war matériel. What was his totally weak force to take on the numerous Wahhābī force at a remote distance from the provincial capital with no [possibility of] aid? His embarking upon what he was not able to do is reckoned as one of the greatest follies.

When he was unable to get the pilgrimage through, he began to distract the people [41] by ordering every so often ridiculous measures to be carried out in various ways. He ordered that every Muslim must let his beard grow, that no one should remain beardless, and that any barber who shaved a Muslim beard would have his hand cut off. So you would see many of the youth of Damascus fleeing to the coast and the Lebanon to avoid letting their beards grow, for it is a custom in the east that once [a man] has let his beard grow, he should not shave it for the rest of his life; and [to do so] is considered the greatest shame. If a man dares to shave his beard after letting it grow, if even out of necessity because of a disease on his face, shame attaches to him as long as he lives and hounds his descendants, who are then called "the house of the beard shaver."

There used to be a parallel to this ignorance among Europeans, for the men let their hair grow like women, though they shaved their beards and mustaches. The custom even grew up among them that the hair was to them what the eyes were among easterners, whose kings and princes used to arrange to have killed or blinded anyone they feared would challenge them for the reins of rule. Likewise, the Europeans used to plot either to have killed one whose challenge they feared or else to cut his hair, for then he would not be considered suitable to rule. One of the bygone kings of France died leaving his wife with two small sons. His brother usurped the kingdom but remained in fear that when his brother's sons reached their majority they would demand their right to rule. Therefore he laid his hands on them and gave their mother the choice of having their hair cut or having them killed. She chose for them to be killed, and they were. The importance of hair remained until Napoleon I Bonaparte abolished this superstition and cut his hair, and the people followed him nonetheless.

When it became customary in the east for young men, even soldiers, to be clean shaven, it became the European fashion to let the beard grow, just the opposite of the east. It is now considered proper for old European men to let their beards grow. Only prelates and clerics, such as deacons, priests and bishops, even the Pope himself, are clean-shaven like women, from whom they are distinguished by shaving their heads, leaving only a hollow ring [of hair] like a grouse nest they call a tonsura.

Let us return to the deeds of Yūsuf Pasha. Once he decided that Muslims must paint their eyes with black collyrium and draw out a long line with the collyrium from the corner of their eyes. Then he issued an edict that when Christian women went out of their houses into the streets they must be covered with a black garment and that their husbands must wear black turbans, while the Jews had to wear red turbans. Likewise, when Christian and Jewish men and women went to the baths they had to wrap themselves in black or red to be distinguished from Muslims. (The black turban used to be worn by the Abbasid caliph, and no other, as a sign of succession from their Prophet, because when he conquered Mecca and entered the Ka'ba [42] he mounted the pulpit and addressed the Muslims wearing a black turban. When the Fatimids came from North Africa and took Egypt from the Abbasids, they decreed that Christians should wear black turbans as a sign of contempt for the Abbasids.)

'ABBUD AL-BAḤRĪ SERVES YŪSUF PASHA; THE FĀRḤĪ FAMILY PLOT AGAINST HIM, BUT HE IS SAVED.

One event that happened during the governorship of Yūsuf Pasha was as follows. There was in his service a man from Homs, a Greek Catholic called 'Abbūd al-Baḥrī. This man was intelligent and skillful and was educated by his father Mīkhāyīl al-Baḥrī, who was renowned for his calligraphy and epistolary style and his knowledge of the Turkish

from Damascus, were the land not "folded up" for those who set out for there so that they arrived in only forty days. The governor of Damascus at that time was one of those who believed in this fraudulent shaykh, who used to go to visit him constantly to receive gifts, like the proverb that says "he who has molasses will attract flies from the caves of Bīsān."

This shaykh had much slandered the Jews, and M'allim Shaḥāda feared that his calumny would influence the governor and cause him to do them injury. Therefore he set a trap with some prayer beads of magnificent large pearls he had. It was customary to string at the end [of prayer beads] an oblong bead, called a "minaret," longer than three or four regular beads; but it was very rare to find one in pearl. He took the "minaret" off and kept it, and as soon as the pilgrims returned from Mecca, he took the prayer beads and presented them as a gift to the governor, who was overjoyed with them but [could not] conceal his disappointment that the "minaret" was not there. He asked M'allim Shaḥāda about it, and he said, "I got these prayer beads from a Persian pilgrim and thought they were suitable for Your Excellency. I asked him about the 'minaret,' and he said that when he bought it the owner told him it had been lost when it fell from his hand while he was out walking one night, and he could not find it. Ones like it are to be had in Mecca. I thought I would ask the pilgrims to buy one."

"That would take a long time," the governor said. "What can be done to get one sooner?"

"There is no faster way than his holiness the saint," he said, "who goes to perform his prayers in Mecca every Friday. He can bring one with him."

"You are right!" the vizier said. Summoning the shaykh and showing him the prayer beads, [he told him] that M'allim Shaḥāda had given it to him but it was missing the "minaret," and asked him to bring him one on Friday when he went to Mecca. The only thing he could do was to reply that he would comply with his wishes, for he realized that this calamity had landed on his head from the hand of M'allim Shaḥāda because of his slander of [the Jews].

That night, under the cover of darkness, he went to M'allim Shaḥāda's house and asked to be let in. When he was shown in and greeted with honor, he asked M'allim Shaḥāda to save him from the predicament he was in by giving him the "minaret" for the prayer beads. At first he denied that he had it and said that [the shaykh] could get one on Friday. The shaykh replied, "You know that this claim of mine is just a means of getting a livelihood out of the gullible. You don't believe it, and I know that I have fallen into this predicament because of my disregard of you. Save me and I promise you I will co-operate with you in whatever you like."

As he gave him the "minaret" he said, "I have made you see the result of your slander. Mend your ways with everyone, and you will always have peace; otherwise you will land in a worse situation at the mercy of someone who will not be clement. Were I such a one, I would have left you to be dishonored before the governor and the people."

He took the "minaret," and when Friday passed as usual, he went to the governor and presented it to him. He also told him about the blessed vision he had had as he was standing in the Sanctuary [at Mecca]. The vision had indicated the righteousness and goodness of M'allim Shaḥāda and commended him from the Apostle—peace be upon him—to his care. And thus a friendship sprang up between them.

ANOTHER STORY TOLD ABOUT THE CLEVERNESS OF JEWS AND THEIR MACHINATIONS TO AVOID PITFALLS.

During the reign of one of the sultans there was a man in the capital so learned and honest, pious in his religion and worship and hardworking at his post that he was appointed Shaykh al-Islām so that decrees would be based on the soundest principles of his sect. He then selected the best of the ulema and made him his Amīn al-Fatwā. The [shaykh] was so honest that all loved him, and even the sultan grew very fond of him. Therefore the grand vizier became jealous of him and began to look for an opportunity to bring him down.

It so happened that one of the shaykh's followers offended one of his neighbors, and the neighbor decided to have his revenge by obtaining a decree from the Shaykh al-Islām. He therefore presented his claim to the Amīn al-Fatwā, but the reply was issued that his claim was invalid. Since he was in the right, he was amazed at the reply. A friend of his advised him to present his complaint to the grand vizier, so he went to him at his house and was able to obtain an interview. He related the transgression he had suffered from his adversary, who was a dependent of the Shaykh al-Islām, and that he had thought it best to block [his adversary] through a decree from his excellency [the shaykh] and had therefore presented his question but received a reply that his claim was invalid. The vizier took the decree from him and promised him he would consider the claim and settle it fairly. Then the vizier secretly summoned some of the ulema upon whom he relied and showed them the decree. They reported that it was contrary to the law, and the vizier was overjoyed to have obtained tangible proof with which he could ruin the Shaykh al-Islām. He kept the decree, and during a session with the sultan in which his majesty was discoursing in praise of the Shaykh al-Islām's religiosity and honesty, the vizier said, "Yes, there are many who make a show of what is pleasing to God and people."

"One gathers from your tone that you think he is a hypocrite and not really as he seems," the sultan replied. "If this can be proven against him, he has committed an outrage in deceiving his lord and deserves death. If the claim is proven to be false, then the punishment will fall upon the claimant. What is the proof of your claim?"

"My proof," said the vizier, "is that he issued an incorrect opinion in which he showed favoritism to his friends." And so saying he took the decree from his pocket and presented it to the sultan, saying, "I did not accuse the Shaykh al-Islām until I learned of his dishonesty. I had this decree investigated by the most learned ulema, and they found it contrary to what it should be. It was my intention that this should not remain unknown to my lord."

Then the sultan summoned some of the Muslim ulema and showed them the decree. When they proclaimed it to be incorrect, his anger waxed and he ordered the Shaykh al-Islām to be brought before him. "I charged you time and again," he said, "to conduct yourself honestly in accordance with the religious law, and thus you prove your honesty to me? How can you deceive the sultan and not fear his wrath? I have no longer any doubt of your fraudulence, which has been proven to me by these deeds of yours my grand vizier has uncovered and acquainted me with."

Now the Shaykh al-Islām was in a real quandry, for he knew himself to be innocent, but there was nothing he could do except plead for mercy and confess his guilt. There must be some reason he could give to protect himself from the sultan's wrath, since he knew of no fault of his that would occasion such anger. The sultan gave him the decree and said, "Here, your signature is evidence against you. I give you three days grace lest it be said that you were punished unjustly." When the Shaykh al-Islām looked at the decree, he realized that the response to the question was incorrect and, giving up all hope of deliverance, returned sadly to his house.

The cause for this occurrence was the desire of bureaucrats to save themselves effort by letting their underlings do their work for them unsupervised. The Shaykh al-Islām had left the job of decrees to the expertise of the Amīn al-Fatwā, who phrased the questions in such a way that in responding the shaykh had only to write on the document one word, *olur* or *olmaz*, which is to say "licit" or "non licit." To understand the import one had to understand the nature of the questions, but the Shaykh al-Islām did not want to take the trouble to read them. In order to save him work, the Amīn al-Fatwā used to place the *olur* decrees in an envelope marked OLUR and the *olmaz* decrees in another envelope marked OLMAZ and present them to him. Without knowing the contents of the decrees, the shaykh would take them one by one and write on them according to the marking of the envelope containing them. The decree over which this incident occurred had been placed by mistake with the *olmaz* decrees and thus became the cause for the Shaykh al-Islām's misfortune, for which he expected to be punished when the three days were up. There was no way he could excuse himself for the Amīn al-Fatwā's error, for he would be told, "Your crime is the greater for having signed the decree without knowing its contents."

The Shaykh al-Islām had a clever Jewish bursar whose company he enjoyed and with whom he used to take a walk every evening after his work was done. The bursar came as usual and found his master so overwhelmed with worry that he did not even greet him. The bursar began to speak but was told, "Be silent. I have no time for you now." He kept silent for a while and then began to speak again. Once more he was told the same thing but with such a look of sadness and dejection in his master's face that the bursar said, "My lord, you know how devoted I am to you. What keeps you from telling me the reason for your grief? Perhaps I can help."

"If it were within the ability of the likes of you," he answered, "I would not keep it from you, but it has to do with the workings of the Muhammadan law, which is a closed book to you."

"Indeed, there is no connection between charcoal and gold," said the bursar, "one being so far beneath the other; yet the goldsmith makes a fire and uses the one to melt the other. To solve your golden problem Your Honor may make use of the charcoal ideas of your Jew. Maybe a fire will emerge and solve it." In his despair and hopelessness the Shaykh al-Islām explained the situation to him, saying that his death would be easier to accept than to confess his inattentiveness to the Amīn al-Fatwā's mistake, and that his predicament was a result of the grand vizier's hatred of him.

The bursar replied, "This is a simple case and should cause you no concern. It has nothing to do with your law, which I know nothing about. To turn it around on the vizier is an easy matter. Let me have the decree." When he had it he said, "Scratch out the word *olmaz* carefully."

"What's the good of scratching it out?" asked the shaykh.

"Do as I say and you'll see the result," he said, and the shaykh scratched it out. Then he said, "Write *olmaz* again in its place."

"What's the use of putting it back the way it was?" he asked.

"I'll tell you when you have finished the operation," he answered. So he wrote *olmaz* again, and the bursar said to the Shaykh al-Islām, "It is done. The case has now rebounded on the head of the vizier. Tomorrow morning go for an interview with His Majesty the Sultan and beg to be allowed to resign your post because, with your study of books of jurisprudence and work, you have no time to fend off the machinations of viziers, who have the luxury for such things. Say, 'Last night I never closed my eyes: I stayed up all night examining the records to find the entry for this decree. When I discovered there that I had signed it *olur*, I was amazed. I passed the decree back and forth in front of the candlelight, and in the light the place of my signature glowed more than anywhere else. In the light of day I discovered that where I had written *olur* had been scratched out and in its place was written *olmaz*.' Give the decree to the sultan and you will be saved."

Thus armed with his bursar's ruse, the Shaykh al-Islām went gladly to the sultan early the next morning and did as the bursar had instructed. [The sultan] issued an order for the vizier to be executed and rewarded the Shaykh al-Islām.*[2]

YUSUF PASHA IS REMOVED FROM THE GOVERNORSHIP OF DAMASCUS AND IS SUCCEEDED BY SULAYMĀN PASHA, THE GOVERNOR OF ṢAYDĀ; HE DOES BATTLE WITH YUSUF PASHA, WHO FLEES TO EGYPT; THE WAHHĀBI QUITS THE ḤAWRĀN.

Let us return to Yūsuf Pasha. Instead of conquering the Hejaz and expelling the Wahhābī as he had hoped, the Wahhābīs reached the Ḥawrān and from there wrote to the leaders of Damascus, calling upon them to surrender, abandon infidelity and enter into the religion of Islam (for they claimed that Sunnis were infidels). Yūsuf Pasha realized that he was unable to repel them, so he sought help from Sulaymān Pasha, the Governor of Ṣaydā, to drive the Wahhābī from Syrian territory. He responded to this request, immediately mobilizing troops and preparing to go himself. He wrote Emir Bashīr to send him at Ṭabariyye as many soldiers from the Lebanon as he could. The emir complied by issuing orders to all parts of the Lebanon that every emir and shaykh [44] come to him as quickly as possible with all the men of their region, Muslim, Shi'ite, Christian and Druze, bearing arms.

All gathered at Ṭabariyye, whence came Sulaymān Pasha with a large number of Turkish, Kurdish, Albanian, North African and Hawwārī troops. The vizier set out for Damascus, accompanied by the emir and notables of his land, with a force the likes of which no vizier in Syria had ever assembled before. When they reached al-Qunayṭra, which is about thirty miles from Damascus, Yūsuf Pasha sent a message for them to return, there being no longer any need for them because the Wahhābīs had learned that Muḥammad 'Alī Pasha, the governor of Egypt, had

Group.

taken control of the Hejaz and driven them out. For that reason they had abandoned the Ḥawrān and returned to their own land. Nonetheless, Sulaymān Pasha kept the troops marching toward Damascus. The reason he did so was that when the Empire had found out that Yūsuf Pasha was incapable of carrying out this undertaking and that, instead of expelling the Wahhābī from the Hejaz, he had actually sent them a delegation on behalf of Damascus, orders were issued for his removal from office, to be replaced by Sulaymān Pasha as governor of Damascus and superintendent of the pilgrimage, in addition to the two provinces of Ṣaydā and Tripoli and their dependencies he already held. He was then to hold all of what is now known as the Province of Syria.

When Sulaymān Pasha, Emir Bashīr and their troops reached the land of Jdayde [and] 'Arṭūz seven miles west of Damascus, Yūsuf Pasha met them with his troops to block them by force from entering Damascus. After a minor skirmish Yūsuf Pasha's troops were defeated, and he fled to Egypt with his retinue, among them M'allim 'Abbūd al-Baḥrī, and took refuge with the governor, Muḥammad-'Alī Pasha, who gained the Empire's consent for him to live in Egypt, where he remained until the end of his life.

Sulaymān Pasha entered Damascus with the troops without incident. All the inhabitants rejoiced that he had been made governor, not only because of Yūsuf Pasha's eccentricities they had had to endure, but more especially because the pilgrimage route, which had been closed for several years, was reopened during his tenure.

From Acre he brought M'allim Ḥāyīm Fārḥī and M'allim Ḥannā al-'Awra the Arabic clerk and his sons, who have been mentioned before. They stayed in the house of M'allim Rūfā'īl, M'allim Ḥāyīm's brother. After things settled down, Emir Bashīr and his men returned to the mountain, and Sulaymān Pasha, when the pilgrimage time was near, set out on the route with the pilgrims, taking with him the necessary ammunitions and soldiers to protect them. Thus the obligation of the pilgrimage was fulfilled, and all returned to their homes in peace.

M'allim Ḥāyīm arranged the offices, services and state taxation of the province in the best possible way. He even forbade the collection of more duties from the people than were due. It is said that one day, when one of the Arabic clerk's sons had been seen to take about three piastres as a tip from someone for whom he had written a document to obtain what he was due, M'allim Ḥāyīm said to the father, "This action is not proper. It is base and should not be done." That evening [45] when the Arabic clerk was seated in the presence of M'allim Ḥāyīm, the son came in with money done up in bags. His father said, "Open them and tell me how much there is." There was more than two hundred fifty piastres. He looked at M'allim Ḥāyīm and said, "Your Honor forbade me to take three piastres. Here are today's proceeds. I wanted to show it to you. The proverb says, 'Take a hair from every beard and they will add up to a beard.'" He replied, "True, but it would be a vile beard no honorable person would want.

THE EMIRS OF RĀSHAYYĀ ARE RELIEVED OF THE BALLĀN REGION.

During the course of that year, 1225 [A.D. 1810], the emirs of Rāshayyā were relieved of their village holdings in the Ballān region, which was annexed to the Damascus treasury. The emirs had paid a fixed annual tax in one lump sum for the Rāshayyā area and Ballān region without dividing the amount into how much was for each of the two. The rulership of Rāshayyā was divided between Emir Efendī al-Shihābī and his cousin Emir Manṣūr, whose brother Emir Bashīr had been treacherously killed by Emir Efendī. Therefore these two were enemies of each other, and each had his own villages and men among whom he lived. However, Emir Efendī was more influential because he supported the Jumblāṭ faction, as did Emir Bashīr the ruler of the Lebanon, to whom all the clans of Syria looked for leadership. Emir Manṣūr sided with the Yazbakī faction, which was isolated by its weakness and whose head, ['Alī] ibn 'Imād, was a refugee in Egypt. The enmity between the two emirs of Rāshayyā resulted in each taking precautions against the other and needing many allies. This occasioned much expense, which in turn forced the emirs to be harsh in extracting money from the peasantry; and the people of the Ballān region bore a heavier burden than the peasantry of their own land, Rāshayyā. The governors of Damascus were too weak to see that the peasants were justly treated by the emirs, who relied for assistance on their leader, the ruler of the Lebanon.

When the province of Damascus came under the command of Sulaymān Pasha, Governor of Ṣaydā, who was the overlord of the Emir of the Lebanon, the people of the Ballān region took advantage of the opportunity and presented their complaint to him. He issued an order to M'allim Ḥāyīm to investigate their complaint and give them relief. He asked them for a record of what the emirs made them pay. They gave him one but inflated it. He then informed the emirs of the people's complaint of excessive demands made on them. They denied it and claimed that they made them pay no more than the old assessments. He asked them for a detailed record, item by item, of what they took. They wrote a record, but they undervalued the amount, recording no more than a quarter of what they had taken, in order to counteract the peasants' claim. They had no notion of what M'allim Ḥāyīm was preparing for them, but after a few days he sent them a reply, saying, "Our efendi desires peace for you and your subjects. He has therefore issued an order to the effect that what you have taken from the Ballān region, according to the record you have submitted, [46] be deducted from the taxes assessed to you, deducting also your expenses for servants to collect the taxes and to protect the region—that is as a gratuity to improve your lot. [Henceforth] you will relinquish the area: you will have peace by being removed from the anxieties of the inhabitants, and the government will have rest from their complaints. Be grateful for such bounty and pray perpetually for his long rule over you." The emirs were no longer in a position to deny the truth of their record, for they would be liable to be charged with the perfidy of having lied to the vizier; and they were compelled to show gratitude and hide their disappointment.

Then M'allim Ḥāyīm summoned the village chiefs from the Ballān region and said to them, "Our efendi has been extremely generous in his compassion for you and issued an order removing the emirs of Rāshayyā from authority over you. You will now be administered as a dependency of the Damascus treasury, along with al-Marj and al-Ghūṭa, to give you relief from the burdens of the emirs and their men. His mercy on you has been great, for he has lifted from you a fifth of what you used to pay the emirs, according to the record submitted by you; you are assessed only four fifths. Pray for His Excellency's long life." These too could not admit that they had exaggerated by half the record of what the emirs charged them, so they expressed their gratitude and thanks. This is what happens to untruthful people: when they try to get out of one scrape, they land in another worse than the first.

THE DRUZE OF THE ALEPPO REGION TAKE REFUGE IN THE LEBANON.

After this it happened that the Druze who lived in al-Jabal al-A'lā in the Aleppo region were subjected to such extreme abuse that they were no longer secure of life and limb, and, although they were strong, they did not consider that they were able to protect themselves because they were too few, while their antagonists were many. Therefore they sought the protection of Emir Bashīr through the good offices of Shaykh Bashīr Jumblāṭ. [The emir] summoned them to Dayr al-Qamar, along with the women and children, and dispersed them throughout the region. Those of their young men who were suitable for service were employed by the emirs and shaykhs of the Lebanon. Shaykh Bashīr Jumblāṭ especially employed many of them, for he was anxious to increase his number of brave horsemen and footsoldiers. His desire for the Aleppans increased when he realized how worthy and brave they were, but he discovered that among them were those who remembered a good deed done to their kind. Let us relate an incident.

SOMEONE IS SENT BY 'ALI AL-'IMĀD IN EGYPT TO ASSASSINATE SHAYKH BASHIR, BUT HE IS APPREHENDED AND EXECUTED.

Shaykh Bashīr had in the public portion of his palace in al-Mukhtāra a small chamber situated at the end of the corrider under the private quarters. There he held public audience in the winter to escape the cold. One day an Aleppan Druze youth came to him, wished him good morning and kissed his hand, as was the custom of the mountain. Then he said, "I have something to tell you confidentially." Those who were present got up and left, except for a lay priest called Father Isṭifān, a Greek Catholic who was a skilled physician in the service of Emir Bashīr and who dwelt with his family in Dayr al-Qamar. He remained seated. The Aleppan said, "I beg his honor the priest [47] to be so kind as to withdraw."

The priest said, "His Excellency the Shaykh conceals nothing from me, but I will nonetheless comply with your wishes." And he left; however, as he was suspicious of this man, he remained on the other side of the doorway, which was covered with a curtain to keep out the cold. Hearing a noise from inside the room, he lifted the curtain and found the Aleppan on top of the shaykh, strangling him with his hands. This priest was advanced in age, but he was nonetheless very strong. He rushed in and, with all the energy he had, with one hand seized the Aleppan by the testicles and with the other pinned his arms, at which point [the Aleppan's] strength failed and he lost consciousness. The priest cried out for the servants, who came running, and ordered them to bind him tightly, which they did. Then he turned to tend to the shaykh, who was unconscious but revived with treatment. The priest chastized him for being alone with someone he did not know and who was as big as an elephant, while the shaykh, although great in intelligence, was small in stature, weak in in body and had many enemies.

When the shaykh had recovered, the traitor was put to torture to confess the reason for his horrible action. After being subjected to numerous tortures over and over again, he confessed that he had been sent from Egypt by Shaykh 'Alī al-'Imād to assassinate him but had not been able to finish the job. He thought little of what he had done [and said] that were it not for the priest he would have finished in five minutes what he had set out to do and left safe and sound. He would have shut the door behind him and told the servants that the shaykh did not want them to let anyone in until he gave them permission, because he was busy reading letters he had brought, and by this ruse he would have had an opportunity to escape. When the shaykh learned of the truth of the matter, he reported the incident to the emir, who congratulated him on his escape from the plot and gave him permission to execute the traitor (capital punishment could not be carried out in the Lebanon except by order of the emir).

EMIR BASHIR SENDS TWO FALCONERS TO BUY FALCONS FROM THE ALEPPO REGION; THE RULER OF RIHĀ IS KIND TO THEM AND IS REWARDED BY THE EMIR.

It was Emir Bashīr's custom to converse with people about what they knew. He conversed with merchants about trade, with farmers about agriculture, with scholars about learning, etc. So also, if he sent any of his people on a mission, no matter how trivial, upon his return he would ask him about everything that had happened to him and everything he had seen and heard. Part of the importance he attached to this lay in his discovery of how truthful a person was, for lying to him and treachery in his service were two things unpardonable in his view.

It happened that he sent two of his falconers to the Aleppo region to buy some birds for hunting, of which he was passionately fond. Upon their return he asked them to narrate everything that had happened to them going and coming. They informed him that they had passed through the town of Rīḥā in the Aleppo region. They had stayed at an inn, as is the custom of travellers, and the innkeeper had asked them where they had come from, where they were going and what their business was. They had said to him, "What concern is it of yours? We are wayfarers who will spend tonight in your place, and tomorrow morning we will be on our way." He replied [48], "What you say is right. It is none of my business, but we are forced by our ruler, Sa'īd Āghā, to report to him on everyone who stays here, where he comes from and where he is going. Occasionally he summons some of them for an interview. Therefore, I am forced to interrogate you." They had then told him that they were falconers in the service of Emir Bashīr, the ruler of Mount Lebanon, and were coming at his order to buy falcons from the plain of al-'Amq and held a laissez-passer with the emir's seal so as not to be hindered.

The [innkeeper] had then left them, but it was not long before a summons arrived from Sa'īd Āghā and they went to meet him. He ordered them to sit down and have coffee. They showed him the laissez-passer with the emir's seal announcing the envoys' business. He read the billet, kissed it, put it to his head[3] and handed it back to them, saying, "His Excellency the Emir is the head of all the clans of Syria. The chieftans consider themselves as his children and their lands as his lands. How can you have stopped in an inn when His Excellency the Emir has a house in our town? You must stay with me, and after three days you will proceed escorted by two of my horsemen, for you are not familiar with the land." They had stayed with him for three days and he had given them as escort two of his best horsemen, whom he had charged not to let the emir's men spend anything on themselves or their mounts but to pay for everything they needed, going and coming. When they returned to him he gave each of them a fine cloak and five hundred piastres, the equivalent of what they would spend to reach the Lebanon.

When the emir was apprised of their report, he was favorably impressed and said, "Perhaps we may be able to reward him for the favors he has done our men with no prior acquaintance between us."

Before much time had passed, Chūpān-oghlī came as vizier to Aleppo, [but the city] revolted and kept him from entering. He fought, entered it by force and decimated it. Then came imperial decrees in the name of many of the leaders of the province, that they be beheaded and their heads sent to the sultanate. One of these was the Sa'īd Āghā who has just been mentioned. As soon as the emir received news of this, he obtained permission from Sulaymān Pasha and sent word to Sa'īd Āghā that he should come to him with whomever he wanted [to bring]. He came to Dayr al-Qamar accompanied by about three hundred individuals with their horses and mules. Among them were two [others] whose heads were sought by the Empire, one of them named Uzun 'Alī and the other Topal 'Alī (that is, 'Alī the Tall and 'Alī the Lame, after the fashion of the Turks to call people by their physical defects). Among those watching as they arrived was this writer. There was an extraordinary resemblance between Sa'īd Āghā and Emir Bashīr, who received them warmly, settled them in the village of Kfar Nabrakh, two miles away from his palace, Bayt al-Dīn, and made arrangements for whatever food and fodder they needed.

After they had dwelt there for about three months, an imperial decree from the sultanate was brought to Sulaymān Pasha by an important deputy. In it was a demand that he turn over the three [49] aforementioned *āghā*s, for it had been reported to the Sublime Porte that they had escaped to the Lebanon. Sulaymān Pasha then sent the deputy, who had with him about forty men variously dressed, to Emir Bashīr. The emir received him with honor, and the interpretor between them was the very wanted man, Sa'īd Āghā, for the emir did not know Turkish and the deputy did not know Sa'īd Āghā. The emir, having installed the deputy in the Dayr al-Qamar seraglio, reported that the road that led from the coast to Damascus and Baghdad was open to all who passed through the Lebanon. "We do not know everyone who passes," [said the emir]. "Moreover, the Lebanon receives all comers. If the wanted men have settled somewhere, we shall search for them, apprehend them and turn them over to you as commanded. This very day I shall send orders to my agents in all parts of the mountain to gather in Dayr al-Qamar, and a search shall be made for the wanted men. Perhaps we may find them."

The emir sent out his orders to all emirs and shaykhs of the Lebanon to assemble, along with all the men of their regions in arms, at Dayr al-Qamar. So many gathered that there was not enough room in Dayr al-Qamar and its environs. "Why this massive gathering?" asked [the deputy]. "These are only the servants of the emirs and shaykhs the emir has summoned," he was told. "They go nowhere without their attendants." Then he told the emir that it would be sufficient to question the elite, so the emir assembled about five hundred men and read the vizier's orders and contents of the imperial decree to them. They all, to a man, replied, "Three months ago we heard that they passed on the Damascus road across the mountain with horses and mules and went on their way. They were said to be from Aleppo, and it is well known that the emir permits no hindrance of travellers." With this, the deputy departed and the gathering dispersed. This gathering has come to be called on the mountain the Halva Gathering because the Christians, who were fasting at the time, were given by the emir huge amounts of bread and sesame-oil halva for breakfast.

After a few days Sa'īd Āghā and those who were with him asked to be sent to Egypt, where they went, but not via the coast. With them the emir sent trusted men since he feared that they might be stopped along the way. They got them to al-'Arīsh, the border of Egypt.

SULAYMĀN AL-ḤAKĪM COMES TO MURDER SHAYKH BASHIR IN HIS HOUSE; HE IS APPREHENDED BUT ESCAPES FROM JAIL.

After that the following took place. A young Druze from the Upper Gharb, named Sulaymān al-Ḥakīm, who was less than twenty years old, came one night to Shaykh Bashīr Jumblāt's house to murder him, but he did not succeed in his plan because the house was well fortified and it was impossible to scale the walls. The youth was apprehended and sent to the emir's prison at Dayr al-Qamar for punishment. One day while I was coming from my father at the palace, I saw that this young man had been brought to the palace with heavy iron shackles around his neck to

Druze.

[50] be flogged in public. His beard and mustache had not grown yet, and he was very slim. They threw him down and put his feet into a thing called a *falaq*, and two cruel men were in charge of beating him with a stiff rod made of oak. At first they beat him savagely, and I felt very sorry for him. However, he bore the painful beating with all patience and did not utter a word but held onto the *falaq* with his hands and raised his back off the ground. They beat him about thirty times on his hands until he let go of the *falaq*, still not uttering a sound. When he had been beaten about a hundred and fifty times with the rod, he lost consciousness and they ceased the beating and threw some water on his face, his feet still in the *falaq*. When he was revived, they began to beat him again, still silent, until blood from his feet flowed all over the *falaq*. Then they stopped beating him and had to carry him into the prison, for he was unable to stand up. All who were watching felt very sorry for him, I most of all.

A few days later when they took his food in to him, they discovered that he was not there, but his shackles were in their place and the prison was well fortified. It was a strongly built chamber, the door to which was inside a gateway that served as the exit gate to the palace. The gate opposite was the entrance, and all around the gateway were platforms where the guards sat by day and slept by night, when the gates were locked behind them. Petty criminals were placed in the prison. It had an arched window that looked out over a broad square around which were the markets. This arched window was also secured by a strong iron grill, and above it was an opening for light about five cubits from the floor and about two-thirds of a cubit in width and length. It was impossible to reach without a ladder, and in the opening was mounted a heavy piece of perforated tile through which the light shone. In one corner of this prison was a small chamber roofed at a height of four cubits, and the only opening in it was a door that let into the prison. Major criminals were imprisoned in this chamber with heavy iron chains around their necks, one end of the chain passed through a hole in the wall of the chamber and fastened outside. They were locked in, and the only time the door was opened was to feed them or to let them out to relieve themselves or to be tortured. It so happened that at that time there was no other prisoner in the prison aside from this youth, and the only trace they ever found of his escape was the perforated tile in the light shaft, which was broken in the middle in a circle about a span in diameter, and next to it an iron spike of the type driven into the ground to tether animals.

The incident was reported to the emir, and he sent clever individuals to examine the tile and see how the prisoner had escaped. After an investigation they reported that the iron collar on the prisoner's neck had been filed off, which was possible. However, it was not possible for a person to get out through the hole in the tile. No matter how thin the escapee may have been, [51] he would not have been able to do it because the edges of the opening were not even and, despite the circularity of it, there were jagged edges that would have cut, due to the way the tile was perforated. If the escapee had gone out feet first, he would have gotten stuck under his arms. If he had gone out head first, the place was so high he would have fallen on his head and been killed.

It was then suspected that the prisoner's escape must have been with the connivance of the prison guards, the sons of Zayn al-Dīn. Since insufficient evidence was found to prove their guilt, the emir made do by punishing their family, who were cast out of his service for ever, in accordance with his rule that no traitor, even a first offender, would be forgiven. When a trusted man died or got too old, his position, along with the living, would go to his son, while the elderly man would retain his income for life, in addition to what his son got with his position. For this reason there were only trusted men in his service. May he rest in peace.

THE SAME PERSON ATTEMPTS TO KILL EMIR BASHIR AND ESCAPES; BUT HE IS APPREHENDED AND HANGED.

One evening a few days later one of the female servants in the emir's household went to the bedroom of the emir's son Emir Amīn to fix his bed but came back screaming that she had found a strange lad in the room. She had grabbed him, but he had hit her on the hand, wrenched her fingers and escaped. The guard of the gate to the private quarters was alerted, and the men set up a watch. They searched for the culprit but found no trace of him, even though the quarters were well fortified and it was not possible to scale the walls or to gain entry by other than the gate that was guarded by trustworthy people. They said that the servant had lied and must have wrenched her fingers some other way, such as by falling on her hand. However, investigation showed that the pair of pistols Emir Amīn always kept at his bedside was missing. There was no longer any doubt of the servant's veracity, but all were perplexed as to how this man could have entered the private quarters and gotten out despite its fortification, the height of its walls and the guard that was maintained day and night at the gate, which was kept locked and opened only when needed.

A few months later some donkey-drivers were bringing their beasts from Damascus to Dayr al-Qamar and carrying some commodities and passengers. They stopped at the source of the Bārūk River, where there was a store in which were sold articles needed by travellers, with shelter for their animals. By chance one of the emir's servants, who was from the village of al-Bārūk, had come to buy something from the store. As he passed by where the donkey drivers were camped, he glanced at the travellers accompanying them and saw a young man among them dressed like a Damascene Christian, yet neither did he have the look of a vagabond about him nor did he display the fatigue that city people bred in comfort would have. On the contrary, he was walking and bounding about as nimbly as a gazelle, unlike the rest of the passengers, who were flat out like corpses. Therefore he became suspicious. He made his purchase from the shop and, returning to the village, told his companions of his doubts concerning this young man and described him to them. One of them said, "This fits the description of Sulaymān al-Ḥakīm, who escaped from our efendi the emir's prison. I know him well. Come on, let's go! If we find out that he is Sulaymān, we'll apprehend him and take him to the emir, who will consider it a real service."

About ten men set out, and when [52] they got near the inn they realized that it was Sulaymān al-Ḥakīm himself. As they approached, he backed away from them. They cried out for him to stop so they could ask him some questions, but he replied, "I can hear you without your coming closer." They asked, "Where are you from and who are your people?" He said, "I am a Christian from Damascus." They said, "Prove it, for your speech indicates that you are from this country and that you are so-and-so." With this he ran away from them. They gave chase but could not catch him. The men of three villages, al-Bārūk, al-Fraydīs and Bathlūn, surrounded him on all sides, but he was as quick as a gazelle and slippery as a fox. Only after they wore him out with fatigue were they able to apprehend him and tie him up. With him they found one of the missing pair of pistols from Emir Amīn's bedroom spoken of previously.

He was sent to the emir, who ordered him kept chained and well guarded in the prison in the palace of Bteddīn[4]. He also ordered a full report on his motives and what he had done. A scribe was sent to take down the interrogation of him. First he was asked about his attempt [on the shaykh's life and told] that they were desirous of learning the truth without torturing him with beatings or other things, that the only way to save himself was to tell the truth. If he promised to repent, the emir would be clement not only with a pardon but probably would make him one of his servants because he admired brave and energetic men. His reply was: "My purpose was the Yazbakī that dwells in every part of me. I will never be rid of it so long as I live. I am in the service of my lord, Shaykh 'Alī al-'Imād, and went into exile with him to Egypt. I returned to kill Shaykh Bashīr Jumblāṭ and Emir Bashīr any way I could, by my master's

Bteddīn.

order. The fortification of Shaykh Bashīr's private quarters prevented me from entering at night. So I tricked them and entered with the water that comes through a narrow pipe. I almost drowned before reaching the inside. I was unsuccessful in my attempt, so I fled through the gate; but fate caused me to fall into their hands, and they put me in the inner prison at Dayr al-Qamar, shackled with iron."

Then he was asked how he had escaped and what he had done that the Zayn al-Dīns acquiesced in his escape. He sighed and said, "Do you think those accursed ones have the slightest mercy in their hearts toward a fellow human being that they would have compassion on me, particularly since I am a Yazbakī and they are Jumblāṭī and my crime was against one with whom they are affiliated. Two of them especially, Abū-Ghawsh and Ṣa'b, beat me with all severity, gritting their teeth as though they were taking revenge on someone who had killed their father. God damn them!" The scribe was taking down everything he said.

Then he said, "My escape came about by chance. One day I was wiping the floor of the prison with the palm of my hand to make it smooth where I sat and slept, since I had no mattress, and the light of day never reached me. It was like being imprisoned in a box: I only saw light when the door was opened to give me food, which I can't complain of since they [53] give prisoners what is put on the emirs' tables. Anyway, I came across a file. Probably some prisoner before me got it to file off his chains and left it behind in prison. First I got the collar off my neck, and then I managed to pull the door off [its hinges] at night and get out into the outer prison, where there was nothing except a few things of the Zayn al-Dīns, among them a tripod they had made in Dayr al-Qamar to send to their house, where they use it for lots of things, among them as a ladder. I found a number of horses and an iron stake. Then I got up to the skylight on the tripod. I broke the perforated tile with the stake enough to get my head and arms out until I was halfway outside. By pressing hard with my palms against the wall I managed to wriggle out of the opening and got down to the ground feet first. Then I fled to Damascus.

"A few days later I decided I wouldn't go back to Egypt without finishing what I had come for, so I came to Bteddīn to kill the emir by strategem, but I found him always surrounded by men. I had no way of reaching him alone except when he was asleep. I found that I could get up from the stables: where the wall is made of cut stone I could get a grip with my fingers and toes and make my way up (something a cat could scarcely do). Then I wondered how to get down, and I saw I could jump from one of the roofs to the ground of the north garden, and I had a sharp dagger with me. So I scaled the wall under the cover of darkness. As soon as I was up I saw a lighted room. I approached and listened. I heard no movement inside. I went in and found a magnificent bed and next to it two pistols. I had no doubt that this was where the emir slept and that he had put the pistols there to shoot a would-be assassin. I took them and stood next to the door to stab the emir in the back when he came through and be done with my job. But before I could position myself, a woman came in and saw me. It is not manly to kill women. She grabbed me and slapped me and went out screaming at the top of her lungs. Everybody in the place came running and there was a commotion. I was afraid the men would gather and hunt me down, no matter how many of them I might kill, so I went out on the roof, headed for the garden, jumped down safely and got out.

"The men ran all over searching the palace. I was exhausted, but I didn't stop until I got to a Yazbakī shaykh's place in the 'Arqūb. I sold him one of the pistols, without telling him what had happened, and kept the other one until you took it from me. The next night I went to Damascus. I hated to go back to Egypt without having done what I came for, so I waited all this time until the affair should be forgotten and there should be no more hope of finding me. This time I came in disguise, hoping to find an opportunity to achieve my goal, but I fell into your hands and wound up here.

"As for [54] your promise that the emir might employ me after pardoning me if I told the truth and promised to repent, well here is my confession in all truthfulness. However, promising to repent and going back on my Yazbakī resolve is not possible. Any time I have the opportunity, you will not be safe from me."

When the report was submitted to the emir, he said, "I would like to have pardoned him and employed him, for his bravery is without equal, but he has warned us of his treachery and must be executed. Hang him at once." When he was hanged, many felt sorry for him.

ḤANNĀ BAYDAR HATCHES A PLAN TO RESCUE THE SONS OF THE NAKAD SHAYKHS FROM AL-JAZZĀR'S PRISON IN THE ṢAYDĀ FORTRESS.

A story told about the brave men of the mountain [is as follows]. Al-Jazzār arrested three young men, sons of the Abū-Nakad shaykhs, and put them in chains in a room inside the Ṣaydā fortress, which is surrounded by the sea and can be approached from the city only across a bridge built on pilings sunk in the water. Although the fathers were not able to effect their release, a man named Ḥannā Baydar, from a Greek village on the Ṣaydā coast, swore he would rescue them by strategem. He owned a donkey on which he carried good-quality kindling to sell in Ṣaydā by the gate to the bridge leading to the fortress. He had such good kindling that the guards of the fortress had forbidden anybody else to buy his goods and bought it all themselves. Recently they had compelled him to bring it right into the fortress itself. As he came constantly, he had begun to come occasionally at the end of the day and then stay the night inside the fortress. He grew friendly with the guards and wandered around the fortress, looking at the various places in it. When he saw the shaykhs in chains, he asked the guards about them, pretending not to know who they were. They told him that they were Druze from the mountain. "Why doesn't our efendi kill them and rid the people of their evil?" he asked and was told, "He must have some reason for keeping them alive."

Then he brought the guards little peasant gifts, once a few small birds caught with birdlime, another time a roll of wafer-thin bread, which city people love but which is not made in bakeries. They were very happy with these gifts and honored him with presents in return. He became so much like one of them that he was able to meet with the prisoners and tell them that he was sent by their fathers to rescue them.

"How can you do that?" they asked. "We are chained inside a fortress surrounded on all sides by the sea. The gate is locked, and the only exit leads to a walled city that has a troup of armed guards stationed at the gate."

"That is all up to me," he said. "You must break your bonds and the bars at the window overlooking the sea. Take this file and use it to help you when I tell you, but not today." Then he went back to his village and expertly made some wafer bread, putting powdered darnel into the dough. This he brought as a gift to his friends the guards, arriving just about the time they were having supper. [55] He distributed it among them and signaled the shaykhs to cut their bonds and the bars as fast as possible. As soon as the guards had eaten, the darnel worked its effect on them and they keeled over. When it was dark, Ḥannā Baydar took a rope he had brought and tied it around the shaykhs one by one and lowered them down from the window to the rock on which the walls of the fortress rested. When he had let them all down, he tied the rope to the window and lowered himself down to them. Then, one by one he swam with them on his back until he got them to the shore outside the city and walked with them to the al-Awwalī bridge, the border of the Lebanon, where horses and men were waiting to accompany them to their anxious families. They rode with their deliverer to Dayr al-Qamar, where a great celebration was made. People used to point out Ḥannā Baydar, who acquired great importance and received gifts from the Nakad shaykhs. He and his family settled in Dayr al-Qamar; and thereafter he did many deeds, in all of which his bravery was apparent and his reputation increased.

ḤANNĀ BAYDAR IS MURDERED; TWO MEN FROM THE LEBANON KILL THE RULER OF ṢAYDĀ IN HIS OFFICE.

When al-Jazzār learned how the shaykhs had escaped from the fortress prison, despite its being guarded, he flew into a rage and promised a great reward to anyone who could bring him Ḥannā Baydar, who had plotted their escape. Word spread, but no one was daring enough to approach the wanted man until a brave Druze from the 'Abdul-Ṣamad family of 'Ammāṭūr in the Shūf got the chance to kill Ḥannā Baydar and took his head to al-Jazzār, hoping for a reward. He was told, "I wanted this bravado alive, not dead." And his hopes were dashed.

Another thing that happened during the days of al-Jazzār and Emir Yūsuf is as follows. There was a *ḥākim* in Ṣaydā, one of those coarse Turks who victimize the common folk, a mean, foul-mouthed, cruel man, especially towards the people of the Lebanon. When he had to do things for them in Ṣaydā, instead of assisting them, he used to savage their rights and abuse them, be they Muslim, Christian or Druze. The worst of his malice was reserved for the Jumblāṭ shaykhs, whose lands in the Lebanon were next to Ṣaydā. Tired of enduring his abuses, they were approached by two of their followers, a Maronite Christian and a Druze from Ba'dharān, who undertook to kill him, to which they gave their assent. The two armed themselves and set out for Ṣaydā, followed by an Egyptian groom of the shaykhs' armed with a wooden cudgel. They wanted to send him back, but he refused, saying, "I'll protect your backs with my cudgel if there are too many for you to handle."

They agreed that the Druze would go into the seraglio and assassinate the *ḥākim* in his office and the Egyptian would guard his rear, while the Christian would wait for them at the city gate and keep it from being closed before they returned. And thus it was: the Druze entered the *ḥākim*'s office and assassinated him [56] and then, brandishing his yataghan[5], rushed the [*ḥākim*'s] men and dispersed them, with the Egyptian guarding his rear and felling with his cudgel anyone who came near them. They got out through the seraglio gate with people coming from all sides. They fought off all who got close, the Druze with the edge of his yataghan and the Egyptian with his cudgel, until they reached the city gate, where they found the Christian keeping it from being shut. The guards had him surrounded on all sides and were exchanging blows with him but could not get him out of the gateway to close it. When the three met they got out of the city safely, the men in pursuit. Just then they passed by a dyer's shop in the farriers' market outside the city. The dyer had a mallet in his hand with which he was pounding the cloth ready for dying. He hit the Egyptian with the mallet and broke his leg. When he fell, his companions turned to save him, but he said, "You can't save me. I'm done for. You mustn't perish because of me. Save yourselves and I'll have my reward." So the Christian and the Druze escaped, for the *ḥākim*'s men were distracted from hunting them down by killing the Egyptian groom [in retaliation] for their master.

THE DARING OF ZAKHKHUR AL-SHAM'UNĪ.

A story told about Zakhkhūr al-Sham'ūnī, a Greek Catholic from Dayr al-Qamar, is as follows. He was hot-tempered, and many instances of his arrogance had occasioned complaint to Emir Yūsuf, the ruler of the mountain. Since the men of [Dayr al-Qamar] were under the jurisdiction of their shaykh Kulayb Abī-Nakad, the emir used to speak to the shaykh about chastizing and reproving him, but the shaykh's talks and threats had no effect on Zakhkhūr. The emir grew so weary of the complaints presented to him that one day he said to the shaykh, "How long are you going to put up with these complaints against Zakhkhūr without killing him? Choose whom you want, me or Zakhkhūr."

"My lord," he replied, "I am your slave. I bring up my men like sons to serve you. I have threatened him repeatedly, but to kill this man of mine is something I cannot do. However, Your Excellency may find some perilous errand to send him on. If he is killed, you will be rid of him. If he carries it out, it will be an expiation for his sins."

"That is suitable," said the emir. "In Ṣaydā there is a one-eyed cobbler, a very bad man. His shop is next to the city gate, and his attacks on the mountain people, regardless of their religion, even Muslims, know no bounds. He treats them to scathing remarks, ridicule and foul curses. If any of them answers him he attacks with a stick. The soldiers stationed at the city gate, instead of stopping him, laugh and are amused by what he does, and so a mountaineer has no one to help him. I have written repeatedly to the *mutasallim* of Ṣaydā, but he has responded that he has inquired of the soldiers stationed at the gate next to the cobbler and of the neighborhood and has proven that the claim is false. You must therefore ask Zakhkhūr to kill this man and bring his ears as evidence of the deed."

That evening the shaykh summoned Zakhkhūr and gave him to understand what had passed between him and the emir [57] and that it had been decided to send him on this dangerous mission, which had been brought about by his refusal to listen to advice. He replied, "What you ask of me to please the emir I do not consider dangerous. It shall be done as you desire. I consider it an honor that he is sending me on this mission."

"Service is well rendered when it is done expeditiously," said the shaykh. "It will take you a day on the road to get there and another to return. I give you three days in Ṣaydā to make arrangements for your job. You should set out tomorrow morning."

The next morning the shaykh sent word to the emir informing him of what had transpired with Zakhkhūr, what he had replied and that he was setting out for Ṣaydā that very day with five days to accomplish his task. The emir replied, "He will probably not return from such a dangerous mission, and we will be well rid of him."

That evening, when the shaykh's gathering had broken up and he had retired for the night, there came a knock on the door [and it was announced] that Zakhkhūr wanted to see him outside. Angrily, he went out and said, "You promised to set out today, and I told the emir that you had gone, yet here you are. Get out of my sight!"

"Don't be angry, master," he said. "I have done what I undertook to do. I went to Ṣaydā, carried out my mission and have come back."

"Have you killed the cobbler and brought his ears?" he asked.

"Yes," he said, "I have them with me. I had very good luck along the way, and it was due to your and the emir's pleasure."

"Come with me," the shaykh said. "Let's tell his excellency what happened to you." So they went to the palace, where the emir had gone in for the night. The shaykh asked to see him, [sending word that] Zakhkhūr had come through the danger and accomplished his mission and was there with him to report what had happened. [The emir] ordered that they be brought in and asked them to be seated.

"Tell us exactly what happened from the moment you left until the moment you returned," the emir said to Zakhkhūr.

"His Honor the shaykh asked me last night to come to him," said Zakhkhūr, "and told me that Your Excellency had ordered the death of the one-eyed cobbler at the Ṣaydā gate, and that I was to set out today to accomplish it. He gave me five days. On account of Your Excellency's intention it struck me when I returned home that I would succeed. I thought it would be better to travel by night by moonlight than in the heat of the day, so I had my supper. Since it is the Fast of Our Lady, I took two loaves of dry bread along for provisions, cheese and yoghurt not being permitted, and asked the Lady of the Fast to aid me in my endeavor."

(I do not consider this strange, for the Italian gentleman Cavarini, while on his way to Beirut, was clever enough to catch three men who were killing and plundering passers-by, and one of them was a Christian I knew. They were brought to Damascus and, before being executed, were offered bread and milk, but the Christian refused to drink the milk because it was a Wednesday.)

"Arming myself with a pistol in my belt and a sharp little axe under my cloak, I set out on the Ṣaydā road. I arrived after midnight and slept outside [the city] until day broke and the city gate was opened. Then I went in and sat down in a coffeehouse near the gate, waiting for my chance. The guard of the gate came and sat down [58] with his troop on a divan reserved for them. I looked at the guard's face and saw malice dripping from it. A little later the one-eyed cobbler came and opened his shop, and villagers began to arrive in the city on business. Whenever this one-eyed man recognized someone as being from the mountain, he would start a quarrel and curse him foully. If he was answered he set upon him with a club. I saw that the guard was amused and laughed at what he was doing, instead of stopping him and rebuking him. I was more affected by him than I was by the one-eyed man. I waited for him to get up to go for lunch at his house or some other business. I was going to follow him into an alley and kill him, which I couldn't do while he was near the guards. But he had brought his lunch and ate it there.

"Then I waited for him to get up for the noon prayer. Two hours after that time I needed to relieve myself, so I asked the owner of the coffeeshop where the place was. He directed me to an empty dyers' *khān* near the coffeeshop. Inside was a vast arch that had been turned into a latrine. I went in and found that it was very dark. The only light was from a doorway littered with filth. I went straight in to get away from the filth and did what I had to do. Just then the head guard came in and squatted down near the door. The place was so dark that he did not see me and turned his back toward the inside. I seized the opportunity and, tiptoeing over to him with the axe in my hand, I struck him on the back of the neck with such a blow that I didn't have to repeat it. I dragged him into the darkness and took all the money I found on him along with his watch, seal and a pair of silver pistols I concealed under my cloak. Then I cut his ears off, and here they are."

"But we sent you to kill the one-eyed man, not to substitute the guard for him!" said [the emir].

"Be tolerant of your slave," he replied, "until I finish my report of everything that happened. When I had finished the job, who should I see coming in but the one-eyed man I was after. He squatted down to do his business like the first one, so quick as a wink I dispatched him to join the other one and dragged him inside. On him I found a little money, which I took, and cut his ears off. Here they are.

"I left the city, and when I got to the al-Awwalī bridge and was inside the Lebanon, I sat down to rest next to the bridge, lit my pipe and called to the innkeeper there to bring me a cup of coffee. Then I looked down at the riverbank below and saw a horseman making his ablutions for the evening prayer. His mare was lovely, grazing by the river's edge. I asked the innkeeper who he was, and he said it was so-and-so, a Mutawālī shaykh from the Shqīf region. I recognized his name because I had heard

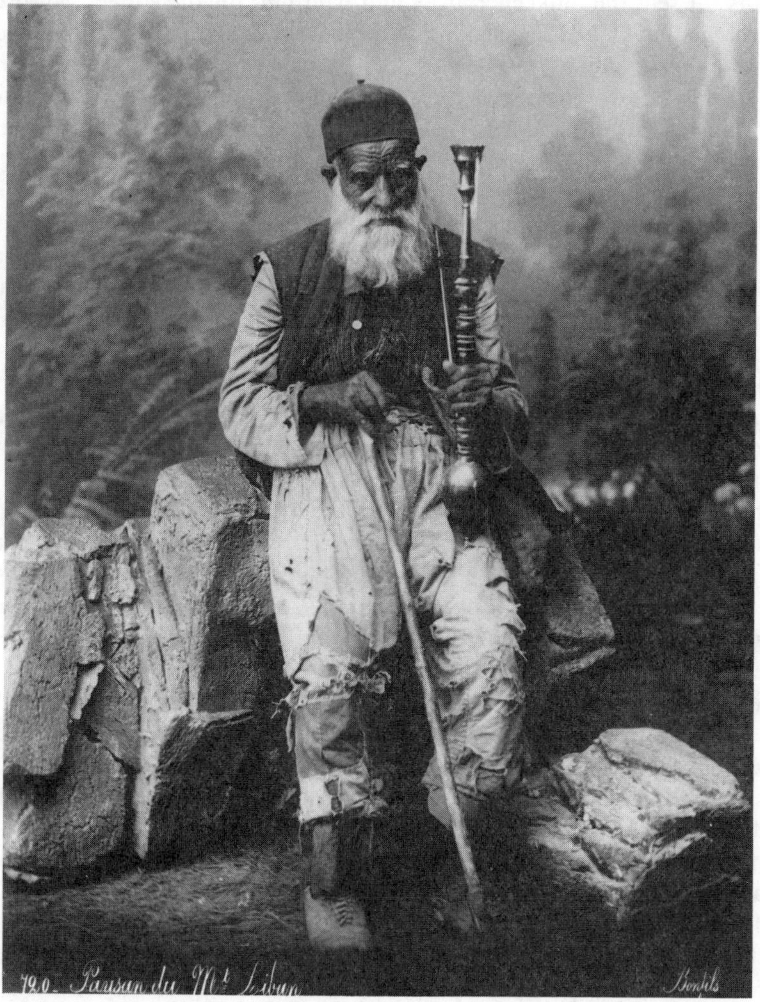
720 - Paysan du Mt Liban
Bonfils

Peasant.

His Honor the Shaykh mention his name and Your Excellency's displeasure with him because he wouldn't cease his shameful deeds."

"What is the upshot of this tale?" the emir asked.

"My lord," said Zakhkhūr, "indulge your slave until I finish my story. I sent the innkeeper away and paid him for the coffee. I waited until the shaykh had finished his ablutions and was starting to pray. Then I went down, and, as [59] he was prostrating, the axe sent his head flying from his body. I stripped him and dumped him into the river, after cutting his ears off, and here they are. Then I gathered his things together, tied them to the horse, put on his robe, got on the horse and rode off.

"When I got to the al-Qanbī crossroads, I found . . ."

"Is there still another tale?" asked the emir.

"Yes, but it's the last," he said. "I saw two Mutawālīs driving ten laden donkeys. Both of them had guns, and when they saw me—apparently they recognized their shaykh's mare under me and his robe on my shoulders—they did not doubt but what I had killed him. They shot at me, but one misfired and the other missed me. I charged them and with the shaykh's sword struck first the one whose gun had misfired, and he fell dead. Then I sent his companion after him and went back and cut their ears off, and here they are. Then I mounted and drove the donkeys ahead of me. They are now, along with the shaykh's mare, tied up outside of town awaiting someone to take possession of them for Your Excellency."

"They, and all you took, are yours," said [the emir]. "Tomorrow morning receive five hundred piastres from the treasury."

Then the shaykh said to the emir, "I beg you to forgive me for not killing such young men I reserve for your service."

"You are right not to do so," he replied, and all returned to their homes.

Among the bravados of the Lebanon I have known and met was the Maronite Shaykh Yūsuf al-Khūrī al-Shalfūn. He was a noble gentleman who lived in Burj al-Barājne outside Beirut. One time a group of people came out from [Beirut] to murder him in the forest, but he drove them off with his sword. Another time there was a conspiracy to ambush him while he was in the city, but as he scattered the gang with his sword, the shops were shut up and the people fled from his might. He left the city brandishing his drawn sword, and no one dared to approach him. Nonetheless he was sociable and of good character, generous as an Arab and never refused a beggar.

He was in the service of Emir Yūsuf's sons, and when the vendetta between them and Emir Bashīr broke out, Yūsuf al-Khūrī was among those who were most upsetting to the emir's plans. A few times he even waylaid supplies bound for the emir's soldiers, seizing them from the men who were guarding them and taking them to Emir Yūsuf's sons' camp.

Horseman.

When Jirjis Bāz and his brother were killed and Emir Yūsuf's sons' eyes were put out, Emir Bashīr ordered Yūsuf al-Khūrī arrested. He could not be caught, although a search was made for him by agents accompanied by strong men to bring him in alive or dead. They scoured the towns and countryside for him but returned with no trace. Some time passed and it was thought that he had fled to Egypt or Aleppo, so the search was abandoned. Then one day, when the emir was sitting in his councilroom, Yūsuf appeared before him, saying, "Your Excellency sent men to take me, but they were not able to do it. However, your order, not men, brings me here. I served your cousins with all energy and sincerity, as a servant should do. If my sincere service to my masters can possibly be construed by Your Excellency as a fault, then here I am. [60] Punish me as you will."

The emir was pleased by his brave speech and told him to rest assured. Then he motioned for him to sit down and take coffee. When he was finished, the emir asked him where he had been hiding that the officers of the search party had not been able to find him.

"I wasn't just in hiding," he replied. "I kept moving around the country from village to village. It often happened that I encountered groups of deputies, but when I attacked them they fled before me. I met so-and-so in such-and-such a place with ten men, but he and his men ran away. So-and-so and so-and-so I encountered with their men in such-and-such places, but they didn't dare confront me. They all knew I wouldn't allow them to take me so long as I was alive, and they couldn't kill me without most of them dying. Trusting in your equity and justice, that you wouldn't condemn me for my energy in serving my masters, I throw myself at your feet, not content to humiliate myself by turning myself in to mere underlings."

The emir was more pleased than ever and asked, "Will you serve me as you served my cousins?"

"Will I have the good fortune one day to shed my blood beneath the feet of your horse?" he replied. The emir ordered a sable fur, put it on him as a sign of his favor and said, "I put you in charge of affairs on the Beirut coast where you live. You are dear and honorable to me, and you will receive whatever makes you happy." He served the emir sincerely and went into exile with him to the Ḥawrān, Cairo and Upper Egypt, remaining faithful in his service until he died, God rest his soul.

AFFAIRS CONCERNING THE MISHĀQA FAMILY; THE WRITER TRAVELS TO EGYPT.

Let us mention some affairs connected to the family of Jirjis

Mishāqa. Even if they are not of much importance, we will mention them to satisfy those who asked for [the account].

After this writer Mīkhāyīl, there were born to Jirjis two male children, Jibrā'īl, who now serves as judge in Zaḥle, born in 1805, and Rūfāīl, who is now a member of the district judicial board in Bayt al-Dīn Palace at Dayr al-Qamar, born in 1809. The number of sons who survived were then five; there were five girls who survived, but there is no need to mention them. Jirjis Mishāqa, fearing for his sons the reversals of fate he had experienced with no trade to live by, was resolved to have them taught trades after they had learned to read and write. He was not satisfied to have them taught a single trade, but as soon as they had learned one he moved them on to another. It was this writer Mīkhāyīl's lot to master four trades, and years later he depended upon two trades aside from the original four.

After having his sons taught a trade, he was determined that they should be remote from contact with rulers, because of what he and his father had suffered from mingling with them. Therefore he decided to send them to their uncles in Egypt to learn commerce. Ibrāhīm, the eldest, was not permitted by his mother to be sent in order that she might see him married early. She got him married at the age of eighteen. Andreos was sent to his uncle [61] Anton at Damietta when he was sixteen. Mīkhāyīl was inclined to learn accounting, but at that time there was no one in Dayr al-Qamar who knew more than how to add. If they had to figure out the price of seven rotls at seventeen and a quarter each for example, they had to write down the price seven times and add it up. His father, however, had learned from his father how to multiply and divide and keep books and taught his sons how to multiply and divide.

From the Jews I used to hear about solar and lunar eclipses before they occurred; they claimed that their *ḥākhām*s knew how to calculate them, not admitting that they got it from Europe written in the almanac for that year, and I fell for it (talk always was that they were a sly folk). I therefore made friends with one of them who was a "reader" (in their parlance that means a learned person) named Isḥāq al-Az'arī. He told me that he was an expert at calculating eclipses. At that time I had no idea what precise calculations, different calendars, knowledge of trigonometry, longitudes and latitudes, meridians and parallax were entailed in that, nor did I know that reading the Talmud was not much help in astronomy. So I begged him to teach me for pay. I went to him for several months, but he kept putting me off with promises, not admitting his ignorance, until finally I despaired and left him.

One day my father sent me on an errand to Pastor Cyrillos Farah, one of the monks who served the spiritual needs of the Catholics at Dayr al-Qamar. I found him reading a manuscript in which were tables and numbers, and the sun and moon were mentioned. I was overjoyed and said to myself, "My wish to learn astronomy has come true, for the father knows it. I'll ask him to teach me." I asked him what the book was. He frowned and said, "It is too deep for you to understand. It is called the *Cyclos* and was compiled by the holy fathers. With it we can determine years in advance when moveable feasts will fall, when the Greek years and months will begin, when the new moon will occur each month, and other things too exalted for common people to comprehend."

In short, I saw that this pastor considered himself equal in knowledge to the philosopher Archimedes or the physicist Isaac Newton, or even more sublime than them, since he could comprehend what was written in the *Cyclos*. At last resort I asked him to allow me to copy the book and be so kind afterwards as to teach me about it, telling him my experience with the Jew. He replied, "My son, those people do not have brilliant scholars like us." Anyway, he said he would let me copy the book, though he would not allow it to be taken away, and teach me about it when he had the chance. I brought all the things I needed to copy it, set to work and finished it in a few days. I found that it was easy to understand and I did not need an instructor, but when Father Cyrillos read it [62] he had to sound out some of the words and sometimes mispronounced them, which was an indication of the extent of his erudition. I left him and worked hard reading the book on my own. Since it was easy I was able to understand the contents well, but I did not get my wish of finding out about eclipses. Because I believed the claims of charlatans that [eclipses] predicted catastrophic events like wars and epidemic or the death of some great person, I was desirous of [knowing about them].

In the year 1814 my uncle Buṭrus 'Anḥūrī, a great merchant, came to us from Damietta to have his daughter's eyes treated. At that time there were no reliable physicians in that country, and the person best known for treating eyes in Syria was Rūfā'īl Nahra al-Ghabghūb, who lived in the village of Ṣaghbīn in the West Biqā'. My father promised to pay him an enormous sum if he would go to Damietta, but he refused. Therefore my uncle was obliged to come to us, and al-Ghabghūb, along with his son Faraḥ, who now lives in Beirut, was summoned to Dayr al-Qamar to treat the girl's eyes. She recovered thanks to him.

When my uncle was rested from the travails of his voyage and getting the eye-doctor to treat his daughter, he took out his books from his trunk, and I looked to see what was written on the covers. On the back of one book I found written "Lalande's Astronomy,"[6] on another "Lalande's Latitudes and Longitudes," on another "Marginalia of the Archimandrite Euthymius Ghāzī on the Englishman Benjamin's Physics," on the fourth "On Physics by Master Rhiga Pilāstanlī," on the fifth "A New Approach for Calculating Eclipses by Buṭrus al-'Anḥūrī," my very own uncle. There were more books too by him and others on various topics. I opened them and found them all written in Arabic. Those that were originally in a foreign language he had translated with the help of Bāsīlī Fakhr, the French consul in Damietta. When I realized what they were, especially the book on eclipses, I was overjoyed, for I believed that when I learned about them, the secrets of the universe would be unlocked for me. I thought that if the prophet David's words were true that "the firmament showeth his handywork,"[7] then astronomy would tell me everything the Creator had done and would do. My limited understanding and narrow learning led me to believe any such fables.

I asked my uncle if he knew astronomy and how he had learned it since, although our country was large and was the seat of the emir, who was called the Sultan of the Dry Land, there was not to be found in it a single person who knew astronomy. He laughed at me and said, "My son, you must know that this country of yours is very small. Compared to the great lands it is no more than a small district."

"How can you call it small," I asked, "when its inhabitants might number four thousand?"

"Damietta contains thirty or forty thousand people," he said, "many of whom are scholars and learned people. I [63] learned astronomy and other things first from my teacher, the famous Shaykh Muḥammad al-Ṣabbāgh al-Mīqātī. Then, when Bonaparte came to Egypt with his French soldiers and took possession of it in 1799, and the English blockaded the sea and cut off commerce, I did not waste my time but worked hard to learn the language of the French, among whom were many scholars. From them I learned the latest discoveries in astronomy, physics and geography. If you want to learn, I will teach you. I have nothing to do and intend to remain with you through the winter and spring to observe meteorological phenomena that do not occur in Egypt. It is now summer; we have much time. If you work hard and open your mind to being taught, you can acquire much of what you desire, and I will strive to be useful to you."

I thanked him for all he would do for me, and the next day I began to study my uncle's book on the new approach, because it was easy to understand and the quickest way for me to learn about eclipses. I finished it in two months, never ceasing to labor at my trade either. Every workday I had two lessons, morning and evening; and holidays were spent entirely, after going to mass, on study. This is how I spent my evenings, and I began to be able to calculate lunar eclipses, which were easier than solar eclipses and did not require as much knowledge as was needed to calculate solar eclipses. But before the time came for my uncle to leave, I was competent in determining longitudes and latitudes, and I understood the parts of astronomy and physics I found easy in the books of Lalande,

Benjamin and others. It was a stroke of good luck for me that my uncle loved the Lebanon: he was gone for a little while and then returned with his family, so I had a further chance to benefit from his learning, in addition to which he also had a powerful, penetrating intellect. Once he knew the principle of something he understood all its ramifications in no time.

In 1817 my father wanted to send me to his brother in Damietta, as he had sent my brother before. My uncle [Buṭrus] approved of the idea and composed a treatise for me containing all I would need to know of the customs, idioms, different weights and measures used in commercial transactions, and how to maintain my health in the climate of that country. He explained some treatments along with prescriptions and sage advice and gave me letters of introduction to his friends there.

I journeyed there at the end of the summer, when the Nile floods and the climate is temperate, the land of Egypt differing from our country, the spring there being very bad and the best weather occurring in the autumn. Instead of saying, as we do, *rabīʻa jamīle* ["nice spring"], they say *kharīfa kwayyisa* ["nice autumn"], *kwayyisa* meaning the same as *jamīle.* When I arrived I settled in my uncle's house, to which my brother Andreos had come about five years before me. I worked copying with him in my uncle's warehouse, where there were two scribes besides us. I also worked a little on my own [64] to make extra money, as the rest of the scribes did. My uncle and brother helped me with their names when necessary, even with loans of cash sometimes, to make payments for which I did not have the ready cash. Thus I built up a bit of capital not to be despised by the likes of me.

One thing that happened during that time in Egypt was that the governor, the famous Muḥammad-ʻAlī Pasha, had sent his intendant Muḥammad Bey to Upper Egypt to oversee, far from Cairo, the training of regular troops,[8] like those of Europe, from which instructors had been sent for. This operation was carried out far away, for fear of an insurrection by the Turkish troops, as had happened to Sultan Selim, who had been killed when he wanted to have a regular army. Therefore Muḥammad-ʻAlī Pasha had sent most of the Turkish troops far away to the Hejaz and ʻAsīr to fight the Wahhābī. Nonetheless, he was not safe from danger. When he learned of a plot of the troops remaining in Cairo to attack him, he barricaded himself in the citadel and sent people to plunder the Khān al-Ḥamzāwī Market to distract the soldiers and give him a chance to make his plans. When his strategem had been made and his mind was easy, he began gradually to cut the soldiers' salaries and ship them to Anatolia.

At that time Alexandria was in ruins, and only a little water reached it, and that only when the Nile flooded. Damietta was the port of Egypt, and these soldiers used to arrive there by riverboat, where sea-going vessels waited to take them to their country. However, we used to hear that anchored ouside the mouth of the river was only one large boat, which had not sailed at all, and all the soldiers that arrived were sent to it. Of the thousands who entered it one by one and then disappeared, never to be heard of again, it was said that when a soldier got on board on one side he was thrown overboard from the other side, after they had tied a jar filled with sand around his neck. But we did not know whether it was true or not. Anyway, he summoned the Turkish soldiers from the Hejaz, officer by officer with his squadrons, and then deported them in this fashion. Only by these means could he get a regular army. As for the shopkeepers in al-Ḥamzāwī who had been plundered, their grief turned to joy when an order was issued by Muḥammad 'Alī Pasha for them to submit in writing the value of what had been plundered and swear an oath to its veracity and then be reimbursed by his treasury. How much stale merchandise that had remained unsold for years but found a brisk market during the pillage were they reimbursed for—and they no longer had to fear insurrections!

During this year the government got its hands on the rice factories and began to sell directly to merchants. In 1818 it got hold of all textile industries, silk, linen and cotton. Little by little it gained control of all products of the region, grains, cottons, linens and leather, and no merchant could buy any of these things to trade except from the government. This state lasted until the governor of Egypt relinquished Syria in 1840, and [65] Muḥammad 'Alī and his descendants gained conditional independence in the internal affairs of Egypt through the offices of the great foreign powers, though they still had to pay an annual sum to the Empire and had to give up the industries and monopoly on the products of the region and grant free trade as well as internal autonomy to craftsmen.

In this year, i.e. 1818, I had a religious crisis, for there were dogma I thought I had to believe, yet no sound mind could accept them—especially since I saw that many of the people of Damietta, both Muslims and Christians, were even more confused than I was. My confusion was added to when I read in Volney's book of travels where he speaks of his journey through Lebanon and his arrival at the ruins of Tadmur.[9] Khawāja Bāsīlī Fakhr. the translator of books from French to Arabic, had translated this book, but at that time there were no presses in Egypt to print it. So Khawāja Mīkhāyīl Surūr, the English consul at Damietta, copied it and, being a relative of mine, asked me to compare the copy against the original to catch mistakes. I did as he asked, and my confusion increased during the comparison, but I remained true to what I had learned from my family.

Musicians.

During this year I endeavored to learn music and how to play stringed instruments and woodwinds, and I acquired what I could. The reason for my interest was that my brother and I were with a group of friends at a wedding, and when the music began to play a man sitting next to me asked me what the mode was that was being played. Before I could confess my ignorance, a man near us, who was from Acre but had been raised in Damietta, was about fifty years old and pretended to refinement and great knowledge, responded to the question by saying about me, "He is a mountaineer still wet behind the ears. He doesn't know anything. I'll tell you what the mode is." I was profoundly affected by the rudeness of this man and said to myself that the people of the Lebanon were far superior to the hoi-poloi of Ṣafad, where he was from, and that my uncle and brother were of much more importance than he was to the people who mattered in Damietta, not to mention others. But I nonetheless remained ignorant of what he spoke of so glibly and had to bear patiently the label he had given me. That night I went to bed fraught with worry, but the next morning I went to one of the best musicians, who knew all types of Arabic instruments, and asked him to teach me to play the easiest one. He chose the *qānūn*[10] for me and fixed an hour at the end of every day to come to me after I had finished my work. During this time I invented a staff on which I could note down the modes he used to teach me. In two months I could easily distinguish the modes, and after that I was able to learn to play other instruments without an instructor. Years later I was able to compose a treatise on this art that has not been superseded.

It happened once that I attended a gathering where that same dilettante 'Akkāwī was I mentioned before. He was asked by one [66] of those present what the name of the mode being sung was. He said it was *ḥijāz*, whereas it was really *sīgāh*, and it is quite impossible to confuse one with the other. I realized then how ignorant he was in this art, so I took the opportunity to have my revenge on him in front of all present for having cut me down once before.

"Sir," I said, "a while back someone asked me about a mode, and you claim to be refined and cultivated, but in your refinement you didn't wait to hear my reply. You probably would have been glad for a Lebanese to confess his ignorance of the art of music, and then you could have displayed your learning and not shame me by saying that the people of the Lebanon were still wet behind the ears; however, it is now obvious to me that after living forty years in Egypt you are still—I would not say it but that you in your refinement chose to—'wet behind the ears,' while we in the Lebanon avoid coarse speech and do not pretend to know what we do not. You claim to know music but cannot distinguish between *ḥijāz* and *sīgāh*, which are as different one from the other as are a Ṣafadī and a Lebanese, which two cannot possibly be confused." He tried to prove that his answer was correct, but those present who knew music showed him that he knew nothing of this art and humiliated him.

Then news reached us of the province of Ṣaydā. 'Alī Pasha, intendant to the governor, Sulaymān Pasha, had died and been replaced by his son 'Abdullāh Bey. Shaykh Bashīr Jumblāṭ had built a mosque with a minaret in his house in al-Mukhtāra and was making a great display of being Muslim. Emir Ḥasan, a cousin of Emir Bashīr, had killed his father and paternal uncle, who were both maternal uncles to the emir, and was also pretending to be Muslim. He [claimed] that he had killed the two of them because they were Christian. He was sent to Acre, and word had it that his execution was being kept secret, but Sulaymān Pasha had sent him to be imprisoned at the capital. Later 'Abdullāh Pasha summoned him to the Lebanon, and his own brother, Emir As'ad, killed him. Then Emir Bashīr executed the *qāḍī* of Dayr al-Qamar, Shaykh Sharaf al-Dīn, who had been afflicted by the loss of an eye but was a clever, well educated man of excellent conduct, though he had been found to be one who satirized piety. A poet said of him after he was killed: "In truth the balance of contentment lies in two unblemished eyes. Did you expect a scale to balance with only one eye?"

Anyway, with these events Emir Bashīr began to suspect—and perhaps he was aided in his suspicions by some of those who hated Shaykh Bashīr Jumblāṭ—that the shaykh had promoted these things to enable him to seize control of the mountain from the hands of the Shihābīs. For that reason he pretended to be a Muslim and built a mosque in his house. In addition he returned to the rightful owners, or to their heirs, all the money he had wrongfully taken throughout his life, which was an enormous amount. It was he who had instigated his cousin Emir Ḥasan to make a show of becoming Muslim and to kill his father and uncle because they had become Christian. It was said he had killed his father inside a church.

When Shaykh Bashīr learned this, he took precautions for his life and made every effort to rid the emir [67] of these suspicions. In truth Shaykh Bashīr was an intelligent man renowned for his knowledge of how to conduct politics agreeable to the customs of the people of the Lebanon and the chiefs of the clans, and moreover it was impossible for any one clan chief to become ruler over the others. However, his opponents can claim that when he saw the emir's power extending, he feared it and wanted to exchange him for a weak emir he could control. In the long run, however, it was clear that Shaykh Bashīr intended to do none of these things. It is sufficient proof to note that, when another was made ruler of the Lebanon, he accompanied the emir and took his men to the Ḥawrān, as will be told in its proper place.

*Let us return to the narration of my stay in Damietta. In Egypt the plague lasted for about five months every year, approximately from the beginning of February until June (Rūmī). Those who feared for their lives would hole up during this period in their houses, taking various means of precaution. The year of my arrival in Damietta my brother Andreos fell victim to this disease but lived through it safely.

Stuck above the door to my uncle's house and the doors of his rooms I found pieces of paper on which was written "Mary conceived immaculately." I asked about them and was told, "They keep the plague from entering a place where they are put over the door. We were assured of that by Father 'Lyās, our learned priest, who is a student at a Greek school.

"When did you put these placards up?" I asked.

"Five years ago," they said.

Then this is just a priests' fable," I said. "My brother got the plague, and he has one over his door."

"Don't be irreligious and sow doubt," they said. "Haven't you heard what it says in the Gospel, 'O ye of little faith'? Don't you know that Father 'Lyās is a pious and learned man? He writes these pieces of paper with great care and puts them under the chalice during the Mass of the Immaculate Conception for this purpose. If he didn't know they were effective, he wouldn't trouble himself to do it. That your brother was afflicted with the disease only proves to us that he is a skeptic with little faith in sacred things. Many people like him have been stricken with the plague, and most of them died because of their lack of faith."

"If Father 'Lyās believes in the efficacy of these placards," I answered, "why does he fear the plague and neglect his congregation, shutting himself up in the house of the *khawāja*s 'Ayrūṭ and forcing Father Anton Maron to serve them in addition to those of his own rite?"

Their final reply was, "You are so stubborn you can't be convinced of anything." I left them to flounder in their error.

The strangest thing I saw about the Egyptians was that, although they are clever, quick to comprehend and sociable—rarely do we find any to equal them in Arab countries—they are prone to exaggeration and gullibility. Now that I have mentioned something that some Christians, despite the [general] soundness of their minds, believed to be true but which no one in his right mind would believe, I will mention another incident, which happened to me with a Muslim gentleman in Damietta.

One day I was on an outing, seated beside the Nile, when one of the ulema, an acquaintance of mine named Shaykh Aḥmad al-Gammāl, came and sat down near me. As soon as I realized who he was, I kissed his hand, for he was acknowledged by the ulema for his superiority in traditional and rational learning,[11] which he had studied with the scholars of the Azhar in Cairo. While we were talking, two boats stopped for about five minutes at a shrine on the opposite bank of the Nile and then went on their way. I said to the shaykh, "I wonder why they stopped. If it was to recite the *Fātiḥa* for the soul of the saint, as is customary, they could have done it without stopping."

"My son," he said, "you should know that this is the shrine of Sayyidnā Abū-'Alī al-Ṣayyād, a son of Sayyidnā Aḥmad al-Badawī. He used to hold gatherings in this place and is the guardian of the River Nile from here to Tanta. From there to the outskirts of Cairo the river is under the protection of Sayyid al-Badawī. The boats stop at the shrine to give something to the custodian so that they will be protected from danger. See how the crocodiles do not dare to approach the river at Damietta for fear of Shaykh Abū-'Alī. He has many evident miracles, one of which is the sheatfish, who are his offspring: they fell into the Nile from the remains of his arm."

I could not restrain myself from saying, "Then it is surprising that the Damiettan proverb says of a mean man that he sinks as low as a sheatfish searching for excrement. They also say of someone who speaks of what is not his business that he is as persistent as a sheatfish in eating shit. Why is it that they tolerate such calumny of it and do not honor it? If what they say is true, how can such a noble being eat filth?"

"The common people are ignorant," he said, "and what they say is of no consequence. What they see a sheatfish doing is only what it seems to be doing. The inner meaning of a thing is known only to true initiates;[12] it is hidden from the gaze of the masses. This is proven in God's holy book, where Our Lord Moses objects to what Our Lord Khiḍr has done, which appears externally to be contradictory to the immaculate divine law, although its inner aspect was true and Moses did not know it, even though he was one of the greatest prophets and Khiḍr was immeasurably beneath him.[13] It is incumbent upon us not to object to what we see of the conduct of saints, which may appear to contradict the law, for these things are all esoteric mysteries and it is not within our capacity to comprehend the meaning."

I refrained from making a reply to this, although the religion of Islam does not accept such fables any more than the Christian religion accepts the superstitions of Father 'Lyās.*[14]

I remained in Damietta for three years, and every year I was imprisoned in the house for about five months because of the plague. I told my brother that it was dangerous to stay in this country for no compelling reason and it would be better for us to return to our family. My brother returned [to the Lebanon] and I stayed to wind up our affairs. At the beginning of 1820 I returned to Dayr al-Qamar and found work dealing in silks, at the management of which I was quite good due to my familiarity with the crafts of textile production; but not half a year had passed before there occurred upheavals in the provincial government of Ṣaydā.

Part Three

1820-1830

THE GOVERNOR OF ṢAYDĀ SULAYMĀN PASHA DIES AND IS SUCCEEDED BY ‘ABDULLĀH PASHA; M‘ALLIM ḤĀYĪM IS KILLED.

Sulaymān Pasha had died before my return from Damietta, and M‘allim Ḥāyīm had thought it wise to obtain the governorship for ‘Abdullāh Bey, the son of the late ‘Alī Pasha, since Sulaymān Pasha had no sons. He did, however, have a nephew, Muṣṭafā Bey, father of the Sulaymān Bey who is now a member of a provincial administrative board in Syria. Those who had loved Sulaymān Pasha told M‘allim Ḥāyīm that he should exert himself to obtain the governorship for Muṣṭafā Bey because he was clement by nature, like his uncle, but [Ḥāyīm] did not listen to them. "‘Abdullāh Bey was born in this country," he said, "and we took great pains to teach him Arabic, nice handwriting and the legal sciences. After the death of his father he was appointed intendant and has experience in governing. It is not right for us to promote over him someone whose Arabic is weak and who neither knows the legal system nor has experience in the government."

At first the Sublime Empire did not consent to let ‘Abdullāh Bey, who was young, have the governorship and held it in abeyance for nine months, [during which time] Emir Bashīr maintained peace throughout the province with his might, of which all the clans were in awe. Finally, through the offices of M‘allim Ḥiziqyāl the Jew, who was then a bursar at the Sublime Porte, he was able to persuade the Empire to appoint ‘Abdullāh Bey to the governorship of Ṣaydā and make him a vizier. [68]

When ‘Abdullāh Pasha took over the office of governor he confirmed all employees in the posts they had held when Sulaymān Pasha died. There was general rejoicing among the people at his succession to office because he had been patronized by Sulaymān Pasha, whose days in office were happy ones for the subjects and officials. Everything remained, as it had been, in M'allim Ḥāyīm's hands—the vizier's treasury was even kept in his house and under his control. However, 'Abdullāh Pasha did not conduct himself with the dignity expected of viziers and consorted with the rabble, mingling with them during *dhikr*s and associating freely with them. M'allim Ḥāyīm, who was filled with wisdom and refinement, was pained at this conduct on the part of his patron and, in true service to him, advised him that it was not proper for people of his station to mix with the vulgar. If he must attend *dhikr*s, then it should be done with suitable people, like the *qāḍī*, the mufti, the dean of the *sharīf*s and the ulema. (Solomon the Wise said: "Reprove not a scorner, lest he hate thee: rebuke a wise man, and he will love you."[1] M'allim Ḥāyīm had the notion that 'Abdullāh Pasha would heed this advice and realize the extent to which his devoted service went, especially since [the pasha] was a learned man. He certainly did not think that ignorance would get the better of him. However, instead of accepting the advice and showing gratitude to the one who had shown him the error of his ways, 'Abdullāh Pasha strayed farther from the path.

He told these scum what his trusty advisor had said, and when they heard, they feared that the Pasha might eventually heed the advice. If M'allim Ḥāyīm persisted in his advice, they would lose one by whose presence among them they benefited. Therefore they began to scheme against him, saying, "This Jew is so arrogant with Muslims that many have begun to kiss his hand as though he were a vizier or a judge. The Koran tells us that they are the worst enemies of true believers. How can a Muslim rely on them and trust them? Your late uncle Sulaymān Pasha was a naive man and was taken in by the chicanery of the Jews. He held the cow by the horns while the Jews drank the milk. His treasury is even kept in the house of this Jew. Does any Muslim know what has gone into or come out of the treasury? Did your uncle know anything about it? The vizier's treasury is the commonwealth of the Muslims: is it permissible to deposit it with a Jew and entrust it to one who is the worst enemy of Muslims, as the Lord of the Universe bears witness to? Is there any evidence greater than this? Anyone who denies it is an infidel. Is it licit to employ a Jew in a governmental department in the interests of Muslims? It was not permitted by any of the Four Imams of the Muslim schools of law. Your late uncle can be excused because he did not know the law, but Your Excellency knows the legal precepts and cannot be excused for neglecting any of them."

'Abdullāh Pasha's [69] wrath against M'allim Ḥāyīm was provoked by the words of these rabble. The next day he demanded that M'allim Ḥāyīm bring the treasury to be put into his custody somewhere inside the seraglio, and he produced it as ordered. Then he ordered him to keep to his house and turn over the office of chief treasury scribe to M'allim Yūsuf Qardāḥī, a Maronite from Ṣaydā—after M'allim Jirjis Masadiyya had refused to accept it.

Thereafter these scum schemed to have M'allim Ḥāyīm killed by two of the vizier's companions who hated the M'allim because he had kept them from obtaining what they wanted, which was not in [the government's] best interests. The two were Shaykh Mas'ūd al-Māḍī from the 'Athlīt coast and 'Umar Efendī al-Baghdādī, whose eyes 'Abdullāh Pasha [later] put out with red-hot irons when his corruption had grown too great to bear.

These two said in one of 'Abdullāh Pasha's gatherings, "All Muslims rejoiced when you lifted the weight of the Jew from their backs, but as much as they rejoiced, they still fear his tricks and sorcery, for he is a skilled sorcerer. Add to that his influence with the Sublime Empire through M'allim Ḥiziqyal, who used his influence to get Your Excellency the governorship to please Ḥāyīm. You may be sure that Ḥāyīm will write to him and tell him what has happened. He who can get a post is not incapable of taking it away, especially since the Jews have great wealth and the Empire craves money, not people. So long as Ḥāyīm is alive you cannot rest from his evil machinations." Therefore 'Abdullāh Pasha decided to kill him, not realizing that that would pose the greatest danger to him because all the Jews would be stirred to take revenge, and they were quite capable of arranging matters to get what they wanted.

That very night he ordered his intendant and brother-in-law, Ibrāhīm Bey the Circassian, to go himself with a few soldiers, strangle Ma'allim Ḥāyīm and throw him into the sea. He went and asked to see Ḥāyīm, who came out and invited him in. In answer he was surrounded by soldiers, a rope was put around his neck and pulled tight until he died, and then they threw him into the sea. The next morning his body was found cast on the shore by the waves. The Jews were not allowed to bury him, and his body was tied to a stone pillar and sunk to the bottom of the sea. All intelligent people in the province, regardless of their religion, were of one accord in their sorrow over the loss of this wise administrator to the government.

Emir Bashīr, the ruler of the Lebanon, was the most aggrieved of all over this loss and expected changes in 'Abdullāh Pasha's policy through his inclination to promote those who had no talent for policy-making. Some of the great merchants withdrew from Acre, some to Beirut and others to the Lebanon, wary of the governor's upheavals when they saw his horrible conduct in killing Ḥāyīm, who had striven and used his influence to acquire the vizierate for him after the Empire had refused to let him have it. Even M'allim Jirjis Masadiyya, the senior treasury clerk, was offered M'allim Ḥāyīm's post, but he refused [70] to accept it, pretending to be sick, and left Acre for a change of climate in Ṣaydā. Then he fled to the Fārḥī house in Damascus and stayed with them in the treasury there. His son, Ibrāhīm Efendī and Niqūlā Efendī, and his grandson Qayṣar Efendī are still in the service of the government of Damascus.

'ABDULLĀH PASHA'S TEMERITY WITH EMIR BASHĪR.

Then 'Abdullāh Pasha began to display his arrogance to the emir, sometimes demanding sums of cash, sometimes demanding certain horses, sometimes demanding jewelry, both things he had been given in the past in token of special services and things [he had inherited] from his ancestors. The emir presented him with whatever he asked for, seeking to conciliate him with letters and messengers. In the emir's employ was M'allim Buṭrus Karāma, a Greek Catholic from Homs, a poet well known for his sharp mind and eloquence and for his good writing style and penmanship. The emir sent him to conciliate 'Abdullāh Pasha. With his powerful intelligence and eloquence he was able to bend the pasha's mind and brought back a letter to the emir announcing his favor toward him. But no sooner was he gone than the corruptors came to the pasha and changed his mind for him, undoing what Buṭrus Karāma had done. He was therefore forced to return to set straight the corruption they had wrought. Their greatest source of provocation to stir up the vizier's wrath was [to say] that Emir Bashīr was at heart a Christian, an infidel, a double-dealer who could not be trusted, who should not rule, "especially among Muslims, of whom there are many thousands in the Lebanon. God will hold you responsible on the Day of Resurrection for putting an infidel ruler over them. This Buṭrus, who is really Karāha ["hatred"] not Karāma ["honor"], this man is a sorcerer who comes and bewitches you, changing your sound ideas to what suits them."

By these means they cast such doubt in the vizier's mind that he summoned Ṣāliḥ al-Ṭarshīḥī, the *qāḍī* of Ṭarshīḥā, a learned and pious man, and demanded that he go to the emir and stay for a few days to observe his conduct with his subjects, especially the Muslims, inquire into his religion, and then come back and tell him the truth. The emir knew everything that went on in the vizier's council chamber because there were members of the vizier's retinue who reported to him. Shaykh Ṣāliḥ went to the emir, stayed a few days and returned without speaking to the emir a word he had been charged with by ʻAbdullāh Pasha.

When Shaykh Ṣāliḥ arrived he reported that he had accomplished his mission. He had examined carefully the conditions of the Muslims, Christians and Druze of the mountain and found that all had nothing but good to say of Emir Bashīr's rule to establish right and maintain security all over the mountain and the surrounding areas. The rights of all were equal in his view, whatever community they came from, and all claims were settled legally. He even forbade judges to take a fee for investigations or for writing cases and opinions, although judges everywhere outside of the Lebanon had the right to do so. Judges on the mountain were given a salary by the emir, and if he learned of their taking anything from plaintiffs or defendants it was an unforgivable sin. [71] All office-holders under him conducted themselves according to this same principle, and no one employed by him could be found to take a bribe or disregard the rights of anyone. As for his religion, when he had asked him about it, he had replied, "This question should be asked of those in charge of mosques, who are employed to discharge religious duties, not of those employed in political administration. His Excellency engaged me to administer the mountain: if in my administration he finds any flaw, then he is obliged in all justice to ask me about it, but it is not my job to know about the rules and regulations of religious affairs. If he wants the mountain to be ruled by a mosque official, he can find plenty of them. Let him send a jurisprudent to rule the mountain instead of me."

Shaykh Ṣāliḥ then said, "I saw that what the emir said was right, for the mountain encompasses many corrupt and villainous people. A pious, religious ruler who is occupied with the discharge of his religious duties would have little strength to control these villains, whose aggression extends to outside of the Lebanon and who are difficult to keep in check. For him to control the brigands of the mountain is a source of peace for the neighboring areas inland and the cities on the coast." The vizier was convinced by what Shaykh Ṣāliḥ said. The emir received word of what he had done and arranged an annual stipend to be sent to him.

It is said that Muṣṭafā Āghā Barbar, the *mutasallim* of Tripoli, who was originally a peasant from al-Qalamūn but was brought up in the service of Emir Ḥasan, Emir Bashīr's brother, and had advanced in the government by virtue of his skill and energy until he had become a *ḥākim* in Tripoli, which was attached to the province of Ṣaydā, was the chief antagonist of Emir Bashīr around ʻAbdullāh Pasha.

[Once again] M'allim Buṭrus Karāma went to ʻAbdullāh Pasha to test the waters after the emir had learned of what had transpired with the *qāḍī* of Ṭarshīḥā. He returned bearing a letter to the emir glowing with words of approval. At the top he had even written the following: "These two lines are in the hand of a miserable servant [of God]. Our honored son, I have tried you and tested you time and time again and have found you to be none other than what the poet says: 'You are true as gold, purified and refined by me and those like me.' Remain safe and sound, and the peace of God be with you."

When the emir saw this he was quite relieved, but M'allim Buṭrus said, "It is impossible that the pasha not change his mind, for his council no longer contains the intelligent M'allim Ḥāyīm, and there is no one around him save the corrupt, who have taken charge of his mind and force him to listen to them. It is impossible that he remain as he is for ten days. I saw conditions in Acre and learned the truth. There are honest men around him who despise his conduct, but it is no longer within their ability to prevent him from acting this way, so many are the corrupt and so great is their hold on his mind. His letter to Your Excellency should be taken as no more than a shortlived opportunity to make your own arrangements, either to declare your disobedience of him or to give up the rulership."

In answer the emir said, "To disobey [72] my overlord is impossible for me to do, but I will think about what the best course of action would be." Immediately he summoned Shaykh Bashīr Jumblāṭ to negotiate what must be done. After consulting with those who could be trusted, it was decided to leave the mountain for the province of Damascus and wait to be restored to 'Abdullāh Pasha's favor. The emir asked Jirjis Mishāqa to report on the cash in the treasury, which was found to be 28,000 piastres (counting a *'amūd* rial as six and a quarter piastres, or a thousand liras). The cash the emir had on hand was little because his expenses were great and, in order to placate 'Abdullāh Pasha, he had taken out loans in his own name and given the pasha whatever he wanted. When he received this report he said to Shaykh Bashīr, "This amount is nothing in comparison to what we will need in exile." He replied that he could make arrangements when necessary. Then the emir warned all his retinue to prepare to move in eight days. That was at the end of February, 1821.

EMIR BASHĪR DEPARTS FOR JABAL ḤAWRĀN.

Eight days later he left with his own three sons and in addition Emir Ḥaydar al-Aḥmad of Shimlān and Emir 'Abbās of Majdal M'ūsh with all their dependents, Shaykh Bashīr Jumblāṭ, his sons and the sons of his brother Shaykh Ḥasan, and the emirs of the House of Arslān and their dependents. All who left with the emir, mounted and on foot, totalled about three thousand persons. Jirjis Mishāqa was accompanied by his sons Ibrāhīm, Andreos and Mikhāyil; the little ones Jibrā'īl and Rūfā'īl were sent to Ṣaydā. In spite of the danger, Shaykh Ḥusayn Shiblī Ḥamāda, the father of the Ḥamāda beys of B'aqlīn, attached himself to the emir's service and showed himself to be energetic and devoted, and the emir loved him very much.

The emir had not been gone two hours when, as he was going down to the village of Kfar Nabrakh to meet his men, a Tatar arrived from Acre with a message from 'Abdullāh Pasha to the emir making demands he was no longer able to meet. He wrote back in appeasement of the pasha that were he capable of meeting the demands he would make no delay, but he had left the mountain and was waiting to be restored to favor. Wherever he settled he would report to his superiors in order that the Empire might know where he was. Then he went down to the village of Ḥammānā, where Muqaddam Abū-'Alī Muzhir, Shaykh Bashīr Jumblāṭ's brother-in-law, lived. He spent two nights there until all the men had arrived. Then he moved to the village of Qabb Ilyās in the West Biqā', a dependency of the province of Damascus. There Muqaddam Abū-'Alī and his sons, Muqaddam Abū-Ḥusayn and Muqaddam As'ad, joined him and he stayed for two days. He ordered Jirjis Mishāqa to send his sons to Damascus because they were unaccustomed to the hardship of exile and to remain himself in his service. They were therefore sent to Damascus. The emir sent a report to 'Abdullāh Pasha explaining that he had passed the borders of the province [73] of Ṣaydā into the Biqā' and was headed for the Ḥawrān, where he would await his orders. Then the emir moved with those accompanying him to Rāshayyā, then to al-Qunayṭra and finally to Jabal al-Drūz in the Ḥawran. From there he dispatched another report to 'Abdullāh Pasha informing him of his arrival and that he awaited his pleasure.

EMIR ḤASAN AND EMIR SALMĀN ARE MADE RULERS OF THE LEBANON, OF WHICH PART IS REMOVED FROM THEIR JURISDICTION.

When 'Abdullāh Pasha learned that the emir had left the mountain, he wrote to the capital to have Emir Ḥasan sent, the one who had killed his own father and uncle and pretended to have converted to Islam (which enjoins respect for one's parents, even if they are unbelievers). He was sent, but before he arrived, the rulership of the mountain was given to two Shihābī emirs, Emir Ḥasan, who was the son of Emir 'Alī son of Emir Ḥaydar, the common ancestor of all the Shihābīs of the Lebanon, and Emir Salmān, the son of Emir Sīd-Aḥmad, who had been blinded by his brother, Emir Yūsuf son of Emir Mulḥim, brother of the above-mentioned Emir 'Alī. To these two was given [the rulership of the Lebanon], but 'Abdullāh Pasha detached from the Lebanon the Kharnūb, Tuffāḥ, Jazzīn and Jabal al-Rīḥān regions and the city of Jbayl. These emirs made a show of being Muslim, and the shaykhs from the mountain who had gone into exile, such as the House of 'Imād and others, returned to their estates.

JIRJIS MISHĀQA'S SONS GO TO DAMASCUS; THEIR FATHER REMAINS WITH THE EMIR.

Jirjis Mishāqa's sons went to Damascus, as ordered by the emir. The vizier of Damascus had been removed from office and the acting ruler was an agent of Darwīsh Pasha, who had been appointed to the governorship of Damascus and was still on his way there. The agent's name was Darwīsh Āghā son of Ja'far Āghā of the Damascene *āghās*. News reached him that the sons of Emir Bashīr's bursar had come to Damascus with chests containing the emir's treasury. He then issued a warrant for their arrest and confiscation of the money, although the emir was bankrupt and they had left their homes, livelihoods and accounts behind on the mountain in haste and had been at pains to scrape together what would tide them over temporarily. When they heard that they were wanted, they hid in a safe place until relief should arrive.

When Emir Bashīr learned that Darwīsh Pasha was coming to the province of Damascus as governor, he sent to him as envoy one of Shaykh Bashīr's trusted men, Yūsuf al-'Akkāwī, a Catholic from Dayr al-Qamar, accompanied by five expert horsemen in livery, empowered to obtain from [the pasha] a guarantee of protection in Jabal Ḥawrān. Yūsuf al-'Akkāwī met with him at Ḥamā and presented the petition and horses, which he accepted, and reported to him what he had been charged to say by the emir. He replied very politely that the emir might be absolutely certain he would do everything in his power to help him, and [the envoy] returned elated. When that became known, the search for the Mishāqa sons was called off, and the emir's followers, such as Shaykh Manṣūr al-Daḥdāḥ and his relatives, Yūsuf al-Khūrī al-Shalfūn, who has been mentioned before, and M'allim Buṭrus Karāma, all went to Damascus, where they stayed for a while.

DARWĪSH PASHA ARRIVES AS GOVERNOR OF DAMASCUS.

The vizier entered Damascus amidst great celebration, and this writer was one of the spectators to his entry outside the city. [74] First were the mobile cannons, followed by criminals trailing their chains. These had been brought from Ma'arra, Hama and Homs, which were dependencies of the province, for execution in Damascus on successive days to inspire dread in the people. Following them came soldiers of various kinds, cavalry and infantry. Next came the Orthodox Patriarch of Damascus with his retinue carrying lighted candles. Then there were the kettle-drums and clarions, followed by the notables of Damascus, and finally the vizier, salaaming right and left, who was preceded by a herald crying for salutations upon the Prophet. After the vizier came another group in which was his intendant. As the mobile cannons fired they were answered by the cannons on the citadel and volleys from the soldiers. The noise of the drums and clarions was unceasing. This took place during Orthodox Eastertide, and one of the vizier's heralds galloped his horse before the Christian spectators, shouting in Greek, "*Christos aneste*!"[2] The Christians were dumbfounded by this action, for they had never before heard these words from the mouth of a Muslim Turk.

It was the custom in Damascus, when the governor issued an order for a prisoner in the citadel to be strangulated, that execution not take place until shortly after the evening call to prayer. A rope would be placed around the [condemned man's] neck, a cannon would be fired and then he would be strangulated and [his body] cast before the citadel gate for the people to see in the morning, so by the sound of a cannon after sundown everyone knew that somebody was being executed. It was Christians and Jews, however, who were forced to do the execution lest the [Muslims] be guilty of the crime of murder, for according to Islamic law guilt attaches to the person who actually performs [the act], not the authority who has it carried out. When a state order was issued that someone be strangulated, there was glee among the officials of the citadel, who spread out into the city. Since they did not dare to perform this task, if they found a Christian or a Jew who was capable of giving, they would press him into service, but one could buy one's way out by paying them money. It sometimes happened that [a Christian or a Jew] would escape from one of them only to fall into the hands of another. Therefore all who knew this was going on would hide for the whole day. At the end of the day they would grab someone who could perform the deed, not releasing him until the condemned man had been strangulated and the officials' pockets had been filled with money. (Thank God such coercion has been forbidden since the Egyptians took over Syria.)

At sundown the day after the vizier's entry a cannon shot was heard from the citadel, and it was known that someone was being executed.

The next morning it was learned that it was Aḥmad Āghā al-Shammāṭ, the head of the millers in Damascus. He had been strangled for the crime of impeding the former vizier's *tūgh* until what was owed to the millers was paid.

The state of this case is as follows. Formerly the viziers in Syria obliged the millers to provision the houses of the vizier and his intendant and all of their servants, retainers and employees down to the grooms, and paid them less than a quarter of the fair price. It happened that in that year, 1235 [1819-20], there was severe inflation in Damascus, and the millers suffered a double loss in provisioning [75] the vizier, who put off payment until they were owed 35,000 piastres in the currency of that time (which would be the equivalent of a thousand English pounds), of which perhaps six thousand liras was due to inflation. Then came the order for the vizier's removal from office, but he still would not pay. As they were in no position to remain silent, their head, Aḥmad al-Shammāṭ, tried to pull the necessary strings with the discharged vizier, but he was unable to recover the debt before the vizier decided to leave without paying what he owed these poor men.

Now it was the custom of the Empire to give viziers three *tūgh*s, which are horsetails about three cubits long dangling from the top of [the vizier's] staff. When a vizier set out on a journey, one day before starting he would send one *tūgh* to the place he would be stopping so that they would be prepared to receive him and have food and fodder ready, without payment of course. The remaining two *tūgh*s went in front of the vizier during his journey. The *tūgh* was said to mean that the Empire ruled the land with its horses' tails.

Anyway, when Aḥmad al-Shammāṭ saw the *tūgh* leaving the city without the vizier's having paid for the provisions, he held it up until the vizier paid, against his will, what he owed. [The former vizier] then told Darwīsh Pasha to kill this man, who had been aggressive in demanding his due. Such was the conduct of office-holders until they were bound by the Empire with its reformed rules and regulations.[3]

The next evening at sunset seventeen cannon shots were heard, and we supposed there must be something going on in the city. About two hours after sundown a young Maronite from Dayr al-Qamar, a servant of the emir named Ghālib Abī-'Ikr, joined us. We asked him about the cannon fire, and he said, "Don't worry about it. I'll tell you about it after you give me something for supper. My companions have locked our rooms and gone out for the evening, and I don't know where they are." After we had given him something to eat he began to tell us [his tale].

About an hour before sunset he was passing by the Khān al-Tūtūn, hoping to run into his comrades and go with them to the Christian quarter for supper, when two imperial musketeers came up to him and asked him if he was Ghālib Abī-'Ikr, and he said he was.

"'Come with us to the seraglio,' they said. 'There's a woman who has filed a complaint against you.'

"'It can't be me,' I said. 'It must be a mix-up with someone else.'

"'We are charged to bring you before the Tufangjī Bāshī. You can exonerate yourself when we get there,' they said. I turned around and saw Ḥannā 'Azzām sitting on a chest. (This Ḥannā was the son of Ibrāhīm 'Azzām, who was hanged by al-Jazzār along with Emir Yūsuf. He later joined the emir's service and gained promotion, being sent to viziers by the emir, but jocularity was the dominant note in his personality.)

"I said to him, 'By your honor, Ḥannā, get me released from these people!'

"He answered, laughing nonchalantly, 'Go along with them. If you are imprisoned, send word to me. Tomorrow, if I have the time and chance, I'll look into your case. If it's nothing major, I'll wait for an opportune day and, if I have business with the vizier and find him in a good mood, I may tell him about your case in the course of [76] our conversation. Maybe he'll permit you to be released.'

"I turned to him and said, 'Let them hang me. It would be easier than putting up with your stupid talk!' His cackling only got worse as I went off with the musketeers. When we reached the 'Aṣrūniyya, they veered toward the citadel. 'I'm supposed to be taken to the seraglio,' I said. 'What do you think you're doing, taking me to the citadel?'

"'It's almost sundown now,' they said, 'and everybody in the citadel has gone home. Spend tonight in the citadel jail, and tomorrow around noon we'll take you to the Tufangjī Bāshī. After that you can return to your cell until the imperials have the leisure to look for the woman and tell her that when she's not busy she can come to the seraglio for notification of the day they will have time to hear her complaint.'

"In exasperation I said, 'I could have done without going into that *khān*!' I went with them into the citadel, where I found by the gateway a group of Christians and Jews sitting weeping. I asked those who had brought me, 'Why are they here?'

"'Now we'll tell you the truth,' they said. 'Our efendi sent out an order today for us to strangulate seventeen prisoners tonight. As usual, we rounded up these people so that each of them could strangulate one [of the prisoners], but we still needed one more. Ḥannā 'Azzām told us where to find you and what to do with you. We really only want you to strangulate one person after the evening call to prayer.'

"'You nearly scared me to death the way you treated me,' I said. 'You could've done me a favor and told me what you wanted. It's no big deal. These people crying here are sissies. Let them go to their families. I'll do it for them.'

"'They're too many for you,' they said.

"'If there were fifty I wouldn't think they were too many,' I said. They consented and sent the others away. When the call to prayer was over they took me to a room and brought me the prisoners one by one, their hands tied and feet shackled. I strangulated them as gently as I could, except for a couple that gave me trouble 'cause they were strong and their necks were thick. They struggled a lot before I could get them to die.

"When I was done I asked them if they had any others for us to strangulate, and instead of showing their appreciation they cursed me. I left the citadel and came down to you in the Christian quarter. That's all."

THE FEUD BETWEEN THE ORTHODOX PATRIARCH SERAPHIM AND THE GREEK CATHOLICS IN DAMASCUS

An event that occurred in Damascus was as follows. When we arrived, the Greek Catholic sect was very upset because of what Lord Seraphim, the Greek Orthodox patriarch, had done to them. At that time his jurisdiction included them, so they were considered subject to him, and their priests were under his orders. They could not hold a funeral or bury their dead or conduct a marriage without his permission, because the Sublime Empire at that time had not officially recognized the Catholic sects that had seceded from their parent bodies. [The patriarch] did not permit them to wear the skullcap or the black head-dress, the clerical garb of the Orthodox; instead, they had to dress [77] like the common people. The punishment of priests was also in his hands.

In 1819 there was a dispute between the Catholics of Aleppo and the Orthodox metropolitan, Gerasimus al-Turkumān, whose sect there numbered about fifty men, while the Greek Catholics were more than fifteen hundred. It is no secret how severe Aleppans can be to someone who opposes their will, for they would rather die than be humiliated. Anyway, the metropolitan, who was an Aleppan, would not back down (later he was removed from Aleppo and became metropolitan of Ṣūr and Ṣaydā, with his seat at Ḥāṣbayyā; and he was a friend of this writer). The matter grew quite serious, eleven Catholics were killed by the authorities, and the matter ended with the removal of the metropolitan. The Aleppo incident cemented the hatred between the two sects throughout the east and opened old Catholic wounds, especially since the Catholic patriarch Ignatius Ṣarrūf had been assassinated seventeen years prior to this by Orthodox men.

Now it happened that a Catholic priest from a village near Damascus

Orthodox bishop.

became the object of the Patriarch Seraphim's wrath for some reason or other, and instead of punishing him himself as a cleric, he sent him to a state prison. Not content to let the rational men of their community placate the patriarch, who was one of those irritable, ill-tempered Greeks who did not act politely even with the important people among his flock, the hot-headed Catholic youth set out for the seat of the government and, in accordance with custom, soothed the rulers' wounds with the balm of gold and obtained the priest's release from prison without the patriarch's consent. They could not leave the matter there and let the priest return to his village in secret, but gathered and went, with the priest before them, to the Christian quarter, where they raised a standard made of a stick with an old shoe on top and cried out, "This is Patriarch Seraphim's standard," in answer to which the crowd roared, "God disgrace him!" Thus they made their way to the Orthodox church and patriarch's house. Naturally such an idiotic ruckus would have raised the patriarch from the dead. Intelligent Catholics were disgraced by this action, which had gone beyond all bounds of tolerance. The patriarch foamed with rage and ordered all Catholic priests to be seized by the authorities, have their beards shaved and be exiled to Arwād Island. They were taken to exile by way of Tripoli.

Now notable Catholics were influential with the governor of Ṣaydā, indeed 'Abdullāh Pasha was greatly inclined in their favor. They told him, "Our priests are monks from Dayr al-Mukhalliṣ, your subjects, and they are charged to perform religious services for the members of their rite in Syria and Egypt. The Orthodox patriarch has never ceased to beleaguer our sect, and Your Excellency knows that during your late uncle's term of office they constantly tried to gain control of our church in Ṣaydā, even sending a representative [78] of the patriarch, Zakhariyyā the Metropolitan of 'Akkār, to take charge of it. But your uncle said that the claimant had to prove his case first in accordance with Islamic law and that we had to deal with each other in a legal manner. Therefore we took the case before the judge, in the presence of the mufti and the ulema in Your Excellency's council chamber when you were the late [governor's] intendant. His case was thrown out and we were given a legal writ invalidating his claim. Now their patriarch in Damascus has had arrested the resident priests, who are your subjects, and exiled them to Arwād Island. But [they will be leaving] via Tripoli, where there is no Catholic to inquire about them. Since Arwād Island is in our efendi's jurisdiction, we beg you mercifully to allow them to go to their monastery, for they will die of hunger on that island where there is no one of our sect in the vicinity to care for them."

The vizier grew angry and said, "This is all the fault of the government clerk there, Na'ūm al-Ghrayyib. Why did he not tell the *mutasallim* he must refer the incident to us and wait for our order? He has no business following the orders of the governor of Damascus!" Immediately he issued an order for the removal and disgrace of the clerk and the *mutasallim* and safe return of the monks to their monastery via Ṣaydā.

The patriarch Seraphim was not content with exiling the priests but complained to the vizier that some of his flock, for whom he was responsible by imperial decree, had disobeyed him at the instigation of Europeans and joined the Catholic sect, which the Empire did not allow its subjects to belong to because of the anathema it contained. They must therefore be made to leave the Catholic sect and obey their patriarch by rejoining the church of their fathers and grandfathers. When the vizier learned the names of the leaders, he summoned them to his council chamber and informed them of the patriarch's demand. They responded, "We know of no one in charge of our beliefs. Your Honor is governor of us all: you do not oppose anyone's religious beliefs, and you force no one to do anything but pay state taxes and conduct himself properly. If we owe him anything in taxes, we will not refrain from paying them. If any of us has committed a crime, let him refer it to you, and Your Excellency can have it investigated and take the necessary steps. If he is not content with that, we will submit to the noble Islamic law. You can refer us both to court, and we will do whatever the law requires us to."

The [vizier] arranged with them that he should see some "keys of gold," which they gave him. Then he told the patriarch, "Your people have denied your claim. You must prove it legally." The patriarch knew that his claim would not be supported by the law, so he gave the vizier enough money to satisfy him to help him enforce his imperial patent without going to court. The vizier said to the Catholics, "The patriarch holds fast to the letter of his imperial patent and cannot be convinced to refer it to court." Then they brought him a *fatwā* to the effect that the implementation of imperial letters patent was limited to what was in accordance with the law, and they also gratified him with money. Then he made excuses to the patriarch based on the contents of the *fatwā*. The vizier kept playing both sides against each other until they had gone overwhelmingly into debt. As soon as he realized that they were incapable of paying more, he forced both parties [79] to refer the matter to the *qāḍī* in his council chamber, with the mufti and the ulema in attendance. It was convened in the evening because it was during the Ramadan fast. The two parties to the suit were present, while the rabble from both sides were gathered outside the council waiting to learn what was taking place.

During that session the case was not resolved, but it was apparent from the way it was going that the decision would go against the patriarch. When the session was adjourned, about half an hour after all had left the seraglio the patriarch returned in terror to the vizier and said, "As I was on my way home, a group of Catholic ruffians followed me to kill me. They cursed me, and my followers were scarcely able to save me from their clutches. I took refuge in Fāris Bey 'Aẓmzāda's house until they were gone, and then I came here to file my complaint so Your Excellency might know what the Catholic leaders are doing: they are having their will done by their underlings, and they will excuse themselves and say that they were ignorant and were not advised of what they were doing. I demand they be punished!"

The vizier lost no time in dispatching all the musketeers to arrest and imprison the Catholics until the necessary steps could be taken early the next morning. It was a dreadful night for the Christians of Damascus, even the Orthodox, because the musketeers could not distinguish between a Catholic and a non-Catholic and refused to believe anyone who told them he was of another sect, thinking it was just a ruse to escape. Since it was Ramadan, the markets, coffeehouses and gaming rooms were open, and musical instruments were being played everywhere. Most Christians were away from their houses making merry, and it was easy to arrest so many of all sects that there was no room in the jails for them and they had to be imprisoned in stables with beasts. That night was spent most miserably.

The next day non-Catholics were sorted out and released. Then they picked out the important Catholics and took them to the seraglio gate, gave them a public bastinado and returned them to prison, where they had to sit and sleep on the damp ground with no mattresses to protect them from detriment [to their health]. They had to resort to the usual balm of gold, and then they were released. They claimed that the patriarch's complaint against them was fabricated, that he had made it up, when he saw that the Islamic law was not going to support his demand, to keep the *qāḍī* from issuing a judgment. God only knows the truth, *but Christians of all denominations in the east should remember their indebtedness to the Jesuit missionaries, who, with their mastery of intrigue, were able to create divisiveness and enmity among the members of every sect. Were it not for their indefatigable efforts in the service of their master, they would not have been able to attain their goal of enthralling all they could to the one who sits in God's holy temple itself like a god.*[4]

The leaders of the Catholic sect feared the machinations of the patriarch, from which it was not possible to escape other than by paying huge sums of money. As their number in the whole kingdom did not exceed fifteen thousand men, and the Orthodox of the kingdom [80] were fifteen million, among them some so rich that any one of them possessed as much as all the Catholics put together, how then were they to resist the patriarch and his claims if the only means they had was to pay bribes to the rulers and judges? They decided therefore to leave their homes and take refuge at Dayr al-Mukhalliş in the Lebanon.

THE MOREA REBELS AGAINST THE EMPIRE, AND THE ORTHODOX PATRIARCH AT THE CAPITAL IS HANGED.

A few days later news came that the Greeks in the Morea and islands of the Mediterranean had rebelled against the Empire, and the Greek leaders in Constantinople and the patriarch had allied themselves with them to liberate the Greek region from Muslim hegemony. Sultan Mahmud had ordered the patriarch hanged. He was executed on Easter Sunday, and many Greeks were killed. Then imperial decrees were issued that dissenting Orthodox leaders were to be killed and the Christians throughout the Ottoman Empire were to be humbled. When the order came to the governor of Damascus, he held a council of the notables and read [the order] aloud. They responded, "There are no dissentors among our Christians. They are all *dhimmīs* who conduct themselves accordingly, and it is not permitted to harass them. Rather, we are all on an equal footing. Our Prophet made a pact with them in which he says, 'On the Day of Resurrection I will oppose any who has presumed upon a *dhimmī.*' We cannot bear the weight of answering for ourselves [in light of this]." It was decided to send to the Empire a declaration of the good conduct of the Christians in the province, of their obedience and payment of state taxes and of their deserving the protection and lovingkindness of the Sublime Sultanate. The Empire relented, but in other regions like Izmir and Cyprus the Orthodox were harassed, and a number of important men of the Orthodox sect were killed. The vizier of Damascus was content to enforce the rule that Christians' outer garments should be dark in color and their shoes should be black, but after they paid him fifty thousand piastres he permitted them to wear red shoes as usual.

The day the proclamation was made, some of the elders of the Daḥdāḥ family, Yūsuf al-Khūrī Shalfūn (who has been mentioned before) and some others, around twenty altogether, were at this writer's house, and they couldn't go out into the street in their red shoes until we got some shoe black. We had to send the servant to the market barefooted, and then we dyed our shoes black.

After the rebellion in the Morea and the hanging of the patriarch, the Orthodox patriarch's standing in Damascus was diminished, and all the Catholic leaders returned who had gone into exile with the priests banished by the patriarch.

THE CHRISTIANS OF THE COAST OF ALL DENOMINATIONS ARE FINED BECAUSE OF THE REBELLION IN THE MOREA.

*In the province of Ṣaydā, 'Abdullāh Pasha ordered amounts of money to be taken from the wealthy Christians, whether Orthodox or Catholic, and called it *zajriyya.* The poll-tax was to be taken from a Christian with the humiliation of having it taken from him in public and being slapped on the back of the neck, [according to 'Abdullāh Pasha's] interpretation of the Koranic text concerning Christians, that "they pay tribute by right of subjection, and they be reduced low."*[5]

Let us return to our narration of Emir Bashīr. We have already mentioned that he left the mountain with no more than 18,000 piastres in cash and that Shaykh Bashīr Jumblāṭ had promised to provide, as a loan to the emir, the necessary funds for those who left their country with him, about three thousand [81] men, of whom five hundred were mounted.

As the emir was constantly in need of cash for expenses, especially his sons' expenses, he sent Jirjis Mishāqa to his sons in Damascus to obtain a loan of 100,000 piastres, the interest on which at that time was 4,000 liras. He sent collateral double the amount of the loan in cashmere shawls, expensive furs and jewelry, along with a promisory note signed and sealed by the emir for the amount of the loan, with a space left blank for the name of the lender. Jirjis Mishāqa and his sons were not acquainted with the bankers of Damascus, but there was there a wealthy silk merchant from Dayr al-Qamar named Buṭrus al-Chāwīsh. They met with him and explained what was needed so that he might direct them to an appropriate banker. He said, "Bankers here do not make loans outside of Damascus, especially when the term is unknown. Nonetheless, I will look around for a loan today and will bring you an answer tomorrow."

The next morning Khawāja Buṭrus brought a respectable-looking man by the name of Muḥammad al-Jūkhī, followed by a black man carrying a heavy sack. We welcomed him, and as soon as he sat down he said, "Khawāja Buṭrus told me of the amount His Excellency the Emir needs. I have brought it in the sack the servant is carrying. Count it." We found that it was all in one denomination, quarter gold "chain" *funduqlī*s, which were rare. We would not have thought so many were in the possession of all the bankers in Damascus. He said, "I chose this denomination because His Excellency the Emir is in exile. All other gold denominations have to be weighed, since some are deficient, and therefore the quarter is the most convenient to spend, because it is small." After taking receipt of the money, Muḥammad al-Jūkhī's name was filled in on the promisory note sent by the emir and given to him. We told him of the collateral and asked him where he wanted it sent. He laughed and said, "His Excellency the Emir sent the promisory note and collateral, thinking that you might get the money from somebody who didn't know who the emir was. I, however, even if I have never met him in person, know of him from afar, and I would be grateful to you if you would introduce me. No matter how much His Excellency may need, I am resolved to give him everything I possess." Then he tore up the note and handed it back, refusing to accept the collateral.

Jirjis Mishāqa sent the money to the emir along with the torn note and reported everything that had happened, adding that the collateral was in his possession at [the emir's] disposal. An answer came, and enclosed was a letter for Muḥammad al-Jūkhī in which the emir expressed his gratitude for the favor he had done him, with no prior acquaintance between them. The hundred thousand piastres sent had arrived with the note he had torn up and returned to him, but [the emir] hoped he would receive the items that had been sent. If he would not accept them as collateral for the loan, would he at least accept them on deposit to be held in safety from harm during exile, for most of the shawls and furs were things that would be ruined by dust and moths. This letter [82] was sent by the emir a document to that effect. Muḥammad accepted and took the items for safekeeping. As soon as the emir returned to his estate, as will be told, he sent for him and installed him in the greatest honor in his palace for his service to his special servants, and paid him every attention. A few days later, as he was setting out for Damascus, [the emir] clothed him in a fur robe of honor and gave him one of his finest horses to ride. He also ordered that the [interest on] the loan be paid double and that he be escorted to Damascus by horsemen. They remained friends until he died.

THE GOVERNOR OF DAMASCUS DEMANDS A THOUSAND PURSES FROM EMIR BASHĪR, WHO REPORTS THIS TO ʻABDULLĀH PASHA.

It was not enough that the emir should be in straitened circumstances and have to borrow money to make ends meet, but the governor of Damascus, Darwīsh Pasha, demanded five thousand piastres to allow his horses to graze in Marj al-Rūm, even though the emir's cavalry had no protection in those lands. The men the emir had with him were sufficient to overwhelm the vizier and drive him from Damascus, but the emir was meticulously obedient to his overlords and responded by writing a letter of appeasement to 'Abdullāh Pasha and sending it by Ḥannā 'Azzām with a verbal message for the governor. Its contents in brief were as follows:

"The emir has been a loyal servant of your grandfather al-Jazzār, of your uncle Sulaymān Pasha and now of you. He has served loyally and faithfully. Recently, perceiving that you are displeased with him, he has removed himself from office and, lest his successor in ruling the mountain have occasion to attribute an ulterior motive to him, has exiled himself to the province of Damascus, content to dwell in the wastelands and borrow to live, awaiting the renewal of your favor to return and live under your grace and favor wherever you please. Having grown old in the service of the governors of Ṣaydā, he cannot take refuge with anyone else. Now the Governor of Damascus demands of him five thousand piastres to permit him to graze his animals in the plains of the Ḥawrān. Had he possessed such a sum, he would have presented it to his benefactor. Now he begs Your Excellency's mercy: write to the Governor of Damascus to lift this demand from him who is one of your servants, or command that the sum be paid from your treasury, for the emir asks favors of no one but his benefactor, or order him to come to you and do with him what you will. The emir has heard of the rebellion of the Greeks in the Morea and that their ships are crossing to the shore of our country and harming wayfarers, occasionally coming inland to harass or kill passers-by. There may be a need for the service of zealous men, and the emir presents himself for this purpose."

'Abdullāh Pasha's answer was: "Our son the emir's words are eligible. Indeed, he will not see from me other than what will gladden him. Let him come to Shifā 'Amr and let him inform me of his arrival. I will let him know what needs to be done." Immediately he ordered the reply written to the emir that he should not delay in coming to Shifā 'Amr and that he should inform him as soon as he arrived. Ḥannā 'Azzām took the reply and returned to the emir, reporting what had transpired with 'Abdullāh [83] Pasha. The emir decided to keep his men, and all the emirs and shaykhs who had accompanied him, in Jabal Ḥawrān and set out with no more than twenty horsemen for Shifā 'Amr.

*Shaykh Bashīr Jumblāṭ met with Emir Ḥaydar al-Aḥmad, who was older than Emir Bashīr and known for his piety, and said, "My lord, I want to say something to you I hope you will keep confidential and not spread abroad. The vizier's displeasure with the emir is due to religion, because when ['Abdullāh's] father 'Alī Pasha died and he was given the post of intendant in his place, the emir went down to Acre to offer condolences. Sulaymān Pasha ordered his intendant 'Abdullāh Pasha to go out a distance of two hours to meet the emir. This was on a Friday. Then the emir left Acre before the next Friday, and 'Abdullāh Pasha took offense. There was much gossip among them concerning the emir, that he was a Christian infidel who should not hold office; but the province was in the hand of Sulaymān Pasha, who loved the emir and gave it little thought, being originally a Georgian Christian. However, 'Abdullāh Pasha's father 'Alī Pasha was a Muslim Circassian and his mother was a *sharīfa* of the Muslims of Jabale. M'allim Ḥāyīm turned him over for his education to fanatical shaykhs, and not only has he turned out more fanatical than they, but he also rewarded M'allim Ḥāyīm for his blunder in obtaining the governorship for him. This mistake caused his death and has brought us to the state we are now in. We must guard against letting ourselves get into a worse predicament.

"It is well known how mercurial 'Abdullāh Pasha is. Just now the emir is heading for Shifā 'Amr, and 'Abdullāh Pasha may summon him to Acre. But this is no longer the time of Sulaymān Pasha, and an intelligent man conducts himself according to the time and place. If he is summoned to Acre, he will have to comply and go with them to the mosque and keep his faith concealed in his heart. Although I am a Druze, I have built a mosque with a minaret in my house, where I have the call to prayer done and pray behind the imam to placate the Muslims, while keeping my religion preserved in my heart where no one can take it away from me. I beg you to convince the emir to comply and not endanger himself. But make as if the words came from you, not from me."

Emir Ḥaydar, a very naive man, met with the emir and advised him as he had been coached by Shaykh Bashīr. When he was finished speaking, it was apparent by the look on the emir's face that he was angry. "Ḥaydar," he said, "until now I always believed you were a staunch Christian, but you make me doubt whether you know the duties of your religion. I recognize from the tenor of your words that they do not come from you, but from Shaykh Bashīr, for in his religious code they are allowed to dissimulate and, to protect themselves from danger, conform to whatever group they find themselves among. Christianity does not allow us to do that, even in mortal danger. If we are questioned about our faith, we are obliged to confess it boldly and unashamedly. What do you think 'Abdullāh Pasha will do to me if I confess to him that I am a Christian? Can he do more than kill me? What could better wash away my sins than to have my white hair spattered with my own blood? Did not Christ say, 'Whoever denies me before men, I also will deny before my Father who is in heaven,'[6] and 'Fear not them that kill the body'?*[7]

‘ABDULLĀH PASHA SUMMONS THE EMIR AND PERMITS HIM TO STAY IN JAZZĪN

Then, escorted by only twenty horsemen, the emir went to Shifā ‘Amr and, as ordered, sent a report of his arrival to the vizier. The reply came that he should select a campsite for himself and those accompanying him. He requested that it be in Jazzīn, which had been removed from the jurisdiction of the mountain. Permission was given and one of the vizier’s agents was ordered to go before him and arrange for the necessary supplies for his horses and followers. The emir wrote to his sons, to the emirs and to Shaykh Bashīr Jumblāṭ, who had remained behind in the Ḥawrān, to tell them what had happened and that they and their retinues should join him at Jazzīn by way of Rāshayyā, and they set out.

Jirjis Mishāqa also set forth, accompanied by two of his sons, Ibrāhīm and Andreos. This writer, his son Mikhāyīl, chose not to go with them but to wait for conditions on the mountain to settle down, for what was the use of his staying in a village outside his homeland where he had no work? Therefore he remained in Damascus studying al-Jamqīnī’s book on astronomy and learning some additional mathematics, geography and music with ‘Allāma Shaykh Muḥammad al-‘Aṭṭār, the famous teacher of traditional and rational sciences, until such time as conditions on the mountain should settle down and he could go up to his homeland.

THE NOTABLES OF THE SOUTH LEBANON COME TO THE EMIR; THE RULERSHIP OF ALL BUT JBAYL IS RESTORED TO HIM.

As soon as Emir Bashīr arrived in Jazzīn, all the notables of the mountain came to him and put themselves at his disposal, utterly disregarding the two emirs who had been put in office over them. This took place before the emir’s retinue came from the Ḥawrān. A few days after they arrived, ‘Abdullāh Pasha restored the rulership of the mountain to the emir, returning to him the regions he had taken from it, with the exception of Jbayl, which, being a seaport, he did not restore. The emir did not return to his house but remained a few days in Jazzīn to arrange his affairs.

THE NORTH LEBANESE AND THEIR PRIESTS REBEL AGAINST PAYING STATE TAXES; THE EMIR GOES TO CORRECT THEM AND IS MET WITH GUNFIRE; JBAYL IS RESTORED TO THE EMIR.

The Christians of Kisrwān and the surrounding regions had held a general assembly with their priests and decided to pay the state taxes only in one lump sum, as had been the ancient custom, and not in eight [separate] taxes, as was the current [arrangement]. The emir advised them that their demand was ill-advised because it was contrary to the assessment and arrangement of the Empire. In the past, when the assessment was made, it had been according to the value of the yield and the coinage; now it was according to the value of the yield and the coinage, and the eight taxes were actually less than the old lump sum. "Do not give the overlords a reason to be angry with you," [he said]. Nevertheless, they did not heed his advice, perhaps imagining it to be a ploy on the emir's part to protect himself from retaliation. The emir went to them himself, hoping to convince them, taking with him only his son Emir Khalīl, Shaykh Nāṣīf Abī-Nakad and his followers, and a few of the emir's followers, about three hundred in all.

When the emir camped outside the village of Liḥfid at the foot of a mountain there [84] that was difficult to scale, about thirteen thousand men gathered above and fired on them. His son and Shaykh Nāṣīf asked permission to go up to them, but he forbade them, saying, "You are too few, and the trail to where they are is not wide enough for two people to pass abreast. I have written to Shaykh Bashīr Jumblāṭ and Shaykh Ḥammūd Abī-Nakad to come to me with men. I have also asked the vizier to give me the city of Jbayl as a center of operations. I have written to the religious leaders to advise their congregations of the danger to themselves. We must be patient and see what happens, so wait here." The gathered multitudes, however, kept up their fire incessantly, and once when he was eating inside his tent, a bullet pierced it, mortally wounding the cupbearer who was standing behind the emir. Then Emir Khalīl and Shaykh Nāṣīf disregarded the emir's advice, saying, "We cannot let these dogs ravish us, who are the lion's people!" They cried out to their men to go up and attack the hordes. They climbed up and found among them priests encouraging them. A pitched battle between the two groups ensued, ending in the defeat of those many thousands. In this fray were lost twelve of Shaykh Nāṣīf's men. He and Emir Khalīl returned to the emir and reported having scattered the

Maronite priest.

multitudes after having killed two hundred of them. That evening an order arrived restoring the city of Jbayl, and the emir ordered a removal to there.

SHAYKH BASHĪR AND SHAYKH ḤAMMŪD NAKAD COME WITH THEIR MEN TO THE EMIR'S ASSISTANCE; AL-ZUQ IS BURNED AND THE PRIEST NAHRA IS KILLED.

Shaykh Bashīr and Shaykh Ḥammūd had gathered around two thousand of their men and set out to join the emir. When they arrived they found the Nahr al-Kalb gap blocked by men from Kisrwān, but they defeated them in a minor skirmish in which a few were killed and others were put to flight. At the order of the shaykhs the Zūq villages were plundered and burned. Along the way Shaykh Bashīr encountered the priest Nahra, who was one of the principal rebels in this insurrection, mounted and fully armed with a large *ṭābiyya*[8] on his head. When Shaykh Bashīr saw him, he said, "Glory be to God, father priest (as the Christians in that region say). How is the father doing? Believe me, I am glad of this chance meeting, but I don't think such a get-up is proper for you. Give your weapons to our followers, for priests should be armed with their book." When he had been disarmed, [Shaykh Bashīr] said, "It is not seemly for a priest to ride a horse. He should ride a mule or a donkey for the sake of humility. Take him down from his horse." Then he said, "I'm afraid you will tire of walking. It would have been better for you to stay at home." And he ordered that he be killed. [The priest] was screaming and pleading, but the shaykh said, "Father, you will forgive us, it would be better to sacrifice you for the sake of your congregation." So they slit his throat, burned him and left him in the open. They then joined the emir, who had chastized the rebels and collected the state imposts for that region.

'ABDULLĀH PASHA ASKS THE EMIR TO SEND HIM JAD'UN AL-BĀHUT AN AN ENVOY.

While the emir was in Jbayl, an order came from 'Abdullāh Pasha to send him Jad'ūn al-Bāḥūṭ, and no one else, [85] to discuss an urgent matter. This Jad'ūn was a prominent Maronite of the Beirut coast, honest in his conduct and trustworthy. The emir employed him as an envoy and sent him to deliberate with the vizier before he employed

Rāshayyā.

M'allim Buṭrus Karāma. He sent him, and he returned, saying, "The pasha informs you that the Jews have conspired with the Empire against him and had him deposed from his post at Ṣaydā, which has been annexed to Darwīsh Pasha, the governor of Damascus, but they have kept it secret until Darwīsh Pasha returns from the pilgrimage. Muṣṭafā Pasha, the governor of Aleppo, and Bahrām Pasha, the governor of Adana, have been assigned to help him. If you stand firm with ['Abdullāh Pasha], he will be able to withstand the forces that will be coming against him. He wishes to know your resolve. If you do not stand with him, he will surrender himself without resistance."

The emir sent [the envoy] back with this reply: "The emir considers himself a servant of no one but you. Do what you will and he will serve you in all you command him to do, even unto shedding his own blood. This is the utmost he is capable of." Then the emir returned to his house in Bteddīn, and the mountain was stabilized.

DARWĪSH PASHA GOES ON THE PILGRIMAGE; DAMASCUS IS GIVEN IN REGENCY TO FAYḌĪ PASHA; THE BIQĀ' IS PILLAGED FIRST BY DAMASCUS TROOPS AND THEN BY MEN FROM THE LEBANON.

Darwīsh Pasha had gone on the pilgrimage, leaving a *qāymaqām* in Damascus named Fayḍī Pasha and a *mutasallim* in the Biqā' named Ḥasan Āghā al-'Abd, who wrought much havoc on the areas belonging to the shaykhs and people of the Lebanon by pillaging their flocks and herds. This was most likely by plan of the *qāymaqām* Fayḍī Pasha, for when complaints were made to him of Ḥasan al-'Abd, neither did he order him to return to the owners what had been taken nor did he chastize him for the offense. Some men of the mountain went and attacked him, plundering the herds of the Biqā' in retaliation for what had been taken from them, and he fled to Damascus.

Then Fayḍī Pasha sent to the Biqā' a *mutasallim*, one of his own people named Amīn Bey. He took up residence in the village of Lālā in the East Biqā'. Shaykh Bashīr dispatched men to kidnap him and sent him to prison in Dayr al-Qamar, where he was left with nothing more to wear than a tunic. This writter saw him in this state. He was a beardless youth who appeared to be an aristocrat. I helped him as much as I could, although I never met him, and this was not wasted on him, for when he was released and went to Egypt and presented himself to the governor's intendant, he provided great aid to a man who told him that Mīkhāyīl Mishāqa was his maternal uncle.

'ALĪ 'IMĀD AND THE YAZBAKĪ SHAYKHS GO TO DAMASCUS; DAMASCENE TROOPS ARE TAKEN TO DRIVE EMIR EFENDĪ FROM RĀSHAYYĀ, AND EMIR MANṢŪR IS INSTALLED IN HIS PLACE.

The 'Imād shaykhs, along with some of their dependents, had taken refuge in Damascus, and through their instigation the rulership of the Rāshayyā region was given to Emir Manṣūr, who was a Yazbakī and and enemy of his cousin Emir Efendī, a Jumblāṭī, then ruler of Rāshayyā. A force was gathered to enable Emir Manṣūr to take the region from Emir Efendī by force. He came to Rāshayyā with his troops and the Yazbakī shaykhs, but Emir Efendī had already reported to Emir Bashīr what the government in Damascus had decided. At once the emir himself came down to Rāshayyā with Sahykh Bashīr Jumblāṭ and cavalry and infantry. When the Damascus troops arrived with Emir Manṣūr, they attacked Rāshayyā with guns, but the men of the Lebanon and Emir Efendī's men held them off. [86] After a few days of battle, the Damascene troops were defeated and fled before Emir Bashīr to Damascus.

In the meantime Darwīsh Pasha had returned from the pilgrimage and sent his insignia to all parts indicating that he was governor of Damascus and Ṣaydā, and he began to muster troops. 'Abdullāh Pasha also began to sign his correspondence as "Superintendent of the Pilgrimage al-Sayyid 'Abdullāh, Governor of Damascus, Ṣaydā and Tripoli, Regent of Gaza, Jaffa and Nabulus, and the Sanjāq of Holy Jerusalem."

THE EMIR IS SUMMONED TO ACRE.

Then the year 1237 of the Hegira began [A.D. 1821-22], and 'Abdullāh Pasha requested Emir Bashīr to come down to him. When he arrived, he did not meet him in his council, as was customary, but waited outside the private quarters and took him in. At once the vizier's mother appeared and greeted him respectfully. Then, putting her hand on the emir's belt, she said, "My son is your lord by virtue of his rank, but in view of age and your efforts on his behalf he is your son. He has acted rashly in the past with even you, not to mention others, and the result of his rash conduct is that his enemies have seized the opportunity to have him deposed by the Empire. We do not know what preparations have been made by his adversaries, the Jews. They may be plotting to have him executed in revenge for M'allim Ḥāyīm, in killing whom my son made an irreparable mistake. Now I ask you to fulfill your promise not to disappoint him."

The emir replied, "I have acknowledged, and continue to acknowledge, my sincere devotion to my benefactor, and I will shed my blood in his service. Let him command the service he wishes rendered that I may carry it out without delay."

'Abdullāh Pasha answered, saying, "I want to strike at Darwīsh Pasha and take Damascus from him before the governors of Aleppo and Adana arrive to reinforce him. When the Empire sees my might and realizes that even so I always render payment of its fiscal demands and carry out all its orders, it will disregard the instigation of the Jews and realize that there is no need to make war and waste money and men in fighting its trusty vizier just to satisfy a whim of the Jews. Moreover, I have friends in the Empire who will help me. Therefore, I need you to take your men to the Banāt Ya'qūb Bridge, and my troops will join [you] there. Together you will march on Damascus and deal a blow to Darwīsh Pasha. Try to capture him and send him to us."

TROOPS FROM ACRE AND THE LEBANON ARE SENT WITH THE EMIR TO ATTACK DARWĪSH PASHA AND TAKE CONTROL OF DAMASCUS.

The emir replied in compliance and issued his orders to the emirs and shaykhs of the Lebanon for all of them to join him with their men in all haste at the Banāt Ya'qūb Bridge. The vizier appointed Ibrāhīm Āghā al-Kurdī as commander. At the bridge about four thousand of his troops gathered, and from the mountain came around twelve thousand under the leadership of their emirs and shaykhs. Together they marched on Damascus. Darwīsh Pasha gathered his troops, along with all those he could muster from Damascus and environs; and to these were added the Yazbakī shaykhs who had fled from the Lebanon and Emir Manṣūr al-Shihābī, who had been driven [87] from Rāshayyā, and their men. He made camp about three miles outside of Damascus at a village called al-Mazze, before which is a broad plain. He stationed the cavalry and artillery outside the town and positioned the infantry behind the walls commanding the plain. As 'Abdullāh Pasha's troops approached al-Mazze, they were fired upon with cannon and guns. Because the road from Acre was too difficult to drag cannon across, ['Abdullāh Pasha's men] had no cannons to confront them with; nonetheless, the cavalry charged and a heated battle took place. Emir Bashīr let the cavalry troops charge and chose from among the infantry around a thousand fearless men and encouraged them on against the walls of the village, from which bullets were pouring down on him like rain. When his men reached the walls and scaled them, they torched the houses of the village in the midst of fighting. When the Damascus cavalry saw smoke rising from the village, the cavalry besetting them and many of their own men and horses killed by bullets from the infantry, they were as easily routed from inside the village as the cavalry had been and were pursued by the Acre troops to near Damascus, where many of them were drowned throwing themselves into the river to escape.

The emir, fearing pillage and plunder, did not allow the troops to enter Damascus but had them return and stay in al-Mazze. More than twelve hundred of the Damascene troops were killed, but only about forty of the Acre forces and the emir's men. One of those taken prisoner was Shaykh Ḥasan Talḥūq, who was pardoned by the emir and sent to the mountain to his father, who had not joined the Yazbakīs. The son was a hot-headed youth, and it was not by great intelligence that he got where he later got.

THE EMIR SENDS SHAYKH 'IZZ AL-DĪN AL-ḤALABĪ TO MEET WITH MUṢṬAFĀ PASHA.

When Darwīsh Pasha realized that his forces had been defeated, he feared for his life and took refuge by shutting himself up in the Damascus citadel, awaiting the arrival of help from the governors of Aleppo and Adana. Then Emir Bashīr sent Shaykh 'Izz al-Dīn al-Ḥalabī, one of the most important Druze elders of the Ḥawrān, to meet with Muṣṭafā Pasha, the governor of Aleppo who was coming to help Darwīsh Pasha, and say, "Darwīsh Pasha is besieged in the Damascus citadel, but the emir, fearing for [the safety of the city], has kept his troops from entering Damascus. If he were determined to enter it and seize Darwīsh Pasha, as 'Abdullāh Pasha has ordered, it would not be difficult for him to do, especially since Darwīsh Pasha treated the emir badly when he sought his protection in the Ḥawrān. Instead of granting him sanctuary and helping him, he demanded of the emir five thousand piastres to allow him to graze his horses in the open country of Jabal Ḥawrān, where the governor's troops have no authority over the bedouin rabble. Therefore the emir does not trust him and will continue his siege until you set foot in Damascus and he receives your order. Then he will remove his troops in respect of your might. This will carry some weight with the Empire and will diminish [88] Darwīsh Pasha's standing, and an order will be issued that he be removed from office and the post be assigned to you."

Shaykh 'Izz al-Dīn brought back a reply that Muṣṭafā Pasha was extremely pleased by the emir's proposal. When the pasha reached Damascus, he wrote to the emir that he was coming, according to imperial order, to assist Darwīsh Pasha and that he was obliged to obey. "You withdraw the troops accompanying you and lift the siege of Damascus," [he wrote]. Immediately the emir withdrew his troops, and every contingent returned to where it had come from. As soon as he arrived home, Emir Bashīr met with Shaykh Bashīr, and they agreed that the emir should go to Egypt and seek the protection of its famous governor, Muḥammad-'Alī Pasha, who could negotiate a pardon from the Empire for 'Abdullāh Pasha. The emir had previously informed Khawāja Ḥannā Baḥrī, a man of influence with [Muḥammad-'Alī Pasha], of what might happen with Darwīsh Pasha, that he might be forced to leave his land, and [inquired] whether he would be received by the pasha in Egypt. The answer came that "it is one of our efendi's special traits to help those who are in trouble and to relieve those who are in straitened circumstances. Come whenever you wish." The emir informed 'Abdullāh Pasha of what he had decided through his envoy Ḥannā 'Azzām. A reply of his approval came, along with a letter from him to Muḥammad-'Alī, craving his assistance with the Empire and exonerating himself with his fidelity in service, [saying] that [the Empire's] displeasure with him was not due to any shortcoming on his part, but rather to the slander of self-interested parties, and asking for [the Empire's] mercy through the good offices of [Muḥammad-'Alī].

EMIR 'ABBĀS IS MADE REGENT OF THE MOUNTAIN, AND EMIR MANṢŪR IS GIVEN THE RULE OF RĀSHAYYĀ.

The emir, fearing that the rulership of the mountain would be given to an emir who would not look after his interests, or who would not be among his partisans, agreed with Shaykh Bashīr that they should promote Emir 'Abbās (the son of Emir As'ad, son of Emir Yūnus, son of Emir Ḥaydar, the progenitor of the Shihābīs on the mountain). He had been raised by the emir, who considered him his eldest son, although he was actually the son of the emir's wife's sister.

The emir went down with his entourage to the village of M'allaqit al-Dāmūr, accompanied by about a thousand men, and got a ship from Beirut in which his sons and a hundred men set sail. Among them was M'allim Buṭrus Karāma and Aḥmad Āghā al-Yūsuf, a Damascene Kurd and dragoman who later advanced in the government until he became Aḥmad Pasha. His son Muḥammad Bey is now a member of the administrative board of the province, and he and his father were both upstanding men. The emir and those left with him arrived in Egypt and were received, but in deference to the Empire he was sent to live in

Upper Egypt in the village of Banī-Yūsuf until Muḥammad-ʻAlī could arrange to have a pardon for ʻAbdullāh Pasha sent from the capital.

As soon as the emir left, Darwīsh Pasha got his troops together and went down to the Biqāʻ valley. There he was joined by Emir ʻAbbās, to whom the rulership of the mountain was turned over. Shaykh Bashīr guaranteed the payment of taxes for him.

In the West Biqāʻ, at the foot of Mount Lebanon in the village of Qabb Ilyās were the ruins of an old fortress left by the Maʻn emirs. Darwīsh Pasha ordered some [89] of the remaining walls razed and posted an agent, a Muslim Aleppan of the ʻAraqtanjī family. To the Empire he reported not only that he had driven Emir Bashīr away and brought Mount Lebanon into submission but that he had also taken control of Qabb Ilyās Fortress, which had been a stronghold of rebellion, and had ordered it destroyed. Then he sent Emir Manṣūr as ruler of the Rāshayyā region, and Emir Efendī was forced to leave his homeland and go with his brother and his children to the Lebanon. The rulership of Marjaʻyūn was given to Shaykh ʻAlī ʻImād, whose chief clerk and administrative officer was Asʻad al-Shidyāq. His encounter with Lord Yūsuf Ḥbaysh, the patriarch of his own sect, the Maronites, and how [the patriarch] killed him, is well known.

Through the intervention of Emir Manṣūr, the rulership of Ḥāṣbayyā was given to the Shihābīs Emir Ḥasan and his brother Emir Ḥusayn Badīʻa. Neither the father nor the grandfather of these two had ruled a region, and consequently they had neither partisans among the shaykhs or inhabitants nor power of which anyone would be wary. The ruling emirs in Ḥāṣbayyā at that time were the three sons of three brothers who were ruling emirs, and they were Emir Sīd-Aḥmad son of Emir Qāsim, the eldest of the three; Emir Salīm son of Emir ʻUthmān, and Emir Saʻd al-Dīn son of Emir ʻAlī, the youngest of the three. Emir Saʻd al-Dīn was older than Emir Salīm, and Emir Sīd-Aḥmad was extremely naive and very religious. Therefore Emir Saʻd al-Dīn held the name and prestige, especially since he had four young brothers, the Emirs Bashīr, Muḥammad, Amīn and Khalīl, mention of whom will come in its proper place.

EMIR EFENDI AND THE ḤĀṢBAYYĀ EMIRS LEAVE RĀSHAYYĀ AND GO TO DAYR AL-QAMAR.

The aforementioned emirs, along with all the emirs of their family, who amounted to around thirty emirs, left Ḥāṣbayyā and went with their entourages to Emir ʻAbbās, because the ruler of the mountain was considered the head of the entire House of Shihāb, even if they were not of the same religion. [Emir 'Abbās] installed them in a palace in Dayr al-Qamar in A.H. 1237 [A.D. 1821-22], and thus they became known to this writer, who has remained friends with them and their children ever since.

DARWĪSH PASHA BESIEGES ACRE.

Then Darwīsh Pasha marched with his troops to Acre. 'Abdullāh Pasha locked the gates and fortified himself inside with his retinue, some soldiers and Arab and Turkish defenders he could trust, about two thousand men. Darwīsh Pasha stationed his troops outside at a distance of three miles in a place called Abā-'Utbe. With him was his administrator M'allim Salmūn Fārḥī, who was determined to have revenge on 'Abdullāh Pasha for their leader Ḥāyīm. Muṣṭafā Pasha, Governor of Aleppo, and Bahrām Pasha, Governor of Adana, also converged on Acre with their troops. It was the custom of the troops to fire three cannon shots after the evening prayer, and 'Abdullāh Pasha answered them from inside Acre with three theatrical rockets to ridicule their cannon shots. Of course, Ottoman viziers in those times did not have sufficient force to conquer a fortified citadel like the Acre Fort, so they talked instead of [waiting until] the supplies of the besieged ones ran out [90] and they were forced to surrender, or else until they were betrayed by some of their own. So they intensified the siege of Acre.

When this writer's uncle Khawāja Buṭrus 'Anḥūrī was obliged to return to Egypt on business, he entrusted to me some documents pertaining to loans to people in the Lebanon and left his son with his paternal aunt. Shaykh Bashīr Jumblāṭ had sold him his silk crop, about seven *qintār*s worth, on a promisory note that had not yet come to term. When he had to leave, the House of Mishāqa promised to pay the amount when it fell due if he had not yet returned. When Emir Bashīr decided to go to Egypt, Mikhāyīl told him he was desirous of going with his father in his service, but that there was a matter of guaranty they owed Shaykh Bashīr. "Take your uncle's documents and his son to the shaykh," he said, "and tell him what you want to do. Offer him the documents and the boy to keep as pledges. Let me know what answer he gives you." I did as the emir commanded, and Shaykh Bashīr said, "Did I ask your uncle for a pledge, or did I draw a document of surety against you all that you should now come to me with such talk? I know you. You stand as guarantee without my asking for a written pledge. Why do you want to go?"

"Out of fear of those who hate the emir, lest they plot some hostility toward us," I answered.

But he replied, "Even if His Excellency our efendi the emir is away from us in person, we are still subject to his command, and for anything to happen to you, it will have to get by me first. Take your cousin and your documents and rest assured in your house and business. We hope that the Creator will make our efendi the emir's way easy and return him to us as soon as possible."

I returned and told the emir what had happened. He said to me, "Stay with your brothers as the shaykh said. Your father will go with me." That very day the emir went to M'allaqit al-Dāmūr, but since he could take no more than a hundred of his retinue on the ship, he sent our father back with the others and gave him a letter for Shaykh Ḥammūd and Shaykh Nāṣīf Abī-Nakad in which he commended him especially and his other servants generally to their care.

I then made my living through the production of silk textiles, which were sent to Damascus, where they had a good market. At that time I wanted to learn about algebra, but I could not find more than a few quires of a text called *A Compendium on Arithmetic* by Bahā' al-'Āmilī,[9] at the end of which were a few terse words on the principles of algebra the author had compressed into about three pages in a most impenetrable style. In Dayr al-Qamar there was no one who knew the name of this science, much less anything about its principles. I devoted myself as far as I could to studying it and understanding what it meant, and the Creator facilitated the attainment of my goal.

During that period I was increasingly in favor with Shaykh Bashīr Jumblāṭ, his sons Shaykh Qāsim and Shaykh Salīm, and his nephews Shaykh 'Alī and Shaykh Qāsim—so much so that they did not let a month go by without inviting me to spend a few days with them at their seat. So also [91] Emir 'Abbās, who lived in Jirjis Bāz's palace at Dayr al-Qamar and with whom I spent every evening to keep him company, would send for me if, for some reason, I was unable to go to him.

One day a note arrived addressed to my father with Emir 'Abbās' seal, requesting the equivalent of 1,500 *'amūd* rials as a loan. I looked through our accounts for bills due us by those who were much richer than we were, but there was not a single bill for more than 150 rials, so I thought, "This loan cannot be met." I took the bill to Emir 'Abbās and asked him whether it was for him personally or for the government. He answered, "It is for the government. Myself, I don't need anything. If you need a loan of a bit of money, I'll give you what you need."

"If it is for the government," I said, "it will have to be distributed equally among the subjects, for nobody like us has more than a hundred rials. So-and-so, who is the richest merchant among us, could subscribe to 180 rials. Would Your Excellency agree to that?"

He laughed and said, "Haven't you realized yet that I am only a banquet-table emir? Everything is in Shaykh Bashīr's hands, for he pledged the taxes of the mountain to the vizier's treasury and then gave me this fellow, a compatriot of yours, of your rite too, as a deputy. He writes down what he knows to do, and I put my seal to what he has written. You know, when I was reading the bills before sealing them, I objected to this bill of yours and to the bill of that fellow you just mentioned, but he got angry and said, 'I know what needs to be done. In the house of Mishāqa there is a father with three sons: a sum like this should not be too much for four men who were so comfortable in the time of your brother-in-law, unlike so-and-so, who was never given rest from demands.' "

"What he says is incorrect," I said. "The emir never charges anyone more than the state tax on land. If he needs a loan, no one is ever compelled to pay. Actually my father used to raise money for loans from those who had ready cash until the silk crop came in, when they would be repaid in good currency at the beginning of the season. Most of the time they ask my father if the emir needs money. The registers of loans and their annual expirations are at home, but I think the name of this person who claims to have been unjustly treated in the emir's time is not among them. It is surprising how he knows of Jirjis Mishāqa's three sons but does not know of the four sons and two brothers of a man who is his own brother-in-law. Since the case depends upon Shaykh Bashīr, I will go myself to al-Mukhtāra and tell him the state of affairs."

I set out immediately, and as I was dismounting there was a servant waiting to say that the shaykh was expecting me. I went with him into the council chamber, where Shaykh Bashīr was with his sons Qāsim and Salīm. After I sat down and had coffee, he said, "We saw you through the spyglass coming in haste down the hill at Jdayde and thought it must be a matter of urgency. I hope everything is all right."

"I intended to go with the emir because I feared some hostility toward us," I said, "but Your Honor thought it better for me to stay at home, since nothing could happen to us without getting by [92] you. That which has come upon us now is from the hand of your appointee. I have come to ask if he is somebody who has gotten by you."

"What has happened to you?" he asked. I explained to him what had happened. His son Shaykh Salīm, who was quick-tempered, said to his father, "Your man has offended Mīkhāyīl? I will go this instant and slay him in his house!"

"This is a simple matter," he said. "Mīkhāyīl will stay with us, and we will all have a good time. We will refer the case to the emir, and it will be resolved satisfactorily." Then I left with his sons to go to their private quarters. We spent that evening with the shaykh, and I slept in his sons' rooms. The next morning I went with them to wish their father good morning. After coffee he gave me a letter from Emir 'Abbās, the contents of which were that he had withdrawn from me and my father half of the request. I asked the shaykh his opinion, and he said, "Everybody is attached to those who are dedicated to him. Your father has been my friend since before you were born, and you have taken after him. I am bound by conscience to protect your interests. As for your brother Ibrāhīm and his partner, your brother Andreos, I do not see them here, nor did I when I was in Dayr al-Qamar. They are in league with our Nakad brothers, Shaykh Ḥammūd and Shaykh Nāṣīf, and I am not obliged to look after the interests of those who are dedicated to others." The reason he spoke thus was that, because of a disagreement between them, Shaykh Nāṣīf had forbidden him to come to Dayr al-Qamar.

I asked his permission to leave, but he would not allow me to go for three days and ordered me to send the emir's bill to my father, now that the demand had been withdrawn. I sent it and acquainted him with what had transpired. My brother Ibrāhīm immediately informed the Nakad shaykhs of my letter and the emir's impost. They seethed with anger and sent an envoy to Emir 'Abbās to withdraw the demand from Ibrāhīm and Andreos Mishāqa. "As for this so-and-so," [they said,] "we will murder him in his bed for trying to sow iniquity and discord among the shaykhs of the country." The demand was withdrawn, but that fellow slept at the palace for a few nights in fear until an abatement of the shaykhs' anger toward him was negotiated.

THE PROVINCE OF ṢAYDĀ IS GIVEN TO MUṢṬAFĀ PASHA, THE GOVERNOR OF ALEPPO, ALONG WITH COMMAND OF THE ARMY AND THE SIEGE OF ACRE; EMIR 'ABBĀS GOES TO CONGRATULATE THE PASHA AND MAKES PEACE BETWEEN THE EMIRS OF ḤĀṢBAYYĀ AND RĀSHAYYĀ.

When five months had passed and Darwīsh Pasha had not succeeded in his siege of Acre, the Empire removed him from office and appointed to the governorship of Ṣaydā Muṣṭafā Pasha, the governor of Aleppo, who was inclined toward Emir Bashīr. He sent a letter to the emir in Egypt requesting his presence. When the order for the removal of Darwīsh Pasha arrived, M'allim Salmūn Fārḥī was so disappointed that he came down with a high fever and died. When Emir 'Abbās went down to the camp in the fields of Acre to congratulate Muṣṭafā Pasha on the post, he asked him if he could make peace between the emirs of Ḥāṣbayyā and Rāshayyā and divide the rule of the region between those who had been appointed and those who had been driven away, in order to put an end to the chaos in that area. He was given permission.

Then the pasha, knowing that Emir ʻAbbās had been promoted to the rulership of the mountain by Emir Bashīr's strategy, to whom he was like a son, said, "I have requested the presence of your father from Egypt, and he will soon be here." He said this, thinking that Emir ʻAbbās would be glad, but inwardly he was disappointed because he hoped [93] that he would continue to rule the Lebanon, for Acre must certainly be taken by siege when supplies were needed and ʻAbdullāh Pasha no longer had enough money to pay his soldiers. When this happened, Emir Bashīr's and his sons' hopes of return would be dashed, and then Shaykh Bashīr Jumblāṭ would necessarily have to support him, since the family of Emir Bashīr would not be able to return. Later I tried to get these thoughts out of his mind when it was apparent to me what he was thinking. I would say to him, "An intelligent man should not let thoughts of what is possible take the place of reality, for impediments may always occur. Idle thoughts may be just as wrong as right. An intelligent person must be wary more of their being wrong than of hoping they are right if he is to protect himself from the evil consequences of mistake." He trusted me enough to listen to me, but he was very indecisive and could never make up his mind.

After returning from Acre, he made peace between the emirs of Wādī al-Taym and divided the Rāshayyā region between Emir Efendī and Emir Manṣūr, each to have specified villages. Each of them got half of Rāshayyā itself, but neither could reside there. Emir Efendī took up residence in the village of ʻAyn ʻAṭā and then moved to Bakkīfā; Emir Manṣūr dwelt in the village of al-Ḍahr al-Aḥmar. Emir Efendī's brother, Emir Jahjāh, and their sons were assigned stipends that were paid half by Emir Efendī and half by Emir Manṣūr, who had no sons or brothers. Ḥāṣbayyā, with its dependencies, the Ḥūle region and its environs, was divided among Emir Ḥasan Badīʻa, Emir Saʻd al-Dīn and Emir Salīm, each getting a third. Emir Ḥusayn[10] Badīʻa and Emir Sīd-Aḥmad ceded their right to rule and were content to take stipends sufficient for their needs, and stipends were arranged for the other emirs, as usual.

Shaykh ʻAlī ʻImād, who had been given the rule of the Marjaʻyūn region, did not conduct himself well either with the inhabitants or with his overlords. Perhaps it was because he was not wealthy, but at any rate his misconduct laid the foundation for a deep-seeded hatred in Muṣṭafā Pasha's heart, and the pasha began to lay in wait for him to fall into his hands, which later did happen and he was killed, as will be narrated in the proper place.

EMIR BASHĪR COMES FROM EGYPT; THE SIEGE IS LIFTED FROM ACRE; SHAYKH BASHĪR JUMBLĀṬ IS FINED.

After Acre had been besieged for nine months, Emir Bashīr returned from Egypt accompanied by Sulaymān Efendī, the *silaḥdār* of the governor of Egypt, bearing an imperial decree pardoning 'Abdullāh Pasha, confirming him as governor of Ṣayda and containing an order for Muṣṭafā Pasha to lift the siege of Acre and return to Aleppo. As ['Abdullāh Pasha] did not have enough cash in his treasury to pay what he owed the soldiers, he informed the emir, who sent him what he needed from the Acre treasury. Then, on the last Friday of Lent [the siege] was lifted. No sooner was it ended than 'Abdullāh Pasha vented his displeasure on all those who had helped Darwīsh Pasha, and none more so than Shaykh Bashīr Jumblāṭ.

The imperial treasury had assessed ['Abdullāh Pasha] for 25,000 purses in the currency [94] of the time (which would be equivalent now to about half a million liras), to cover the expenses of [imperial] soldiers during the siege of Acre. He had spent everything he had during the siege, and the Empire had taken from him the province of Tripoli and the *liwā'* of Gaza and Jaffa, promising to return them when he finished paying what was demanded. He then distributed the Empire's demand over the province and said to the emir, "The mountain is part of what is left to me of the province and has to pay a fifth of the demand. *If it is possible to get it all from the 'Yazīdī'[11] Bashīr Jumblāṭ, that would be best."

"A third should be enough for him," said [the emir]. "The subjects and myself will bear the rest." The emir asked Shaykh Bashīr for 1500 purses. (The currency of the imperial treasury was the *'amūd* rial, the value of which was six and a quarter piastres.) He began by sending it to my father. The emir came up to collect the taxes, and as often as a large amount was gathered he sent it to the treasury in Acre with this writer. Every time I took a payment, I found the vizier himself waiting for me with the bursar in the treasury, for the pasha's horsemen would precede me and bring news of my coming. He would ask me, "Have you brought the Yazīdī's money separate, as I told you?" I would answer yes. Then he would say to the bursar Shaykh 'Abbās, "As soon as the number of the purse Mīkhāyīl is talking about is recorded, write on it 'to be kept.' Seal it and send it to my private quarters." He would do as he was ordered. Once Shaykh 'Abbās asked him what his purpose was in doing that. "It's for my personal expenditures," he said, "since it is money from a Yazīdī. The rest is contaminated with *dhimmī* money taken from them illegally. It is not permitted for us to take it."

"If they conduct themselves according to the stipulations of the *dhimma*," [Shaykh 'Abbās] said, "then it is correct." He pointed to me and said, "Doesn't Mīkhāyīl here abide by the provisions of the *dhimma* in his dress and arms?" I was afraid of the import of his words, for the pasha was very fanatical about his religion, but he burst out laughing and said, "Don't try to make yourself into one of the ulema, for I know how ignorant your are. You have a big beard but a little brain. I'll show you your ignorance with one question: is it legally permitted for us to compel a *dhimmī* to pay anything more than the poll-tax? How then can we force on him things he does not have to do? In our fight with Darwīsh Pasha didn't many thousands of them defend us for free and shed their blood in our service? So also during the tenure of our late uncle did many thousands of them serve us in resisting the Wahhābī and getting rid of the Kurd Yūsuf Pasha. Many of their men perished with no profit accruing to them from us, whereas no Muslim would serve us without personal gain, first among them you, learned master who claims to know so much. Do you want us to deal with them on a contractual basis? They would profit, and the loss would be ours. Tell me, do they wear white and arm themselves to please me or to spite me? If they do this and we keep silent, then we are equal. But if we forbid them and they refuse to obey, then we would have to treat them as we do the rabble in the streets. You ought to know what you are talking about before you speak."

When I heard the vizier's words, my concern left me and I felt sorry that the old man had been humiliated. I spoke very harshly of the vizier's mean words after he had gone, but [Shaykh 'Abbās] apologized for him, saying that he had not meant anything bad. Thereafter he became one of my special friends, and I profited through him to the tune of about two thousand rials.*[12]

Anyway, Shaykh Bashīr paid what was demanded of him but then, expecting the peace to be broken, decamped to Rāshayyā, seeking asylum with the governor of Damascus, who wrote concerning him to 'Abdullāh Pasha, who wrote to Emir Bashīr on his behalf. He was given assurances that it was safe for him to return to his home, and he came back accompanied by an envoy from the governor of Damascus, 'Abdullāh Efendī Muhrdār, an intelligent person who was quite adroit in the arts and literature. When the shaykh appeared for an interview with the emir, he did not come with ten or twenty men as usual, but with about a thousand men in arms. His intention may have been to make a show of the power of the shaykhs of the Lebanon and their allegiance to their emir for the benefit of the governor's envoy, however the emir took this act to indicate that Shaykh Bashīr mistrusted the amnesty given him and feared treachery. Such thoughts, resulting from the way the interview was conducted, stirred up the emir's wrath and made him certain that the shaykh would never return to his old loyalty to him. Moreover, the religious leaders of both sides introduced doubts into their minds that estranged each from the other.

Experience has shown that any temporal affair religious leaders meddle in will inevitably turn out badly. It is incorrect to say that these leaders have evil intentions or motives. Far from it! But we can only compare them to a jeweler who does not know how to make charcoal and, if he tries, will botch the job. If I want to resole my shoes, I do not need to consult a watchmaker but have to rely on the advice of a cobbler, who knows more about it than a watchmaker. So also, if an affair is a spiritual one, I rely on the advice of the clergy; but if it is physical, I rely on the advice of those who treat the body. If you probe the causes for chaos in all countries of the world, seldom will you find a cause other than the meddling of religious leaders in temporal affairs. An intelligent person must stop his ears and not listen to what they say about worldly affairs, just as he must not listen to what worldly people have to say about spiritual affairs. This, I think, will not be contradicted by anyone except those who are too blind to see.

SHAYKH BASHĪR GOES TO THE ḤAWRĀN.

After a while the emir demanded from Shaykh Bashīr a thousand purses over and above what he had already paid. He paid some of it and sent his emissary, the Catholic from Dayr al-Qamar who has been mentioned before [Yūsuf al-'Akkāwī], [95] to mollify the emir into letting him pay the rest little by little. His motive for this was to give himself some time, and that very night he went to the Ḥawrān with his men. The news did not reach the emir until the next morning, when Shaykh Bashīr and his men had already reached safety in the province of Damascus. [The emissary] was greatly afraid that the emir would think he had come to deceive him, knowing beforehand what Shaykh Bashīr had decided to do. However, the emir did not blame the servant for conducting himself according to his master's wishes and assured him that he was safe and could stay in his house.

Then various complaints started pouring in, for it is usual for suits to begin when someone has fallen from high position. Ibrāhīm Mishāqa, who was an expert in legal affairs, was sent to defend these cases, which he did; and in the end no charges were made. Some time later influence began to be used with the emir to get [Ibrāhīm Mishāqa] employed as clerk of correspondence. He even sought to collect on past favors by endeavoring to get the emir to discharge Abū-Ibrāhīm[13] from his post so that he could take his place; this he did by writing false accusations the emir was pleased not to believe. However, Ibrāhīm's father persisted in pleading with [the emir] to have an examination made in the presence of the slanderer in order either to prove the charge or to exonerate him publicly. After repeated pleading, the emir allowed it, and when the accounts and books were audited by the slanderer himself, it turned out that there was a surplus due Ibrāhīm's father in the amount of three thousand piastres, the value of the rial being seven piastres. The books were sealed by the examiners and the slanderer and presented to the emir, who summoned Ibrāhīm's father and said, "The result of this investigation you requested is that you have gained three thousand piastres."

"My lord," he said, "there is no surplus here. The three thousand you have set down for me in the ledger of stipends I left in the treasury for when I need it. My request for an examination was to prove my innocence to the slanderer and to those who listened to him, not to prove it to Your Excellency, for you well know the loyalty of all your servants. Now that I have been exonerated publicly, I beg you to let me stay at home and pray for Your Excellency for the rest of my life. Thank God I have five sons who have been raised in your establishment, and each of them is able to take care of the expenses of our family. If you approve, command my post to be given to this man who is fighting to get it. He has done other things against me, aside from this, as M'allim Ghanṭūs 'Āzar and others know, which I could not begin to describe. Thank God he has not succeeded in any of them."

"When you are too old to work," replied the emir, "one of your sons will have your post. But you are not feeble yet, so go back to work." He bent over to kiss the emir's hand and withdraw, but the emir told him to sit down. He summoned the slanderer and asked him, "This examination ledger, is it in your hand? Is this your signature and your seal?" He said yes. "How much did we get by this audit, counting what Abū-Ibrāhīm is paid from our treasury for his sons to invest?"

"Nothing," he said. "He gets the surplus."

"This is what comes of his listening to your slander of him," the emir said. "Although he knew that I [96] would accept no slander of him, he was not content but that an investigation be made by you in order to show his innocence to those before whom you have dragged his name through the mud. Moreover, your dishonesty is now apparent to all. Know you that my servants are not brought up to act as you have. Watch out for my stick for such a thing lest you get from me something you won't like. Now, write with your own pen a receipt from me to Abū-Ibrāhīm for 12,000 piastres and give it to him with your own hand as a sign of his loyalty and your disgrace." He wrote it in execution of the emir's command, and the two of them withdrew, one happy and the other humiliated.

JONAS KING COMES FROM AMERICA; AS'AD AL-SHIDYĀQ IS ATTACHED TO HIM.

At that time an American named Jonas King came to Dayr al-Qamar bearing a letter of introduction to a merchant named Yūsuf al-Dūmānī, whose house was opposite the Mishāqa house and one of whose sons had married one of the Mishāqa girls. He received [the American] in his house, and we were much thrown together because of the proximity of our houses. He spoke Arabic well, but everybody was distressed by him, for, although he was handsome and youthful, they believed he was English and therefore had no religion. They had been inculcated by their priests to believe this, and many of them would remonstrate with him and say, "Why is it that you English have no religion?"

"That is a mistake," he would say. "We are Christians." They were still not convinced, but he treated everybody with all kindness nonetheless. We spent most evenings with him. My family felt very sorry for him because he was not Catholic and was going to Hell, and I used to laugh inwardly at both groups. I admired this man's good qualities, but I used to wonder how he could have a good mind and yet believe religious fables any sound intellect would reject.

He used to travel to various places and then return to Dayr al-Qamar. Once he asked us to find him someone to teach him Syriac. Now we knew of the sons of Yūsuf al-Shidyāq on the Beirut coast, who copied books for us for a fee. Their handwriting was beautiful and they had been educated at the Maronite school, which taught Syriac and Arabic. We brought him young As'ad, son of Yūsuf al-Shidyāq, and arranged a monthly stipend. He taught him Syriac in a short period of time and returned to his home grateful for what Mr. Jonas King had done for him, for he began to write for him in Arabic what he needed.

*Later [As'ad] became absorbed in the study of scripture, which led him to reject Roman excesses. That was what caused Lord Yūsuf Ḥbaysh, the patriarch of his sect, to imprison him for a long time and treat him with all cruelty, cutting off his livelihood and having him starved and beaten. That was in accordance with the Roman doctrine [that says] "we must annihilate heretics, and the ends justify the means." No matter whether such conduct is permitted or rejected by the Christian religion, both men are now dead and will stand for judgment before the Ultimate Judge.

IT COMES TO LIGHT THAT THE MONKS OF DAYR AL-MUKHALLIŞ HAVE EMBEZZLED SOME OF THE PROPERTY OF THE HOUSE OF MISHĀQA.

After Jirjis Mishāqa returned from exile with Emir Bashīr in Jabal Ḥawrān, he received a letter from Father Buṭrus Kaḥīl, the abbot of Dayr al-Mukhalliṣ, informing him that "the Nakad shaykhs are claiming the right to the al-Wardiyye plantation your late father donated to the monks. We are ignorant of what they hope to gain, and beg you to inform us how we should act with them."

He replied, "All our family papers were lost when Salīm Pasha's troops entered Şūr by force and ransacked the place. Therefore we do not know how to answer you. Send us the document you have from our father that we may know what reply to make." He was sent a bag full of papers marked "Documents pertaining to the House of Mishāqa." He opened it and found therein a number of documents, some from Ibrāhīm Mishāqa and others from his father Jirjis Mishāqa. He also found a wrapper marked "Wardiyye documents," which contained not only a deed from Ibrāhīm Mishāqa endowing the plantation to the Monastery of the Savior but also documents pertaining to the purchase of the plantation from its original owners. One of the documents was signed and sealed by Shaykh Kulayb Abī-Nakad and registered at the court in Şaydā. Then he found a deed from the Şaydā court pertaining to the joint ownership of much property, houses and orchards in Şaydā, with equal shares belonging to Ibrāhīm Mishāqa and the monks. It was authenticated by the signatures and seals of the abbot of the monastery and its four managers. Then he found a ledger in the hand of the general director at that time, Father Mīkhāyīl 'Arrāj, containing entries of the income of this partnership and deductions made by the monastery against Ibrāhīm Mishāqa for masses and such things. The account went until the year of Ibrāhīm's death. Jirjis knew nothing about this, and the monks had not informed him of it when he was in dire straits and had gone to them hoping to find something of his father's being held by them.

He replied to the abbot and sent him the papers pertaining to the Wardiyye plantation, along with an inquiry about the partnership in real estate. The abbot answered, "My son, there is no longer any partnership. It is over. That is why you see the monastery's seals torn from the deed." This was not correct, however, for the seals were intact and the income ledger was there.

When this answer arrived, Lord Theodosius Ḥabīb, the Metropolitan of Acre, happened to be at the Mishāqa house. He looked over [the letter] and said, "He cannot possibly deny the claim. I know it well from the time I was a deacon in the service of the abbot Father 'Arrāj. Your family has many things deposited with the monks, but I do not know the details." Then he was shown the ledger of the partnership. "This is none other than Father 'Arrāj's handwriting," he said.

Then Jirjis Mishāqa gave his son Ibrāhīm a copy of the deed to find where it was registered in the Ṣaydā court, to make the necessary investigations and then demand of the abbot what the law required. He set out for the Ṣaydā court, where he found the registration of the deed. Then he located four of the properties of the partnership in the hands of persons other than the monks. When he requested the documents of ownership, he found two of them in the name of the monks and Ibrāhīm Mishāqa and two of them in the name of the monks only, the latter dated after Ibrāhīm's death. He copied down these documents word for word and went to the abbot, whom he informed of all he had learned, and from whom he demanded restitution, but the abbot answered, "This is a claim that goes back to before my days. Neither have I ever heard of it nor do I want you to prosecute claims against the monks, whose greatest patrons were your ancestors."

Ibrāhīm returned and told his father what had happened. The monks sent Father Euthymius Mishāqa to his brother to stop him from proceeding with this case, and thus by dint of sheer nerve his legal rights were embezzled.

Thank God I managed to slip through the cracks of this madness by staying out of it. I only mention it as a warning to those of my family and their descendants who are still embroiled in it.*[14]

EMIR 'ABBĀS SENDS THE WRITER AS AN EMISSARY TO EMIR BASHĪR TO RESOLVE THE MISUNDERSTANDING BETWEEN THEM.

Feeling himself declining in Emir Bashīr's favor, Emir 'Abbās began to fear for his life. He summoned me for an interview in the village of Majdal M'ūsh, told me of the decline in favor he had perceived and asked me to mediate between them, since his servants had no standing with the emir. Aside from me, he did not trust anyone else of the emir's entourage to act honestly on his behalf. I accepted the charge and went back and forth repeatedly between them. Emir Bashīr complained of instances that indicated that Emir 'Abbās was in collusion with Shaykh Bashīr Jumblāṭ, who was out of favor. Although he considered him like a son, his alliance with the enemy was taken as a grave sin. [97] Emir 'Abbās denied the charge and said, "I don't like the emir to treat me like a disobedient child," and then he gave evidence countering the emir's charge.

My mind was so overwhelmed trying to fathom the true state of affairs that I confessed to the emir, "Your servant is expert in knowing how to derive numerical and quantitative unknowns, but my mind is not capable of finding a way to derive the unknown of this political affair."

He laughed at what I said and replied, "The reason for your inability to solve it is your lack of experience in politics. I will teach you how to discover this unknown. The Christians say of one who has renounced his faith that he must purchase it back from where he sold it. Emir 'Abbās sold my favor for that of Shaykh Bashīr Jumblāṭ, who has recently come to the B'albak region to stir up sedition on the mountain. If [Emir 'Abbās] is still as fond of me as he claims, let him go deal him a blow."

"Does he have enough men to fight Shaykh Bashīr's multitude?" I asked.

"I will provide more than enough men," said the emir, "but he must lead them. Ask him to do it, and let me know what answer he makes." I then went to Emir 'Abbās, happy that I had put an end to the altercation so easily, and reported to him the purport of the emir's words.

"If I do that," he said, "I would be like someone who became a Muslim after the noon prayer and died before the evening prayer: he would be an apostate from his own religion, but Islam would not recognize him as a Muslim."

"I beg you to listen to what I have to say," I said. "If you approve, accept it; if not, reject it. I don't think my affection for Shaykh Bashīr is any less than your own, beause he merits love by his good actions. I always pray for the Creator to end the ill feeling between him and His Excellency the Emir, who is our benefactor. We cannot forget our indebtedness to him, and we crave well-being always for his family, all of whom are under his protection, he being the eldest and highest in station and rank. We have seen all too clearly how foolish it is to join those who oppose him, whether of his family or otherwise, just as we have seen how rewarding it is to conduct oneself in a manner pleasing to him. The analogy you were pleased to make is applicable to the reverse of the present situation, for the hypothetical man in it leaves a religion he knows for one he does not and thereby fails to get what he wants. More applicable to this situation, begging your pardon, would be the prodigal son mentioned in the Gospel, who returns to his father's embrace and is accepted with gladness and rejoicing. Thank God there has been no sin like those of the prodigal son, and we hope our father [the emir] will receive us even better than [that son's] father did him.

"I wonder what it profits Shaykh Bashīr for you to be under a cloud with the Emir. If you were in his favor as you used to be, it would be more in the interests of Shaykh Bashīr, for you could curry favor with the emir on his behalf. He has never been inimical before. Indeed the shaykh has to his credit many, many services. Can one doubt that there is room for hope in the emir's wrath after his services to 'Abdullāh Pasha and his efforts to lift the siege and gain the sultan's favor for him? [98] After the way the emir relied on Muḥammad-'Alī, the Governor of Egypt, was there any question of his assistance, even if it was against 'Abdullāh Pasha's will? My advice is that you go now yourself to the emir and go to see your aunt or his sons as usual and confront the emir with the words, 'Your son is here and has nothing more to say than "Do with him as you will.'" If you so please, I will go with you. You won't be disappointed."

I stayed with him for two days, exhausting myself trying to bring him around to my way of thinking, but he would not bend. Therefore I returned to the emir and told him that Emir 'Abbās was sorry he could not undertake this service, but it was beneath his dignity to go himself to fight a [mere] shaykh. The emir grabbed me by the ear and said, "Now you'll see with your own eyes how to derive political unknowns. Remember it! If Emir 'Abbās summons you, tell him you are sorry but I have forbidden you to go." Then the emir sent men to deal a blow to Shaykh Bashīr, who did not confront them and withdrew instead to the 'Akkār region.

THE EMPIRE SEEKS MUṢṬAFĀ ĀGHĀ BARBAR'S HEAD, AND HE SEEKS ASYLUM WITH THE EMIR.

In the meantime an imperial decree went forth for the head of Muṣṭafā Āghā Barbar. He came to the Lebanon seeking asylum with the emir, who received him with all honor and appointed a residence for him and his people in the village of Shwayfāt until he could obtain a pardon for him through the offices of the governor of Egypt, and thus a friendship sprang up between them, after they had been enemies.

INSURRECTION AGAINST THE EMIR BEGINS IN THE SOUTH LEBANON FROM 'IMĀD AND JUMBLĀṬ.

Then the Christian year 1825[15] began, corresponding to 1240 of the Hegira. In the month of February the news came to Emir Bashīr that Emir Salmān and his brother Emir Fāris, Emir 'Abbās and his brother Emir Ḥasan, Shaykh 'Alī 'Imād and his cousins, and Shaykh 'Alī Jumblāṭ and his brother Shaykh Qāsim (the sons of Shaykh Ḥasan, brother of Shaykh Bashīr) had assembled with their men at al-Mukhtāra,

Shaykh Bashīr's seat, where they numbered about twelve thousand men, mounted and on foot, awaiting the arrival of Shaykh Bashīr from the 'Akkār region to attack Emir Bashīr. They had also forbidden [the emir's] servants who were from their region to go to him, so that day the servants did not come to the emir's palace as usual. There were usually more than fifteen hundred of his followers around him, but that day there were no more than one hundred forty-three persons, among whom were Shaykh Ḥusayn Shiblī Ḥamādī and his relatives and the employees from Dayr al-Qamar and environs. The rest were cooks, bakers and grooms.

The emir made a report of the situation to 'Abdullāh Pasha, who issued orders abroad to muster soldiers and assemble at the al-Awwalī bridge and await the emir's orders. Later he went down himself and pitched his tent at the bridge. The emir also reported the situation to the governor of Egypt through his son Emir Amīn, who had set out for there with a gift of magnificent horses for Muḥammad-'Alī Pasha's stables. When he received the report, he ordered the preparation [99] of a sufficiently large force to be at Emir Amīn's disposal to go to the Lebanon. He also wrote a notice to those who were not in obedience to the emir, threatening them and warning them of the consequences of opposition.

Shaykh Bashīr was in no haste to return from 'Akkār, fearing instability on the part of Shaykh 'Alī 'Imād, who might bring him to the brink of warfare with the emir and then back out. Therefore he bided his time until after the outbreak of hostilities.

This gave the emir a chance to make his own plans. On the one hand he sent messages with wise elders not to provoke bloodshed and destruction of the country, that he would get them everything possible to make them happy. On the other hand he tried to win to his faction every possible person of importance in the country. The first thing he did was to win over Shaykh Ḥammūd and Shaykh Nāṣīf Abī-Nakad. They were near him and controlled the men of Dayr al-Qamar and the Manāṣif and Shaḥḥār regions, the best men of the mountain, who naturally were inclined to the emir and many of whom were in his service. Through them he won over the shaykhs of the Upper Gharb, the House of Talḥūq of the Yazbakī faction. They came to Bteddīn with their men. Of the Yazbakīs there came also with his men Shaykh Shiblī 'Abdul-Malik, who had already declared himself with the emir. Then Muṣṭafā Āghā Barbar came with forty of his cavalrymen. From B'aqlīn came all the allies of the House of Ḥamādī, both Christian and Druze. Then Shaykh Nāṣīf Abī-Nakad came with his band to the emir, and his cousin Shaykh Ḥammūd remained at Dayr al-Qamar.

Eight days later the shaykhs, emirs and their men at al-Mukhtāra had formed a huge multitude, so they moved to the village of al-Samqāniyye, about one mile away from the emir's seat. The emir sent wise elders to them to make peace, but they remained determined. The next morning, when the emir learned that they had begun to move to al-Samqāniyye, he sent Emir Bashīr al-Qāsim to bring the troops stationed at the al-Awwalī bridge. Shaykh Nāṣīf also wrote to his cousin to send him only five hundred footsoldiers from Dayr al-Qamar and to leave the rest there as a precaution against treachery from the men of the Lower Gharb, especially from Lady Habbūs Arslān, the grandmother of Emir Muṣṭafā, the present *qāymaqām* of the Shūf, because they were Jumblāṭīs.

THE EMIR IS ATTACKED, AND THREE BATTLES ARE FOUGHT.

The morning of the next day guns were being moved in the direction of al-Samqāniyye against the guards stationed on the road by the emir. Emir Khalīl rode out to them accompanied by some of the emir's cavalry. He put up a brave fight, but they were too many and drove him so far back that their bullets almost reached the emir's palace. Then he issued an order to Shaykh Nāṣīf to come with his men to his aid, and he rode forth with his followers and the men of Dayr al-Qamar. When he arrived, a pitched battle broke out between the two sides until the men of al-Samqāniyye were driven back and took cover behind the fortified walls of an elders' retreathouse far from the village. The men fired from behind the walls, and the cavalry fought in the open. In the heat of the battle, [100] Emir Bashīr al-Qāsim arrived back from the al-Awwalī bridge accompanied by sixty-five Hawwārī cavalrymen and thirty Albanian footsoldiers. They fought hard, and Shaykh 'Alī 'Imād received a bullet wound in the arm. The battle ended with victory for the emir's party and few killed on either side. The emir's adversaries returned to al-Mukhtāra and evacuated al-Samqāniyye. That day the rain poured down on the combattants.

The next day, because of this victory for the emir's party, many of the Jumblāṭ and 'Imād men abandoned their shaykhs and came to the emir to beg his pardon, which they received. After this battle Shaykh Bashīr Jumblāṭ came from 'Akkār to the masses assembled at his house. This gave the emir a few days' respite to gather men, a task made easier by the victory of his party at the Battle of al-Samqāniyye and the wounding of Shaykh 'Alī 'Imād, whose party were more than ten thousand strong, while the emir's men who fought them were less than a thousand.

Many of the men of the Shūf and the 'Arqūb came to the emir, as did Emir Qāyidbayh (who later became *qāymaqām* of the Christians), accompanied by two thousand men on foot from the Matn. Emir Muḥammad al-Shihābī brought his followers on behalf of his brother Emir Sa'd al-Dīn at Ḥāṣbayyā. Of the vizier's troops came about three thousand cavalrymen and infantry, Kurds, Turks, Albanians, North Africans, Hawwārīs and artillerymen with cannons.

When a few days had passed without fighting, one night the Jumblāṭīs sent a band in secret to the village of B'aqlīn to murder the House of Ḥamāda and their partisans, who were about fifteen hundred men, both horsemen and footsoldiers.[16] They took them by surprise around midnight. Hearing the sound of gunfire and shouts, the people in Dayr al-Qamar ran with their weapons to help the Ḥamādī family. Emir Khalīl also rode out with his men to drive off the attackers, who had been able to set fire to all the buildings, while the Ḥamādīs kept them at bay until the men from Dayr al-Qamar could arrive with reinforcements. When Emir Khalīl and his men arrived to help, the attackers, completely routed, turned and fled.

The next morning the men left al-Mukhtāra and went up to the plain of Biq'āthā and the Samqāniyye heights. The men of the 'Arqūb went to help by way of 'Ayn Wazīh and, under the leadership of their shaykhs, covered the plain and the hills for a distance of five miles.

The emir met them with his men under the leadership of their emirs and shaykhs and with the vizier's troops. The battle started early in the day. The emir had come down below al-Samqāniyye, keeping about half his men with himself outside the battlefield, watching the progress of the battle and sending in aid to those he saw faltering against their adversaries. That day Muṣṭafā Āghā Barbar brought his cavalry into the battlefield and displayed bravery and daring that were attested to by the fiercest men. The battle lasted until two hours before sundown, when both sides [101] withdrew. Fifteen were slain from the emir's party, but they brought back twenty-nine of their opponents' heads to be sent to 'Abdullāh Pasha with Qāsim Āghā Abū-Sayf, who spent that night in the Mishāqa house, accompanied on his way down by his friend 'Abdullāh Āghā Shānātā and his men. During this battle Shaykh 'Alī Jumblāṭ was wounded by a bullet, and there was no hope of recovery. The son of Abu-Zayd Āghā, an officer of the Hawwārī troops, was also killed.

A few days later the emir rode out intending to disperse the masses that had gathered against him. 'Abdullāh Āghā Shānātā advised him to take the cannons to fire on them and annihilate them. "If I were able to drive them off without injuring one human soul," he answered, "I would do it, for they are poor peasants who have been bullied into this by their shaykhs. Is it not enough that they have been kept from making their living and thrown into mortal danger on the battlefield? Should I, who am charged by God and the Empire to shepherd them and protect them, annihilate them with my own hand? I will do my utmost to avoid bloodshed, and therefore you see that my reward for taking prisoners is double what for I give for the head of a slain man. I hope thereby to avoid excessive slaughter." These words this writer heard from the mouth of 'Abdullāh Āghā himself.

The emir sent the vizier's troops by way of al-Kaḥlūniyye to al-Jdayde, and brought the mountain soldiers to the Biq'āthā plain above al-Jdayde. Shaykh Bashīr made his camp below al-Mukhtāra opposite al-Jdayde, with the Bārūk River between them. That day the children of Dayr al-Qamar, boys from the age of twelve and up, armed themselves with slingshots and went out with the soldiers to fight. Their chief was M'allim Khalīl 'Aṭiyya, the engineer mentioned once before. The brave Jews of Dayr al-Qamar, such as Mūsā Sha'bān, his brother Abū-Ḥasan and Shmūyil Bārūkh also came out for battle. Shmūyil stood as leader of two hundred infantrymen.

Shaykh Bashīr sent his men to meet the advancing soldiers at al-Jdayde, his cavalry met the cavalry coming into the plain from the direction of al-Kaḥlūniyye, and the footsoldiers came together and began to scale the mountain above al-Jdayde to fight the emir's troops, but the boys injured them severely by hurling stones with their slingshots and rolling down rocks on them as they climbed up. The engineer instructed them how to roll down the proper rocks to hit the climbers. A pitched battle was fought until the emir's troops gained the victory and got them out of al-Jdayde, following them until they drove them away, vanquished.

The emir saw the women of the Shūf running off into the hills and feared lest the Turkish troops arrive and consider them fair game. (A Lebanese will permit bloodshed to protect the honor of his enemy's women sooner than his own.) When the emir saw the women fleeing, he reached the Jdayde bridge first and prevented the troops from crossing to go after the defeated men. To the leaders [102] of the troops he said, "The victory God has given you over the wretches is sufficient. Let us withdraw so they can carry off their dead." They turned back, but the emir stayed on the bridge until the troops were gone, and only then did he ride behind them with his men. A mere twenty-two heads were taken, and they were sent to the vizier with Qāsim Āghā.

That night many men of the Shūf and the 'Arqūb came to the emir to be reinstated to favor by confessing their fault and claiming that they had been forced by fear of ruination to follow their shaykhs. He forgave them and told them to return to their homes.

THE EMIRS AND SHAYKHS FLEE THE LEBANON.

The emirs and shaykhs who had gathered fled that night from the country, scattering in various directions. The emir disbanded his own and the vizier's troops, sending each to his home, and distributed the expenses of the vizier's troops over those who had been in league with his adversaries. All property of the House of Jumblāṭ was confiscated by the Acre treasury to be at the emir's disposal on condition that he pay annually, in lieu of taxes, 350,000 piastres to the treasury and 50,000 piastres to the vizier's mother. The vizier ordered the mosque and minaret at al-Mukhtāra destroyed [on the pretext] that it had been built without permission of the overlords and that, on the testimony of reliable Muslim soldiers, there was found in the minaret a graven image of a calf. (Of course, there was no truth to this claim. The Druze curse the calf, which has a different significance for them, but they pretend to be angry when a calf is cursed so that people will do it even more.) Anyway, it was razed, as was Shaykh Bashīr's house, which had cost more than a million *'amūd* rials to build.

DAMASCENE TROOPS ARREST THE SHAYKHS; 'ALĪ AL-'IMĀD IS KILLED AT DAMASCUS, AND THE REST ARE SENT TO ACRE, WHERE SHAYKH BASHĪR JUMBLĀṬ AND SHAYKH AMĪN AL-'IMĀD ARE EXECUTED.

Muṣṭafā Pasha had previously been relieved of the governorship of Aleppo and come to Damascus as governor. When he heard of Emir Bashīr's victory and the flight of his opponents to the province of Damascus, he sent Kurdish troops to arrest any of the leaders they could find. As soon as Shaykh Bashīr left the Lebanon and entered the province of Damascus, he sent his wounded nephew, Shaykh 'Alī, to hide among the Druze in the Ballān region, where he died. Shaykh Bashīr and his sons Shaykh Qāsim and Shaykh Salīm, as well as Shaykh 'Alī and Shaykh Amīn al-'Imād, were surprised by Kurdish troops from Damascus. Shaykh Bashīr wanted to fight, but Shaykh 'Alī did not agree and chose to surrender. When the soldiers had them surrounded, they stripped them of their weapons and, taking their horses and all the goods and possessions they had with them, put them on broken-down nags and took them to the Damascus seraglio. When Muṣṭafā Pasha saw them, he issued an order for Shaykh Bashīr, his sons and Shaykh Amīn al-'Imād to be placed under guard in the citadel. Because of the prior experiences [the pasha] had had with Shaykh 'Alī al-'Imād when he was under the vizier at the siege of Acre, as has been mentioned, he ordered him executed, and he was cut to pieces before he could dismount from his horse.

When news of this reached 'Abdullāh Pasha, he requested that Shaykh Bashīr and those with him be sent to Acre. [103] They were sent and placed under guard. After some months he ordered Shaykh Bashīr and Shaykh Amīn al-'Imād killed, and they were strangulated and thrown before the city gate for all to see. Shaykh Bashīr's two sons were kept in detention, where they died during an epidemic of the plague.

THE FUGITIVE EMIRS LEAVE HOMS AND ENTER THE LEBANON; THEY ARE ARRESTED, THEIR EYES ARE PUT OUT AND THEIR TONGUES ARE CUT OFF.

Emir Salmān and his brother Emir Fāris, and Emir 'Abbās and his brother Emir Ḥasan all went to Homs, where they stayed but a few days and then returned to the Matn in the Lebanon before the emir's anger at them had cooled down. He immediately dispatched one of his *bulūkbāshīs*, Shaykh 'Alam al-Dīn Dhibyān, escorted by a squadron of cavalry and infantry, to find them in the Matn, hold them under arrest and report to him until he could order what should be done. 'Alam al-Dīn came across them by chance on the open road and arrested Emir Salmān, his brother Emir Fāris and Emir 'Abbās, whose brother Emir Ḥasan escaped and fled to Egypt. The three emirs who had been seized, however, were held by 'Alam al-Dīn in Dayr al-Kaḥḥāle, and a report was sent to the emir. He sent his son Emir Khalīl, who had them brought and placed in a cell. This was the 14th of Rajab 1240 [4 March 1825]. That night the emir's order was issued to cut off their tongues and put out their eyes. The cutting out of their tongues was done by a Maronite monk, who held their tongues with a grapple, pulled them out and cut them off with a knife, cauterizing the wounds with a piece of red-hot pottery to stop the bleeding. Then came Qāsim al-'Arab, who had put out the eyes of Emir Yūsuf's sons, to blind them, which he did with irons heated in the fire. He repeated this for three successive days, under the supervision of a Christian surgeon I had often seen eating at the emir's table and claiming to be a specialist. After the three days they mounted each emir on a mule and sent them to their houses.

Some time later, when the emir had relented toward them, Emir Salmān perceived that one of his eyes was all right, but the lids had been stuck together by the irons. He asked the emir's permission to have the lids opened, which he gave, and he was able to see again. His brother and Emir 'Abbās, however, remained blind.

EMIR ḤASAN AND HIS BROTHER EMIR ḤUSAYN BADĪ'A ARE KILLED AT ḤĀSBAYYĀ.

As for the emirs of Ḥāṣbayyā, the emir realized that Emir Ḥasan and Emir Ḥusayn Badī'a had been in league with those who had amassed against him. Emir Sa'd al-Dīn came to congratulate the emir on his victory and deliberated with him in this regard. His brother Emir Muḥammad, who had remained with the emir after taking part in the battles, was sent to Ḥāṣbayyā; and the two aforementioned emirs were killed.[17]

It was customary for the emirs of Ḥāṣbayyā to have appointed by the emir a superintendent of affairs, whom they called in their dialect a *kyakhye*[18]. They had had a man who was one of Shaykh Bashīr's trusted people, and he had made [104] their lives so miserable with his arrogance and objections to everything they did that they were sick and tired of him. Emir Sa'd al-Dīn asked the emir to allow Mikhāyil Mishāqa to be his manager, and permission was granted. Therefore I went with him, and their affection for me and mine for them increased to such an extent that the whole princely family considered me one of them. When I decided to establish permanent residence among them, they gave me vast estates in the Ḥūle district, which they held as *mālikāna*,[19] with their own lands below the waters of the Nahr al-Liddān, anciently known as the City of Dan. They exempted [my estate] from taxes and gave me a village, a dependency of al-Qunayṭra, which was an endowment of which they emirs had the gift. I closed my silk business in Dayr al-Qamar and switched to agriculture.

Emir Sa'd al-Dīn and his cousin Emir Salīm no longer had any rival for the rulership of the region. Shaykh Abū-Ṣa'b Shams, who had married Shaykh Bashīr Jumblāṭ's sister and whose sons were by her, had of course cooperated with his in-law in the insurrection on the mountain. He and his sons, Shaykh Amīn and Shaykh Khalīl, were therefore placed under arrest. The sons of his brother, Shaykh Aḥmad, and Shaykh Qāsim, the father of the Salīm Bey Shams is alive today, made no objection at all. However, there was a score to settle with the shaykhs of the Qays family, who were originally from the village of Kfar Nabrakh, which belonged to the House of 'Imād al-Dīn, the leaders of the insurrection on the mountain. Therefore they fled their homes. The feud with the Shams family was mediated by this writer, and they were lightly fined. When they had returned I hoped they would remain quiet so I could get them restored to favor with the emirs, but the fear that the emirs would do them in preyed on their minds and they fled their homes. The emirs' wrath was once again stirred up, and they ordered Shaykh Abū-Ṣa'b's house destroyed but not those of his nephews or of Shaykh Bashīr Qays, the *qāḍī* of the region. His house had been an asylum for the poor, so I begged that it be left for my residence, my intention being to protect a house that fed and sheltered the unfortunate. I got my wish and moved into the house. During that year the Druze of Ḥāṣbayyā were subjected to many humiliations.

THE REASON FOR THE AUTHOR'S DESIRE TO LEARN WHAT HE COULD OF MEDICINE.

In the year 1828 this writer contracted quartan fever, and at that time quinine was not known to the physicians of the Syria. I went home to Dayr al-Qamar for treatment, as the physicians there excelled their brethren in other Arab lands. With much effort I was able to recover in five months, and I then determined to learn about the art of medicine, which was a particularly difficult task since there were no schools or presses for books, and indeed even teachers were hard to find. Nonetheless, the balance of my mind was tipped in favor of being able, with industry, to attain my desire by reading the textbooks on this art that were available. Since these were in my own language, there was nothing except my own idleness to keep me from understanding the contents: with assiduity then, it should be possible to learn. [105] Therefore I acquired what medical texts in Arabic I could and began to read. I was able to understand the jist, but I was stumped by the technical terminology taken from foreign languages like French or Greek, and especially by the authors' inconsistency in terminology. For example, one called a fever "daily," another called it "cathemerous," and a third called it "quotidian," all three meaning the same thing. To understand such inconsistencies I had to resort to some physicians.

After a time my uncle Buṭrus 'Anḥūrī came from Egypt for a change of climate, as his health was not good. He stayed a number of months, and that gave me a chance to learn from him some things of which I was ignorant. That same year one of the emirs fell ill, and I brought him Emir Bashīr's physician, the Neapolitan doctor José Carlini. He remained for time, during which I learned many things that had lately been discovered. He left with us his son-in-law, a young man from Izmir he had brought with him, to complete the treatment of some illnesses in the princely family. Recognizing that he was skilled, I represented to them that it would be good to engage him as a physician on a permanent basis. They agreed, and he did not disappoint me. The emirs gave him a house to live in, and he brought his family. From him I acquired much useful knowledge, and I began to practice medicine gratis, my intention being to acquire some practical experience. When that physician's reputation reached the ears of the governor of Damascus, he summoned him there to treat someone who was ill and kept him.

THE REASON FOR THE DISAGREEMENT BETWEEN 'ABDULLĀH PASHA AND MUḤAMMAD-'ALĪ PASHA, THE GOVERNOR OF EGYPT.

Let us return to news of the province of Ṣaydā. The state taxes on the peasants of Egypt were burdensome, but they were fairly light on the peasants of Ṣaydā. This resulted in the migration of many peasants from Egypt to Gaza and Jaffa. Muḥammad-'Alī Pasha wrote to 'Abdullāh Pasha to send them back where they had come from, but he decided not to comply. Ibrāhīm Āghā al-Kurdī advised him to obey the governor of Egypt, who was like a father to him and had previously done him a favor, but ['Abdullāh Pasha] grew angry at him, and this reached the hearing of the emir, who sent an envoy to make clear to 'Abdullāh Pasha that such a step was contrary to his best interests and would have fearful consequences, and that he should not forget what he owed him.

"I know the emir's bravery," he replied. "How could I be unaware of it now? The Empire would never have allowed the siege to be lifted from me unless its soldiers were incapable of conquering Acre, a feat that Bonaparte couldn't accomplish either. Then it was fortified by one wall; now it is fortified by two walls so strong all the kings on earth could not take it. What can Muḥammad-'Alī do to me? Is he more than a vizier? I am a vizier like him. Let the emir be as brave as I expect him to be. Likewise inform the emir that this year it will not be permitted to take silkworm cocoons from the mountain to Egypt." (Because of the great heat in Egypt, cocoons hatched before the mulberry leaves, and so cocoons had to be taken from the mountain, where the cooler climate delayed the hatching.)

This [106] conduct annoyed the governor of Egypt, because 'Abdullāh Pasha should have considered himself much in Muḥammad-'Alī Pasha's debt, and therefore everybody expected a different turn from the governor of Egypt.

EMIR EFENDĪ TREACHEROUSLY MURDERS EMIR MANṢŪR.

In A.H. 1243 [A.D. 1827-28] Emir Efendī betrayed his cousin Emir Manṣūr by bribing a woman from the village of Ḍahr al-Aḥmar to keep a lookout until it was a late hour, when [Emir Manṣūr] had gone to bed and his men were not around him. She was then to bring him word secretly in his village, Bakkīfā, which was about two miles away. When she got the chance, she went and informed Emir Efendī. After midnight he went with a group of men and surrounded [Emir Manṣūr's] house. They climbed up on the roof of the sleeping quarters but did not dare to go in, for he, being brave and never without his weapons, would have killed many of them. They made a hole in the roof and fired on him until they killed him. Then they looted all the weapons and horses he had, leaving his wife only her personal possessions. Emir Efendī was left alone in the rule of Rāshayyā and no longer had a rival.

When Emir Bashīr was informed of the murder of Emir Manṣūr, he flew into a rage at Emir Efendī, for it was he who had made the truce between them. Emir Efendī then went to Ḥāṣbayyā and tried to get the emirs there to win back the emir's favor for him. Emir Sa'd al-Dīn went to Emir Bashīr, conciliating him until he was reconciled to Emir Efendī, who later repaid [Emir Sa'd al-Dīn] poorly for this favor.

Emir Efendī had taken in Emir Aḥmad and Emir Bashīr, his sister's two sons by Emir Ḥasan Badī'a, who, along with his brother, had been executed with the emir's permission for having had a hand in the Jumblāṭ-'Imād insurrection, and assigned them a larger stipend than that of any other Ḥāṣbayyā emirs who were their peers. In 1245 [A.D. 1829-30] Emir Salīm, the son of Emir Sa'd al-Dīn's paternal uncle and co-ruler of Ḥāṣbayyā, died at the age of thirty, leaving behind his son Emir Muḥammad, a minor, under the guardianship of this writer. To achieve his goal, Emir Efendī schemed to get the emir to issue an order doubling his sister's sons' stipends. Emir Sa'd al-Dīn paid the double stipend in accordance with the emir's order, but then the family rose up against him and also sought increases, [claiming that] the others were enemies while they were of his own faction. If he were to give them what they demanded, there would have been nothing left of the income of the region for him to live on; and if he offended his own partisans, he would lose them. Therefore he decided to stop paying the increase ordered by Emir Bashīr. I tried my best to dissuade him, because he was going to make the emir angry, and that would be to his own detriment. I gave him many rational arguments until, at my wit's end, I said, "Let us pay this month's stipend and then take the opportunity to pay a visit to Emir Bashīr, inform him of the predicament he has put us in with regard to the family's demand and the necessity of being equitable, and ask him to resolve it. He will assuredly agree, and we will be safe from the evil consequences that must certainly follow if you continue in your present resolve." Contrary to his habit, all my words [107] had no affect on his resolution, and he had just gone into his private quarters, ordering me to pay the old stipend, when Emir Aḥmad's courier came.

The courier came, and he would accept nothing but the amount of the new arrangement. If we were going to give him the old amount, he said, he would not take anything. It occurred to me that later everybody would think this was my doing because they all believed that the emir acted on my advice, even though he was opposed to most of it. I wrote him a note and sent it into his private quarters, saying: "I implore you again to pay Emir Aḥmad's stipend as His Excellency the Emir ordered. The courier has come and will not consent to take the amount you have ordered. I beg you to allow me to pay the increase for this month, even if from my own personal salary. This will allow you to go to your father and end the dispute by his command."

He returned the note to me, and on it was written an answer in his hand and with his signature: "I am not accustomed to have you refer to me so much in an affair like this. I have repeatedly had you to understand that I will not allow the increase to be paid. If the messenger is not content to take the old stipend, he may do as he pleases. I will not be annoyed by this affair again."

I informed the messenger of my note and the answer, and he left taking nothing. Four days later I received a letter from my brother Andreos summoning me for an interview with the emir. I set out immediately, knowing what the summons was for. When the emir received me, he ordered me to sit down and have coffee as usual, without, however, his usual friendly manner.

"Why have you acted thus in the matter of Emir Aḥmad's stipend?" he asked.

"I am a servant," I relied. "My only function is to carry out the orders of my master. The question must be answered by my master. Had I known the queston before coming, I would have asked your son, Emir Sa'd al-Dīn, for an answer."

"I know that Emir Sa'd al-Dīn relies on your opinion," he said, "and for that reason Emir Efendī attributes the state of affairs to your doing."

"Yes," I said, "Emir Sa'd al-Dīn does rely on my opinion, but only when it does not affect his purse. If Your Excellency thinks I have lost my mind, then I am not to blame. If you attach any significance to your training of me, you should not suspect me of consenting to anything that would run counter to your will and be detrimental to my master's interest. If Emir Efendī attributes the state of affairs to my doing, well, he is of your noble family and it is not fitting for me to make answer more than that he relies on the opinions and reports of persons who were not trained by Your Excellency, as I was, and does not ascertain the truth or falsehood of such reports before passing them on to Your Excellency and putting his signature and seal to an accusation of your servant."

Then I showed him my note to Emir Sa'd al-Dīn and his answer to it. After reading it he said, "Emir Efendī's accusation forced me summon you to learn the truth so I could give him a proper reply. You go back to your job and make Emir Sa'd al-Dīn understand that he is mistaken in what he has done. Now that Emir Sa'd al-Dīn has unloosed the bonds of contention with his own hand, it is not for me to oppose his adversary." [108]

Emir Efendī sent emissaries to Damascus to ask for the Ḥāṣbayyā region in the name of his nephew, Emir Aḥmad. I went myself to Damascus but was unable to undo their action completely, first of all because they had undertaken to pay a large sum to the vizier's treasury. Secondly, the shaykhs of the House of Qays, whom the Druze were inclined to follow because they were elders, had taken refuge in Damascus and sided with them. The Druze *shaykh al-khalwa* and *qāḍī* were also with them. Thirdly, Emir Bashīr had withdrawn his support from Emir Sa'd al-Dīn. After much effort [on my part] Emir Sa'd al-Dīn was left with half the region, and Emir Aḥmad was given the half that had been in the late Emir Salīm's name. When Emir Aḥmad was unable to fulfill his promise to the Damascus treasury, Emir Bashīr gave over two thirds of the region to Emir Sa'd al-Dīn, who was to pay two thirds of the impost to the treasury, and one third was given to Emir Aḥmad. Had the emir not done that, the governor of Damascus would later have demanded of Emir Sa'd al-Dīn the amount for half the region that Emir Aḥmad had promised. Thus the country was divided between the two of them by Emir Bashīr's compromise. Emir Aḥmad, however, did not dare to live in Ḥāṣbayyā and resided in the village of 'Ayn Ḥirshā, a dependency of Rāshayyā near the Ḥāṣbayyā region.

NABULUS IS ANNEXED TO THE PROVINCE OF ṢAYDĀ AND REVOLTS; SĀNŪR FORTRESS IS CONQUERED BY THE EMIR'S MEN.

Then the year 1246 began [June 1830]. During this year the Nabulus region revolted against 'Abdullāh Pasha because, by imperial order, it had been severed from the Province of Damascus and made a dependency of the Province of Ṣaydā. This was easy for him to have done because the vizier of Damascus had complained that [the region] was unruly and the impost of six hundred purses could not be collected without his going there himself with soldiers, the cost of which was more than the yield of the region. 'Abdullāh Pasha undertook to pay two thousand purses annually to the Empire and was given the region. When the state taxes were demanded of the people at the same rate as other subjects, that being more than they had been paying to the vizier of Damascus, they revolted. He dispatched troops with cannons and cavalry, and [the people] fought and fortified themselves in the citadels. Then the troops went against Sānūr Fortress, which al-Jazzār had not been able to subdue, and besieged it, but futilely. The inhabitants sallied forth and engaged the [soldiers], and the people outside [the fort] also plundered the supplies on the roads and engaged the guards.

When 'Abdullāh Pasha realized that his troops were not strong enough to take the fortress, he asked Emir Bashīr for reinforcements. [The emir] went down himself, escorted by about fifteen hundred of his men, both mounted and on foot. To accompany him he also appointed Shaykh Nāṣīf Abī-Nakad, who was renowned for his bravery, with about a thousand of his followers and the men of Dayr al-Qamar. The emirs of Ḥāṣbayyā and Rāshayyā and some shaykhs of the mountain joined the emir with about two thousand horses and men. All told, they were fewer than five thousand.

The emir and his men camped next to the vizier's camp, [109] opposite Sānūr Fortress. He then wrote guarantees of amnesty for all the prominent people of the Nabulus region and those who were besieged in the fortress, along with warnings and threats of the seriousness of revolt against their overlords and to take this opportunity, which they would not have again. If they rejected this advice, he would have to implement the vizier's order to destroy the insurgents. He gave them three days to reply. Some of them surrendered and came to the emir, trusting in his amnesty, which he gave them, sending them back to warn the rest of the consequences. They returned, but only a few accepted to surrender, for those who were inside the fortress refused to listen to advice. Many thousands gathered in the village of 'Ajje near the camp. The emir's group begged him to strike at them before they became too many, but he would not permit it, his intention being to end the affair without bloodshed.

One day, however, some of the emir's soldiers were drinking at a nearby spring when some men from the 'Ajje multitudes ambushed and massacred them. Among those killed were four youths from Dayr al-Qamar, Shaykh Nāṣīf Abī-Nakad's men. When he heard this, he could no longer be restrained by the emir's prohibition of fighting and drove his men before him to attack the 'Ajje multitudes. They fired on them like rain and did not stop until they had entered the hamlet by force, battling incessantly. When the rest of the emir's troops and the vizier's soldiers saw the battle fray, they hastened to assist Shaykh Nāṣīf, and defeat was dealt to the insurgents, whose losses were great, and the troops ransacked the hamlet. In this battle one of Ḥusayn Ḥamādī's sons was killed, and the emir wrote to console [the father], addressing him as "dear brother," by which address the family was elevated to the rank of shaykh, after having been prominent commoners.

After this victory cannon and shells were deployed, and frontal attacks were repeatedly made on the fortress. Those who were inside were so beset, with no hope of help from their region, that they surrendered to the emir, who pardoned them all. The fortress was destroyed, the state taxes were collected and the soldiers were sent home.

Part Four

1831-1840

THE MUSLIMS OF DAMASCUS REVOLT AGAINST THE GOVERNOR, SALĪM PASHA, AND KILL HIM.

Then began the year 1247 [June 1831], during which commenced significant events in Syria that led to the overthrow of rulers and spread of war. The former governor, Salīm Pasha, had imposed on the people of Damascus a new payment to his treasury, a trifling monthly impost on establishments inside the town such as storehouses and shops, but the people were not accustomed to pay anything at all on such things, not even on orchards or land. The only levy the government had on Damascus was the customs impost on goods imported from outside the province—not on goods leaving the province—which amounted to about two thousand purses. They also had the polltax on Christians and Jews, which varied according to the number of persons, and the tax on grapes and churches. The new impost caused a revolt [110] against the vizier, who holed up in the citadel while his troops remained outside, for inside there was neither fodder nor food. The townspeople expelled the soldiers, [but] one of the officers, a strapping Turk called Qāḍī Qirān, fought mightily against the insurgents until they cornered him in a mosque in the Mazz al-Qaṣab quarter on the outskirts of the city. He sought amnesty and left Damascus with his soldiers.

The Christians would have feared aggression from the hot-headed Muslims were it not for 'Alī Āghā Khazīna-Kātibī, one of the Damascus *āghā*s, an intelligent man, not at all fanatical, to whom the Christians were much attached because of his good character and kind dealings with all. He was one of those robust bravados who was formidable with the sword and the pen and could wield his left hand as well as his right. I saw him do it with my own eyes when I asked him to show me and he was kind enough to do it. He split a reed with a blow of the sword with each hand and wrote a line in beautiful script, half with his right hand and half with his left. (Having seen that, I am emboldened now to write with my left hand, since my right side is paralyzed.) Anyway, 'Alī Āghā took it upon himself to protect the Christians and Jews from attack by the lower elements. Then, from Acre came the Chorbajī al-Dārānī, who had taken refuge there from Salīm Pasha. It is said that, because he had enormous influence with the leaders of Damascus, 'Abdullāh Pasha sent him to implement what would happen later.

Salīm Pasha, being in dire straits in the citadel for lack of food, sought quarter with the insurgents and was given amnesty. He was taken to a house they had prepared for him, but the guards set around him were in league with the insurgents and knew what their adversaries would do to win. Some of the [insurgents] attacked, and he barricaded himself in the council chamber but they set fire to it and he perished in the blaze. Then the prominent men of Damascus gathered and arranged an interim government. They were expecting the advent of imperial forces to take revenge when news arrived that troops had left Egypt for Syria, and their fear subsided a bit. When the Egyptian troops set forth, the Empire ignored what the people of Damascus had done and dispatched a governor named 'Alaww Pasha.

IBRĀHĪM PASHA BRINGS EGYPTIAN TROOPS TO BESIEGE 'ABDULLĀH PASHA AT THE ACRE FORT.

When 'Abdullāh Pasha, the Governor of Ṣaydā, heard that the Egyptian troops had embarked, he hastened to make ready all he needed for a siege and announced a devaluation in commercial prices of about ten per cent. To Emir Bashīr came an emissary with a letter from Shaykh Ḥusayn 'Abdul-Hādī, an eminent shaykh from Nabulus, informing him of the arrival of the Egyptian troops at Gaza under Ibrāhīm Pasha, son of the governor Muḥammad-'Alī Pasha, and asking how he should conduct himself, in defiance or compliance. The emir replied that he should comply and that the best thing was for the shaykh to set out [111] ahead of him and, just before they reached Acre, he would come down to them.

I had gone to the emir to find out how Emir Sa'd al-Dīn should act in this affair. "When the Acre affair is over," he said, "I will let Emir Sa'd al-Dīn and the others know what to do. For the time being he should comply with the governor of Egypt, as usual." I wrote to [Emir Sa'd al-Dīn] of the answer I had been given and went down to Beirut to tend to some affairs of my own. When I arrived I learned that the Egyptian troops had landed at Acre and that an order from Ibrāhīm Pasha had gone to the emir to attend him. The next day I set out for Acre, and when I got there I saw twenty-two battleships stationed, eight to the north, eight to the west and six to the south in front of Burj al-Dibbān, and cannon and rockets on Tall al-Fukhār, all of them pounding Acre incessantly, and Acre, which could not even be seen for the smoke of gunpowder, pounding them in return. The shelling lasted from morning until an hour and a half before sunset. The ships went off to Haifa and did not return. I learned that the ships that day had shelled Acre more than seventy thousand times, and most of the ships had been disabled by Acre's firing on them.[1]

I stayed there around twenty days watching the events. Each of the three or four nights about five thousand soldiers went away from the Egyptian camp under the cover of darkness, but the dawning rays of the sun would show the soldiers of Acre that the Egyptian troops were still coming down upon them. The Egyptians dug crooked trenches they called "rat tracks" and made barricades near the city walls, where they mounted cannons, rockets and mortars. They completed these works during the night to protect themselves from fire from Acre. The battle raged between the barricades and walls of Acre day and night. The Egyptians concentrated their fire on Burj 'Alī, near the city gate, which was, along with the wall, more than sixty cubits thick. The only part that could be hit was about three cubits that rose above the wall, the rest being hidden by the earthenworks that lay beyond a deep trench. Outside the trench the ground was high, level with the highest parts of the wall where the slits were for the cannons. I could see that they would not be able to conquer Acre from the land unless they could fill up the trench. I suggested this to Khawāja Ḥannā Baḥrī, and he replied, "The engineers with us are perfectly competent. They will certainly do what needs to be done."

Inside Acre were about three thousand brave and experienced soldiers. They would come out and try to entice the Egyptians into moving in front of the cannons on the wall, but the Egyptian officers were too perceptive to fall for this. Messages from the Empire and others reached Acre by night with people who swam in from the sea in the dark. One [112] night there occurred a commotion in the camp. Then shots and shouts were heard, then peasant songs in praise of 'Abdullāh Pasha. We thought it was what they call an enemy raid on the camp until it was established that six hundred men from Nabulus had agreed to break through the Egyptian lines and enter Acre to help the vizier. They rushed into the camp, brandishing weapons and striking down anyone who opposed them. As the troops were unable to fire on them inside the camp without hitting their own, they got through to the Acre side. Then they fired on them, but the darkness prevented them from being hit, and they reached Acre safely. Every night they could be heard on the walls chanting victory for 'Abdullāh Pasha.

Khawāja Yūḥannā Baḥrī, who had been sent by Muḥammad-'Alī Pasha to his son Ibrāhīm Pasha as an assistant and commissioner for ordnance and finance in the council, had taken direct charge of all necessary arrangements throughout the province. He was one of those individuals who was skilled, intelligent and honest in all he said and did, whether it concerned his master or the subjects. What had to be done he did in the best manner possible.

Acre pounded and was pounded incessantly day and night. I returned to Dayr al-Qamar after I had learned everything I could, down to the number of soldiers, eight regiments of footsoldiers, eighteen thousand in number, eight regiments of cavalry, four thousand in number, and about two thousand Hanādī Arab horsemen. The cannons, rockets and mortars were thirty to forty pieces and a rock crusher. After meeting with Emir Amīn, his father's deputy, to assure him of his father's safety and inform him of the events at the camp, I went to Ḥāṣbayyā and reported to Emir Sa'd al-Dīn that the Egyptians were greatly prepared but that it was not to be hoped that they would conquer Acre in a short time, since it would not be easy to take from the sea, the walls on the land side were extremely strong and well fortified, and the cannons could strike only the tops of the walls, which were hidden by the high earthenworks on the other side of the trench wall.

THE NAKAD SHAYKHS UNITE WITH THE IMPERIAL FORCES; 'UTHMĀN PASHA COMES AS GOVERNOR OF TRIPOLI, BUT HE FLEES BEFORE IBRĀHĪM PASHA.

Before the Egyptian troops arrived, the Nakad shaykhs had united with the imperial forces. Ibrāhīm Pasha sent Ya'qūb Bey Mīrālāy with his troops to Dayr al-Qamar as a guard while the emir was away at the Acre camp. Later the Empire sent 'Uthmān Pasha al-Labīb as governor of Tripoli, and he entered [the city]. Ibrāhīm Pasha then took a detachment of his soldiers there, and ['Uthmān Pasha] fled before him. After he had made arrangements in Tripoli, he went to Homs and from there to M'allaqit Zaḥle, and thence to the Acre camp.

Against [Ibrāhīm Pasha] the Empire sent troops under the leadership of the governor of Aleppo, Inje Bayraqdār Pasha, who brought his men to Homs and then moved his camp to Tall al-Nabī [113] Mindaw, below the village of al-Quṣayr on the banks of the Orontes, to wait for the arrival of the regular troops to join them and march to Acre through

B'albak and the Biqā'. Ibrāhīm Pasha sent a squadron accompanied by cannon and stationed them on the road in the village of M'allaqit Zaḥle, the lease-hold of Emir Bashīr's sons.

The siege of Acre lasted from the beginning of the month of Jumādā I [until] Dhūl-Ḥijja. The trench was filled up, and Ibrāhīm Pasha and the Egyptian troops attacked the walls of Acre but were repelled by the men and cannons. On the 28th of that month 1247 [29 May 1832],[2] Ibrāhīm Pasha addressed his soldiers, recounting their valor in the wars of the Morea and the Hejaz and their past victories over strong enemies, not weaklings like those who were beleaguered in Acre. To retreat would be an unacceptable humiliation for the Egyptian army, which was known throughout the world for its bravery. Therefore, they would attack the walls of Acre that very day, and the cannons would be brought up behind them to blast any soldier who returned without having taken the walls. Then he led the army and took the walls by storm from both sides.

The first to mount the walls on horseback was Salīm Bey Oṭūzīr, colonel of the artillery, and Ibrāhīm Āghā al-Rishmānī, a Maronite equestrian instructor from Dayr al-Qamar, and behind them was Ibrāhīm Pasha. Ibrāhīm Āghā was killed by a bullet that struck him from the inner wall of Acre. Then the Egyptian soldiers swarmed over the walls and engaged 'Abdullāh Pasha's men, whose numbers had been reduced by casualty and wounds and who therefore took refuge behind the inner wall. When 'Abdullāh Pasha saw that the impregnable walls were taken and that he had only three hundred fifty fighting men left, he surrendered to Ibrāhīm Pasha and opened the gates.[3]

The Egyptian army entered and plundered the town. 'Abdullāh Pasha was treated with honor and sent to Egypt, where Muḥammad-'Alī received him warmly and arranged a stipend commensurate with his rank to cover his expenses. He dwelt there for a time and then asked to go to the capital, where he lived for a while. Then, requesting the sultanate to let him spend his remaining days in the Hejaz, he was sent there, and there he died. After the conquest of Acre Yūḥannā Baḥrī was promoted to the rank of *amīr-liwā'* and was addressed as Baḥrī Bey.

Ibrāhīm Pasha had signed his official correspondence: "al-Ḥājj Ibrāhīm, Vâli of Jidda and the Hejaz[4], presently military governor of Acre." However, after the conquest of Acre he changed his signature to "military governor of Arabia." After he had consolidated Acre, issued orders for the repair of the walls that had been destroyed and for stocking supplies and matériel, stationed the necessary soldiers and artillerymen for guarding it, and brought many soldiers from Egypt, he left with his troops for Damascus, accompanied by Emir Bashīr, who wrote to his son Emir Amīn to send him some of his men and to the emirs of Ḥāṣbayyā and Rāshayyā to join him in Damascus. I therefore set out for Damascus in the company of Emir Sa'd al-Dīn. [114]

THE EGYPTIANS TAKE CONTROL OF DAMASCUS AND ENGAGE IMPERIAL FORCES AT HOMS.

'Alaww Pasha,[5] the governor of Damascus, had gathered a force of Kurds and locals and taken them out to fight Ibrāhīm Pasha to keep him from entering the city. About ten thousand went out to encounter him. He saw them from afar through the telescope and distinguished the detachment of Kurdish cavalry from the Damascene detachment. He sent the Arab Hanādī cavalry against the Kurds and notified the regular troops to meet the Damascenes but not to hurt them and to fire only into the air. When the two sides met and the Damascenes heard the sound of constant gunfire, they took flight. The Kurds stood their ground, but finally they too were defeated, the Hanādīs in pursuit, killing all they could.

When 'Alaww Pasha learned of the defeat of his forces, he fled as fast as he could from Damascus, which was then entered by Ibrāhīm Pasha. He did not allow his soldiers to molest anyone and immediately sent out a herald to announce amnesty and for everyone to go peacefully about his business. He stayed in Damascus until Monday, the 4th of Ṣafar, and advised the *efendī*s of Damascus that they should accompany him. There he left M'allim Buṭrus Karāma to arrange an advisory council and installed as regent one of his elite, Aḥmad Bey, the step-son of Kurd Yūsuf Pasha, a former governor of Damascus who has been mentioned previously.

On Tuesday, the 5th of Ṣafar, he left Damascus for al-Qaṭṭīne, and Emir Bashīr and the emirs of Ḥāṣbayyā and Rāshayyā went to the village of 'Adhrā. That day I checked the number of soldiers: eleven thousand footsoldiers, two thousand regular cavalry, three thousand Hanādī cavalry, forty-three cannons, and three thousand transport camels for supplies and matériel. Accompanying Ibrāhīm Pasha was 'Abbās Pasha, son of his late brother Tosun Pasha, and his cousin Yeğen Aḥmad Pasha. On Wednesday he took his troops to al-Nabk, and the emir's people stayed in the village of Dayr 'Aṭiyye. There the emir mediated the return of the notables of Damascus to their homes. On Thursday he reached Ḥasiyye. On Friday he turned off the Homs road onto the road to al-Quṣayr, and the army stopped on the banks of the Orontes at Tall al-Nabī Mindaw, where the Ottoman troops had been camped, for when the news of the conquest of Acre was received, they had withdrawn to Homs, which was about fifteen miles away.

Ibrāhīm usually had his troops move out three hours before daylight to reach a stopping place before noon. That same day, as he neared al-Nabī Mindaw, the rest of the troops, about six thousand, arrived from Tripoli and M'allaqit Zaḥle. That made the total army, along with the emir's men, around twenty thousand. Word had it that there were no more than twelve thousand soldiers in Homs. Ibrāhīm Pasha met with the leaders of the army, and they made the necessary arrangements for engaging the enemy. At midnight the Hanādī horsemen were sent to Homs to harass the soldiers. Ibrāhīm Pasha did not move out with his troops before dawn as usual but waited until daylight. On Saturday [115] the 9th of Ṣafar 1248 [8 July 1832] he divided his infantry into three divisions, with about two miles in between. In each division every *yūzbāshī* led his men in three divisions, followed by the next at a distance roughly equal to the length of the preceding line. Alongside the middle division was Emir Bashīr and the other emirs with their men and transport camels behind the emirs. Alongside the right division was 'Abbās Pasha and half the regular cavalry with half the cannons. Alongside the left division was Yeğen Aḥmad Pasha and the rest of the cavalry and cannons. Ibrāhīm Pasha galloped on his steed among the ranks, then the marshal cadence was beaten and the ranks marched across that broad plain, banners streaming over their heads. It was a stirring sight.

When the troops had marched for less than an hour, they rested. At 6:15, according to the Arabic hour,[6] they reached the village of Qaṭṭīne, about three miles from Homs. Part of the army spread out to the northwest toward the Orontes and part to the southeast, thus covering about five miles, with 'Abbās Pasha and the cannons to the right and Aḥmad Pasha to the left of the core. Ibrāhīm Pasha made his headquarters in the middle of the ranks on Tall Qaṭṭīne and ordered the emir to make camp, with the emirs and men who were with him, to the left of the troops near the Orontes and not to enter the battlefield. Therefore he camped near a high, cone-shaped hill, and the men propped their weapons up to eat and rest.

The Hanādī horsemen swarmed back to Ibrāhīm Pasha with the heads they had cut off and the prisoners they had taken from the Turkish troops. He rewarded them and praised their bravery. The Turkish camp was at Tall Bābā 'Umar, at a distance of two miles, and a number of cannons had been mounted on the hill. That day there was a strong wind from the northwest blowing at our backs and stirring up dust in the Turks' faces. Since the ground was flat and covered with fine sand, and it was summertime—and the dirt had been further pulverized by the horses' hooves—the air was so full of dust it was difficult for men and horses to face it. This was a great advantage to Ibrāhīm Pasha's troops and a tremendous catastrophe for his adversaries.

I climbed to the top of the hill with some others to watch the battle. The Hanādīs attacked the Turkish cavalry like savage beasts snatching their prey from among the multitudes. It was ten of them against a hundred, and if they were too many for them, they did not draw back but rather some or all of them moved laterally to help their comrades, attacking their adversaries and driving them back from their positions.

Three hours before sunset we saw a horseman hastening from the battlefield to Ibrāhīm Pasha, who was just then riding alone to [116] the Hanādī. I sent word to the emir, who was inside his tent to be out of the wind and dust. He immediately came to the top of the hill and took the telescope to see what was happening in the field. I was emboldened to say, "These are the twelve thousand of the enemy you spoke of in Damascus?"

"We said that," he responded, "and yet not half of those with us came here. How would it have been if we had said that they were sixty or seventy thousand? No one would have come. Don't be fooled by their numbers: they will run away when they hear *firsī* being ripped." (By this he meant the sound of the regular army's guns being fired. The word *firsī* in the dialect of the mountain people means the cotton cloth known as calico). While we were speaking, a Turkish bullet whizzed by us, for their troops had advanced beyond the others in our direction. I feared the emir would be hit, and not by chance but by design, so I begged him to go down to his tent out of the wind and dust.

"You are afraid of bullets," he said, "and that is not like your compatriots."

"If I am afraid," I said, "it is only for Your Excellency's sake. You are our inspiration, and if you go down to your tent and your servant goes down too, then I can be afraid for myself. I entreat you to test me and go down." My only purpose in this was to get him to go down.

"One must take precaution when not compelled to face danger," he said. "It would be foolhardy to remain here in danger, and I would insist that everyone around me go down; but we are in no danger, for the bullets landing here have no force to them but are only falling after having been spent. They do not dig into the earth, for you see them lying on the ground." Then the Hanādīs, who were in our direction, kept retreating, their foes attacking them and driving them back. The emir said, "No doubt the Nakad shaykhs are with those people, for this is their type of assault." (Later the emir ascertained that the Nakadīs were with the Mar'ash troops.)

IMPERIAL TROOPS ARE ENGAGED AT HOMS.

Then I looked in the direction of the enemy and from afar caught a glimpse of regular troops. I stared hard, but the whirl of dust kept me from making out the distance well. I informed the emir, who said, "Up until this morning, when our spy came from their camp, they were fifty-five thousand, and there were no regular troops among them." He looked with the telescope but saw no one. Then I spied the rows of red fezzes and the glitter of weapons and banners in the sunlight. I told the emir that what I had said was confirmed and that they certainly outnumbered us. I indicated to him where they were, and, looking again with the telescope, he saw them and said, "These troops must have just arrived at the camp."

It was two and a quarter hours to sunset. Just then a mounted spearsman came to the troops from Ibrāhīm Pasha, and immediately the horses and cannons drew up in a single wall to either side of him, 'Abbās Pasha with the right-hand cavalry [117] and Aḥmad Pasha with the left. The marshal music was sounded, and they marched to meet the adversary. The enemy before us fled before the troops, pursued by the Hanādī horsemen snapping at their heels. The right flank was attacked by about five thousand Turkish cavalry, but 'Abbās Pasha repelled them with cannon fire and kept moving. Then perhaps five thousand Turkish cavalrymen grouped and attacked all together, but they were met with cannon spray and routed, leaving behind more than two thousand slain. When the regular Egyptian troops reached the battlefield, they were met by the more numerous regular Turkish troops. One hour before sunset the battle raged between the two sides with continuous fire of guns and cannon. Likewise from the barricades on Tall Bābā 'Umar cannon were fired and bombs were hurled at the Egyptians. It was a frightful hour, during which the very gates of hell were opened. At sundown the noise of guns was quieted, leaving only the pounding of cannon until an hour and a half after sunset, when total silence reigned. The news of complete victory reached the emir: Inje Bayraqdār Pasha and all the viziers with him had fled for their lives; part of the Turkish troops were dead or wounded, and part had been taken prisoner or scattered.

HOMS IS ENTERED AND SURRENDERS TO EMIR BASHIR.

On Sunday morning the emir entered Homs, the horses having trod over dead bodies for a mile on the Bābā 'Umar plain, and the reins of power were turned over to the emir. Among the prisoners were found eight hundred Armenians in the service of the army. These he released and sent to the Orthodox metropolitan. The military prisoners were one complete unit, aside from miscellaneous individuals, and they were sent to Acre in the company of Shaykh Ḥusayn Talḥūq, who has been mentioned previously. The wounded Turks were around six hundred and fifty, and they, along with our own wounded, were turned over to the physicians. He ordered the *qāḍī* and *muftī* of the town to bury the dead and charged this writer to make an inventory of what the fleeing viziers had left behind. Their camp was by the Orontes near the al-Mīmās bridge. I found that they had left their tents with their furnishings—the bureau scribe had even left his silver inkpot, pens and paper lying on the ground. Food was left burning over the fire, and medicine chests, rolls of dressing and shrouds, a great number of furs and mantles for awards and much matériel were all left behind. There was found in the Sīdī Khālid quarter a storehouse filled with enough Hejazi coffee beans to supply a city. I completed my mission, and everything was put in its place.

The city of Homs had good soil, temperate climate, and vast lands surrounded by many villages, but through neglect and inattention most of it had been devastated by marauding bedouins from the desert. The inhabitants of the city numbered around twenty thousand, a quarter of whom were Christians, mostly [118] Orthodox with a few Catholics and Jacobites, who had a metropolitan there. Three quarters of the population were Muslims. I did not see a single Christian there not lit up with intoxicants, but many of them wrote a beautiful hand. From among them come some individuals known for intelligence and cleverness, although the majority are foolish. Too many tales are told of their naiveté for me to begin to tell them, but I will mention one thing I saw with my own eyes.

The day after we entered Homs reports were received by the emir that there were local people dead and wounded in the vicinity of Tall Bābā 'Umar and an investigation was being sought. He sent me for this purpose, and I found eight men lying on the ground, four dead and four alive but wounded. When I asked them who had done this to them, they replied, "We came here to have a look at the soldiers' place and found a bomb filled and its wick exposed. We wanted to have a chance to see it go up and come down, so we lit the wick and stood around it to see it go up. We don't know what kept it from going up, but it exploded and did to us as you see."

Having given permission to bury the dead and treat the wounded, I returned to report the incident to the emir. "Write up the incident," he said, "so that M'allim Buṭrus Karāma may realize the degree of his compatriots' intelligence."

Later, during one of my meeting with Baḥrī Bey, he asked me what I had seen of Homs. I praised its good climate and said, "I found, however, that they have a bone to pick with Your Excellency and M'allim Buṭrus Karāma."

"How so?" he asked.

"They say that you have appropriated for yourselves their share of intelligence and left them impoverished in that respect," I said. He asked the reason for this, and I told him the story of the bomb.

A RE-OUTBREAK OF CHOLERA IN HOMS.

Cholera had appeared in Homs, but it had passed before the Egyptian troops arrived. However, a few days after the battle it reappeared and began to spread. Because of what clinical tests had proven to me, I believed that it was infectious and that those who denied it were mistaken. I therefore refused to eat anything other than bread, thyme and cherry preserves, and under my cloak I carried a piece of camphor, and I advised the emirs and their people to do the same. The Christians among them followed my orders, but the Muslims and Druze, because of their belief in fate, which is unsanctioned by religious law, mostly did not hearken to advice, and more than half of them died, while only the very few Christians who did not follow my order were afflicted. The disease spread rapidly throughout the town and was highly fatal, with four out of every five patients dying. One day the number of fatalities reached two hundred forty-eight, although it was a small town. I treated many, but treatment was successful only in cases where the illness was slight, and they may have recovered without it. After staying there a month and a half, I returned home.

During that year my father Jirjis Mishāqa died, having long been an invalid at home. After his death his position was given to his son Andreos. [119]

IBRĀHĪM PASHA PURSUES THE IMPERIAL TROOPS AND ENCOUNTERS ḤUSAYN PASHA; HE DOES BATTLE WITH THE GRAND VIZIER, WHO IS TAKEN PRISONER.

Ibrāhīm Pasha remained in Homs for one day. On Monday the 10th of Ṣafar 1248 [9 July 1832] he left with his troops and headed for Aleppo. Before reaching there he was met by Ḥusayn Pasha, who was advancing to encounter him with forty thousand soldiers. They fought, and Ḥusayn Pasha was defeated, leaving Ibrāhīm Pasha to continue on his way. The city of Aleppo opened its gates to him, and he consolidated the rule there, dispatched a *ḥākim* to the province of Urfa and marched into Turkey, seizing control of Adana without encounter because fear of his might had the entire country in its grip. He marched to Konya, whose protectors fled, and entered it with his troops, of which only twelve thousand remained with him since he had left some to guard the regions he had conquered and others had died in battle or of cholera.

Then he heard that the grand vizier had arrived near Konya with 150,000 troops, artillery and much war matériel. It was a bitterly cold day, snowing heavily and densely overcast. Ibrāhīm Pasha had only his few soldiers commanded by the Frenchman Sulaymān Pasha,[7] who had taken part in many battles in his time with Napoleon Bonaparte, serving with him as a lieutenant at Acre. The two armies met, and the battle raged. The grand vizier was one of those brave types who rode his steed among his soldiers, encouraging and stirring them to fight. The fog was heavy, and the smoke of gunpowder prevented the soldiers from seeing each other, and then the darkness of night fell. When Ibrāhīm Pasha assessed the situation, with the profusion of his adversaries and the paucity of his own men, he gave up all hope of escape and thought that he and his men would surely fall prey to the enemy. While he was in this state of despair, Sulaymān Pasha passed by him and, perceiving that he had given up hope, said in all severity, "You are still ignorant of the art of warfare. You cannot distinguish between victor and vanquished: our adversary's strategy has been diminished to the point of collapse, while our troops' strategy is in the best possible situation. Take courage and don't shrink from resisting. I believe our few troops are sufficient to overcome the adversary." Ibrāhīm Pasha took courage from these words and inspired his men to fight.

The grand vizier was parading among the front ranks of his troops to encourage them, but because of the thickness of the fog and snow and proximity of his troops to the Egyptians he was surrounded by Egyptian soldiers and taken prisoner to Ibrāhīm Pasha, who immediately came forward to receive him with the respect due his rank. He dispatched a herald to the Turkish troops to announce that the grand vizier had been taken prisoner. They then scattered, leaving behind their matériel as booty for the Egyptians. Ibrāhīm Pasha, however, took the vizier to Konya, whence he sent him to his father in Alexandria, and dispatched communiqués of his victory to all the parts of Syria and Turkey that had succombed to his might.

After his men had rested, he set out for the province of Kütahya. There too the rulers fled before him, leaving no one to resist him [120] in his path, for the entire country was in fear and trembling of his might. He entered Kütahya peacefully. The Hanādī horsemen went to Izmir, which was still ruled directly by the central government, [to seize] certain goods, and they met with no resistance.

IBRĀHĪM PASHA HALTS HIS ADVANCE; SHARĪF PASHA IS SENT AS *ḤUKMDĀR* TO SYRIA.

At that point [Ibrāhīm Pasha] received letters from the English and French embassies calling for a halt to his advance until an order from his father should come, for negotiations were being held with the sultanate to resolve the dispute. He stopped until it was settled that the provinces of Ṣaydā, Tripoli, Damascus and Aleppo, along with Adana in Turkey, should remain in the hands of the Vâli of Egypt but that he should abandon his other conquests. Then [Ibrāhīm Pasha] returned with his troops to Syria.

Sharīf Pasha, a relative of the Vâli of Egypt, then came to Damascus as *ḥukmdār* over Syria from Aleppo to Gaza. Some time later the Empire gave him the rank of *mīrmīrān* and the title of pasha. He was an intelligent man, eminent and skilled, but he was severe to the extreme on those who made mistakes and never forgave or had mercy on a criminal. He had many killed by beating with the whip, and those who merited twenty blows with a rod received five hundred lashes with a whip, each lash equivalent to twenty blows of a rod, and mostly these beatings were carried out in his presence. For administering beatings he had a young Egyptian, an evil, cruel man named 'Alī, who boasted that he could draw blood from his victim's feet in four blows. I saw him beat a man who was unconscious with blood pouring from his feet, and this was in the sight of the pasha, who nonetheless was an extremely equitable and truthful man who kept his promises.

His administration of the province and the council were excellent. Anyone who had a complaint of the judgments of the provincial councils could appeal his case to the Damascus Council. The minutes of the councils and depositions of plaintiffs and council members were recorded word for word with the signatures and seals of the council, and none of the men of authority had the power that is current now—even the pasha, the *ḥukmdār* of the province, could not overrule a decision. If it was necessary for him to act in the council, he had to appear like any plaintiff, and the council would rule as it saw fit. The council minutes, with detailed drafts, were handed over to Baḥrī Bey to revise in accordance with his charge from Muḥammad-'Alī Pasha. If he found a report or judgment by one of the council members not in accordance with strict justice, he would write a disputation of it in which he pointed out the error and send it to the council. If [his judgment on] the mistake was correct, they amended it; otherwise they would dispute with Baḥrī Bey. Such deliberations were repeated until it was right. Such a procedure kept anyone from being tyrannized, and the council members had to take care to know the correct procedures, not as we see now, as the poet says:

I went to market to buy an ass,
The donkey-trader frowned and said:
"Don't you see they have all become council members
at the government's gate?" [121]

THE EGYPTIANS IMPOSE THE *I'ĀNA* TAX PER CAPITA.

Then the Egyptians instituted an annual per capita tax called *i'āna.* It was based on a man's ability to pay: a rich man would pay 500 piastres annually, and on down to 15 piastres, such that the [average] would be 100 piastres per capita or more. At that time the *'amūd* rial was fifteen piastres. This demand was difficult for both Muslims and Christians to bear, especially for villagers, who had a tax based on their land and cultivation as well as a tax on the number of livestock and beehives and a per capita tax on individuals. Added to this for Christians was the per capita poll-tax in regions like Ḥāṣbayyā.

Emir Sa'd al-Dīn was in a quandry because on the one hand it was obligatory to obey his overlords, but on the other his subjects could not bear the burden of this demand. He therefore sent me to Damascus with a carte blanche sealed by him to write on his behalf whatever was necessary for the government and the council. I went to Damascus and found the council clerk a very able man, and between us a close friendship grew up. I presented on behalf of the emir a response to Sharīf Pasha's order, saying that I had been sent as a deputy to make arrangements with the council for the *i'āna* tax on the Ḥāṣbayyā region. The pasha referred the response to the council, so I took it to the clerk, who promised me that it would be taken care of quickly. I begged him to put me off until last, which was in our best interests, and then I induced the deputies of the region to complain more bitterly of the harshness of this imposition. They complained and asked for mercy. Buṭrus Karāma endeavored to get the *i'āna* rate for the Lebanon reduced to fifty piastres and then had the population set at forty thousand, exempting emirs, shaykhs and religious persons such as Muslim teachers and preachers, [Christian] bishops, priests, and monks, and Druze elders, hermits and preachers. The total *i'āna* imposed on the population of Mount Lebanon had been 4000 purses, and after the adjustment of rates on the region it was more or less the same. The Biqā' had the least with 35 piastres. I then made an effort to get Ḥāṣbayyā in last place and wound up with 30 piastres. They did not do well by Damascus in the adjustment of rates, and its rate fell at about 110 piastres, making the total assessment for [the city] 4000-odd purses per annum. Since most of the inhabitants were poor artisans, even though there were a few rich men among them, it was impossible to impose more than the 500 piastres stipulated by the High Council. For this reason the guilds were hard pressed and the population began to decline, creating a deficiency that would accrue as a loss to the country.

THE EMIR HAS THE NAKAD SHAYKHS' HOUSES RAZED AT DAYR AL-QAMAR.

As soon as Emir Bashīr returned from Homs, he ordered the Nakads' houses destroyed and their property confiscated. The houses were razed, but their property was kept from confiscation by the House of Mishāqa's claim to debts owed them by [the Nakadīs]. The shaykhs settled down in exile in Egypt along with the Jumblāṭ and ʻImād shaykhs, except for Shaykh Saʻīd Jumblāṭ, who had entered the military. [122]

THE EGYPTIANS STRIP THE CLAN CHIEFS OF THEIR AUTONOMY.

Then the Egyptian government began to curtail the independence of the shaykhs, who, by paying a fixed tribute to the treasury, had ruled as autocrats in their territories. [Instead,] the taxes of a region were recorded in detail by the treasury, and the emirs were made agents of the treasury, with fixed stipends not to exceed one tenth of a region's income. Gradually they were removed from their regions and outsiders were put in their place. Emir Bashīr, however, obtained from the Vâli of Egypt an absolute decree [of autonomy] for himself so that Sharīf Pasha could not interfere with him in anything but had to leave him to act independently in the Lebanon, as was his custom. This distinction was too much for Sharīf Pasha to tolerate, and he lay in wait for a chance to humiliate the emir.

First of all, the Ḥarfūsh emirs of Bʻalbak were relieved of their autonomy and given stipends. Then at the beginning of 1250 [1834] the same thing was done to the emirs of Ḥāṣbayyā and Rāshayyā. At that point I decided to reside in Damascus, where I went, got married and bought a house to live in, although I remained supervisor of Emir Saʻd al-Dīn's affairs with the government and the council and had his seal carte blanche.

THE CLANS TURN AGAINST THE EGYPTIANS FOR CHANGING CUSTOM AND BEGIN TO REBEL.

When the Egyptians began to alter the customs of the clans and institute more taxation of the inhabitants than they were accustomed to pay, the people began to despise them and, wishing for the rule of the Turks back again, manifested signs of rebellion. The Egyptians were forced to increase the soldiery to guard their new position. Then the

Nuṣayrīs in the mountains of Latakia rebelled against them, and the *ḥākim* sent troops from the Lebanon, Ḥāṣbayyā and Rāshayyā to combat them. These troops were led by the emirs, who entered those mountains, took possession of most places and were victorious in their engagements. However, because they failed to maintain the necessary discipline and took their adversaries too lightly, their situation turned into defeat, many of their men were killed and their gains were lost. They returned to Latakia humiliated until the government dispatched a large force to subdue the mountains.

THE INSTITUTION OF MILITARY CONSCRIPTION.

Then the government began to conscript individuals from the peasantry, but they were taken at random. A soldier had no fixed period of service after which he would be free to return to his family, but rather his service was as everlasting as hell. Therefore youths fled to places where they would be safe. When the government demanded individuals for the military from Emir Bashīr, he did not make this a reason for young men to run away but rather distributed the number over the Muslims and Druze of the Lebanon based on the number of men in each village. He also ordered that no one be taken against his will. The villages placated an individual with money and then brought him to the seat of government, where he was asked whether he had come of his own free will or by force. If he answered of his own will, he was accepted; otherwise, he was allowed to go his own way. In this operation no young man of the mountain was forced to flee. In cities like Damascus, however, the soldiers would burst into town all of a sudden while the people were busy with their affairs and seize all the young men they came across. Anyone the physician found [123] healthy was conscripted into the military, even if he was the sole support of aged parents. Even if someone was taken whose brother was already in the military and who had no one else to care for his parents, they would not release him.

NABULUS REBELS AND THWARTS IBRĀHĪM PASHA.

When the Nabulus region felt the weight of the Egyptian government's imposition, which was something they were not used to, they rebelled. Ibrāhīm Pasha took his troops there, but the people fought him, and his men were not numerous enough to humble them. Aside from their sheer numbers, they were also among the strongest men of

Syria and well trained by constant internecine warfare, but they would always unite against a foe who attacked any of them. Ibrāhīm Pasha was hard put to fight them and nearly fell into their hands. News of his trouble reached his father in Alexandria, and he immediately came himself to the port of Jaffa. When he arrived he found that his son had extricated himself from his adversaries with a severe loss of his own troops, and therefore he began to plot to bring them into obedience. After a while he summoned some of their leaders and had them beheaded in front of the seraglio gate in Damascus. Muḥammad-ʻAlī Pasha returned to Alexandria when he saw that his son was safe.

THE DRUZE OF THE ḤAWRĀN AND ARABS OF THE LIJĀH REBEL.

In the year 1253 [1837-38] the Druze of Jabal Ḥawrān rebelled against the government because of the imposition of new taxes. Ibrāhīm Pasha was absent in the Shmāl region, taking measures against new developments against him by the sultanate, and could not come. Therefore Sharīf Pasha the *ḥukmdār* sent against them 450 Hawwāra horsemen, thinking they would be sufficient to subjugate the Druze because the mountains were easy for cavalry to manage and there were no more than 1600 men in toto, mere peasants in their shaykhs' villages. As the soldiers were camped for the night, however, they fell upon them, massacred them and took their horses and weapons. Only a few managed to escape under the cover of darkness.

When the news reached Sharīf Pasha, he sent against them about 6,000 regular troops, infantry and cavalry, with cannons. The Druze, however, after the massacre of the Hawwāra, made an alliance with the al-Sulūṭ bedouins and took their families to the Lijāh.[8] When the soldiers arrived and fought, they were beaten. News of this instilled fear in the troops and encouraged the Druze outside to come help their people, especially since the Lijāh was difficult to maneuver in. It was a vast area, twenty miles long and fifteen miles wide, with many rocks, caves and fissures in the ground that no outsider could know how to navigate. Many battles took place there, and the soldiers were always defeated with many dead and wounded. When auxiliaries came they were too weak to fight before the battle ever began, for their determination was undermined by news of prior defeat dealt by the enemy hosts, who were actually fewer than a fourth of the soldiers, and the impossibility of the terrain. Nothing, of course, was ever attributed to bad planning on the part of the commanders or to the cowardice that afflicted them all. [124]

Ḥāṣbayyā.

SHIBLI AL-'ARYĀN TAKES A BAND OF DRUZE AND TWO EMIRS TO FIGHT EMIR SA'D AL-DIN.

As the soldiers increased, so did the Druze, who were reinforced by other Druze from the Lebanon, Ḥāṣbayyā and Rāshayyā. Among them was Shaykh Shiblī al-'Aryān (who is now Shiblī Pasha in the imperial service), a brave young man who had been brought up in the service of Emir Efendī and who had performed heroic acts in the Egyptian wars that later gave cause for his promotion in the Egyptian service, and even later in the imperial service. Before he arrived in the Lijāh, Ibrāhīm Pasha's deputy ruler in Rāshayyā had been killed, and [Shiblī] had gone to Ḥāṣbayyā with a group of men along with Emir Bashīr and Emir 'Alī, the sons of the Badī'a emirs who had been murdered, to take revenge on Emir Sa'd al-Dīn.

At that time [Emir Sa'd al-Dīn] had with him Emir Maḥmūd, the son of Emir Khalīl and grandson of Emir Bashīr the Great, with some of his servants. Jibrā'īl Mishāqa was also there by chance on business. Emir Sa'd al-Dīn gathered the emirs and their followers into his palace and sent word to Emir Bashīr of what was happening.

Shiblī al-'Aryān arrived in Ḥāṣbayyā with his band, intending to take the palace by storm. Kept at bay with gunfire, he withdrew and concentrated his fire on the palace windows. Emir Muḥammad, Emir Sa'd al-Dīn's brother, was fighting from the southern side, where his quarters were, with some of the emirs and protecting the palace gate to the west. His brother, Emir Bashīr, was guarding the northern side, where his quarters were, with some of his men. Emir Sa'd al-Dīn's quarters were on the eastern side, which faced the adversaries' positions, and there Jibrā'īl Mishāqa and some of the emir's followers were. A pitched battle was fought and constant assaults were made, but the men came out to defend under the cover from the eastern side of the palace, until many of al-'Aryān's men were killed. Of the emir's group only his brother Emir Muḥammad was killed by a bullet that struck him in the head. It was he who had slain with his own hand Emir Ḥusayn Badī'a, whose son Emir 'Alī had come with al-'Aryān to take revenge on his father's murderer.

The next day al-'Aryān heard that Emir Khalīl was approaching to save his son Emir Maḥmūd and deal a blow to those who were amassed against him. Therefore he retreated with his people and headed for the Lijāh. Had he not had with him two Shihābī emirs, he would not have dared to fight Emir Sa'd al-Dīn, for it was an established custom in the land of the Druze that no one would raise a weapon against a Shihābī emir unless he had another emir with him. When Emir Khalīl reached Ḥāṣbayyā, the others had scattered, so he took his son and returned home.

THE WAR WITH THE DRUZE OF THE ḤAWRĀN IS INTENSIFIED; SHARIF PASHA LEADS A LARGE FORCE AGAINST THEM BUT IS DEFEATED.

The war in the Lijāh was intensified, but the Druze always gained the victory. Beasts of burden were continually leaving Damascus carrying supplies for the soldiers and returning bearing the wounded. It was deemed necessary for the French *mīr al-liwā'* Clot Bey, Inspector General of Health to come from Egypt with several physicians to assist the military physicians, who were insufficient to deal with so many wounded and ill. When the Druze damage to the Egyptian army [125] worsened, Sharīf Pasha himself took a huge contingent and, camping beside the Lijāh, undertook a fierce offensive that drove back the Druze, with Sharīf Pasha and his troops entering the Lijāh in pursuit. At the end of the day, in a place in the middle of the Lijāh that was difficult to negotiate, the Druze who had been driven back returned, some of them lying in ambush behind rocks and in caves. They poured down on the Egyptians, whose resolve had been worn down with fighting and marching through rocky debris all day, and began to slaughter them like sheep. Only with great effort was Sharīf Pasha able to save himself by fleeing outside the Lijāh, but most of his soldiers perished in this engagement. Not only did the Druze gain possession of weapons and supplies, but the Egyptians were filled with mortal dread of the might of the Druze, whose resolve was further strengthened and whose numbers increased with help arriving from outside. Raiding parties were scattered, and supplies and matériel coming to the soldiers from Acre were seized.

IBRĀHIM PASHA RETURNS FROM ALEPPO, ENTERS THE LIJĀH AND IS ROUTED.

When Ibrāhīm Pasha learned of the state his soldiers were in and what had happened to Sharīf Pasha, he went to Damascus and made ready a force to combat the Druze. He fought them repeatedly from the camp but could not gain victory because his soldiers were afraid. Then he planned to combat them from the direction of Ṣalkhad, from which he could get to the Dāma plain inside the Lijāh, which was suitable for military operations. He sent in some Kurdish horsemen. The Druze fought them a little but were scattered by them. Then came the Kurdish cavalry followed by Ibrāhīm Pasha with the regular army. When the Kurds reached the Dāma plain, the Druze poured down on them and defeated them severely. Although Ibrāhīm Pasha was defending them with the regular troops, it was useless because his soldiers, fearing the might of the Druze, were put to rout by them. [The Druze] pursued them and slew them by trapping them in narrow passes. Ibrāhīm Pasha was scarcely able to escape outside the Lijāh with those of his men who remained. There were too many encounters to chronicle in detail or even to write of the important ones. Suffice it to say that from not one of them did the Egyptian troops emerge victorious.

IBRĀHĪM PASHA POISONS THE WATER.

Ibrāhīm Pasha then determined to drive them out with thirst, for there are no springs inside the Lijāh. In winter they get water from reservoirs of rainwater, and in summer from springs on the outskirts of the Lijāh. Ibrāhīm Pasha decided to poison these waters with corrosive sublimate and asked Clot Bey to do it. He replied, "My job is to preserve health, not to kill human beings. Even so it is unthinkable for a person like you to ask a subject to help you perform perfidious acts, especially when women and children drink this water. Is it permitted to destroy them for the crimes of their menfolk?"

"I am not going to deceive them," he said. "I will tell them what I am going to do."

"No," he answered, "this cannot be, for the innocent will perish of thirst. I will not permit it." Ibrāhīm Pasha, however, would not back down from his resolve [126] and forced the Egyptian chemists who were in the camp to do it. He bought all the sublimate available in Damascus and had it dissolved according to his order and put into the waters that his soldiers and cannons could not protect. Although [the Druze] attacked, defeated the soldiers and got some water, they were not able to get enough, and many died of thirst.

THE DRUZE MOVE TO RĀSHAYYĀ AND MASSACRE THE BATTALION GUARDING IT; IBRĀHĪM PASHA COMES FROM DAMASCUS AND ENCOUNTERS SHAYKH NĀSIR AL-DIN AL-'IMĀD.

After the waters were poisoned, the [Druze] were forced to leave the Lijāh and take up positions in Rāshayyā, the 'Arqūb and Ḥāṣbayyā. The rulers had stationed a battalion of soldiers in Emir Efendī's palace at Rāshayyā. The Druze besieged it, but since there was not enough water or supplies there, they were forced to surrender and return to Damascus. As they were leaving the region, they were followed to the village of al-Ḍahr al-Aḥmar, about three miles away, where they were all massacred. Not one of them escaped. When news of this reached Ibrāhīm Pasha, he wrote to Emir Bashīr to send troops to Ḥāṣbayyā with his son Emir Khalīl and to remain there at his disposal. With him he dispatched three thousand horsemen and footsoldiers, and they camped at Ḥāṣbayyā.

Then Ibrāhīm Pasha came from Damascus with troops, headed for Rāshayyā via al-Dīmās, where the road was flat. When he reached the top of Wādī Bakkā he came across Shaykh Nāṣir al-Dīn 'Imād coming from the Lebanon with a thousand armed Druze from the mountain to help the rebels in Rāshayyā. Fighting broke out, and the Egyptians gave the Druze a hard time in a pitched battle. Shaykh Nāṣir al-Dīn, who was one of the bravest heros of his time in the Lebanon, encouraged his men, but unfortunately for them he was fatally struck by a bullet and fell. His men took refuge on a hill that was fortified by rocks and trees but had no water. The soldiers hemmed them in on all sides, yet they continued to defend themselves, not seeking quarter and enduring their thirst, until their gunpower gave out. Assaults were made on them constantly from every direction, and they fought with whatever sharp weapons and rocks they could find. However, the soldiers kept firing on them until they were all killed. Ibrāhīm Pasha wrote in his letter to Sharīf Pasha that only one of them escaped, for he had seen him running away and not taking refuge on the hill with his comrades. However, what I later understood from the people of Yanṭā, near the site of the battle, was that more than forty had escaped. Perhaps Ibrāhīm Pasha had not seen more than the one he reported.

THE DRUZE BATTLE FROM JIN'AM, DEMAND QUARTER AND SURRENDER THEIR WEAPONS.

When news of Ibrāhīm Pasha's approach reached the Druze in Rāshayyā, they fled to the field of Jin'am in the Ḥāṣbayyā region, near the village of Shab'ā, which is inhabited solely by Muslims and Christians. To the east of Jin'am lies Mount Hermon, and to the west is Mount al-Wusṭānī, which is difficult to scale and divides Ḥāṣbayyā and some of its villages from the field of Jin'am.

When the battle of Bakkā was over, Ibrāhīm Pasha went to Rāshayyā and found that the Druze [127] had fled to Jin'am, where many from Ḥāṣbayyā, Rāshayyā and the Ballān region had gathered. Shiblī al-'Aryān came to them from the Lijāh accompanied by Emir Bashīr and Emir 'Alī Badī'a, who had been with him at the storming of the Ḥāṣbayyā palace.

Ibrāhīm Pasha sent an order to Emir Khalīl at Ḥāṣbayyā to meet him with his men at Jin'am at a certain hour on a certain day. He took his men to the village of Shwayyā in the foothills of Mount al-Wusṭānī. Since the Druze were on the other side, to reach them he had to scale the mountain, on which were posted Druze lookouts. The road was tortuous and narrow for single travelers, much less for groups, and his mistakes were compounded: first he ascended before the appointed hour; and second, he was supposed to lay low with his troops in the foothills and send a detachment to eliminate the Druze lookouts at the summit, and only when the summit was taken was he to take the rest of his troops up. Instead, he scoffed at remaining where he was and, two hours before the rendezvous, led his entire troop up all together. The watches immediately summoned men from their party and fired on the climbers, attacked them and sent them in rout back to Ḥāṣbayyā. They also killed a good many of them.

After that the sound of Ibrāhīm Pasha's cannons in Jin'am was heard in Ḥāṣbayyā, so Emir Khalīl and his band and the emirs of Ḥāṣbayyā set out to join him. When they arrived, a decisive defeat had been dealt to the Druze, who sent Ḥasan al-Bayṭār, one of the elders of Rāshayyā, to Ibrāhīm Pasha to seek quarter. Ibrāhīm Pasha had met with him many times and had always enjoyed talking to him, so when he saw that his cloak was in shreds, he said, "Are you still alive?"

"As Your Excellency can see," he answered, "my cloak has been shredded by bullets, but the Creator has not permitted me to be killed. If you desire me dead, I am at your mercy."

"I do not wish the death of any of my subjects," he said, "but your band have been trying to get themselves killed."

"They are now aware of their folly," the shaykh replied, "and seek quarter and pardon for their past offenses."

"They may have it on condition that they surrender their weapons," he said.

"They will submit to anything you command," said Ḥasan al-Bayṭār. "Let your order for quarter be issued, and let an agent come with me to collect the weapons and they will surrender them." The order was written, the agent was dispatched, and they handed over their weapons.

After giving quarter to the Druze throngs and ordering their weapons to be collected, Ibrāhīm Pasha left Emir Khalīl and the Ḥāṣbayyā emirs there to complete the collection and disperse the bands, returning himself to Damascus. When the bands had departed, Emir Bashīr and Emir 'Alī Badī'a were followed by Emir Sa'd al-Dīn's brothers, Emir Bashīr and Emir Khalīl, who attacked them, killed them and, raising their heads on their lances, set out for Ḥāṣbayyā.

THE HERMITAGES OF AL-BAYYĀDA IN ḤĀSBAYYĀ ARE PLUNDERED; SOME INFORMATION ON THE RELIGIOUS BOOKS OF THE DRUZE.

In the course of these battles the hermitages of the elders in al-Bayyāḍa were plundered. Above [128] Ḥāṣbayyā were grouped around fifty of these hermitages, which were inhabited by pious elders and forbidden to women, something like Christian monasteries. There was nothing like them in Druze realms. While some of the elders were unmarried, the wives and children of those who were married lived in villages and could be visited at will.

Here I would like to mention briefly something of this sect, for I am acquainted with all their beliefs and have read assiduously the *111 Treatises* with the commentaries of Emir al-Sayyid (i.e., Emir 'Abdullāh al-Tanūkhī, who is buried in 'Abayh and is one of the greatest saints of the Druze) and others to learn what they mean, for they are full of symbols. What is absolutely certain is that the common prattle about them, which is offensive to human dignity, is mere fabrication without a grain of truth to it. However, their practice of doctrinal concealment has led to their being accused of abominations with which they have no connection whatsoever. For their concealment they may be excused because they live under a law that grants security only to Christians, Jews and Mazdaeans, who may live on their land by paying the poll-tax; but the possessions, lives and honor of any others are fair game. And according to the soundest opinions, an act of contrition on the part of the Druze would not be acceptable [to Islam]. For that reason they are enjoined in their religious books to conceal their beliefs, discussion of their religion with an outsider being considered "spiritual adultery."

A *jāhil*[9] who reveals what is forbidden is not permitted to study their books or to discuss religious matters, even if he repents. If a person commits unjustifiable homocide or adultery, he is given a harsh act of contrition and absolute penitence with weeping for his excessive behavior; he must also go around to the elders and ask their pardon, and even then they will not permit him to read their books, which they revere as we do the Gospel, but will give him only the commentaries.

[An elder] must abstain totally from alcoholic beverages, waterpipes and tobacco and from eating any forbidden food, which is taken to mean that one must not eat with rulers, usurers or priests, for it is they who compete with heirs for a dead man's property. One must wear the modest garb of the elders, which consists of a calico robe, dyed either a dark color or white, with round sleeves unsplit at the openings. Over this [is worn] a cloak and on the head a white cap or turban. It is not

Druze shaykhs.

permitted to wear ornate silk fabrics, although those who live among Muslims in the cities do wear silk for dissimulation. An elder must guard his tongue from uttering oaths and curses and from foolish talk or any word that is immodest or impolite, such as "excrement", which they call *hazā* (for *kharā*), and "horns" (*qurūn*), which they call "weapons" (*sawāliḥ*). The cat they call *bsayn* or *biss.*[10] Thus they avoid all words that have unbecoming connotations.

Even when they want to exaggerate, instead of saying, for instance, "I wouldn't do that if you gave me a thousand piastres" (though they would do it for ten), they will take precaution by saying "I wouldn't do that if you gave me a portion of a thousand piastres," since a portion [129] might be less than ten, and so forth.

As for their marriage customs, it is an utter lie that brothers marry their sisters and fathers marry their daughters, as they are accused of doing, for they do not permit endogamous marriage closer than first cousins. They may not have more than one wife, who can be divorced but can never be taken back or gazed upon again.[11] If a woman is divorced through her own fault, the religious leaders rule that the husband may take half of her property, and if the fault is the husband's, the wife takes half of what he owns. As for inheritance, one may will his property to anyone he chooses, as Europeans do.[12] This method makes children behave well to their parents lest the property be alienated from them altogether or left to one and not another. About half of the Druze men are elders, and the rate of literacy among them is generally one in ten. Nowadays, with the introduction of schools in the Lebanon, this rate will increase. There is scarcely a Druze woman who is ignorant or who does not know how to read, and the reason for this is that girls are always with their mothers and have the opportunity to be taught, while males are with their fathers making a living and only rarely have time to learn.

The Druze avoid foul language more than any other sect. They are content with their lives, they are not covetous, they are modest in their dress and social intercourse, and they are neighborly to those who are honest with them. They bear injustice with patience when they see it is inevitable. Their self-respect is beyond comparison to others. To strike one of them with a weapon and speak decorously is more acceptable to them than to give a fabulous gift with insulting speech. However, they will brook no interference by outsiders in their religious affairs. They give more reverence to the Four Evangelists than Christians do, and of the Companions [of the Prophet Muḥammad] they give more reverence than Muslims to Salmān al-Fārisī, al-Miqdād, Abū-Dharr al-Ghifārī, 'Ammār ibn Yāsir and 'Uthmān al-Najāshī. They believe in the truth of many verses of the Gospel and the Koran. They revere all the Greek philosophers, especially Asclepius, whom they call Ishqilubyūs, then Pythagoras the Wise, then Jethro the priest of Midian, then Yusawwi'[13] the True Messiah. It was Pythagoras the Wise who founded the belief in transmigration of souls, but they do not agree with him in his prohibition of his disciples from eating meat, for they do not prohibit it, except for those who are very severe in their piety and who also refrain from the use of many pleasurable things that are permitted. It is not necessary to explain any more of the good qualities of this sect to persuade people of understanding to approve of them.

When you see members of [130] different religions hating each other over a difference in belief, it is contrary to reason to approve of such a thing, because the profit and loss of belief accrue to the believer alone and, since it pertains to the afterlife, it harms no one else. If for the next life X chooses a path he believes best, why should it concern Y if he is on a different path, which he considers best? A discussion of this would entail more than there is room for here. I only say that in temporal affairs we should respect nations according to their conduct with us; we do not have to look upon them with hatred because they differ from us in otherworldly affairs, for that does not affect us one way or another. We must work shoulder to shoulder with them for mutual benefit and hold out to them love and respect and consider them and ourselves as one family: it is sufficient to say that they are different. It is in the interests of both parties to be in accord and harmony. Their laws are based upon the best custom, and both [Christians and Druze] are subject to the rule of a law that commands the debasement of one and destruction of another. Each of the two should find no one more sympathetic than the other. The Druze does unto others as he would have them do unto him, so we must do unto them as we would have them do unto us. Thus our peace of mind will last, and they will support us.

I have already mentioned the instigation of the Druze to oppose the Christians and how this planned sedition was countered by the good policy of Shaykh Najm al-'Uqaylī, who was renowned for his good mind, acuity and honesty.

EMIR SA'D AL-DIN IS DETAINED BY EMIR BASHIR IN THE LEBANON FOR HIS BROTHERS' MURDER OF THE BADI'A EMIRS.

Let us return to Ibrāhīm Pasha. When he learned of the murder of the two emirs who had sought quarter and Shiblī al-'Aryān's violation of [the emir's] amnesty, he ordered Emir Sa'd al-Dīn to be detained by Emir Bashīr in the Lebanon and his two murderous brothers to be bound. He himself rode with his troops to the Ballān region in search of Shiblī al-'Aryān, who he found had fled to Jurd in east B'albak, so he turned back in search of him there. Shiblī sought quarter and offered an apology for having treacherously killed the two emirs after they had received quarter. He was given amnesty, threw down his weapons and surrendered himself. Ibrāhīm Pasha ordered him to pick up his weapons and accompany him to Damascus, where he employed him as an officer over three thousand horsemen. As *ḥākim* over Ḥāṣbayyā he appointed Muḥammad Āghā Swaydān, who held an *īkī qapūlī* lease on Ḥasiyye and vicinity. He was an intelligent and pious man who was well informed on history, manly and brave, of good character and treated Christians well, especially during the Incident of 1860 in Damascus, when he protected the Christians of his region and of nearby Homs as well as those who came from outside seeking asylum with him, about three thousand souls in all. In fact, he was held in such awe that in the regions near him no one was harmed. He is presently an invalid in his home in the village of Qāra.

THE FUGITIVE EMIR KHALIL HAPPENS UPON ḤUSAYN AL-ṬARĀBULSI, A WANTED MAN.

Emir Bashīr and Emir Khalīl, the two murderers, took flight from the authorities and hid for a long time, [131] each in a different place. Ḥusayn al-Ṭarābulsī, a Mutawālī from the Bshāra region who was renowned for his audacity and had eleven sons, had to his credit many acts of aggression on the population at large and on wayfarers, whom he had plundered and killed. Ibrāhīm Pasha ordered him arrested, but he could not be caught. One day Ḥusayn happened to be passing through Marja'yūn coming up from al-Ḥūle, where he had taken some plunder, when Emir Khalīl ran into him and determined to seize him by strategem and honeyed words. [Ḥusayn] fired on him and missed. Emir Khalīl attacked him before he could reload his gun and, with the help of his servant, was able to take him. He disarmed him, ordered him to be bound and brought him outside Ḥāṣbayyā. He sent him in with his servant, fettered, and turned him over to Muḥammad Āghā Swaydān the *ḥākim*. A report was made to Ibrāhīm Pasha, who said, "It is strange indeed that of two fugitives from the law on charges of murder, one catches the other and turns him in to prison."

One of those present replied, "The one who was seized killed for greed and plunder of property with no fear of the might of the law, while the one who seized him only took revenge on his brother's murderers. His flight was in fear of the might of the law and in expectation of eventual clemency: he neither disturbed the peace of wayfarers nor gave vexation to the government. Indeed, he displayed his affection and loyalty by seizing a wanted man and turning him in."

"I have no doubt of the loyalty of the Shihābī emirs in my service," said Ibrāhīm Pasha, "but their revenge for their brother was taken in violation of my quarter, but I forgive them their crime in return for their loyalty." He then ordered Emir Sa'd al-Dīn released and amnesty for his brothers, whose stipends were paid. Ḥusayn al-Ṭarābulsī was hanged in Ḥāṣbayyā, and the rulership of Ḥāṣbayyā and Rāshayyā was later restored to the Shihābī emirs.

During these wars and rebellions this writer suffered losses that almost reduced me to poverty. I held the village of Ayyib in the Lijāh, which I had taken from the government on a promise to develop it. I made some development and attracted peasants to it, but the next year the rebels plundered it and wrecked it. I also had two villages in the Ḥūle, al-Khraybe and al-Manṣūra. Just at threshing time the crops and animals were plundered, and [the loss] was dreadful. Added to this were the state tax-farms I held for a period of three years. Due to the wars and destruction of the roads there was a drop in income, and I lost what I had. I had been practicing medicine for free, but when these blows to my livelihood piled up on me I began to take fees. The long residence of Clot Bey in Damascus was a great help to me, for he liked me and used to summon me to assist him in his operations. He gave me not only all the medical texts that had been translated into Arabic and printed in Egypt but surgical implements as well. Then I was appointed by the government as Chief Physician of Damascus, although I was not competent to hold such a post. During that period I studied the *Isagoge* on logic with Father [132] Yūsuf Ḥaddād, a Greek Orthodox. Then I read a commentary with His Excellency Sharīf Maḥmūd Efendī al-Ḥamzāwī, who was renowned for his learning and intelligence, his fine nature and good character. He is now the *muftī* of Damascus, and it is truly said that he is the first man of Syria. I acquired the basics of this discipline, but I never worked hard enough to master it.

THE DISAPPEARANCE OF PADRE TOMA IN DAMASCUS

Many things happened during the period of Egyptian rule that are not important enough to mention, but during 1255 [A.D. 1840] there did occur the disappearance of the Capuchin Padre Toma, a Sardinian by origin, and his servant. A search was made for them, and when first they entered his cell they found burnt food on the fire and his and his servant's belongings, along with a bit of cash, untouched in their chests.

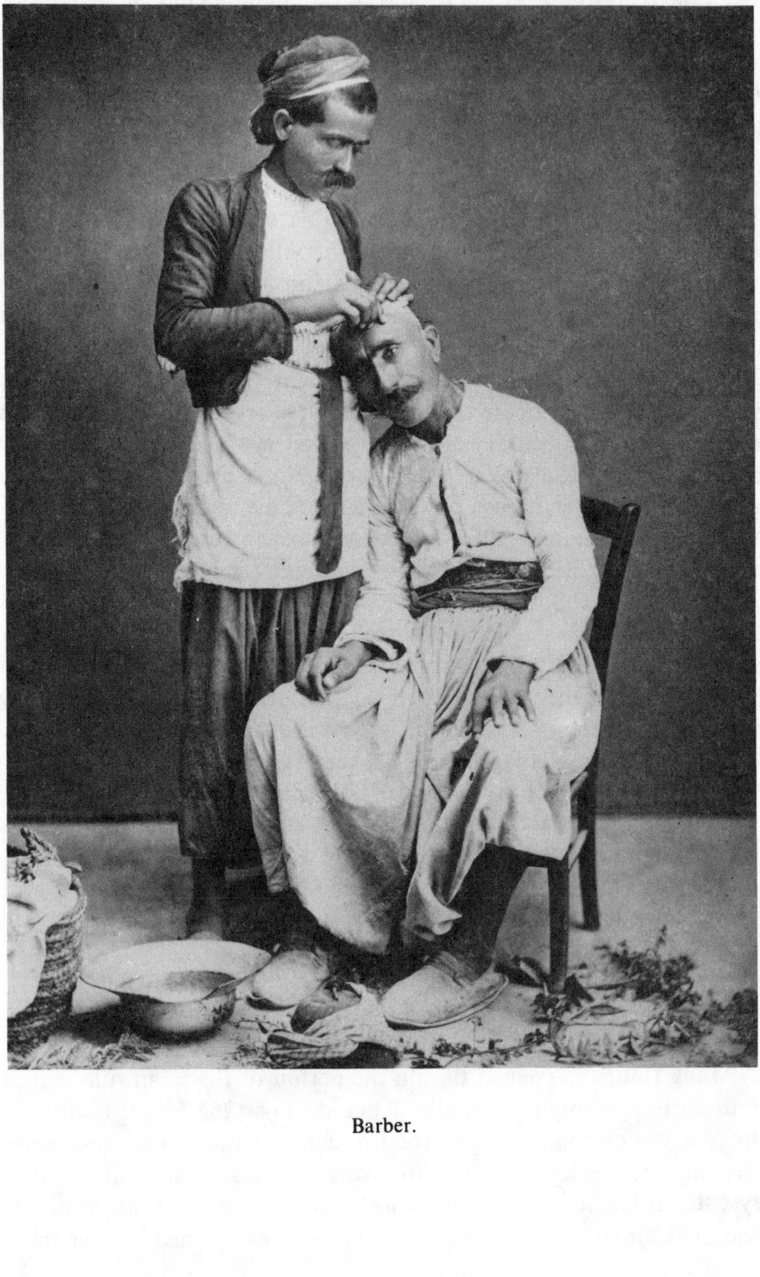

Barber.

The search was intensified, and it was learned that Padre Toma had entered the Jewish quarter toward the end of the day and no one had seen him since. Inasmuch as he practiced medicine and gave innoculations against smallpox, he was wont to go all over the city, yet he divided his time among the quarters routinely. In the morning he went to the farthest Muslim quarters and then headed back toward the Christian quarter, where he returned to his cell for lunch and a nap, resting for about an hour. After that he went around the Christian quarter and then, at the end of the day, entered the Jewish quarter, returning to his cell in the evening. This routine was never varied except in case of emergency.

Now it happened that the padre had some summer clothes he wished to sell at auction, so he wrote notices to put up in Christian churches and the Jewish synagogue on the very day he disappeared. Some of them were found pasted up in all the churches, but not in the Jewish synagogue or in the Greek Orthodox church. Since the padre had been seen to enter the Jewish quarter before going to the Orthodox church, it was surmised that he had gone into the Jewish quarter to put up a notice before going on to the Orthodox church, and that the Jews had murdered him and taken down the notice he had put up there in order to do away with any trace of him.

The day after this was voiced around, a notice was found pasted in the place where such announcements were customarily hung, next to the barbershop of Sallūm the Jew. The investigators had not previously seen a notice in this place, so they asked Sallūm who had put it up. He said a Christian he did not know. They asked him what he had stuck it up with, and he said with some red paste. When they took it down they found that it was as he said, although the other notices in the churches were stuck down on all four sides with white flour paste of the type the padre used for consecration. Therefore suspicion of the padre's murder fell on [Sallūm], who was thought first to have destroyed the notice pasted in the Jewish quarter in order to cover up the evidence, but after being questioned about it, to have stuck in its place the notice for the Greek Orthodox church the padre had still had with him. [Sallūm] was arrested, but then they began to suspect every Tom, Dick and Harry of the Jews, high and low alike. The severity of the *ḥukmdār* [133] Sharīf Pasha has already been mentioned, and he dealt with them by subjecting them to torture, during which many of them died. Monsieur de Ratti-Menton, the French consul, was very active in this case.

[Some] considered this to be a ritual act on the part of the Jews to take Christian blood to spread on the unleavened bread they eat during Passover and for use in other things too, which it is not necessary to mention, although in Jewish law it is strictly forbidden to eat blood. True, their law allows them to treat outsiders differently than their own

Group of Jews.

in matters such as usury, which they are forbidden to take from a Jew but are allowed to take from an outsider. So also is an ignorant physician permitted to practice on an outsider but forbidden to treat a Jew. This much cannot be denied, but a death sentence cannot be given without the judgment of the Sanhedrin (i.e., council), which has not existed since the destruction of the Temple and extinction of their state. In general the prominent [Jews] who were tortured and forced to confess to the truth of the charge did so only in order to be killed and escape further torture, and the end result of this calamity was to force them to be more fanatical in defending every Jew from the charges against them, even if the charges were true. More specifically, if they were asked about a criminal they knew, it was impossible to get them to reveal anything. I can state with certainty that the prominent Jews who were imprisoned in this case were innocent. Among them were the three Harārī sons, Hārūn, Isḥāq and Dāūd, and Mūsā Abū'l-'Āfiya, Mūsā al-Salāniklī and Ḥākhām Ya'qūb al-'Ayntābī. It is impossible to think of them undertaking such a horrendous thing, for no one who knew them could imagine them having the boldness to slaughter a chicken, much less a human being. After severe tortures they confessed, except for Mūsā al-Salāniklī, who maintained his innocence even though he was more cruelly tortured than the rest.

One day I was with Sharīf Pasha on business, and [Mūsā] was brought to confess to charge. He denied it, so he was ordered to be tortured in the presence of the pasha. One of the tortures was to stick reed splinters under his fingernails, but he insisted on his innocence. However, after Mūsā Abū'l-'Āfiya had been much tortured, he said, "So long as I remain in the Jewish religion I cannot divulge what they have done, but if I leave [that religion] I can confess." He then embraced Islam, and when he was garbed in a Muslim turban and given the name Muḥammad Efendī, he began to disclose that it was permitted by the Jews to kill outsiders, that they had killed Padre Toma and taken his blood. Indeed he was not slow to confess everything his adversary wanted to hear. Sharīf Pasha asked them where the padre's blood was that had been kept, and they all claimed that it had been turned over to Mūsā al-Salāniklī, who was tortured even more cruelly but kept denying the charge altogether. They remained imprisoned for a few months until the famous Jew Montefiore[14] came from England to Alexandria and obtained from Muḥammad-'Alī Pasha a decree of pardon—not exoneration—of them for Sharīf Pasha. [134] (It was widely said that it cost him 60,000 purses for Muḥammad-'Alī and 3,000 purses for his court, though we never knew the truth.) After that they were released. Another group of Jews was charged with the murder of the padre's servant, but they managed to hide from the law until the pardon was issued.

The confession that was wrung from those who had been imprisoned on the charge was insufficient as evidence because it had been obtained under torture and could not be considered. What weighed heavily, however, was the discovery in that very Jewish quarter of traces of the padre's body and clothing, which were pointed out by some of the defendants. The investigation of this case, from beginning to end, was not attended by a single Muslim or Christian but was undertaken exclusively by Sharīf Pasha himself with a scribe of depositions. Twenty-two days after the event he summoned Sallūm the barber, who was imprisoned in isolation from his companions and had grown emaciated from the severity of his torture, and addressed him indulgently, saying, "I want to save you. I do not wish for you to die under torture, but I cannot release you until I learn the truth of the case and locate Padre Toma's body. If you will tell me the truth and I find you to be honest, I will grant you amnesty even if you are the murderer. If you do not tell the truth, you will die under torture."

He then confessed that after the padre had been killed in Dāūd al-Harārī's house, "his servant came and summoned me to help him remove the body. I went with him, and we stripped the flesh with a big knife, broke the large bones and threw them into a sewer that flows through a vault under the Sūq al-Jum'a marketplace. We also shredded the padre's clothes and threw them and the flesh into the same place. That's the truth."

The pasha had him returned to his cell and had Dāūd al-Harārī's servant brought. Addressing him in the same manner as before, he said, "I summoned the barber and gave him amnesty if he would confess the truth. I have his confession here, and you are his accomplice in removing the padre's body. Now, if your confessions match, the amnesty will include you both. Otherwise you will both be punished until you die." His confession corroborated the barber's, and he was taken back to his cell.

The next morning the pasha himself rode to the Jewish quarter, taking one of them along to point out to him where they had thrown the padre's limbs and belongings. He indicated that if they dug a little they would find the vault into which they had thrown the padre's limbs. The pasha sent him back to his cell alone. Then he returned and brought the other without telling him where the first suspect had indicated, and he pointed out the very same place. When he was taken to Dāūd al-Harārī's house, showed the five knives that were there and asked to point out the one they had used, he pointed out one of them. Then [the pasha] ordered him taken back to his cell and had the other one brought. He indicated the same knife as [135] his companion and was returned to his cell. There was no longer any doubt of the truth of their statements.

He ordered the vault to be opened and men to go down into the vaulted sewer and bring out any bones and material they found. They dug down to the vault, finding traces of blood around the rim, and then descended into the sewer. They had just begun to pick up the bones when a tremendous flood of water surged through, nearly drowning them, as they said. Some claimed that when the vault was opened all the Jewish houses released the water in their cisterns in order to flush away all traces of the padre, though this was never proven. However, they did bring out a number of bones and pieces of clothing they took to the pasha, who sent them to the French consul and ordered them examined by physicians and surgeons, both military and civil. I was among those invited for the examination, which was conducted in the presence of the French consul and the consul for Austria, Signore Marlato. The bones were examined: among them were animal bones, but those that were established to be human were set aside. There was part of an upper jawbone with a tuft of beard still attached. After the examination of the bones was completed, the pieces of cloth were examined. They were shredded beyond recognition, but a black fez, which was part of the padres' costume, was found. Signore Marlato wrote in his deposition that Padre Toma was his father confessor and he knew beyond a doubt that this was his fez. Then was found a piece of broadcloth from the hem of a robe. When I examined it carefully I had no doubt that it was from Padre Toma's clothing. Then another piece of the same broadcloth was found, from the shoulder of a robe, and stuck to it was a piece from the edge of a cap such as the padres wore when it was cold. I was then even more certain, and I will now state the reason.

Some months before the padre disappeared, I was passing by the shop of a draper from whom I purchased winter material for my family. He showed me a piece of broadcloth as thick as felt. It had come in a shipment of broadcloth, but since no one was desirous of buying it, he was going to sent it back. If I wanted it he would give it to me for a good price. I thought it would do nicely for a robe for traveling in the snow, so I took at a very low price ten and a half ells, which was enough for trousers and a *kākūla*. As it was being cut, Padre Toma passed by and asked me what I was doing. When I told him, he said, "This would do nicely for me during the winter." And he took the rest, which was less than six ells. He asked the merchant if he had any more, but he said that not in all Damascus was any like it to be found. He had it made into an outer robe for the winter, and the two pieces of broadcloth found with the bones were of that very same broadcloth that in all Damascus only the padre and I had.

After the investigation was completed, written up and sealed by the investigators, it was turned over to the French consul. What I feel certain happened is that Padre Toma was murdered by only the Harārī servant and the barber out of greed for the money he had with him. They must have asked him to visit a sick person and taken him by surprise. When the padre's servant [136] saw that his master was gone long past his usual time, he set out to ask for him in the Jewish quarter. The murderers took him [on the pretext of] leading him to [the padre], fell upon him and murdered him too to keep him silent. The correspondence of their confessions proved the charge against them. However, the zealousness of Jewish leaders to defend the crimes of ignorant members [of their community] gave them a bitter draught. They attempt to establish the innocence of all members of their community, whereas, just like all groups, there are good and bad among them.

THE GOVERNANCE OF ALEPPO IS TAKEN FROM DAMASCUS AND GIVEN TO MIR AL-LIWĀ' ISMĀ'IL BEY.

During this year, A.H. 1255 [1839-40] the governorship of Aleppo was taken from Sharīf Pasha, and Ismā'īl Bey Mīr-Liwā' was stationed there as a military governor. Sultan Mahmud also sent many troops there to get the Egyptians out of Syria. Ibrāhīm Pasha wrote to Emir Bashīr to send troops to protect Damascus as a precaution against unrest, for most of the Egyptian soldiers were with Ibrāhīm Pasha. Emir Bashīr sent his son Emir Khalīl, who, accompanied by five hundred mountain men, made camp in the fields outside of Damascus. Ibrāhīm Pasha headed for Aleppo, where he gathered his troops and entered Turkey to meet the troops that were advancing on the Sultan's order to wrest Syria from him. He encountered them at Nizzīb, where a fierce combat took place and the imperial forces were almost victorious over the Egyptians. However, Ibrāhīm Pasha's bravery and experience in strategy won him the day with such a decisive triumph over the imperial forces that the *sar'askar* was forced to flee, leaving all his matériel as booty for the Egyptians—he was not able to save even his private papers, which fell into Ibrāhīm Pasha's hands. Among them was found an imperial decree appointing to the governorship of Damascus 'Alī Āghā Khazīna-Kātibī, who has been mentioned before, and a letter from the Empire to the *sar'askar* ordering him to send the decree of appointment to 'Alī Āghā as soon as he reached Aleppo, for the Empire had learned of his friendship with 'Alī Āghā from a former *amīn al-ṣurra.* Kāmil Efendi (for whom, when he later became governor of Damascus, I was family physician. I learned from his son 'Alī Bey that Khazīna-Kātibī was unaware of his appointment as governor and that ['Alī Bey's] father had been instrumental in obtaining this office for him because he had liked him when he met him in Damascus.) Ibrāhīm Pasha sent Ismā'īl Bey, the *ḥukmdār* of Aleppo, to Sharīf Pasha, the *ḥukmdār* of Damascus, and 'Alī Āghā was held under arrest in quarters in the government seat.

THE REASON FOR THE EXECUTION OF 'ALI ĀGHĀ KHAZINA-KĀTIBI AT DAMASCUS.

Sharīf Pasha had been vexed by 'Alī Āghā's standing with Ibrāhīm Pasha, so he convened a council to establish charges he trumped up against him. A number of sessions were held, and 'Alī Āghā was able to prove his innocence, as he truly was, but they never mentioned the decree of governorship to him. Finally all that was left for him to do was to write one more reponse and present it to the last session of the council. Everybody was expecting, as was I, that he would be exonerated and released the next day, for I had been informed of everything that went on during the sessions by Emir Maḥmūd, [137] Emir Bashīr's grandson who was in Damascus and attended the tribunal at Sharīf Pasha's order. But the next day he was not allowed to present his reponse but was summarily beheaded that morning in front of the seraglio gate and left lying there till the end of the day for all to see. He was seventy-two years old, but he was as vigorous as a fifty-year-old. It was a grievous day for all the people of Damascus, Muslims, Christians and Jews, because he had treated everyone well. No one expected he would come to such a horrible end at the hands of the Egyptians, for he had been very friendly with Ibrāhīm Pasha, who had also been strongly attached to him and had stayed in 'Alī Āghā's house when he came to Damascus. They were together day and night, and [the pasha] had taken such pleasure in his company and his telling of anecdotes that he had taken him with him on some of his excursions. He had gone with him to Nabulus, when Ibrāhīm Pasha had been in so much trouble, and great chivalry had been displayed by 'Alī Āghā and his men, some of whom had been killed in the battlefield. When Muḥammad-'Alī Pasha came to Jaffa, he had gone with Ibrāhīm Pasha to meet him. All his services had been rendered gratis, and he never accepted a position for himself from which he might profit, although Ibrāhīm Pasha had repeatedly offered him lucrative posts.

Once, when he and Ibrāhīm Pasha were at a drinking party with some officials in Jaffa, Ibrāhīm Pasha, in a state of intoxication, asked 'Alī Āghā, "How long are you going to refuse the posts I offer you in my service?"

"I am your servant in all you desire," he replied, "except for official posts, which I will not accept."

Ḥasan Bey al-Kaḥḥāla, the Damascene *mutasallim* of Jerusalem, was present and said to him, "Didn't you serve as *mutasallim* in Latakia and later as *mutasallim* in Hama?"

Ibrāhīm Pasha was fired up by the wine and said to 'Alī Āghā, "Were the viziers you served greater than me?"

"Oh, no," he said, "but they didn't ask me to account for my actions. The Egyptian state, however, punishes its servant if he accepts a gift of so much as a chicken, imprisons him and summons a Copt with his spectacles to write a formal charge and look at me sidelong as though I had murdered his father, saying, 'So-and-so has made a deposition, and so-and-so has made a deposition,' and the charge is for a chicken or a radish. I'm not going to make myself a prisoner for things like that, or for anybody's deposition. It's better for me to be free to accept a bull or a camel as a gift and not have to answer for it."

"I can arrange a post that will bring you more than you could ever hope for from gifts," said Ibrāhīm Pasha, "and then you would have no excuse."

"When God wanted to create heaven and earth," he said, "he made the fish in the sea, the animals on the dry land and the birds in the air. He made a paradise of every kind of tree anyone could wish for. Then he thought it would be good to create our father Adam, so he made him in his likeness, in absolute perfection, breathed into him the spirit of prophecy and made him ruler of all creatures, beasts, fish, birds, trees and grass, with no other human being to contend with. God kept for himself only one tree and forbade [138] it to Adam, but he disobeyed God and ate from it, even though he was a prophet. Now, no matter what you may give me, you cannot give me what God gave Adam, who nonetheless stretched forth his hand to what God had forbidden him. I am his son, and my nature must perforce be like his: I would not be restrained by your prohibition, and you would punish me. It is better for me to remain outside of official posts." Ibrāhīm Pasha agreed with this answer.

SHARIF PASHA KILLS EMIR JAWĀD AL-ḤARFUSH EVEN THOUGH HE HAD TURNED HIMSELF IN TO EMIR BASHIR'S PRISON.

Because the emirs of the House of Ḥarfūsh had been relieved of the B'albak region, from the proceeds of which they had lived and which they had ruled for many generations, they never ceased fomenting strife, because the pensions the government had given them were a pittance in relation to what they had realized from their land before it was taken over. Emir Jawād, one of the leaders, made open rebellion, but, since he did not stay put in any one place, the law was unable to lay hold on him until he himself tired of being a hounded fugitive and went to Emir Bashīr with three of his men and turned himself in. The emir released him and promised to try to obtain a pardon for him from the authorities.

As Ibrāhīm Pasha was absent in Aleppo, the emir had to write to the *ḥukmdār* Sharīf Pasha, who replied that the emir should send Emir Jawād and his men to Damascus immediately. Then he said to Emir Maḥmūd, who was still in Damascus, "I intend to kill Emir Jawād as soon as he arrives here. Will this anger your grandfather the emir?" [Emir Maḥmūd] answered that he did not know and would have to ask him. At once he sent word to his grandfather, and the reply came before Emir Jawād reached Damascus, along with a letter for Baḥrī Bey indicating that if a pardon was not possible, he hoped that his punishment would be commuted to something other than death since [Emir Jawād] had come of his own accord in obedience to [the emir]. The utmost was done to dissuade Sharīf Pasha to wait at least for an order from Ibrāhīm Pasha, but he replied, "I have written him concerning my desire to have him killed, and in order to defame the emir in Acre he himself killed the Nabulus shaykhs who had taken refuge with the emir." When Emir Jawād arrived, he summoned him to his office, sat him down and talked to him for a long time and dismissed him. Then he appointed agents to kill him and his followers, and they were beheaded before the seraglio gate. Such conduct pained the emir greatly and undermined his trust in the Egyptians, from whom he began to expect a loss of favor, as had happened to others.

It is obvious that the instinct for self love in all animals increases according to rank. Human beings are the highest, so [self love] makes them strive to eliminate everything that keeps them from getting what they want. Those who hold the highest power strive to destroy those who are beneath them in power in order to strengthen their own influence, and therefore you see a sultan endeavoring to weaken the power of his ministers, who strive to weaken the power of emirs, who try to weaken the power of shaykhs, who in turn weaken the ability of the peasantry to resist the authorities over them who are so desirous of expropriating the fruits of their labor. [139] The Egyptians constantly tried to disarm the populace in order to weaken their power to resist oppression and enfeeble the clan chiefs by enfeebling their men so they would be able to destroy them and then govern the peasantry as they wished, without opposition.

SULTAN MAHMUD DIES AND IS SUCCEEDED BY HIS SON 'ABDUL-MAJID KHĀN.

During this year, A.H. 1255 [1839] Sultan Maḥmūd died and was succeeded in the sultanate by his son Sultan 'Abdul-Majīd, who began the enactment of reforms in the conduct of the empire according to equitable rules and regulations.

Ibrāhīm Pasha had no rest from uprisings against him in various parts of Syria over the new levies the peasantry were not accustomed to pay. Before he could put down an uprising in one place, another would break out elsewhere. In general the time the Egyptians were in Syria passed in ceaseless struggles with the Empire and subjects, although there was great equity among the subjects under [Egyptian] rule and equality among the various communities: right was given where it was due, and no one was forced to pay for his rights. The councils gave decisions in cases without cost, and council members received a sufficient stipend from the government. Crimes could not be bought off with what was called "cash penalty," and no municipal council spent its income for government officials' personal benefit on things like carpets for the governor and *daftardār*'s houses, tribunals and offices and bureaux, about fifty altogether, oil for illumination of government buildings during Ramadan, banquets given by the governor for visiting dignitaries, repair of government structures, or other such things from which a town derives no benefit at all.

Let us mention an affair connected with Ibrāhīm Pasha to illustrate this. The effluent from certain parts of Damascus collected in a trench beyond the city walls in the direction of Bāb Sharqī, and horrible stenches from there plagued the houses of the nearby quarters, most of which were Christian, though some were Muslim. This filth sat there putrifying until the end of summer, when it dried up and was taken away by orchard owners and replaced by other useless stuff. It was possible to divert the drainage to the Nahr 'Aqrabā[ni], which irrigated only agricultural land and carried off much refuse from Damascus. However, a governmental order was needed to route it through land endowed to Muslim lepers. The inhabitants of the quarter petitioned Ibrāhīm Pasha for permission to divert the effluent at their own expense and for authorization to route it through the lepers' land, which it would benefit. He wrote to Sharīf Pasha to investigate the claim of detriment [to health] with physicians; if it was established to be so, a survey was to be made by engineers. If it was to be diverted through the endowment land, an estimate of the costs necessary to implement the project and a report of the cost-benefit should be made. Sharīf Pasha carried out the order and found out that [as it was] it was injurious to [the health of] all the inhabitants and could be diverted. A comparison of expenses was made and reports were sent [140] to Ibrāhīm Pasha, who ordered the necessary action to be undertaken at government expense, for [the government] was obliged to protect its subjects from harm, and they should not be charged for such a thing. And it was all done according to his order.

Another example is as follows. Once the butchers raised the price of meat so exorbitantly an executive order had to be issued to stabilize the price, and several advisory council members were appointed for that purpose. They bought a sheep, slaughtered it, averaged the expenses and weight and added to the price a fair profit for the butcher. It was announced that that was to be the price, and that it was not to be increased unless the council learned of an increase in price of sheep. After a while, although the price of sheep had not increased, it was brought to the attention of the authorities that the butchers not only had not acted according to the council's decision but also had kept selling at the old, high price. Ibrāhīm Pasha's order was issued that the difference be collected from them and that, instead of going to the treasury, it was to be spent on things of general benefit to the population, and this was done.

SIGNORE RICHARD WOOD, DRAGOMAN OF THE BRITISH EMBASSY, COMES TO KISRWĀN.

Then the year A.H. 1256 [1840-41] began. Previously Signore Richard Wood,[15] a dragoman for the British Embassy in the capital, had gone to Kisrwān. (He is now English consul general and Her Majesty's representative in Tunis.) He was there ostensibly to learn Arabic, for which he had engaged a tutor, Arsānyūs al-Fākhūrī, a Maronite priest, though his undercover purpose was to create means to undermine the Egyptian government in Syria. He took up residence in Kisrwān.

THE ANGLO-AUSTRIAN ALLIANCE WITH THE OTTOMANS AGAINST THE EGYPTIANS.

It was then learned that the English and Austrians had made a pact with the Ottoman Empire against the Egyptians,[16] and their ships appeared off the coast of Beirut with Ottoman ships. French ships also arrived, but they were unallied with the others. Egypt thought that France would take up defense with her, and so the Egyptians declined to accept the terms offered them, which were that the hereditary government of Egypt by primogeniture would be given to the descendants of Muḥammad-ʻAlī Pasha; Egypt would have autonomy in her internal affairs so long as she paid the Empire 60,000 purses annually; her soldiers and battleships would be fixed at a certain number; and Syria would remain in [Muḥammad-'Alī's] hands only for the duration of his life. All other [regions] held by him, such as the Hejaz and Crete, would be given back to the Empire. If he did not agree, in ten days Syria would be taken from him and he would be left with Egypt. Then another ten-day period of grace would ensue, after which, if he did not agree, Egypt would also be taken. Were it not for Muḥammad-'Alī's confidence that France would help him, he would not have refused the offer.

REBELLION SURFACES IN KISRWĀN; IBRĀHĪM PASHA FIGHTS BUT IS DRIVEN OUT; ENGLISH, AUSTRIAN AND OTTOMAN SHIPS COME TO BEIRUT; FRENCH SHIPS REMAIN NEUTRAL.

Ibrāhīm Pasha was faced with the reality of a rebellion in Jabal Kisrwān instigated by Signore Wood, who had summoned to help him Emir Khanjar al-Ḥarfūsh, from whose family B'albak had been taken and who was a cavalier renowned for his bravery and daring. It was said that with them were English agents provocateurs. Ibrāhīm Pasha took twelve thousand regular infantry soldiers against them, [141] leaving Sharīf Pasha as ruler in Damascus to place the English and Austrian consuls under house arrest and prevent them from seeing anyone if war broke out between their states and the Egyptians. He sent Yūḥannā Bey al-Baḥrī to stay in Emir Bashīr's palace and had the emir send his brave grandson Emir Majīd to accompany him. When Ibrāhīm Pasha arrived at the mountain with his soldiers, the men met him and a battle took place. The Egyptian troops were repeatedly defeated for a number of days, never achieving a victory. The English consul in Damascus, Mr. Wood, sent Rūfā'īl Mishāqa in secret to the emir to inform him of the decision of the allies and to tell him that the best course of action was to comply with the Empire. Rūfā'īl went and delivered his message. To the emir came also a secret request to send an emissary to meet with Admiral Napier in Beirut harbor. He sent Ibrāhīm Mishāqa in secret via Ṣaydā, from where he went clandestinely by sea to Admiral Napier. After deliberations, he returned to the emir via Ṣaydā. This was all done without the knowledge of Baḥrī Bey, who was resident in Bteddīn to keep an eye on the emir's actions. The emir was told of what the emissary had been given to understand by Admiral Napier, who, among other things, had said, "Ibrāhīm, tell your emir that Syria is at present at the mercy of the wing of this hat of mine. Let him not deceive himself: the Egyptians must absolutely be expelled."

THE VALI OF EGYPT REFUSES THE TERMS OFFERED HIM.

When Muḥammad-'Alī Pasha refused to accept the terms offered him, an order was issued to expel the Egyptians from Syria by force. Before the bombardment of Beirut, Baḥrī Bey returned to Damascus, where the authorities were executing anyone accused of speaking about the progress of the war. One night Signore Marlato, the Austrian consul, spent the evening with me, and talk turned to the presence of the ships at Beirut. I said that they would do best to concentrate first on the weak spots, and lastly to besiege Acre, so that there would be time to conquer it.

"Do you think so?" he asked.

"I am not alone," I said. "Everybody thinks so."

"They are there primarily because of the many foreign merchants who might be injured," he said. "What do you think the likelihood is that Acre will withstand the English?"

"Ibrāhīm Pasha battled it for seven months," I replied, "although those inside were weak. Now those inside are strong. The fortification has been increased, so we must calculate the strength of the English over the Egyptians with a view to the fact that their position is stronger now than it was in the past."

He laughed and said, "Woe betide the nation that falls subject to the wrath of the English."

"Acre is very strong," I said, "and Ibrāhīm Pasha has increased its fortifications."

"I know it well after its fortification," he said. "It will hold up under English fire for six hours, no more."

That evening one of Baḥrī Bey's relatives who was a friend of mine was present. He had heard everything that had transpired, and I was worried that the news would reach the authorities from someone other than me. As the party was breaking up I asked my friend [142] to go immediately to Baḥrī Bey and tell him for me what had been said. The next morning a messenger came to ask me to meet with Baḥrī Bey.

"So-and-so has told me what the Austrian consul said to you," he said. "I want to verify with you that there is no more or no less of it." I told him what had taken place. "Now I want you to get out of him whether England and Austria are going to fight with the imperial fleet. Let me know as soon as possible."

"The consul does not spend every evening with me," I replied. "If I go to him with such a question, he may have suspicions that will prevent him from telling the truth. I beg you to give me time to think of the best way."

That evening the consul came to me, although it was extremely rare for him to come on two successive evenings. When we spoke I said, "I am still thinking about what you said, that Acre can be taken in six hours. I wonder if the ships are really there to protect the property of foreigners in Beirut, as you said last night, and maintain neutrality, or are they there to bombard along with the Ottoman ships."

"The only reason England and Austria are here is to bombard," he said, "but the French will stay neutral."

The next morning I went to Baḥrī Bey and told him what had happened. He appeared to be more worried and asked me to repeat my words again, which I did. "God will punish the French," he said, "if they remain neutral, because by doing so they will destroy our efendi [Ibrāhīm Pasha]. Were it not for their promises of assistance, our efendi would not have challenged the English and made an adversary of them."

"Bonaparte vexed the kings of the earth but was unable to take Acre when it had only one wall and Jazzār Pasha was inside," I said. "His ability could scarcely have matched that of one battalion of Egyptian troops, in the face of only a few of whom the imperial hosts have been unable to stand. Now Acre has two walls and has been fortified many times more than before, and inside are Ibrāhīm Pasha's soldiers, not Jazzār Pasha's weak forces."

"Bonaparte was unable to take Acre not because of its fortifications but because of the English force that came against him. Add to that the revolt of the French republic against him, which cut off aid and hoped he would be destroyed here in this land, so he was forced to abandon Acre. Otherwise what is Acre? What is something greater than Acre in relation to the might of the great kings? Were the power of the Turks alone coming against our efendi, he would not care how great their numbers and preparation were. I have heard him say many times that in their wars the women of the Morea were braver than the Turks. You have seen him with your own eyes do battle in Homs, you have seen how huge hosts flee from a few Egyptian soldiers. As though it were not enough that we have to worry about repelling an enemy approaching from outside, we are forced to contend with the Maronites of north Lebanon, who deny the good done by Egypt to the Christians."

"Will you permit me to speak candidly, without [143] restraint? Otherwise I will remain silent," I said.

"I wish you would speak with complete freedom about whatever you wish," he said, "especially regarding the situation in Mount Lebanon and how to stop the deterioration there, for, if the Lebanon is with us, it is our backbone for more than Acre. Since you know it well, you must know what is good and what is bad for it."

"It is a rule proven by experience that if the usurper of a country does not do well in his policy and institutes measures unfamiliar to the people," I said, "then it will certainly fall into another's hand as it fell into his.

"Firstly, the Lebanon used to pay the provincial treasury thirteen hundred purses annually. Then you imposed an increase of four thousand purses annually and constantly demand men to help you in your wars without paying them for the time they are kept from making a living for their families. Many of them are killed, their wives are widowed and their children orphaned. They lose their means of livelihood, and all they get in return is hunger, nakedness, wailing and weeping. They are in severe poverty: there are no poorer than they in all Syria. True, the Lebanon produces from a thousand to fifteen hundred *qinṭār*s of silk, but most of it belongs to the emirs, shaykhs, monks and people of cities like Beirut and Tripoli. The people retain little of the produce of the mountain, and the population is around 300,000. They have no land for planting grain to eat and are forced to buy from outside. The price they get from producing silk and other things goes to buy grain. If you take away the rocks from their arable lands, you would not have enough left to equal the fields of one village in Damascus, Homs or Hama. That is why you see some of them living from service to the emirs or entering monasteries or becoming priests in order to live from religious service to the peasants. Others leave their land to serve city people, and many of the old men, with their wives and children, go from door to door in the cities begging a crust of bread to stave off hunger. You see no city from Aleppo to Egypt not crowded with these Lebanese.

"Secondly, which clan chief have you left in peace as he was, or not humiliated and taken his territory? That which used to accrue to him and be spent on the people, you have appropriated to your treasury. Yes, only Emir Bashīr has been left as he was in the Lebanon, and that by special order of Muḥammad-ʿAlī Pasha; however, afterwards you imposed on the poor of his territory an increase of four thousand purses a year more than the old assessment, making the amount due about three times what it had been. If this were not enough, you took extreme action, doing things that blackened his good name, which was considerable among all the inhabitants of Syria, by demanding that he turn over men who had taken refuge with him to negotiate clemency with you. When he sent them to you, instead of accepting [144] his plea, you cut their heads off.

"Thirdly, Syria is not used to servility, as Egypt has been since the time of the Pharaohs. [Syrians] have grown up in freedom and are familiar with their clan customs; they cannot be reduced to servility in a short period of time. You have been hasty in trying to make them servile by taking their sons for the military without establishing a term of service. A man whose son is taken knows that he will not return unless

Peasant.

he is disabled in battle and no longer able to work, if indeed he escapes from death in these neverending wars. Moreover, only sons are taken in disregard for the old age of parents or the tender years of infants, all of whom are dependent upon them. These things I have mentioned are enough to account for the people's turning [against you]. Only those not liable to ruin, such as merchants who have no sons eligible for the military and others like them, desire the Egyptian government to remain because it maintains law and order internally and externally.

"As for northern Mount Lebanon, before the Egyptians took over Syria, it was always inclined to resist Emir Bashīr. In 1236, or 1821, they mounted a widespread rebellion against him. The clergy supported them and the patriarch remained silent, particularly during the patriarchy of Yūsuf Ḥbaysh."

"How do you know," asked Baḥrī Bey, "that the patriarch does not support the emir? They are of the same sect."

"I knew him before he entered the clergy, when his name was Shaykh Ya'qūb of the House of Ḥbaysh, an important family in Kisrwān. Because of his ecclesiastical learning he was promoted to what he became. In 1811 or thereabouts I was apprenticed to a trade with the sons of Fransīs Bāz, whose uncles Jirjis and 'Abdul-Aḥad were killed by the emir. Shaykh Ya'qūb lived in Dayr al-Qamar for a long time while he had pending in the Islamic court with Shaykh Sharaf al-Dīn al-Qāḍī a case against a man named Shaykh Shamsīn, who, I think, was of the Khāzin family, partisans of Shaykh Bashīr Jumblāṭ. Shaykh Ya'qūb spent most of his time with the Bāz sons, studying language with one of them. He used to attribute the lack of success of his case to the emir's desire to spite him, and this he did in language that eloquently bespoke of his hatred for and envy of the emir. This I heard myself from his own mouth. Since he is light-complected[17] and quick-tempered, I do not think that clerical garb would go far in changing that, especially since it is said that his major characteristic is a love of status. A holder of spiritual rank should be balanced by his equal in temporal rank. The patriarchate of the Lebanon should be balanced by the emirate. Emir Bashīr has never been one to let the clergy have free rein to go beyond their religious boundaries and meddle in temporal affairs. This has always been a bone of contention between him and them. [145]

"If the south Lebanon is not consolidated, the contagion will spread from the north, for the Maronites [in the south] are about half the population, and they are the fiercest Maronites of the mountain. The shaykhs who bind them together with the Druze to act as one are Jumblāṭ, 'Imād and Nakad, who have been exiled to Egypt. If they are placated and returned appeased to their places, they can stabilize the south, and the north will fear them. This is what I think, though I may be mistaken."

"I too think the best course of action would be to bring the shaykhs back," he replied.

THE SHIPS BOMBARD BEIRUT, THEN ṢAYDĀ, AND TAKE CONTROL OF THEM.

When the fleet bombarded and took control of Beirut, Ibrāhīm Pasha ordered Sharīf Pasha to place the English and Austrian consuls under house arrest and station military guards at the gates. A few days later Sharīf Pasha received a letter from Ibrāhīm Pasha in which he stated, "The English consul's house has two gates. What is the use of guarding only one of them?" And that was true. Talks with the Druze of the Ḥawrān were being concluded by a dragoman of mine, and there was no necessity for the English consul to talk and broadcast announcements. I was concluding what had to be done in secret, not out of hatred for the Egyptians or in partisanship with the Turks, but acting as an agent of the state to which I belonged. When it assisted the Egyptians I acted in accordance with its wishes; when it assisted the Turks, I conducted myself so. In both cases I endeavored to avoid the pitfall of personal ruin while striving to help the underdog as much as I could.

The failure of the Egyptian troops was realized, as the men of Kisrwān were assisted with men and war matériel. The Egyptian army, afflicted by malaise and demoralization from constant warfare and loss of men, began to detest its own government. When Ibrāhīm Pasha saw that his army fell back in all engagements, he took it to Zaḥle in the West Biqā‘ and waited for his voracious adversary to follow him. There was level ground suitable for military operations, and he could pounce upon his opponent. However, the people of the mountain would not meet soldiers on level ground and were satisfied with the gains they had made in driving the army from their land.

EMIR BASHIR GOES DOWN TO ṢAYDĀ, PROMISED THE GOVERNORSHIP OF THE MOUNTAIN, BUT HE IS SENT TO BEIRUT AND THEN EXILED TO MALTA.

In the course of its actions in the mountain, the Empire had taken control of Ṣaydā, whence a guarantee of quarter was dispatched to Emir Bashīr if he would come down to Ṣaydā on a determined day to receive orders for the mountain. Immediately he sent word to his grandson Emir Majīd to escape from Ibrāhīm Pasha's camp and come to him in all haste. He told Andreos Mishāqa to take inventory of the available cash in his personal quarters, which was found to be 8,370 purses, which which was then equivalent to 64,000 French pounds. He ordered 8,000 purses put [146] in sacks marked with the amounts, placed in a strongbox and brought to him with the key. [Andreos] did as he was ordered, asking, "What shall I do with the rest of the money?"

"Leave it out to be sent to the patriarch," he said.

"Our lord the patriarch is not presently in need," he said. "You need it more."

The emir sighed and said, "I need to send it to the patriarch now more than anything I know of." (This well illustrates his lack of reliance on him.)

As soon as Emir Majīd received his grandfather's order he managed to escape from the Egyptian camp, but he was not able to reach his grandfather until the very day the emir was supposed to arrive in Ṣaydā, and the emir could not go down before his grandson escaped lest Ibrāhīm Pasha get angry and kill him. The next day the emir went down to Ṣaydā with all his sons and grandsons. Khālid Pasha came out with soldiers to meet him and greeted him with all honor. He wrote to Beirut of the emir's arrival in Ṣaydā, and in response they asked for him to come to them, so he set out as requested. During the interview they chastized him for disobedience and accepted no apology, giving him the choice of residence anywhere he wished, other than Syria and France. He chose the English in Malta and was given some time to arrange him affairs. He made him arrangements, and the patriarch sent him Father Niqūlā Murād to accompany him for religious service (or better, to spy on the emir's activity). The emir set forth with his whole family and coterie—including Father Niqūlā—to Malta, where they took up residence.

The governance of the Lebanon was given to Emir Bashīr al-Qāsim, who has been mentioned previously. He was weak in strategy and implementation of rule and so was welcomed by the emirs, shaykhs, patriarchs, bishops and even governors of the area because he was incapable of opposing them, and they were unconcerned with the common welfare. His weakness strengthened their hold and weakened the ability of the peasantry to resist their rapacity, which the former Emir Bashīr, who is known as the Great, never let happen. One can see with one's own eyes what the notables of the Lebanon came to after him. They have called him the weakest of their leaders, who shed much of their blood and the blood of the peasants, but they never established that he dealt illegally with a single person. Is the present situation of the leaders of the country in general better than it was? Were those who were killed during his period of office—and they justly killed—more than half a generation? Would their number equal the number who have been unjustly killed in one day in one town after he left the Lebanon? Let a fair comparison be made.

Ibrāhīm Pasha remained in Zaḥle with his soldiers, as has previously been said. One day a rumor spread in Damascus that Firdaws Bey had come to his brothers in Damascus. He was the son of 'Alī Āghā, a *mamlūk* of Nāṣīf Pasha al-'Aẓm, who was with the grand vizier during the French campaign in Egypt in 1801. 'Alī Āghā had married [Nāṣīf Pasha's] daughter and by her had sons and daughters, one of whom Sharīf Pasha [147] had married. Firdaws Bey was with the imperial troops. One day Baḥrī Bey summoned me and asked me whether I knew Firdaws Bey had come to Damascus and whether I had gone to greet him. I replied, "I had heard of his arrival and, by chance, I met his brother 'Ākif Bey at someone's house and asked about him. He told me that he was in Beirut, not in Damascus."

"Word has it that he has come to Damascus and is in hiding in their house," he said. "I want to learn the truth. They are friends of yours, and you are a physician with access everywhere. I want you to investigate the rumor."

I had already ascertained that he had come by way of Ḥāṣbayyā, where he had asked Emir Sa'd al-Dīn for men to get him to Damascus in safety. They dressed him in mountain clothes, and [Emir Sa'd al-Dīn] sent with him his brother Emir Khalīl, who escorted him to the gates of Damascus and then returned [to Ḥāṣbayyā]. But how could I make myself party to the arrest of a man they would most likely kill? Therefore I said, "The beys are my friends, and I visit them, but, not being their physician, I do not enter the private quarters. Even a physician does not enter private quarters unless asked to."

"Who is their physician?" he asked.

"Rūqān Ṣaydaḥ," I replied, "whose daughter you want your nephew to marry." That answer satisfied him.

Damascus then had a special ruler called a *mutasallim*, Ḥāfiẓ Bey, a son of the 'Abdullāh al-'Aẓm who had been deposed from the governorship of Damascus when the Wahhābī took possession of the Hejaz and cut off the pilgrimage route. This bey was one of those who had been friendly to the Egyptian rule. As he was also a relative of Firdaws Bey, Ḥāfiẓ Bey[18] found out that Firdaws Bey had been in Damascus and met clandestinely with Sharīf Pasha in his house before returning to Beirut.

"You must report this to our efendi Ibrāhīm Pasha," [Ḥāfiẓ Bey said to Baḥrī Bey].

"If it is relevant, but I must have proof to defend ourselves with when it is denied."

"It is relevant," he said. "Come, let us have lunch together at my house. There you will see the truth of the affair."

He went with him, and after lunch he put Baḥrī Bey in a small chamber in his quarters with a curtain hung over the door. Then he summoned a nephew of Firdaws Bey and asked, "At what time will your uncle Firdaws Bey be coming out of the private quarters so I may see him?"

"My uncle left three days ago," he said. "He has not been gone from us above two days."

"Then he did not wait to meet with your in-law Sharīf Pasha?"

"The pasha came to him the second night, and they spent the evening together by themselves upstairs. The next night my uncle left."

After this he dismissed [the boy] and asked Baḥrī Bey, "Do you have any doubt left?"

"No," he said, "but pretend you have no knowledge of this affair so that we may remain in Ibrāhīm Pasha's good graces and conduct ourselves according to his will."

Baḥrī Bey was no longer able to keep this secret from Ibrāhīm Pasha if, on the one hand, he was to remain loyal or if, on the other, he wanted to protect himself from danger if the news reached Ibrāhīm Pasha from Ḥāfiẓ Bey that Baḥrī Bey knew of the affair and had not reported it. Yet he was afraid of [148] harming Sharīf Pasha, who was a special friend of his and had always watched out for his and 'Abbūd al-Baḥrī's interests.

The strategy I learned of in this affair to avoid Ibrāhīm Pasha's retribution was [as follows]. Baḥrī Bey met with Sharīf Pasha and told him what had happened, saying, "Your life is in danger. If you flee, perhaps you may not lose all your wealth and possessions. If I keep the news from Ibrāhīm Pasha but the person who told me does not keep it from him, he will consider me a traitor and kill us both." They agreed on the following plan of action: Baḥrī Bey wrote clandestinely to Ibrāhīm Pasha to summon him to report on Sharīf Pasha. The Sharīf Pasha was told: "It is necessary to speak with you on an important matter, [but] the present situation does not allow you to leave Damascus. You will therefore send us Baḥrī Bey for me to speak with." Sharīf Pasha informed Baḥrī Bey of this, and he went quickly and reported to Ibrāhīm Pasha what he knew of Sharīf Pasha's actions. [Ibrāhīm Pasha] flew into a rage and said, "He must be killed!"

"Yes," said [Baḥrī Bey], "but we should look to the consequences before acting. If you allow me to speak, I shall speak." He gave permission and Baḥrī Bey began, saying, "Sharīf Pasha was no stranger to you. He was one of your relatives. You raised him and treated him well and increased his rank and annual stipend from the treasury to three thousand purses, although there is no authority for giving someone of his rank more than five thousand piastres a month. He has also acquired more estates in Egypt and Syria than can be counted. In addition to this, you made him military governor over Syria, and there is no greater position than that. If you cannot be confident of such a person, can it be expected that pashas and lower ranks in your service be trustworthy? They are not related to you and have not acquired anything like what Sharīf Pasha has. If your adversaries plot to corrupt the most intelligent person you have to rely on, a relative who has been showered with your beneficence and has no military force they are in awe of, can we hope they will not plot to corrupt our military leaders, of whom they are in awe? Now, if you kill Sharīf Pasha, we fear that there will be others like him among the military hierarchy who will turn against [you], rebellion will break out among the troops and the adversary will grow in strength against us. The best thing for you to do now is to take the troops down to Damascus and do what you think appropriate."

Ibrāhīm Pasha was pleased by Baḥrī Bey's idea and went to Damascus, where his troops began to assemble.

THE ALLIED FLEET BOMBARDS AND SEIZES ACRE.

The English and Austrian consuls were expelled from Damascus and were seen safely to the province of Ṣaydā. Then the Anglo-Austro-Ottoman fleet went to Acre [149] and did battle. They were easily able to take it by superior force in the space of three hours and twenty minutes. The rapid conquest was aided by there being many crates of gunpowder that had come from Egypt and had not been stored but were left in the open between the two walls. During the battle a bomb fell among them, and they caught fire, [exploding] in such an unexpected fashion that the soldiers inside Acre fled, leaving no one to defend it, and so it was taken. When the coast was cleared of the Egyptian army, the Empire took possession of the lands adjacent to the coast without doing battle. It also seized control of the Biqā' and B'albak when Ibrāhīm Pasha left Zaḥle with his soldiers for Damascus. Then Emir Sa'd al-Dīn al-Shihābī went to Khālid Pasha in Ṣaydā and got arms for the men of Ḥāṣbayyā, whose weapons had been taken by the Egyptians.

Aḥmad Āghā al-Yūsuf al-Kurdī, who has been mentioned before, was appointed *ḥākim* of Damascus and given troops to drive Ibrāhīm Pasha out and take possession [of the province]. He came to the village of Sa'sa', about twenty miles west of Damascus. The news reached Ibrāhīm Pasha on a dark and rainy night; he left immediately, taking some soldiers and two cannons to confront [Aḥmad Āghā], and battle broke out. Ibrāhīm Pasha scored a victory, and the others were scattered in defeat, Ibrāhīm Pasha returning with his troops to Damascus. Then Aḥmad Āghā al-Yūsuf took his men and camped in the village of al-Baṭrūne, a dependency of the al-Zubdānī area, about twenty-five miles from Damascus, waiting for Ibrāhīm Pasha to leave so he could enter [the city].

Ibrāhīm Pasha held a tribunal with the pashas and emirs of his army, Sharīf Pasha and Baḥrī Bey, who was first of all charged by Ibrāhīm Pasha with being a traitor for having been in correspondence with the enemy. Baḥrī Bey denied it, and the tribunal asked for proof of the charge, either the correspondence with Baḥrī Bey's signature or some [other] proof sufficient to establish the charge. Ibrāhīm Pasha replied, "It is impossible that the enemy should turn over to us the correspondence with his signature, but it is sufficient proof that Baḥrī Bey rented a house for his family in the Christian quarter. If he were not secure from the enemy, he would not have done it."

A reply to this was asked of Baḥrī Bey, who stated, "The weather is very cold in this season, and I have children and a wife eight months pregnant. Since her family is in Damascus, I asked our efendi to permit me to leave them with their relatives, and he granted permission." He produced the written permission from Ibrāhīm Pasha and said, "Nonetheless, if our efendi wishes to retract his permission, I will take my family with me, even if they die on the road. If I had contact with the enemy, I would not have given my grain to the troops and taken a voucher for it against the treasury of Egypt." He produced the voucher. The tribunal declared him innocent. The charge was probably a connivance between the two of them for some purpose or other.

Then Ibrāhīm [150] Pasha charged Sharīf Pasha with treason. Baḥrī Bey spoke in his defense, but Ibrāhīm Pasha insulted him by saying, "This does not concern you. You are here to judge, not to defend." And he fell silent. Sharīf Pasha denied the charge.

"I ordered you to place a guard over the English consul and forbade him to meet with anybody," said Ibrāhīm Pasha. "Yet you left a door [unguarded] for anyone he wanted to come through. If I heard of it on Mount Lebanon, how is it you didn't hear of it here in Damascus? It is impossible. Moreover, Firdaws Bey, your brother-in-law, came here on behalf of the enemy, and you met with him in his house. Shouldn't you have arrested him?"

"Firdaws Bey did not come, and my visit to their house one night was to see my wife's family, as people are accustomed to do during Ramadan," said Sharīf Pasha.

"Was it or was it not being rumored in Damascus that Firdaws Bey was here?" asked Ibrāhīm Pasha.

"Yes, it was rumored," he said.

"That you did not look for him and that you did not inform me of what was rumored prove that you knew he was here and that you intended to keep it quiet for reasons of your own," said Ibrāhīm Pasha. The tribunal agreed with this. Then Ibrāhīm Pasha said, "What proves your collusion with the enemy is your intention to keep all your womenfolk in Damascus, although I gave you permission to keep only your Damascene wife at her family's house, not the rest, who are from my father's harem. You were to take them with you, but you would be content with nothing less than keeping them all here, even those who have no connection to this country.

"Moreover, as our troops have gathered in Damascus, we are in need of grain for the soldiers and fodder for the horses, mules and camels. All our followers who had grain have offered it to us and taken vouchers on the Egyptian treasury in payment. Orders were issued under your seal to all villages of Damascus to tender their grain at the [established] price, with hoarding punishable by death. I myself went to the villages and, finding grain stored in some of them, hanged two of the owners. You have such-and-such amounts of grain stored in such-and-such a place you did not tender. Do you intend to keep it as booty for our enemies, or is it rather because you feel so safe from them?"

Sharīf Pasha did not have sufficient proof to refute the charge, so Ibrāhīm Pasha ordered his sword taken and him kept under guard in the barracks by a general, Muṣṭafā Pasha, and held incommunicado to all save Baḥrī Bey, and this order was carried out.

IBRĀHĪM PASHA AND HIS TROOPS LEAVE DAMASCUS FOR EGYPT.

Ibrāhīm Pasha again received orders from his father to return quickly to Egypt. When his troops from Aleppo and Turkey were all gathered in Damascus, around seventy thousand of them, he decided to quit Damascus. At that time Baḥrī Bey called for me and said, "My brother Germanos is advanced in years and cannot withstand the hardship of travel to Egypt by land during these bitterly cold and rainy days; he and his small son must be kept hidden by you until [151] the country settles down, for turmoil may break out when we evacuate. Aḥmad Āghā al-Yūsuf, who is coming as governor, is a special friend of yours. Through him you may arrange a safe conduct for my brother and his family, for you are their physician."

On the night before the sixth of Dhū'l-Qa'da 1256 [30 December 1840], when the Egyptians were to depart Damascus, I summoned Khawāja Germanos and his son Bāsīlā under the cover of darkness and hid them from prying eyes with a Druze youth from my town who was a sergeant in the Egyptian army.

The next morning the Egyptian army began to move out along the

Ḥawrān road, and by evening not one of them or their followers was left. Ibrāhīm Pasha stood at the seraglio gate, surrounded by the notables of Damascus bidding him farewell. He turned to them and said, "Take care lest anything disturb the peace of the city between now and the time a ruler comes. If the least disruption occurs, I will come back myself and take revenge on you." They promised him to maintain order, so he mounted and set off after his troops.

The next day I remained at home in order to check on the situation in the town, for it was now without a ruler. At noon I received news that a Christian youth, the son of Khalīl al-Ṣaydnāwī, had been killed. The Christians were blaming the Jews for his death because he had not been acquainted with the ignorant Muslim of the Maydān district who had killed him. The Jews were being suspected because the victim had humiliated them in the Padre Toma affair, and so [it was thought that] they had taken revenge by arranging for a Muslim to kill him.

Part Five

1840-1873

AḤMAD ĀGHĀ AL-YŪSUF ENTERS DAMASCUS AS RULER ON BEHALF OF THE EMPIRE.

On the third day Aḥmad Āghā al-Yūsuf entered Damascus with a troop of soldiers, the rule was turned over to him and a proclamation of law and order was made. He executed two poor Kurds and patrolled the city himself. The Christians, who had worn white turbans during the Egyptian reign, had now put on black turbans for fear of being exposed to degradation by ignorant Muslims. When he spied some of these Christians he told them publicly that they should wear what they were accustomed to and that he would take retribution on any who opposed them. The day after his arrival I went to greet him and congratulate him on his appointment. I told him about Khawāja Germanos and his son, who were at my house, and asked for a safe conduct for them.

"The good the Baḥrī family has done cannot be forgotten by me or anyone," he said. "They have a family member in me." Immediately he gave me a sealed decree of imperial immunity to keep as a document from the sultanate itself. I asked permission to bring them to him that evening and returned with the paper and, giving it to Khawāja Germanos, told him what had happened. He breathed a sigh of relief but was still wary of hindrance by rabble in the street. Shaykh Ḥammūd Nakad had previously come to Damascus and stayed with me for a period of time while I was using my influence on his behalf. Then he took a house for himself and settled in Damascus. I summoned four of his strongest armed men, each of whom could handle a multitude, and after sunset we set out with Khawāja Germanos and found Aḥmad Āghā waiting for us in his private quarters. He received the *khawāja* graciously [152], offered him sherbets, coffee and tobacco and very kindly told him that he was prepared to do whatever he wanted. [Khawāja Germanos] departed thanking [God] for [Aḥmad Āghā's] good character.

NAJĪB PASHA IS MADE GOVERNOR OF DAMASCUS; 'ALAWW PASHA IS POSTED TO THE HEJAZ; SIGNORE WOOD COMES TO DAMASCUS AS BRITISH CONSUL.

Then 'Alaww Pasha, who had fled from the Egyptians, came to Damascus. [In theory] the governorship was still his because the Empire had not officially recognized the Egyptian rule in Syria. A few days later he was posted to the Hejaz; and Najīb Pasha, the father of Maḥmūd Nadīm Pasha the former grand vizier, arrived in Damascus as governor. He had been Muḥammad-'Alī Pasha's *qapūkatkhudā* in the capital, and therefore he summoned Khawāja Germanos for an interview and received him with all respect.

Signore Wood was appointed by the Empire to make all necessary arrangements in the Damascus area and the province and to oversee [imperial] agents. In his official correspondence he signed himself "Richard Wood, Deputy of the Sublime Empire." Thereafter the British consulate in Damascus was given to him, and he remained by imperial decree as a supervisor of provincial tax collectors. A word in praise or dispraise from him was influential with [the Empire]. He advised that two persons be discharged, and the Empire discharged them as he had advised. All communities and sects of the Damascus area—emirs, shaykhs, ulema, religious leaders, chieftains of tribes and clans, and peasants—loved him very much for his conduct with everyone. He employed me as a dragoman.

EMIR BASHĪR IS BROUGHT BACK TO THE CAPITAL FROM MALTA.

Let us return to Emir Bashīr the Great. After he took up residence in Malta with his sons and grandsons and all the rest of his coterie (including Father Niqūlā Murād), M'allim Buṭrus Karāma went to the capital to work on the emir's behalf at the Sublime Porte. After a while he summoned Emir Amīn, the emir's youngest and most intelligent son. After some time he was promised they would all be allowed to return to their country if his father would come to [Constantinople] from Malta. He wrote to his father, who proceeded at once with those who were with him to await imperial forgiveness. Khalīl Pasha, the sultan's son-in-law, had gone to Beirut to make [financial] arrangements for the Lebanon that would be satisfactory to the Empire; however, he was unable to effect its wishes and returned to the capital. [His lack of success] was attributed not to any shortcoming in his ability or to uncooperativeness on the part of the people of the Lebanon to change their custom, but to the emir's being in the capital, so without an inquest [the emir] and all with him were exiled to Safranbolu.[1] They were sent out into the sea on a raw, stormy day and were almost engulfed, but they arrived safely in the place of exile. Then Shaykh Ḥammūd Abī-Nakad followed them into exile and remained with them away from his family until he died. Emir Qāsim, the emir's eldest son, also died there.

After a while it was found that their exile had no effect on the situation in the Lebanon, so they were brought back to the capital. Then a deal was made that the Empire would give the rulership of the mountain to Emir Amīn and the old emir would stay in the capital until the son went to the Lebanon. If his dealings were honest, then the father would be permitted to return to his home. [153] As soon as Father Niqūlā discovered this plan, he wrote to his master. Immediately a petition was sent to the Sublime Porte, saying that they had heard of the Empire's intention to send Emir Amīn, who was more tyrannical than his father: all implementation of the rulership of the mountain was to be in his hands, and if he came there the country would be ruined. They complained bitterly of both Emir Amīn and his father. The letter was signed by all the emirs, shaykhs and bishops of the Maronite sect and presented to the Empire. However, in the capital a decision had already been made to send Emir Amīn, who went to the Grand Vizier Rashīd Pasha to receive orders for the rulership of the Lebanon. The vizier handed him the petition against him and said, "We have approved you, but what can we do if your bishops and leaders of your community do not want you?" He left in despair, and several days later he converted to Islam, saying that it was a mistake to belong to a religion whose leaders were like that.

THE DEATH OF EMIR BASHĪR AND HIS SONS IN THE CAPITAL.

[Emir Amīn] was followed [in his conversion] by Emir Majīd and Emir Mas'ūd, sons of his brothers Emir Qāsim and Emir Khalīl, who died of grief some time later. Four months later Emir Amīn died a Muslim. Thus their father also, in the extremity of grief over his sons and helpless old age, died of no apparent illness at the age of eighty-four. The Empire celebrated his funeral, and he was buried in the Armenian

Catholic church.[2] Thereafter his family returned to Syria. Emir Majīd died a Maronite, but Emir Mas'ūd died a Muslim. The Bayt al-Dīn palace was sold for a pittance to the Empire by the emir's widow and was turned into the residence of the chief administrative officer of the Lebanon. Thus ended the rule of the Shihābs.

THE JUMBLĀṬ, 'IMĀD AND NAKAD SHAYKHS RETURN FROM EGYPT.

Shaykh Nu'mān Jumblāṭ, Shaykh Khaṭṭār 'Imād and Shaykh Nāṣīf Nakad, all of whom had been in Egypt, forbidden to return [to the Lebanon], were awarded the rank of *mīrālāy* and given the title of bey by Muḥammad-'Alī Pasha (eventually the shaykhs of the mountain all unduly assumed this title, which should not be used unless properly bestowed, except at the ministerial level.). He then ordered them to return with their retinues to their homeland, which may have been at Ibrāhīm Pasha's request, but [in any case] they did not reach there until after he had left Syria and arrived in Gaza, and Zakariyyā Pasha had arrived in Jaffa with imperial troops. Ibrāhīm Pasha had no further need of them, so they went to Jaffa and then to the mountain, where their men rejoiced at their arrival. Nāṣīf Bey was met outside Ṣaydā by the notables of Dayr al-Qamar with rejoicing, singing and firing of guns. Since the shaykhs' houses had been destroyed, the Mishāqa family invited him to stay with them until he could make other arrangements. He accepted their invitation because they were special friends of his.

Shaykh Sa'īd Jumblāṭ, who was an officer in the regular Egyptian army, managed to slip out before Ibrāhīm Pasha left Damascus and make his way to his house. He got back all his possessions, which had been confiscated to the treasury during the governorship of 'Abdullāh Pasha sixteen years before. [154] Inasmuch as the property, which was tied up in lien for its income, had been included in the state property of the Lebanon, the treasury kept on taking everything due it from the Lebanon and lost nothing.

STATE TAX ASSESSMENT IS BEGUN IN THE LEBANON.

When the Empire wanted to assess the state taxes on the mountain at what the people had paid to Emir Bashīr the Great, the Druze did not object. However, the Christians of Kisrwān and vicinity and their leaders objected to this, claiming that they had been tyrannized by the amount taken from them before. They held many meetings attended by prominent men and metropolitans of the Maronite sect to discuss this matter. It was not possible to yield to the wishes of the Empire, and they complained bitterly and represented to the provincial governor that their income should be based on the fact that they netted from an oke of silk no more than twelve piastres (even if they had made it a hundred and twenty, no one would have believed them, because an oke of silk sold for more than that).

They should have made their basis of comparison a true one and explained that only one third of the property belonged to the three hundred thousand persons on the mountain. The other two thirds belonged to the emirs, shaykhs, endowments of monasteries, patriarchs, metropolitans, churches and Druze temples, most of which were exempt from state taxation. The burden was borne by the poor, and of their income there was not enough left to provide a minimal standard of living. Therefore, thousands of mountain people, old men, old women, wives and children, were begging in the cities, and thousands more worked for wages carrying rocks, earth and clay for construction, while thousands more were in service in the houses and shops of city dwellers in Syria and Egypt. All of this was due to their inability to make a living in their native land, for the soil of the Lebanon could never produce enough for those who lived there, no matter how hard they worked.

The Lebanon, from the borders of Ṣaydā to near Tripoli, does not exceed in length twenty French leagues, or in width, from al-Dāmūr to Rās al-Jabal, which divides it from the Biqā', around eight leagues. Its area is approximately a hundred and sixty leagues square, much of which barren landscape in which crops do not thrive—not to mention the stones and rocky land in which nothing can be planted. In general half of the Lebanon is not fit for planting anything; the other half, eighty square leagues, contains 3,750 persons per league, whereas the land of Europe, with all its crowding and overpopulation, does not have more than a quarter the population per league that the Lebanon has with its population of 300,000. It is known that no matter how expertly cultivation of the earth is carried out, a square league cannot produce enough for a thousand persons to live on. Therefore, the generality of the people of the Lebanon were hard put to maintain even an impoverished existence. The nobility, although their holdings were vast, had less income than expenditure—indeed most of them were sunk in a sea of debts, and half their income went to pay interest to traders [155] in cities outside the Lebanon.

It would have been better for the people to reveal their poverty to the Empire, for it would doubtlessly have had mercy on them and done something for their relief and emelioration of their situation. However, their leaders' policy only permited them to make a show of strength to the Empire so that it would fear their might. With this policy, which is not suited to our age, they made the Empire detest the people of the Lebanon, and they brought down upon their own poor people one disaster after another—and on themselves too. The [nobility] had formerly been autonomous in their regions, but they began gradually to decline from their former estate until they reached the level of commoners. True, there are still some of them engaged in official positions such as *qāymaqām* and bureau chief, but such positions do not distinguish them from commoners as they used to, for they can also be held by any person of merit from the common folk. Emirs, shaykhs and guildmen are all alike: they can be appointed and discharged. Whatever distinction the nobility of the Lebanon had has been wiped out.

The leaders of those enclaves were not content to complain and make false representations but even wrote petitions to the Empire concerning their complaints. One of the things they wrote was that the poll-tax should be paid by those who needed the Empire's protection, but they did not need it, for they could protect their neighbors. This they submitted to the governor to forward to the Empire. He advised them to revise it, and they did go over it several times, but they only increased in arrogance and conceit, so the governor was obliged to forward it. When one of them informed me of the contents of the petition, I was heartsick. He asked me why I was so distressed, and I replied, "This is no complaint of inability to pay the state taxes assessed on land. Subjects have the right to complain to their overlord of a burden, and he is bound by conscience to adjust it to what can be borne. But in the matter of the poll-tax, it is impossible to cease paying it. First of all, it must be paid as a matter of religion, for Lord Christ commanded it to be paid and 'rendered unto Caesar.' Secondly, when the Muslims conquered Syria, they made a pact with the Christians to pay the poll-tax: if they do not pay it, their community will have broken faith and the sultan's community will be legally bound to make war on them. A refusal by the Lebanese to pay the poll-tax will necessarily have dire consequences."

THE EMPIRE HAS A CHANGE OF HEART TOWARD THE CHRISTIANS OF THE LEBANON BECAUSE OF THEIR MISCONDUCT.

The Christians' misconduct and lack of foresight made them think they had might, but in comparison to the might of the Empire it was that of a sparrow against a hawk. Nonetheless, the outward display of firm resolve made the Empire mistrust them, especially when they openly proclaimed their allegiance to a foreign state that was alien to them. In addition to this was Emir Bashīr al-Qāsim's incompetence to rule the Lebanon, mainly because of his jocularity and coarse speech with Druze leaders, who were repulsed by such a thing, especially since they had grown up during the time of Emir Bashīr the Great, who was never seen to jest or to utter an indecorous word, even about his enemies.

The Druze made the most of the Empire's change of heart toward the Christians [156] of the Lebanon, especially when friction broke out between the people of Dayr al-Qamar and B'aqlīn. A Christian from Dayr al-Qamar was hunting with his gun on B'aqlīn land, and a Druze from there objected. Bad blood surfaced between them, and helpers came to both sides, the fray ending in the discharge of weapons. The cry reached Dayr al-Qamar that the people of B'aqlīn had killed their men, so the Nakad shaykhs got on their horses and rode to the place to quell the disturbance, and the men of Dayr al-Qamar too came armed and running. When they arrived they found the men of B'aqlīn gathered together and some men slain. Shots were fired and a fierce battle was fought until the B'aqlīn men were driven back with all those who had come to help them. The Dayr al-Qamar men did not leave until they had penned [the B'aqlīn men] in their village. Even after all this the shaykhs were still able to separate the two parties. There were four Christians of Dayr al-Qamar killed, and thirty-two of the Druze of B'aqlīn. The B'aqlīn Druze had been particularly friendly with the Christians of Dayr al-Qamar, but this incident changed that and provoked all the Druze to take revenge on Dayr al-Qamar, especially since Jumblāṭ and 'Imād, who did not have a town as the Nakads did, wanted to diminish the Nakads' strength, which lay in their men, but [the Nakads] were unaware of it. This occurred in 1841.

When the news reached Damascus I was on my way to see Sulaymān Efendī, the commisioner of supplies for the Pilgrimage, on business pertaining to the emirs. He asked me what I knew of the B'aqlīn incident. I told him simply what I had heard. It never occurred to me that the province of Damascus had any connection to what went on in the province of Ṣaydā. At that time Najīb Pasha, one of the most intelligent men of the elite corps of the Empire, was governor of Damascus. He relied especially on Sulaymān Efendī in his affairs because he was one of the few men skilled in administration. He was originally a Jew who had converted to Islam with his father in Jaffa.

Thereafter I used to see many prominent Druze of the Lebanon in the streets of Damascus, and I chanced to meet some of them at Sulaymān Efendī's. At that time I suspected that clandestine arrangements had been made by the government against the Christians of the Lebanon. Then I learned that Shaykh Qāsim al-Qāḍī from Dayr al-Qamar had come to Damascus and and returned to the mountain, taking with him loads of bullets and guns. I had seen him at Sulaymān Efendī's. I then decided that he intended to attack Dayr al-Qamar, but I could not conceive that the Nakad shaykhs would permit such a thing in their own town, which contained the best of their men. Then I thought that Shaykh Qāsim al-Qāḍī was a close relative of theirs and would not do anything against their will.

There were many people from Dayr al-Qamar in Damascus, both merchants and craftsmen. I met with the reasonable ones, and we discussed what was going on and what things might come to, and that all this had come about over hunting quail. It was in the best interest of the town and countryside to mediate a truce [157] in a manner that would prevent injury from occurring. We parted with an understanding that they would write to the notables of Dayr al-Qamar about it, but nothing ever came of it.

HOSTILITIES BREAK OUT BETWEEN THE CHRISTIANS AND THE DRUZE OF THE LEBANON, AND THE EMPIRE CLANDESTINELY AIDS THE DRUZE.

One day, while the people of Dayr al-Qamar were going about their business, the Druze of the Manāṣif, who had entered the town by night and hidden in Druze houses, unnoticed by the Christians, sprang at them. At the same time Shaykh Khaṭṭār al-'Imād came with his men from the upper part of town in the north, and Shaykh Sa'īd Jumblāṭ appeared with the men of the Shūf from the east. His brother Nu'mān Bey, fearing the consequences, had turned back half way there. The people of B'aqlīn came from the lower part of town in the south and spread out to the west. Against the Druze were many Christians, and the fire of war between the two sides blazed up.

*[3]The Christians whose houses were near the Druze sought refuge with the shaykhs, but they killed them. Not only that, but they killed the Christians who served them and had gone from their homes into exile with them. The war between the two sides grew fierce. The Mishāqa family, however, were safe because of their friendship with the Nakad shaykhs, and Shaykh Ḥammūd lived near them. One of them yelled to Ibrāhīm,[4] "Stay quiet in your house. This doesn't concern you." But his only son Khalīl was then in the marketplace with his uncle Rūfā'īl, and when a rumor spread that he had been shot, Ibrāhīm went to see what had happened to his son. The women of the quarter gathered in the Mishāqa house with everything of value they had, for they knew of

Dayr al-Qamar.

their friendship with the Nakad shaykhs. However, their hope was in vain: the Mishāqa house was assaulted with gunfire from the direction of Shaykh Ḥammūd's house by about seventy armed men. Andreos Mishāqa was killed along with a builder who was working there. All the women in the house gathered with an aged servant in a chamber overlooking the town and locked the door. The Druze, quite unlike their custom to respect womenfolk, attacked and tried to break down the door, not to outrage the women but out of greed for plunder. The servant stood behind the door, and when they could not break it down they fired at the door, shattering it and killing the servant. The women screamed as loud as they could, but there was no one in the house to come to their defense, for Andreos had been killed, Jibrā'īl had gone to the Maronite patriarch to try to settle the dispute between the two sides, and Ibrāhīm had gone to look for his son.

When the insurrection began, Rūfā'īl was in the marketplace conducting business, confident in the presence of Shaykh Ḥammūd near the house, but when he heard the sound of gunfire in that very house and the women's screams, he rushed there with four young men of the neighborhood. When they arrived and found the house filled with Druze and the women screaming and crying for help, the only thing he could do was to attack with his four companions. They fired until they drove them from the house by force, but of the four one was killed in this fray. It was never known how many of their adversaries they had hit. They got the women out and took them to the palace, which was fortified, for the emir was in residence and the men would guard it well.

The Druze were unable to take possession of more than the western section of town, where the houses were widely spaced and Shaykh Ḥammūd lived. The Druze quarter above was impossible to guard, especially since many of the young men of the town were away working in Ṣaydā, Beirut and Damascus. Nonetheless, the Druze were many and waylaid all who came to help Dayr al-Qamar. That day Shaykh 'Abbās, son of Nāṣīf Bey Abī-Nakad, made a drive with a huge host from the Nakad square toward the house of the Ṣūṣa *khawāja*s, around which were three churches. (It was the custom in the mountain in times of unrest to place valuables inside houses of worship, where they would be respected by the victor.) There [Shaykh 'Abbās, fired upon by] the Christians, fell from his steed, mortally wounded by a bullet. Those who were with him fell back, but the fighting continued.

The next day three hundred Druze assaulted the lower, western part of town and approached the Catholic church of St. Elias. Eight individuals went to drive them off, among them Rūfā'īl Mishāqa and Niqūlā Jabbūr al-Ṣūṣa, whose bullet had struck Shaykh 'Abbās. These eight resisted the attackers and drove them from town. Not content with that, they pursued them past the built-up part of town to the *khshākhīsh* (the mountain word for cemetary[5]). M'allim Buṭrus Karāma's house overlooking the cemetary had been occupied by the Druze of B'aqlīn, and when they saw the eight in pursuit of their fleeing partisans, they opened fire on them. Niqūlā al-Ṣūṣa was hit in the stomach and died before reaching his house; Rūfā'īl Mishāqa was hit in the arm. It became infected, and after much treatment he recovered, although he developed a fistula that never healed and has lasted until today.

That day Shaykh Qāsim al-Qāḍī, who has been previously mentioned as having taken bullets and guns from Damascus, attacked the town from below the Church of St. Elias with a host of his men. In fierce fighting a number of the attackers were killed, among them this Shaykh Qāsim, and the rest were routed.

When the Druze took possession of a house, they looted everything and burned it. In the Mishāqa house was untold wealth in silks, fabrics from their looms and cash, aside from the furnishings of the house such as carpets, brass and silver and what the neighbors had deposited with them, thinking that since they were friends of the shaykhs [they would be safe]. They were the first to be inflicted with death, plunder of their property and burning of their house.

Two days passed and no one came to help. Nor did the vizier of the province give an order for the Druze to be stopped. On the third day the Christians of al-Bārūk moved and came to Bteddīn, but when they saw Dayr al-Qamar surrounded by the adversary and the smoke of fire and gunpowder inside the town, they did not dare to approach. Among them was a brave Greek Catholic named Ibrāhīm Ṣaqir who tried to embolden them, the fiercest men of the Lebanon, but they would not advance and returned to their homes. This very Ibrāhīm, however, went toward the town with his cousins, the Druze firing on them from outside and the people of Dayr al-Qamar firing from inside the town, thinking they were more adversaries, until he got near and waved a handkerchief. Then they directed their fire at the Druze who were firing on him, so he could reach the town in safety. Shaykh Ḥammūd had taken control of the Sidonian quarter, torched it and reached the back of the garden attached to Buṭrus al-Chāwīsh's house, in which were eighteen men. It was surrounded, and the number of men grew and grew (it is said there were more than five hundred), but they could not take it for the fire of the beleaguered men inside. Ibrāhīm Ṣaqir and his cousins went to help the Chāwīsh house, entering from the side the Druze had not taken. When he was inside, he got up on a low garden wall and fired his carbine at the Druze host. Then he fired pistols, and so did his cousins and all those in the Chāwīsh house. He drew his sword and jumped down from the wall into the midst of the enemy, shouting at them to frighten them and strengthen his comrades' resolve. They did as he had done, wielding their swords and yataghans and giving their opponents no opportunity to reload their guns. They wounded and killed many and drove the rest from the quarter by force.

The third day passed in attacks and counterattacks, and the battle had its ups and downs, but the Druze were unable to reach the Khunūq quarter on the eastern side of town, because the houses were too close together and their own houses were too far away. The fighting continued into the fourth day, when al-Sayyid 'Abdul-Fattāḥ Ḥamādī al-Iskandarī came as an emissary from the vizier and the Druze hosts withdrew to their homes. He returned, taking Emir Bashīr with him, and many of the Christians of Dayr al-Qamar left their homes because of the imposts their shaykhs still placed on them, even though they had been reduced to poverty with the burning of their houses and pillaging of their property in the marketplaces. The Mishāqa family went to their brother in Damascus until the situation on the mountain should calm down. Then the *mīrālāy* Muṣṭafā Bey brought imperial troops into Dayr al-Qamar, but it was apparent from his conduct that he favored the Druze over the Christians.

In this affray 109 Christians were killed, including those who had sought refuge with the shaykhs and been treacherously murdered and those who had been killed on the roads. The number of Druze slain was never known for certain because they kept it quiet, but it was ascertained that thirteen of their shaykhs were killed. The Christians said that they opened no cemetary vault to bury their dead without finding many dead Druze therein. It is no wonder that they lost so many, because one who assaults another within his own walls is more liable to be shot.

When the people of Dayr al-Qamar saw their shaykhs' behavior, they turned totally against them and begged the government to relieve them of the rulers of the mountain and send a ruler on behalf of the provincial governor. This request was granted.

THE DRUZE WITH SHIBLĪ AL-'ARYĀN AND HIS GOVERNMENT-APPOINTED TROOPS ATTACK ZAḤLE; HE IS WOUNDED, AND THE DRUZE ARE DEFEATED IN A FIERCE BATTLE.

One month after the Dayr al-Qamar incident the Druze gathered to attack the Christians of Zaḥle. They were joined by Shiblī Āghā al-'Aryān and the government-appointed horsemen of whom he was in charge. They drew up opposite Zaḥle and assaulted. Fierce battles took place, but they were unable to cross because the people of Zaḥle had no enemy within, as Dayr al-Qamar had. After a number of encounters the affair ended with the defeat of the Druze, many of whom were slain. Shiblī Āghā al-'Aryān was hit in the neck by a bullet; for a while he lingered at death's door, but after a time he recovered. This uprising ended, but the people of Zaḥle began to construct barricades around the town to protect themselves from enemy treachery. When the authorities learned of this, they forbade it and decreed that they must tear down what they had constructed, and it was done. (This may have been to facilitate a later attack.)

After this, the Druze of the lower Shūf provoked a fight with the Christians of Jazzīn. The Christians met them under the leadership of Abū-Samra, a young man from the village of Bkāsīn near Jazzīn. He caught the Druze unaware, and they fled. He pursued them to their villages, Nīḥā and others in the lower Shūf renowned for fierce men, but they did not stand to face him until he entered the village of 'Ammāṭūr, the chief village of the Shūf, bent on destruction. In the meanwhile the regular troops stationed in al-Mukhtāra with Sa'īd Bey Jumblāṭ had arrived to take revenge on the men of Jazzīn. They did not want to face [the soldiers] and so returned to their homes, although about forty of them were seized and sent to the governor in Beirut. After a time they were released.*

'UMAR PASHA ARRIVES AS MILITARY GOVERNOR OF THE LEBANON.

Some time later the brave 'Umar Pasha came on behalf of the Empire as a military governor over the Lebanon. He was originally an Austrian who, deserting the army, had gone to Ottoman lands, become a Muslim and joined the imperial service, in which he had advanced. Upon arrival he smoothed over the situation on the mountain, seized prominent Druze shaykhs and sent them under guard to the governor in Beirut. This was done so that the people could see that the incidents had not occurred with the connivance of the government or in vengeance.

A short while later the Druze assembled against 'Umar Pasha and cut off the water supply to the Bteddīn palace, his residence. He went out to them himself and threatened them, and they released the water. Next they continued to gather in the lower Shūf, where they were joined by Shiblī al-'Aryān and his horsemen, even though he was employed by the government of Damascus. 'Umar Pasha summoned around two hundred Albanian soldiers from Ṣaydā. The Druze ambushed them at Nahr al-Ḥammām, but they scattered their attackers and reached 'Umar Pasha. When Shiblī al-'Aryān, with his cavalry and the Druze hosts, had advanced to al-Samqāniyye, less than half an hour away from the Bteddīn palace, they were enjoined in battle by ʻUmar Pasha and his forces. He ordered them attacked, and they did not stand for even half an hour before they scattered to save themselves. It appeared that the Empire did not approve of this action, for a short time later ʻUmar Pasha was dismissed.

Then an arrangement was made whereby the mountain was divided into two by the Beirut-Damascus road.[6] The north, in which there were scarcely a thousand Druze, was ruled by a Christian emir, and the south by a Druze emir, although there were three times as many Christians as Druze in the south, and it was they who had borne afflictions, not the northerners. Dayr al-Qamar was outside both divisions, for the inhabitants had requested that it be ruled by a special agent of the provincial governor.[7]

THE CHRISTIANS OF ḤĀṢBAYYĀ MOVE TO ZAḤLE TO DISTANCE THEMSELVES FROM TROUBLE; THE DRUZE FALL UPON THEM ON THE WAY AND MASSACRE THEM, AIDED BY ARMED MEN FROM THE BIQĀʻ.

In 1847 an uprising broke out against the Christians of Ḥāṣbayyā. Since the Druze there were fewer than the Christians, they were joined by the Druze of the Ḥawrān. The Christians, however, chose to leave their homes and go to live in Zaḥle, away from the strife. They departed from Ḥāṣbayyā with their belongings, escorted by Emir Bashīr, the brother of Emir Saʻd al-Dīn. When they reached the fields of Rāshayyā, they were fired upon by the Druze. They defended themselves as well as they could, and Emir Bashīr left nothing to be desired in his defense of them. In the end the Druze defeated them and killed around three hundred of them, looting everything they had. Those who fled were killed by armed men from the Biqāʻ, while those who returned to Ḥāṣbayyā were slain by the Druze there. However, those who gathered around Emir Bashīr reached Zaḥle in safety.

A few days later the government of Damascus summoned Emir Bashīr and appointed him to the rulership of Ḥāṣbayyā, but it would allow no prosecution of the criminals. The Christians, based on what they had seen in this incident and what had happened previously in Dayr al-Qamar and Jazzīn, did not think the Empire innocent in this action, which had been deliberately done to weaken them. This cannot be doubted by any intelligent person.

THE WRITER GOES A SECOND TIME TO EGYPT.

During this year[8] I journeyed to Egypt, where I stayed for eight months. I met often with the *amīr al-liwā'* Clot Bey, the supervisor general of health who has been mentioned before. Since I had a desire to see some practical anatomy, [329] he ordered the teachers of the Qaṣr al-'Aynī school to allow me to attend their surgical and post-mortem operations, to which I paid careful attention. Then he invited to his house some of the teachers who had studied in Paris, the most famous of whom were three gentlemen, Aḥmad Efendī, Ḥusayn Efendī al-Rashīdī and Ibrāhīm Efendī al-Badāwī. He ordered them to examine me. At first I balked at this because I had never studied in a school, but he insisted and I gave in. My examination took place, and thank God they did not pose a single question I didn't know. They approved of my answers and gave me a certificate signed and sealed by the Bey.

I toured the ancient monuments, entered the pyramids at Giza, saw the observatory at Būlāq and the Engineers' Palace, met with the learned Rifā'at Bey and saw Pompey's Pillar and the obelisk in Alexandria, along with everything one could want to know about in that marvelous realm, and then I returned to my home in Damascus, overwhelmed by the kindness of the Egyptians.

THE WRITER JOINS THE EVANGELICAL SECT; HE IS PERSECUTED BY THE PATRIARCH MAXIMUS AND FORCED TO WRITE RESPONSES.

When I returned I was absorbed by religious ideas. Sometimes I thought I must not know what Voltaire, Rousseau and the likes of them had known. How could those philosophers submit to the everlasting damnation of their souls and reject all religions? If they had found proof of the turth of any one of them, they would have joined it. Other times I would revise my thinking, for the sage Newton, who was more learned and intelligent than any of the others, realized through the power of his intellect the force of gravity that dominated all existence by merely observing an apple fall from a tree. He also realized, without ever going there, that the earth was flat for twenty-six miles around both poles. [330] These were things that the most brilliant minds had not comprehended. With all his vast erudition and towering intellect, he was the fiercest in clinging to religion and in opposing those who rejected it.

During this period I came across a book translated into Arabic and printed in Malta. It was written by Mister Keith, an Englishman, and was entitled *Evidence of the Truth of the Christian Religion.*[9] I determined to read it, intending to have a look at the methods the clergy uses to hoodwink the common people and spread their fabrications among the feeble-minded. When I had read a bit of it, I began to believe in the excellence of this learned man, for I saw that he spoke a language unlike that used by the scholars of my church, who wrote of things that were abhorrent to nature and unacceptable to sound minds. Thereafter I began to read the book more closely, comparing his quotations with their sources in scripture. I had no sooner finished reading it and checking his citations than I was convinced of the truth of the Christian religion. What the leaders of my church taught and the fables they told had no basis whatsoever in Christianity; it was all an invention of priests, and not only was it unsupported by scripture, but most if it flatly contradicted it. It was simply to enhance the power of the ecclesiastical mantle, to amass the wealth of the people and to enslave them.

When I realized the truth of the situation, that there was no true Christianity except that which scripture explicitly states to us, I thought it best to leave my church, to abandon my standing with my brothers and relatives, preferring [331] a clear conscience by being among the few evangelicals in Damascus, whom the traditionalists call heretics because they reject the teachings of hypocrisy and consider God's Word sufficient.

After reading repeatedly the scriptures, three books by traditionalists in refutation of Protestant belief and numerous books by Protestants in refutation of the traditionalists, I left my church in 1848. My inquiry led me to believe that the Protestants were the only Christians who acted in accordance with the Gospel and who did not swerve from it in any way, and that the Papists were the farthest of all from the teaching of the Gospel—and this only if we can count them as Christians at all and not relegate them to being a nation of heathens beyond the pale of Christianity.

Then I made myself known as an evangelical. When the Patriarch Maximus was unable to convince me of the truth of the Papist sect and bring me back to his party, he directed at me in his sermons, his writings, his conversations and his exhortations all the anathema commanded by Papist dogma. He left no stone unturned to injure me and made me realize what the enemies of a man of truth can inflict upon him. I bore it all patiently, for I had the strongest proof of the truth of what I had embraced. Yes, I wrote much against their teachings, but I never interfered with them. When they published slander of unshakeable evangelical beliefs, I took up the cause and revealed to them the error of their teaching with proofs from scripture. [332] He anathematized me with his word and that of his congregations, so I anathematized him with God's word and that of His Prophets and apostles. In all I wrote eight works against their teaching. They were printed and became well known, although I was not learned enough to undertake such a labor: (1) *The Reason to Follow the Gospel*, 1848; (2) *Evangelical Responses to Traditionalist Fables*, 1852; (3) *A Response to a Friend of the Catholic Sect in Homs to Persuade Him of the Truth of the Evangelical Sect, of Which He Was Convinced and Joined*, 1852; (4) *Unveiling the Face of the Anti-Christ*, 1860; (5) *Gospel Proofs Against the Fables of the Papists: A Refutation of a Work by the Jesuits*, 1863; (6) *Exoneration of One Falsely Accused by the Patriarch Maximus Maẓlūm*, 1854; (7) *A Refutation of Pope Pius IX's Encyclical Inviting the Protestants to Enlightenment Through His Vatican Council*; (8) *Proof of the Weakness of Man: A Response to a Friend Who Follows the Teachings of Voltaire.*

Books that have not been printed: (1) A treatise on the career of the Patriarch Maximus and his scheming to attain the position he has, though he was of an obscure origin. I sent him a copy of this because he had published an [account of his] career filled with boasting and containing scarcely a shred of truth, attributed to one of the bishops of his see and published in Arabic and French. [333] (2) A treatise in refutation of what Ibn al-Ḥamūya addressed to me as a catechism for his people criticizing the evangelical sect; (3) "The Shihābī Treatise" on the fundamentals of Arabic musical modes, written at the request of a Shihābī emir,[10] (4) a long work on arithmetic entitled *al-Tuḥfa al-Mishāqiyya*, and (5) *Kitāb al-mu'īn* on the calculation of days, months and years, with appendices containing tables of correspondences for a hundred years for the Western, Greek, Coptic, Hebrew and Islamic months, and the occurrences of solar and lunar eclipses for the longitude and latitude of Damascus beginning in 1870.

I will always be grateful to the loyalty of Mister Wood, the British consul in Damascus, who, although a Catholic, earnestly defended me against the Patriarch Maximus' attacks. I do not deny that, according to papist doctrine, the patriarch's position obliged him to annihilate those who opposed their teachings. How many thousands of their opponents have they annihilated in the past? But we are thankful for the Creator's kindness and blessings that those who came after them have broken their vainglory, as the Apostle John says in his Revelation. After the death of the patriarch I was free of opposition. He was followed in rapid succession by two patriarchs, Lord Clemendos and then Lord Gregorios, who is [patriarch] now. I had been friends with both of them from childhood and remained so. They did nothing to vex me, and I am not barred [334] from visiting or friendly relations with the present [patriarch], even though he is a student of the Propaganda.

I confess that the Catholic clergy in the east, along with most of their followers, still have the old Christian spirit and do not accept the excesses of the western theologians.

In 1858, when the governor of Damascus was Muḥammad Pasha Qibrişlī, the Druze of the Ḥawrān rebelled. He took troops and fought them, but without success. They seized his cannons, and he returned to Damascus without them. Mister Wood, the English consul, got them back and turned them over to the government.

In 1859 I was appointed as vice-consul at Damascus for the United States of America.

In 1860 Ṣādiq Efendī, who is now vizier, came to Damascus as supervisor of the political bureau, and his counterpart went to Beirut. Then the governorship of Damascus was given to the general of the army corps, Aḥmad Pasha, who got along very well with everyone. Ṣādiq Efendī did not have much contact with *cancellieres*' offices but met often with some of the Druze shaykhs from the mountain and the emissaries of those who were not present themselves. Whenever an incident occurred on the mountain he used to go himself. From these interferences of his it was thought that the efendi's presence had something to do with the policy for the mountain, veiled under the name of policy for foreigners, for when his work was done he returned to the capital and was not replaced by anyone for dealing with foreigners.

A Christian said that he had seen in [Ṣādiq Efendī's] reception hall a letter from the capital [335] in which he was told: "Now that you have finished your work, give instructions to the governor to act accordingly and come to the capital." After Ṣādiq Efendī left Damascus, the governor's conduct toward the Christians changed, which proves that he received instructions he had not had before. His subsequent acts will be described later.

The Druze of the Lebanon began to provoke strife by killing a group of Christians on the open road. A band of them also came by night to the monastery at 'Ammīq, near Dayr al-Qamar, and murdered the abbot, Athanasius Na'ūm while he was asleep in his bed. Then the Druze of the Nakad estates came to Dayr al-Qamar and fought a little, with a few on both sides killed, before retreating. It was apparent from Sa'īd Bey Jumblāṭ's conduct that he was aware of the plan carried out in Dayr al-Qamar but was unable to publicize it. He went to the Bteddīn palace and summoned the Catholic metropolitan, Jibrā'īl and Rūfā'īl Mishāqa and a number of other friends of his, and took them to his house in al-Mukhtāra. Rūfā'īl Mishāqa returned to Dayr al-Qamar on business, and after it was taken care of he decided to take his family down to his brother Ibrāhīm, who had settled in Beirut after the Incident of 1841. His son Khalīl worked as a dragoman and *cancelliere* in the

Dragoman.

British consulate general. Ṭāhir Pasha, who had come with imperial troops and taken up residence at Dayr al-Qamar, forbade him to leave the town, as he had also forbidden the rest of the Christians to leave. The Druze shaykhs were very hesitant to meet with him. [336] Rūfā'īl wrote to his brother Ibrāhīm of what was happening. He in turn reported it to the [consul] general, who immediately wrote in strong terms to Bashīr Bey Nakad to send Rūfā'īl and his family out of Dayr al-Qamar at once and get them to Beirut in safety. After repeated writing, one of Bashīr Bey's strongmen came to Dayr al-Qamar and took them to Beirut. The consul general also wrote to Bashīr Bey Jumblāṭ, charging him with [the safety of] Jibrā'īl, as did the British consul in Damascus. In truth it was not necessary to caution Sa'īd Bey, for had he been able to prevent the uprising he would have, but his hands were tied and he was powerless to prevent it.

Ṭāhir Pasha disarmed all the Christians. Inasmuch as the town was surrounded by Druze on the outside and had imperial troops inside, they could not resist. Sa'īd Bey took the Christians who were with him and the metropolitan and delivered them to Ṣaydā in safety. The very day Ṭāhir Pasha finished disarming the Christians, the Druze came in to slaughter them like sheep, even those who fled to the troops in the palace. Had they fled to their enemies they might have found some compassion in them, but the soldiers helped to slaughter them until blood flowed in rivers. They did not leave a single Christian who did not have a Druze to protect him or help him escape. The pillage, killing and burning lasted for three days. The governor, whose residence was in al-Ḥāzmiyye outside Beirut, received word of the massacre the very day it took place, but he did not budge. The consuls repeatedly pleaded with him to go up to Dayr al-Qamar [337] to save lives; he could have reached it in five hours, but it took him three days. Buṭrus al-Chāwīsh's house was still surrounded, but the vizier did not allow him to be informed of his rescue until [the house] had been taken and smoke from it could be seen rising in the air. The town was in utter ruins: only women wailing over their slain men and children were left—without food, furnishings, clothing aside from what was on their backs, or shelter, for everything they possessed had been plundered, their houses torched and their men killed. They became refugees in the cities to beg their daily bread, a sight that would melt a heart of stone.

The Druze then spread out in pursuit of the Christians, from the gates of Beirut to the gates of Ṣaydā and Ṣūr, killing everyone they could find, even monks in monasteries, which they ransacked and burned. By chance they came upon Emir Bashīr al-Qāsim, their former ruler, going down to Beirut, and killed him.

Then the Druze went to Jazzīn and the surrounding region. Since there had been no imperial troops there to disarm them, they were able to oppose their adversaries. After some men from both sides were killed, the victory went to the Druze, and the Christians of that region scattered outside the Lebanon. Among them was a man who reached the village of Jbā' in the Shqīf region and sought and received refuge with Shaykh 'Abdullāh Ni'ma, a scholar who had attained the degree of *mujtahid* in the Shi'ite sect. Now, this shaykh had excellent qualities, his conduct was praised by those [338] of all sects who knew him, and he carried more weight among the Shi'ites than a patriarch does among Christians; nevertheless, some of the Druze pursued the Christian into Shaykh 'Abdullāh's house, murdered him before the shaykh's very eyes and looted his house. When the Mutawālī shaykhs heard that their leader had been dishonored, they rose up against the Druze. However, the vizier prevented them, reaching them from Beirut in one day. Had he traveled the way he did to Dayr al-Qamar, he would not have come in less than a full week! Upon arrival he forbade the Mutawālī shaykhs to oppose the Druze.

Emir Sa'd al-Dīn had resigned the rulership of Ḥāṣbayyā and gone to live in Damascus, and the rulership had been given to his son Emir Aḥmad, who was greatly favored by Aḥmad Pasha, the Governor of Beirut, who addressed him like a father. He asked him to go to Ḥāṣbayyā to collect the outstanding taxes to the treasury and gave him troops to accompany him. When the emir informed me of that, I said, "This is not a good time either for him to leave Damascus or for the outstanding taxes to be collected, since all that remains is owed by the Druze and their shaykhs; the Muslims and Christians have paid everything they owed. Therefore, the whole [financial] burden of the troops to collect will fall upon the Druze and no one else. Most likely there will be an uprising against you, particularly during this time of insurrection in the Lebanon and dispute between your house and Sa'īd Bey Jumblāṭ. It is patently obvious that the government stretches forth its hand to help the Druze. It would be better for you to make an excuse to the governor for not being able to undertake the collection at this time, at least until things in the Lebanon settle down. [339] If we annoy the Druze now and they do not revolt, they will go to help their cohorts in the Lebanon, and there will be no one for us to collect from anyway."

The emir approved of what I said and offered an apology to the governor, who refused to accept it and ordered him to take the troops. It did not occur to me that a trap was being laid for him. He set out with the soldiers commanded by a *mīrālāy* and took them to the emirs' palace. He also had a cannon. When he demanded of the people the outstanding taxes for the treasury, the Druze openly proclaimed their disobedience, gathering in the villages of Shwayyā and 'Ayn Qinyā above Ḥāṣbayyā. The Druze of Rāshayyā also came to help them, bringing with them Shaykh Abū-Ṣāliḥ, their religious leader, a pious man around ninety years old whose word was unquestioningly obeyed. The Druze of the Ballān and Majdal Shams, a dependency of the Ḥūle, who were renowned for their bravery, came ready to attack Ḥāṣbayyā. The Christians met them with gunfire, and after a minor battle in which a few from both sides were killed, the Christians were driven back and fortified themselves in the palace. The Druze attacked, looted and burned the houses, the soldiers never venturing forth from the palace to defend them.

Emir Sa'd al-Dīn kept insisting that the *mīrālāy* take action, so he ordered his troops to fire on the Druze, but they fired without hitting them. They fired the cannon once but claimed it didn't work. The Druze did not dare to attack the palace because it was too strong and there were armed men inside. In this fray Shaykh Kanj Abū-Ṣāliḥ from Majdal Shams was severely wounded and hovered for a time at death's door. The *mīrālāy* grieved over him and went to visit him in Shwayyā. The day he died [340] he awarded his brother a sable in his stead. Then he said to the beleaguered Christians, "I cannot get the Druze away from you unless you hand over your weapons." In view of their situation, they were in no position to argue lest the troops join the Druze against them. So they handed over all their weapons, which he had loaded on donkeys as though sending them to Damascus. As soon as they left Ḥāṣbayyā, the Druze took them, and the Christians had no doubt that he was in connivance with them. Therefore some of them decided to flee to Marja'yūn, which was about four miles away, but the soldiers commanded the windows of the palace and would not allow anyone to leave.

The consuls of Damascus demanded that the governor send an officer of the Kurdish troops to bring the Christians from Ḥāṣbayyā to Damascus, and it was decided to dispatch Aḥmad Bey Ajalyaqīn, who requested permission to fire upon the Druze if they interfered with the Christians escorted by him. When permission was denied, he replied, "I cannot allow my name to be dishonored by bringing the Christians out and then not defending them from their enemy." In his stead the vizier sent one of his aides to Rāshayyā and summoned from the Biqā' Shaykh Kanj al-'Imād, son of the Shaykh Nāṣir al-Dīn who had been killed battling Ibrāhīm Pasha at Wādī Bakkā. He came for an interview, bringing with him about thirty poor Christians who had taken refuge with him. After his meeting with the aide they went together to Ḥāṣbayyā.

A few days prior to this 'Alī Bey Ḥamādī had brought men from the Shūf and remained outside of town. When Shaykh Kanj and the aide arrived, they entered the town and met with the *mīrālāy*. The next day [341] the Druze were let into the palace and killed all the Christians inside, some with guns, some with swords and others with axes, while the soldiers watched. Those who ran among the soldiers to protect themselves were pushed out at spear point to be killed by the murderers; they also killed the Christians who had come with Shaykh Kanj. Then they went to Emir Sa'd al-Dīn's quarters and killed him and his son-in-law Emir Jahjāh intentionally, though they also killed four other emirs by mistake, thinking they were Christian peasants. The other emirs were not harmed, but their houses were sacked, as was Emir Sa'd al-Dīn's, and the palaces that were the emirs' houses were burned.

That same day the Druze of the Ḥawrān killed the emirs of Rāshayyā, only two of them remaining alive, and looted their houses and those of all the Christians, many of whom had taken refuge with the military in the palace. The Druze were let in and killed them all. The only Christians who escaped were those who had distanced themselves from the soldiers and sought refuge with Druze who protected them from being killed.

The Druze of the Ḥawrān went in the company of Shaykh Ismā'īl al-Aṭrash to help with the fighting in Zaḥle, where they had failed in 1841. Although the government had forbidden the people of Zaḥle to build barricades to obstruct attackers, the Druze of the mountain remained wary of it nonetheless, especially since the inhabitants, after witnessing the conduct of the government troops with the people of Dayr al-Qamar, had not allowed the [troops] to enter and forced them to camp outside with the Druze who were gathering for attack. When Ismā'īl [342] al-Aṭrash arrived in the village of Kanākir in Wādī 'l-'Ajam, he found Christians from the Ballān region who had taken refuge with the Shaykh al-Islām Khlayfa. He killed a hundred and thirty-five men he found, some of whom had been hidden and others were only laborers who had been hired for harvesting the crops. Then he set out with his band for Rāshayyā, where he did what has already been stated. From there he joined those who had gathered against Zaḥle.

According to rumor, the commander of the imperial troops urged them to be quick in attacking Zaḥle, so the assault was launched and a defense was made by the men. Ismā'īl al-Aṭrash and his men were said to have been driven back after fighting for two days and not meeting with success, and the Druze of the mountain were fiercer fighters than they. The people of Zaḥle were fewer than their opponents and received no aid from the mountain, only promises they were expecting to be kept. One day while fighting their attackers in the lower part of town, a host of horsemen came from the upper part, and they believed they were the promised help, since their banners resembled Christian banners; but this was a trick on the part of Khaṭṭār Bey al-'Imād to take revenge for his son 'Alī, who had been killed in the war. When they entered the town they began to kill all they could find and to pillage and burn the houses. The cries and wails of women and children arose, so the men of Zaḥle left the battle and returned to see what was going on in their houses, followed by their adversaries. Many of the Muslims of the villages of the Biqā' were harassed and forced to take refuge [343] in flight with their womenfolk to the mountains. Then the churches and houses were sacked and burned.

With this the mountain war ended. Christian houses, churches and monasteries were destroyed, an enormous number of men and monks were killed, and everything the opponents could lay their hands on was looted. It was all the result of over self-reliance and lack of foresight. The catastrophe that befell Zaḥle in loss of men was but little in comparison to Dayr al-Qamar and Ḥāṣbayyā, and this was due to the fact that [Zaḥle] had not accepted to have imperial troops in the town and therefore lost no more than around a hundred men.

THE MASSACRE OF THE CHRISTIANS OF DAMASCUS AND THE REASONS THEREFOR.

The Damascus incident had no connection with the incidents in the Lebanon but had special causes that grew out of the conduct of ignorant Christians when the intelligent among them no longer had the power to curb them. As the Empire began to implement reforms and equality among its subjects regardless of their religious affiliation, the ignorant Christians went too far in their interpretation of equality and thought that the small did not have to submit to the great, and the low did not have to respect the high. Indeed they thought that humble Christians were on a par with exalted Muslims. They did not want to understand that, just as equality was based on regulations and legal rights, the people of stature had to maintain their proper dignity before whatever community, especially when it came to Christians vis-à-vis Muslims. They should have known that the leaders and important people of the area were [344] Muslims, as the power structure, with its viziers, soldiers and might, was all Muslim. The Christians in Syria were the smaller and weaker portion in everything, and in all regards the Christians should have not only paid great respect to the Muslims but given total obedience to the authorities.

Let us leave this talk of the conduct of the ignorant and look at what happened when the government's orders were disobeyed. The poll-tax was lifted from the Christians, and they were made the equals of Muslims. This equality meant that they were to be treated equally in

Zaḥle.

the matter of military conscription, upon which the defense of the country and maintenance of peace among the subjects depended. Either because the Empire knew that not only did the Christians detest entering the military but they were also unsuited to it because of the timidity they inherited from their fathers and grandfathers, or because the Empire was looking for excuses to keep from taking Christians into the military, it exempted them from service on condition that they pay fifty Ottoman liras per person, whereas if a Muslim was permitted an exemption from the military he had to pay a hundred liras. The Christians of Damascus would not agree to pay the exemption fee and requested that they present men, as Muslims universally did. They believed that the Empire would not accept Christians into the military, and thus they would escape paying, although, had the authorities acceded to their request and instituted a lottery, they would have made them pay double the exemption fee and not given them any special consideration [345] on account of the timidity resulting from their former degradation.

During the governorship of Maḥmūd Nadīm Pasha, the former grand vizier, in Damascus a demand for the military exemption fee was made of the Christians, but they were too pigheaded to pay it. I was on familiar terms with him and suggested that, in view of the position of the Damascene Christians, the best way to end this affair was to institute a military lottery for the Christians, since those who were well-off could get the money themselves to pay the exemption fee or could get it from their fathers. This left the poor, who suffered from the draft, but they could be paid for either by their community or from church funds, and thus the burden would be lighter for everyone. The annual flat tax per capita on all members of the community was also hard for the poor to bear, for most of the time they have more offspring than the rich do. A poor man may have five or six children, while a rich man may have only one or two, or none. If the tax is levied [equally] on all individuals, it is unfair to the poor, even when [a poor man and a rich man] have an equal number of children. The governor replied, "This is true, but we must follow the regulations established by the Empire. We cannot disregard them."

In 1860, when it was firmly insisted that the Christians pay the military exemption fee for years past and present, it was a hard burden for the poor to bear, for they were scarcely able to pay for one year, much less for several years at once. Every new demand was made retroactive for several years prior to the enactment, in flagrant disregard of the palliatives that should have [346] been used to get the subjects to accept new measures, as the Arabs had done when they conquered a country. They imposed the poll-tax to be paid the following year in order to make it more acceptable. Now, however, if the government imposes a new tax, such as the one on dwellings, and it is announced in '73, it expects to be paid retroactively from the beginning of '71, and that is difficult for subjects to do. Apparently the reason for this is that the Empire orders the imposition of a new tax, but it is hung up for a long time in committee while the arrangements for implementation are being made. When it is finally enacted, the demand is made backdated to the [initial] approval of the imposition.

Such circumstances made poor Christians unable to pay what was asked of them, so the government summoned the leaders of the Christian community and demanded that they either collect what was owed or be imprisoned until they came up with it. They apologized for their inability to collect and begged that [they be allowed to] present a detailed ledger of the amount owed by each person, to be collected by government agents. The governor did not agree and ordered them imprisoned until they promised to pay the full amount owed by the Christians. This they were not able to do, so they were put in prison for a few days until they ran out of patience and their businesses came to a standstill, as a result of which the poor craftsmen who worked in their shops ceased to have the price of bread for their families. Their outcry was great, and they went to the Greek Orthodox patriarchate to ask for relief.

The Patriarch Irenaeus [347] was away, and his deputy, Metropolitan Joseph, the Bishop of 'Akkār, was a man with an odd way of expressing himself. Imagining the poor people's outcry to be much more than it was, he wrote, without thinking, to the governorate that "the Christians are in rebellion and have conspired to kill me." All he meant to show was the lengths to which they had been driven by their poverty and inability to pay what they owed. He did not take into consideration what measures the government would take to deal with rebels, for it was well known that the Muslims of the city, small and great alike, even council members, were displeased by the arrogant way the Christians conducted themselves with them, who were accustomed to degrade [Christians] and apologize for the mere mention of them, as they would do for the mention of filth. They would say to someone they were addressing, "So-and-so the Christian—may you be beyond mentioning him," or "you are too noble to mention him." The Turks, with all crudeness, would refer to a Christian as *bir gâvur*, "an infidel," though the speaker might not be worthy to groom the Christian's donkey. During the present sultan's reign such nonsense has been forbidden, but the prohibition is disregarded outside of cultured circles, for commonly even in government offices there are many Turks who use derogatory expressions with Christians.

The metropolitan's letter became a weighty document in the hands of the government and councils to prove that the Christians were in rebellion, and Islamic law provides for the annihilation of rebels. However, outwardly the government refrained from doing such things, especially since the Muslims of Damascus were not in good odor with the Empire because of their past conduct, their murder of imperial viziers and their refusal either to accept the new impositions [348] or to pay the back taxes they owed the treasury. Therefore [the Empire] strove to incite the Muslims against the Christians and so have its revenge on both of them. The actions of the authorities prove this.

Aḥmad Pasha, the governor, had cannon mounted at the gate to the Umayyad Mosque at the time of Friday prayer to make clear that the Muslims would be protected from Christian treachery, and by such means he stirred up the wrath of the Muslims against them, even though the Muslims and troops in Damascus were more than 30,000, not counting the Muslims in the surrounding villages, who were more than 100,000, among whom there were not more than 500 weak Christians. [The Muslims] had many weapons, the citadel and cannons, while the men of all Christian sects were only 3,000, and only rarely could so much as a hunting rifle be found among them. Most of them took their chickens to the butcher for slaughter because it was impossible for a Christian to screw up the courage to cut a chicken's head off himself. Could then any rational person imagine that the Christians might murder Muslims? However, when they saw how the pasha was and that his desire was in line with theirs, the ignorant among them—not the intelligent—were incited to annihilate the Christians, most of whom kept to their houses. So also did the Muslims and Druze of the villages of Damascus change toward the Christians.

It was harvest time, and many of the poorer Christians of the mountains had brought their families to the villages of Damascus and the Ḥawrān to live during the harvest. These people were gripped with fear, unable to return to their homes, because no roads were safe for Christians. If the Damascenes had had a safe [349] route to any of the seaports, there would not have been a single Christian left in Damascus. However, they chose to remain open to a probable, impending danger rather than expose themselves to the certain danger of the roads.

The consuls here made great efforts to speak to the governor about how to prevent civil strife. He not only did nothing, but he no longer permitted them access to him. Finally they requested that he meet with one of them as a representative of the group, and he replied that he would. They sent Monsieur Yorgaki, the vice-consul of Greece, since he was expert in Turkish and knew how to deal with Turks; but he returned in despair of the governor's doing anything positive. During their conversation he had said, "If Your Excellency does not try to prevent the harm that is about to befall the Christians of Damascus, you will be responsible to the Empire, especially since the consuls have repeatedly warned you."

In response he said, "If they ask me anything, your documents are in my pocket to answer for me."

While this was going on, news of the capture of Zaḥle reached the authorities, and there was such rejoicing and celebration in Damascus, with lighting of fires in the marketplaces during the day, you would have thought the Empire had conquered Russia. However, the Sharīf Maḥmūd Efendī al-Ḥamzāwī, who has been previously mentioned, exhibited his displeasure with all this and ordered the fires put out in the marketplaces near his house.

Then the Christians grew more fearful and despaired of the authorities' protecting them. Damascus was filled with the poor foreign [Christians] who were away from their homelands working at the harvest in the villages of Damascus and the Ḥawrān and, having no security of life or limb from the Druze and ignorant Muslims and unable to reach their homes via the open road, [350] fled to Damascus. So also came all the Christians who were able to escape from Ḥāṣbayyā and Rāshayyā. The Christian quarter was jammed with poor strangers who did not even have enough to eat. As there were not enough places to shelter them, most of them, their wives and children slept in the lanes around the churches, with no bed save the ground and no cover save the sky. The Damascene Christians, despite their own hardships and fear and the vast numbers of their own poor, were moved by Christian commiseration to provide for the relief of their poor foreign brethren by whatever means they could, and they devoted an oven to the making of bread for them to live on and distributed it free.

EMIR 'ABDUL-QĀDIR AL-JAZĀYIRĪ AND SOME OTHER PIOUS MUSLIMS UNDERTAKE TO RESCUE THE CHRISTIANS.

The Christians who were well-off, even those employed as clerks by the government, no longer were secure of their lives if they ventured forth into the streets to go to work. So they remained at home, trusting in God to send them relief. The government offices came to a standstill, since most of the clerks were Christian. The indignation of ignorant Muslims grew by the day, and Druze poured into Damascus from all directions. The governor, Aḥmad Pasha, who was also general of the army corps, did nothing to quell the disturbance—not even an indication that that he was displeased. The Christians would have despaired of a strong hand to protect them from the impending disaster were it not for the manliness and highmindedness of the Sharīf [351] Emir 'Abdul-Qādir al-Ḥasanī al-Jazāyirī,[11] who was anxious to preserve the good name of his religion. This outstanding man, whose excellence was well known to the kings and inhabitants of the earth, never rested a moment in his attempts to allay the revolt. There was not a single leader of the city, ulema, *āghā* or village shaykh, with whom he did not speak, warning them of the serious consequences of revolt, over and above its impermissibility in the Islamic religion. He alarmed them so much that he obtained promises from them all that they would support him in preventing any disturbance of the peace.

On the 7th and 8th of July, 1860, things quieted down in the city, and the Christians breathed a sigh of relief. The government ordered the clerks to come to the seraglio to work. On Monday morning, the 10th of July, the clerks went to their jobs and those who were left at home felt safe enough to go about their business in the marketplace. That afternoon the authorities ordered some of the Muslims who had been jailed for crimes against Christians to be paraded through the markets in chains, ostensibly to teach them a lesson (whereas the real reason was to provoke the Muslims against the Christians). When they reached the market at Bāb al-Barīd, the Muslims rebelled and broke their bonds, crying out against the Christians. Some of those in the marketplaces took refuge in the houses of Muslim aristocrats and others hid in merchants' shops, for it was the custom to shut the doors of shops when a disturbance was going on in the town, and the insurgents would respect them. [352] Still others went to protect their homes.

It was hoped that the Muslims would not enter a private home without the owner's permission, as was the custom dictated by the Islamic religion; but such hopes proved false. They entered houses, killed the men and looted their property. There was nothing forbidden by their religious law they did not violate. They sacked the churches and monasteries of all rites, killing the monks and also Mister Graham, an English missionary—they even killed old blind monks and peasants. Most of the poor strangers mentioned above, who had no place of shelter except the streets, were killed. The leper colony in Damascus was assaulted, where lepers from various parts had gathered in the hopes of alleviating their misery, living on Christian charity and thinking that the climate of Damascus, whose inhabitants were not afflicted with this disease, would be beneficial. The residences were torched, and the Monastery of Terra Santa was not only sacked and burned, but all eight of the Spanish monks were slain. One of them had managed to escape, but he was pursued and killed. The French Lazarist monastery was very strong, and His Excellency Emir 'Abdul-Qādir was able to reach it and save the monks' lives. He did not have a chance, however, to save it from being burned, for he was occupied night and day rescuing people.

On the first day of the incident Ṣāliḥ Zakī Bey Mīrālāy came with a battalion to protect the Christian quarter, and when it was attacked by the insurgents he fired on them [353] without injuring anyone, and they ran away. Had he been left to quell the disturbance, he could have done so; but the authorities did not let him and hurled imprecations at him from the citadel. Therefore he was obliged to withdraw with his troops. Later they charged him with insubordination, demoted him and exiled him to the capital. In truth his only crime was to have prevented the insurgents from murdering Christians, as can be established by the facts.

That evening Emir 'Abdul-Qādir went to the governor and met with the Muslim council members. They deliberated about what was happening, and Emir 'Abdul-Qādir testified that according to Islamic law it was not permissible. If the insurgents did not cease their actions, the authorities would be religiously obliged to fight them. The *muftī*, Ṭāhir Efendī, was present and could not deny it. They agreed, and Emir 'Abdul-Qādir returned to arm his men and accompany the vizier to fight the insurgents. While he was preparing his band word from the governor came ordering him to desist, so all he could do was to try to save as many as possible. [The emir] ordered his band to patrol the Christian quarter and bring him everyone they could find, man, woman and child. This was also done by His Excellency Sharīf As'ad Efendī Ḥamza, the brother of the aforementioned Maḥmūd Efendī; he armed himself and his coterie to rescue every Christian he could find, take him to his house and provide him with necessities. [354] So also were there many religious and virtuous Muslims, such as Shaykh Salīm al-'Aṭṭār, an important member of the ulema, who followed the example of Emir 'Abdul-Qādir and took Christian men and their families into their homes.

We saw none more zealous and compassionate than Ṣāliḥ Āghā Chorbajī al-Mahāyinī, Sa'īd Āghā al-Nūrī and 'Umar Āghā al-'Ābid in the Maydān quarter. Despite the ferocity and lawlessness of the Maydān men, he was able to keep them under control and protect all the Christians of the Maydān. He sent his relatives with men to the Christian quarter in the city, and they rescued hundreds of men, women and children and took them to their houses.

On Tuesday, the second day of the insurrection, things quieted down somewhat, but on Wednesday, the third day, Christians were treated extremely cruelly and pressure was brought to bear on pious Muslims, who were warned that anyone who had a Christian hidden in his house and did not turn him over to be killed would have his house burned down. The insurgents entered the house of one such who dreaded having his dwelling burned, and snatched the children hidden there from their mothers' arms and slaughtered them before their very eyes.

The reason this was done was that a man came up to the Ṣāliḥiyye quarter and cried out: "Some builders were at work on the house of Shaykh 'Abdullāh al-Ḥalabī, the dean of the ulema. Christians hidden nearby fired on the Muslim workers and killed some of them. The house has caught fire, and the shaykh wants you to come help." Although there was no basis whatsoever to this story, the Muslims and Kurds of Ṣāliḥiyye rose up and made an assault on Damascus, deciding to inflict damage on Emir 'Abdul-Qādir. They massed near his house, around which many Christians had gathered in refuge. The emir went out armed and escorted by a band [355] of North Africans to confront them. He told them to cease their heinous acts and if they did not go away he would fire on them. Fearing his might, they withdrew from the vicinity. Nonetheless, that day many injuries were done to Christians and many hundreds were killed. Kurdish officers like Ismā'īl Āghā Shamdīn, Farḥāt Āghā and others encouraged the attacks, galloping in front of the governor's palace boasting of their bravery in falling upon those who were helpless to defend themselves. The Christians of Damascus lay before them like sheep before butchers.

The governor gave not the slightest indication of being displeased by Christian massacre. True, the morning before the afternoon of the insurgence he had ordered the Christian clerks to come to the seraglio to man their offices, and when it broke out he immediately summoned the clerks to the military seraglio for their protection, but it was not out of compassion for them but rather to safeguard government operations only they knew how to perform.

Many Christians who lived at the end of the city in Bāb Sharqī had fled along with the metropolitan of the Syriac Catholics, before the arrival of the insurgents, to the village of Ṣaydnāyā, where there were many fierce Christians. There was also a strong Greek Orthodox monastery. They reached it safely and entered the monastery, where the Christians of the village had fortified themselves in fear of the Muslims of their town and the vicinity. Da'ās Āghā al-Jayrūdī set out to attack them with the horsemen appointed to him by the government. [356] He was joined by many Muslims of the countryside and assaulted the monastery, but he was unable to defeat the men inside, who came out to confront him and defended themselves passionately. Finally they drove him away and felt secure of their lives from the aggression of those who would shed their blood and plunder their possessions unjustly.

PROOFS THAT THE UPRISING AGAINST THE CHRISTIANS WAS PLANNED BY THE AUTHORITIES.

Among the acts of the military in Damascus toward the Christians that prove that what happened was with government connivance are the following. First, the governor refused to stop the insurgents, although, had he ridden alone through the streets making a show of his displeasure, they would have stopped. Second, as has been previously reported, Ṣāliḥ Zakī Bey, whose hindrance of the insurgents was disapproved of by the authorities, was ordered out of the Christian quarter. Third, when Emir ʻAbdul-Qādir determined to stop the insurgents, and the *muftī* and council members, in the presence of the governor, declared the necessity of doing so, he was later forbidden. Fourth, the authorities stationed troops at the entrances to the Christian quarter to permit only armed Muslims to enter to kill Christians. Fifth, when the military saw that the insurgents were satisfied with killing and looting, they fired cannons over the straw roofs in the Ṭāliʻ al-Qubba quarter until they caught fire and burned the Christian houses. Sixth, a Jew reported to the authorities that the fire had spread to his house. The military was ordered to take the fire engine and put it out, but when they arrived they found that the fire had not spread to his house but to his Christian neighbor's. They refused to put it out and said that when it reached the Jew's house they would extinguish it. Seventh, which proves beyond a doubt that what happened was at the order of the authorities, that the Muslims [357] and Druze were not acting outside of their will in what they did, and which is stronger than any of the allegations adduced before, is that the abasement of Jews, more than any other community, is strongly intrenched among Muslims. The Koran defines the Jews as more inimical to Muslims, and the Christians as the closest of all people to them in affection; and this they believe to be God's word. The greed of the insurgents for plunder cannot be doubted, just as there is no doubt of the wealth of the Jews in Damascus, yet not only did the insurgents not bother a single Jewish house, they actually deposited their loot with the Jews until they had finished the job, and the Jews set out iced sugarcane juice at their doors for the insurgents to drink. Therefore the authorities must not have permitted them to harm the Jews as they did the Christians.

EMIR ʻABDUL-QĀDIR ASKS THE GOVERNOR TO TAKE CHRISTIANS INTO THE CITADEL; ṢĀLIḤ ĀGHĀ AL-MAHĀYINĪ PROTECTS THE CHRISTIANS OF THE MAYDĀN.

When Emir ʻAbdul-Qādir no longer had the facilities in his house to shelter the thousands of Christian men, women and children who had gathered there, he could find no place large or safe enough to keep them in. Thinking it would be best to put them in the citadel, the gates of which were guarded by soldiers, he made a request of the governor to that effect, and permission was granted. All the Christians he had collected were sent to the citadel, guarded along the way by the armed North Africans who never ceased day or night to search for Christians in hiding among the ruins and in wells, where many were found, both alive and dead, some having starved to death and others killed by bullets shot by the insurgents through openings in the rocks to kill any hidden inside. The smoke of conflagrations blocked out the light of the sun to the Wādī al-Zaydānī plain, [358] which was filled with the smoke of Damascus, although it was twenty-five miles away.

Five days later, as there were no more Christians coming to the citadel, an order was given to separate the men from the women, and they were petrified that what had happened in Dayr al-Qamar and Ḥāṣbayyā would happen to them, that the soldiers would let the Druze in among them to kill them all. This fear was justified, for the next day Ṣāliḥ Āghā Mahāyinī learned that a host of Druze was approaching to annihilate both the Christians of the Maydān, who were under his protection, and the rest in the citadel. He mounted and went with his band from the Maydān to confront them. When he met them, he addressed them civilly and said, "It is shameful for manly and religious people to act like this. You had best cease and desist. Moreover, I will persevere in my assistance to those who have taken refuge with me as long as I remain alive. You know what men I have at my command. If you do not heed my advice and return, each and every one of you, to your homes without entering the city, you will force me to take steps that neither you nor I will enjoy. What has already happened is enough." They obeyed him and returned to where they had come from.

MUʻAMMAR PASHA ARRIVES AS GOVERNOR AND QUELLS THE INSURRECTION.

The great peril for Christians lasted eight days, and then Muʻammar Pasha came as governor of Damascus. As soon as he arrived he had heralded through the streets a proclamation of general amnesty and forthwith forbade any aggression against Christians, and this proves that the insurgents were not in opposition to the will of the authorities.

The Christians in the outlying villages, and those who chanced to pass through, were given the choice by the Muslims of embracing Islam [359] or being killed. Those who were frightened into converting were circumcised and their lives were spared, but those who refused were slain. In Damascus, however, those who became Muslims were not spared but were slain along with the rest, even after converting.

WHAT HAPPENED TO THE WRITER DURING THE INSURRECTION.

Inasmuch as the one who requested me to write this brief work asked me to include especially accounts of what happened to our family, I should mention here what befell me during the Damascus Incident. On Monday afternoon the 10th[12] of July 1860, I was asleep. I was awakened and told that the Muslims in the city had risen up against the Christians. Just then none of my men or grown sons was there. Nāṣīf was with Mister Brant, the British consul for whom he worked in the chancellery, and Salīm was at the Orthodox patriarchal school learning Turkish. I went to the door of my house to see what was going on and found people running madly. From them I learned that the Muslims had turned on the Christians, so I locked the door and was waiting for the consul's kavass to arrive when two assistants of the precinct officer brought me one of my men. He was a Christian who had taken refuge at the officer's house, who had sent him to me. A short time later the Muslim kavass arrived, and I sent him to Emir 'Abdul-Qādir to ask for men to escort me there. He returned alone, saying, "The emir was out. Just then he returned home and gave me six of his men, but they couldn't get here because they were unarmed and the streets were crowded with insurgents. They can't protect you without weapons." Then I began to wish they would arm themselves and come. [360] I had a few weapons, and if they had only come I would have given them to them.

When I was waiting, a host of insurgents attacked my house. When they could not get the door open they began to beat it with axes. They broke it in and entered the outer part of house and garden, which was overlooked by arches with iron grillwork in them. They fired through them into the inner part of the house and set to work beating down the door. When I realized what danger I was in, and Emir 'Abdul-Qādir's men had not yet arrived to help, I left through the back door, taking

Dervish.

with me some cash to use in case of emergency. I did not think it a good idea to carry arms because it would only exacerbate the insurgents. The Muslim kavass followed me with his sword, and my nine-year-old son Ibrāhīm and his six-year-old sister also followed me. I headed for the street leading to Emir 'Abdul-Qādir's house, but I was confronted by a group of insurgents who ran at me brandishing weapons. I threw a handful of money at them, and they knocked each other over to get at it, and so I escaped them by returning to the street leading to the officer's post. Before reaching it I was confronted by another group of armed men making for me. I did as I had done before and distracted them by throwing money in their path. I headed back, death behind me and before me.

I entered a miserable quarter, through which one could pass into the street to the emir's house, and hoped that the men of that quarter had gone out to make holy war in the Christian quarters and large streets and would not be at home. I was wrong, however, for the men had returned [361] to get their weapons, and there they stood before me. I had nowhere to run. They surrounded me to strip me and kill me. My son and daughter were screaming, "Kill us instead of our father!" One of these wretches struck my daughter on the head with an ax, and he will answer for her blood. Another fired at me from a distance of six paces and missed, but I was wounded on my right temple by a blow with an ax, and my right side, face and arm were crushed by a blow with a cudgel. There were so many crowding around me that it was impossible to fire without hitting others. I tried to trick them and said, "I was going to the officer bey on important business. I couldn't get to him with all that's going on. Take me to him." Among the crowd were some men who knew me, and they said, "We ought to take him to the bey." After looting all the cash left on me and taking my watch and even my head-dress, they took me there, followed by a large group of people.

Along the way we were joined by a dervish with a green turban, long hair hanging down and painted eyes. In his hand he held a long staff, and attached to the top was a large sickle he stretched out over the men, who were staring at me, to cut off my head, but he could not do it. When I arrived near the precinct officer's post at the Bāb Tūmā cross-roads, the [officer] met me and took me by the hand, expressing sorrow over my affliction, dismissed the men and then put me in one of his men's houses, where there was no one except an old woman [362] who was the landlady. They send me with the kavass to an upper apartment overlooking the street.

There were three hours of daylight remaining. I began to think of my family and what had happened to each of them. If they were hungry, who would feed them? I didn't even know if the house had remained unburned for them to take shelter in. What bed would they sleep in? What would they cover themselves with? The looters had entered the house before I got out. My little children had been with me, but I hadn't seen them again. I didn't know that had happened to them, especially my injured daughter, who wouldn't know how to bandage her wound. Was there anyone among all these cruel people who would have compassion on her and tie her bandage? They had wounded her before they wounded me. My wife and her nursing infant, her mother and aunt I had left in the house—what had happened to them? Had the women fallen prey to the mob, or had there been some pious Muslims to have compassion on them? I wondered what had become of my elder sons. Were they still alive? Such thoughts kept me from thinking about the agony of my own wounds. Gunfire, looting, the burning of Christian houses, and the influx of Muslims and Druze from the villages continued without cease.

I looked out of the apartment window down to the street and saw Christian men with their families coming to the officer's. I thought, how can he have put me here in this obscure place and not taken me into his house, when those he was taking in were not superior to me in station? Then I decided that he intended [363] to do away with me but couldn't do it openly. By night he would send people to kill me, and they would also kill the kavass who was with me so no one would know who the murderer was. I found that it was impossible to hide my thoughts from him lest he be killed because of me. I told him what my thoughts were, that he should leave me and save himself.

"And what will you do?" he asked.

"Trusting in God," I said, "I'll wait until it's dark, when there probably won't be many people in the street. I'll go to the officer's house, where there are many Muslims and Christians. He can't do anything to me in front of them. His house is only three hundred steps from here. I can reach it in two or three minutes. If the Creator lets me arrive safely, I'll immediately summon men from Emir 'Abdul-Qādir to come and take me to him."

"Your idea is sound," he said. "If the officer wants to do you in, he won't send anybody before it's good and dark and the street's empty, so nobody will know who did it. I don't want to leave you. I'll stay with you until you get to the officer's house, then I'll go tell the emir. If I go out now, I'm afraid they'll make me tell where you are."

I waited for it to get dark. The street filled with people pouring in from the villages, bent on killing and looting. When it began to get dark I saw seven men approaching the door of the house. They knocked, and the old woman opened the door.

"Where is Mikhāyil Mishāqa?" they asked.

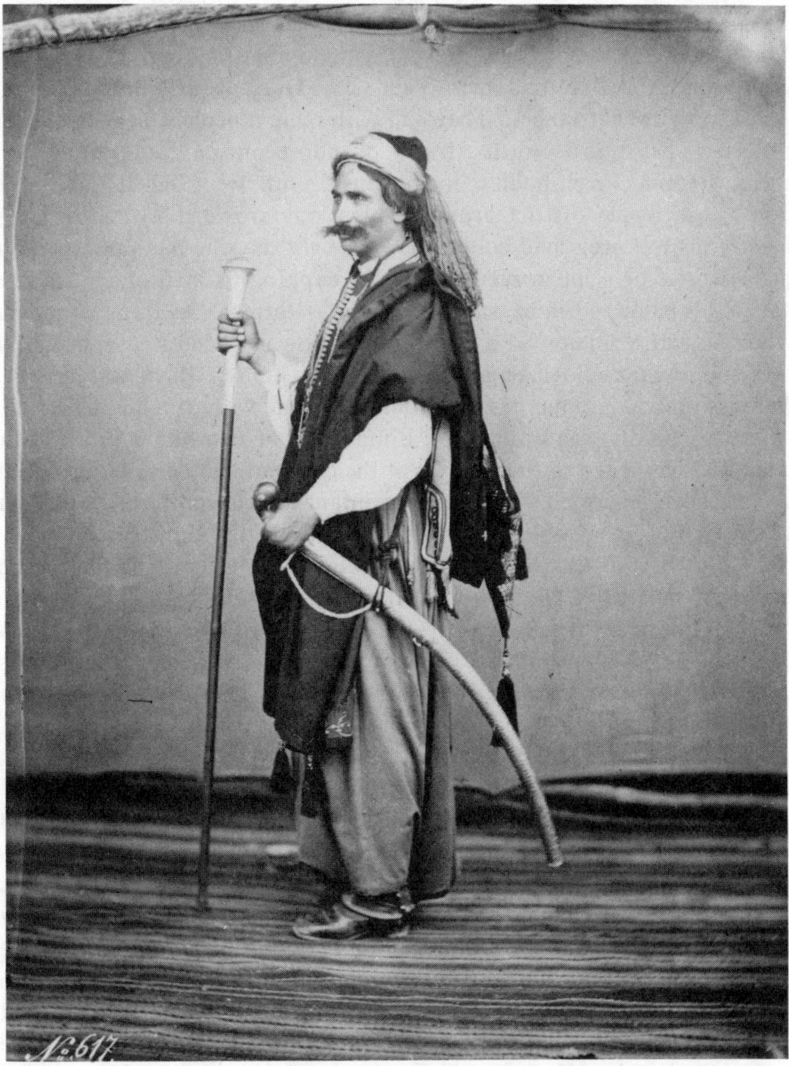

Cavass.

"He's in the upper apartment," she said. [364] At that moment I despaired of my life.

"Save yourself!" I said to the kavass. "Scale the walls. At least it will be known who came asking for me."

While we were talking, one of the men shouted out, "Mikhāyil, come down! It's your friend Sayyid Muḥammad al-Sawṭarī. I've come with Emir 'Abdul-Qādir's men to get you. Don't be afraid."

I went down to them. They had with them a nephew of the precinct officer. They put a North African burnoose on me, and I went with them, stepping over bodies in the lanes, until we reached the emir's house, the whole district around which was crowded with Christians he and his followers had collected. For eight days he had not taken off his weapons or slept in his bed, simply napping on a straw mat by the gate of his palace when he was overcome with fatigue. As I was wounded, when Sayyid Muḥammad al-Sawṭarī saw how crowded it was, he asked the emir if he could take me to rest at his house, which was nearby. Permission was granted, and he took me home with him and asked me where my family was so he could bring them. I told him I didn't know what had happened to them. Two of the children had been with me, but we had been separated. There was an infant with its mother, a youngster at the Orthodox school and the eldest in the British Consulate.

"The British Consulate alone of all the consulates has not been harmed," he said. "Don't worry about your son there. I'll go now to look for the rest of your family and bring them to you. But they may be afraid of coming with me, since they don't know me. The kavass will have to come with me to reassure them." They set out together and searched until they found them and brought them to me, all except my son Salīm. He went back out to look for him but couldn't find him or any word of him. We imagined that he was among the slain.

Then I asked Sayyid Muḥammad al-Sawṭarī how he had found out where I was. He told me that when news had reached them of what was going on in Bāb al-Barīd, they had thought it was a local disturbance and the authorities would keep it from spreading. They shut the Mazz al-Qaṣab gates leading into the Christian quarter to prevent the people of that quarter from joining the insurgents. Then a band of Kurds from Ṣāliḥiyye came and broke down the gate. Fearing for my house, he went there and was told what had happened to me and that I had gone to the precinct officer's. He went there and asked for me, but [the officer] denied any knowledge of me. He returned to Emir 'Abdul-Qādir and informed him what had happened. The emir gave him six armed North Africans to get me from the precinct officer, [whom they were to tell that] the emir knew I had reached him. He and the North Africans came and applied pressure on the officer, who was obliged to send his nephew to show them where I was.

That very night Mister Brant, the British consul, came to ask after me and reassure me of my son Nāṣīf. However, for three days there was no word of my son Salīm, although he was not discovered among the dead in the streets or among the ruins. When the warning was given that if Muslims hiding Christians in their houses did not turn them over to be killed, their houses would be burned, [366] a Turkish Muslim came to the British consul and told him that he was married to 'Alī Āghā Khazīna-Kātibī's daughter, who had let the outer portion of his house to Mister Robson, a British missionary they feared the insurgents would attack. Also with them was Salīm, Mishāqa's son, whom his wife had taken in and hidden. My son Nāṣīf sent word to me where his brother was, and a North African soldier had gone to fetch him to the consulate. Then I breathed a sigh of relief.

However, I was still anxious of an attack on Emir 'Abdul-Qādir, for the Muslim rabble were enraged with him for protecting Christians. I sent my son Ibrāhīm to his brothers in the British Consulate, which was crowded with Christians and Europeans who had taken refuge there when they saw that it was respected by the insurgents. The consul had not neglected to take precaution and had summoned soldiers from the authorities and from Emir 'Abdul-Qādir to guard the premises.

I was occupied tending to my wounds and the bruises on my limbs resulting from the cudgel blow. In addition I was penniless and did not have the wherewithal to buy even the barest necessities of clothing. The roads were blocked, and it was impossible to reach the things I needed. A renowned member of the ulema gave me a robe (my own was covered with blood) and a few *shūshe* rials I prized double their worth because I needed them so much. I bought the things I was most in need of. My son Nāṣīf also sent [367] me what money he had with him. Only when Mu'ammar Pasha came and proclaimed amnesty did I venture into the streets to get some money from outside to buy the clothing my family and I needed.

I stayed a month at Sayyid Muḥammad al-Sawṭarī's until my wounds had healed. My house had not been burned because it was surrounded by Muslim houses, but they had stripped the wood and tile, broken down the trees and done all the damage they possibly could. It was impossible to live in. The Sharīf Maḥmūd Efendī Ḥamza, who is now the Muftī of Damascus, vacated his outer house and invited me to stay there. I moved in with my family until Fu'ād Pasha, the Foreign Minister, came and gave me a house to live in until what had been destroyed in my house was repaired.

One thing that consoled me in my affliction was that while I was in the efendī's house, one of the greatest *sharif*s of the Shi'ite ulema, Sayyid Muḥammad Amīn, the *muftī* of Bshāra, came to inquire after me.

"My dear friend," he said, "what has happened to you?"

"As you see," I replied.

"Your blood has been shed, your womenfolk cursed and your houses destroyed by some of the Muslims of Damascus," he said. "Has anything else happened to you?"

"Isn't that enough?" I asked.

"A reasonable person takes solace in the affliction of others," he said. "I have read in the histories of Islam that those who killed the children of their prophet, cursed his womenfolk and destroyed the Noble Ka'ba were Muslims of Damascus. Take solace in the affliction of the Muslims by the Damascenes." [368]

THE FOREIGN MINISTER FU'ĀD PASHA COMES TO DAMASCUS.

It has been explained how Fu'ād Pasha came to Syria and what he did. During the insurrection in the Lebanon and the continual killing of Christians, plunder of their property and burning of their houses, the authorities did not exhibit the slightest concern to prevent injury. On the contrary, the viziers and government agents were like rabbit hunters loosing ferocious beasts to rip their prey to shreds. The situation lasted more than three months until the news had reached the furthest corners of the globe, but in the capital no attention was paid to remedying the situation. However, when the great foreign powers saw that the Empire failed to act to protect the lives and property of its Christian subjects, they decided to send fleets and troops to Syria to put down the on-going strife. Only then did the Empire send to correct the situation the most intelligent and competent of its men, Fu'ād Pasha, the Minister of Foreign Affairs. However, he made no haste to get to Syria; if he had, the Damascus Incident would not have happened. On the contrary he delayed getting there as much as he could, but when the French fleet and troops reached Cyprus headed for Beirut, he could not delay any longer and was forced to go to Beirut. The French fleet and troops arrived, and immediately the troubles ceased everywhere.

Fu'ād Pasha came to Damascus and ordered everything that had been pillaged from Damascus and the villages to be collected. These things were received by agents without documentation on the individuals from whom they were received, which left the door wide open for the agents [369] to pilfer valuables. Another mistake was made when one of those who brought plunder was arrested for being a known bandit, and this frightened others off. When it was announced that the authorities would search Muslim houses, and no one in whose possession articles belonging to the Christians were found would escape severe punishment, the Muslims threw everything they had into the streets to be picked over by the Jews, who also bought valuables from the looters at very low prices. It was not safe for Christians to enter Muslim quarters to search through what had been thrown into the streets, and they did not have the money to buy valuables even if the Muslims had let them see them. Thus the uprising cost both Muslims and Christians and was profited from by the Jews, not only in what has already been explained but also in what is yet to come of the Muslims' loss of men through execution and exile. Taxes were imposed on them to cover what the sultanate had borrowed from the Jews at exorbitant rates of interest, 30% and 36%. The Christians were given vouchers as indemnification, but since they needed cash, most of them were bought up by Jews at discounted rates.

Then Fu'ād Pasha entered the citadel and saw the plight of the Christian men, women and children there: naked and hungry, sleeping on the ground with no bedding, and no cover over the slain. [370] Here a woman with no one to care for her wept over her dead husband and her abandoned infants; another bemoaned her dead children or aged parents. Another wept over the loss of her brothers. Men too cried over their fathers, mothers, brothers and sisters. When he saw this sad scene, tears rolled down his cheeks (though one of the afflicted claimed that these tears were out of disappointment that there were so many left alive). He ordered that housing be arranged for those who wanted to live in Damascus and that those who wanted to go to Beirut be given the necessary pack animals to get their things there. In Damascus itself they vacated enough Muslim houses for the remaining Christians. He ordered that some mosques be given over for religious services, but this was not agreed to because it would only have incensed the Muslims. Instead they took over some houses near the Christian quarter for services. Daily bread was arranged according to the number of people in Damascus and Beirut, and they were given calico to clothe the naked, to be distributed by priests.

CERTAIN NOTABLES OF DAMASCUS ARE EXILED.

Then [Fu'ād Pasha] exiled Ṭāhir Efendī the Mufti of the Ḥanafīs, 'Umar Efendī al-Ghazzī the Mufti of the Shāfi'īs, Aḥmad Efendī 'Ajlānī the Dean of the *Sharīf*s, Shaykh 'Abdullāh Efendī al-Ḥalabī the Shaykh al-ʻUlamā, Aḥmad Efendī al-Ḥusaynī, ʻAbdullāh Bey al-ʻAẓm and his son ʻAlī Bey (who is now ʻAlī Pasha), ʻAbdullāh Bey the grandson of Nāṣīf Pasha and brother of Firdaws Bey (who has been mentioned before), Muḥammad Bey al-ʻAẓma, and Muḥammad Saʻīd Bey Shamdīn al-Kurdī. [371] Some of these he sent to Cyprus, some to Rhodes and some to Greece for five years. The dean, al-Ghazzī, ʻAbdullāh Bey al-ʻAẓm and Muḥammad Bey al-ʻAẓma all died in exile; the rest returned to their homes. Shaykh ʻAbdullāh al-Ḥalabī was given an annual pension from the government treasury of 18,000 piastres, Ṭāhir Efendī was appointed *qāḍī* of Hama, and ʻAlī Bey al-ʻAẓm and Muḥammad Saʻīd Bey became pashas.

Aḥmad Pasha, the general of the army corps and governor of Damascus, was sent to the capital on a steamship. It was said that there his credentials were taken from him and then he was sent back to Damascus, where he was shot to death along with the *mīrālāy* who was present at the massacre of Christians at Ḥāṣbayyā and the *bimbāshī* who was with the troops at the Rāshayyā massacre. Ṭāhir Pasha, who was present at the Dayr al-Qamar massacre, remained at his post and retained his importance.

A TRIBUNAL IS HELD TO INVESTIGATE CRIMES PERPETRATED DURING THE UPRISING.

Fu'ād Pasha then held a tribunal for investigating the crimes of the murderers and looters. He called it an "extraordinary tribunal." As consultant legist was Muḥammad Rushdī Shirwānī Efendī, who is now vizier of the Prime Ministry. The Christians were asked to present their charges against individuals who killed and looted for the tribunal to investigate. They replied, "We only know the individuals who took us into their homes and were kind to us. Those of us who encountered the aggressors are no longer alive to talk about it. All we know is what Your Excellency has seen, that the streets are filled with our dead [372] and our houses are heaps of rubbish. Our men, women and children are naked and would not have bare sustenance were it not for good Muslims."

Then he ordered the persons responsible for the Muslim quarters to present him lists of the inhabitants of the quarters who were armed at the time of the uprising. The lists were presented and handed over to the tribunal for investigation. Those whose names were written therein were arrested, although many of them had fled. Among those arrested were the precinct officer of our quarter and his two nephews. His son was cleared.

THE GUILTY ARE DIVIDED INTO THREE CATEGORIES: HANGING, EXECUTION BY FIRING SQUAD AND EXILE.

Investigation was made, and those who were proven innocent were released, while those whose guilt was proven were divided into three categories according to the seriousness of their crimes.

In the first category were 54 individuals, among whom were the officer of our quarter, his two nephews and six of those who had wounded me, among them the *shaykh* with a scythe who had tried to cut my head off. These were sentenced to hanging fully clothed. They were hanged in various parts of the city, except for one who escaped from the hands of the officer and became a highway robber. [Later] he was caught, brought before the authorities and pardoned.

Of the second category were 111 persons, among whom was Muṣṭafā Bey, son of 'Ākif Bey and grandson of Nāṣīf Pasha al-'Aẓm, a regular army officer who was present at the massacre at Ḥāṣbayyā. He had a young Christian employed by him as a servant, who, when the massacre was going on, clung to his feet for protection, but he pushed him away [373] with his weapon into the mob to be killed. It was said that he himself supervised the burning of the Orthodox church in Damascus, although he was a man of learning and had socialized with Christians and others. Among them were also some Kurdish *efendī*s and *āghā*s; they were shot, although one of them, a friend of the officer in charge of execution, escaped. When they were being lined up before the firing squad, he told him to fall to the ground when he heard the officer shout "Fire!" In this way he would not be hit by a bullet. His family took him away safe and sound, but he died a week later.

Those of the third category who were fit for military service were inducted; those who were not fit were exiled for a fixed period. The villagers who had killed and looted, whether Muslim or Druze, were not charged.

THE PROCEEDINGS OF THE COMMISSION TO EVALUATE AND INDEMNIFY CHRISTIAN LOSSES.

When the commissioners of the foreign powers met, it was decided that the Empire should pay the Christians reparations for their losses, and the churches and houses that had been destroyed should be rebuilt. A commission was established with Muḥammad Rushdī Efendī presiding; the other members were from various communities and sects. The Christians employed by the government strove with all their influence to ascertain the value of the things that had been looted and burned, hearing testimony from the master architect appointed by the government and from Muslim experts. They did not take into consideration the cost of decoration, such as carving, paint, etc., but considered only the cost of basic construction, [374] for the major building costs of Damascene houses were in decorative ornament. Even the government, when it instituted a new tax on houses, did not assess them as simple edifices but rather according to the amount of ornamentation. Claims for cash robberies were not considered.

After investigation they gave out vouchers,[13] which the needy sold to Jewish bankers at 20% and 30% discounts, receiving for the price Ottoman liras valued at 127 piastres, whereas the value at the time of the investigation had been 214 piastres. The authorities were glad of the devaluation of the price it had to pay. Demands on the treasury were taken with the lira as only 100 piastres. After the vouchers were issued, it was announced that the price of the lira was 100 piastres and the vouchers could be redeemed for consular scrip,[14] after a discount of 17%. The result of such actions was that the holders of indemnifications wound up with only half the value. When Qapūlī Pasha came, those who were holding vouchers got only half the value again.

The Christians of the villages of Damascus were not given anything like the value of their loss, but were awarded a lump sum of the total amount of looted goods, to be divided among them as the authorities saw fit. The tax rolls were reviewed for a hundred years and the land tax was figured as for a year in which nothing could be planted, because of the devastation and loss of men, plus the tax for military exemption, plus the tax owed by those who had been slain and those who had fled, plus old outstanding amounts. They appointed cavalrymen to collect and charged [the villagers] with providing food for the collectors [375] and fodder for their horses. Those who owed an amount equal to the indemnification received a receipt for it and were left alone by the tax collectors.

Those who were owed more than their assessment were not paid the difference, which they would have been glad to leave to reduce their taxes in coming years, but [the authorities] only agreed to commute [the excess] to the amounts owed in state taxes by Druze who had run away from their homes, which the government could not collect. They requested the authorities to keep the difference until it could collect the outstanding amounts from the Druze, since [Christians] were incapable of demanding [anything] from [the Druze]. Only now do they deduct the amount owed the treasury and cancel the tax collection, as was done with those who had no excess, although it was not possible to cancel the collection until legal instruments had been obtained that they had received all they were due. This was done eight years after the fact. Such is the compensation received by the Christian villagers of Damascus after eight years!

Then Fu'ād Pasha imposed a tax of 150,000 purses on the province of Damascus, of which 8000 purses was stipulated for the Druze of the Ḥawrān, with the approval of the commission and the foreign consuls; but nothing was ever collected. The rest of the tax was distributed over towns and individuals in Damascus, many of whom had had nothing to do with the riots. [376]

To investigate the losses of foreigners a mixed commission was set up in Beirut. When Fu'ād Pasha summoned me for an interview and told me of the constitution of this commission, he said that I would have to go to Beirut to process my claim. I said, "During the time of terror I did not leave Damascus. I beg you not to make me leave it now. There are those here who can give an opinion on my losses."

"All right," he said. "Select whom you want for your side so we can appoint them with those on our side to give an opinion on the claim."

"I don't need to select anybody," I said. "I believe in the honesty of your people. I'll be satisfied with their opinion. I will not even appear before them."

He asked me to write down the names of those I wanted, so I wrote the names of Shirwānīzāda, Muftī Efendī and three other government officials. The ones selected met and asked me for a legal instrument of my acceptance of their decision and a list of my losses. I gave them what they asked for. They made an estimate and presented it to Fu'ād Pasha, who added an extra amount and ordered it to be processed. Thus my claim was taken care of without my attendance, and it was only a quarter less than I had asked for, though others were halved. The ones who really suffered, however, received no more than a quarter of what the government authorized: one quarter went in expenses; another quarter was gobbled up by bureaucrats on behalf of the government; and another quarter went in profit to Jewish bankers and others. All in all, the Empire, Muslims and Christians suffered loss; [377] but the Empire compensated itself by degrading and humiliating its subjects [by demanding payment of] every tax that had ever been imposed on them, even the outstanding amounts in Damascus governors had worn themselves ragged trying to collect. The first thing Fu'ād Pasha did was to collect them with all ease, for the clans no longer had chiefs to wear down the authorities by resisting taxation, and orders had to be obeyed by all.

In Mount Lebanon, Ḥāṣbayyā and Rāshayyā many Druze were arrested. Fu'ād Pasha wanted to execute five hundred of them, but the Christians would not give their approval until after a legal hearing, when those condemned by law could be executed. He did not agree; even had he agreed, no one would have been executed because the law cannot condemn without testimony by peers. It was impossible to get a Druze to testify against another Druze in these incidents, Christian testimony could not be accepted because the enmity between the two groups was too well known, and there was no third party to testify except Druze supporters. The matter ended in no one's being executed, though some were exiled for specific periods. The leaders of the Druze, beys and shaykhs, were arrested, except for Khaṭṭār Bey al-'Imād and Bashīr Bey Nakad, both of whom fled to the Ḥawrān. Those who were arrested were detained under guard in Beirut, where they were interrogated and sentenced to exile. They were exiled for specific periods, at the end of which they returned to their homes. Some, like Shaykh Ḥusayn Talḥūq, were given pensions from the treasury. Sa'īd Bey Jumblāṭ [378] died in Beirut before being exiled; some say he was poisoned. Khaṭṭār Bey al-'Imād was killed like his father and son, and this came about as follows.

Some Druze in the Ḥawrān started a fight in order to plunder some supplies that were being carried to the soldiers thereabouts and guarded by eighty soldiers armed with six-shooters (called *shishkhāna*). [The Druze] were unable to plunder them and were beaten off. Then the Druze from the villages, along with Khaṭṭār Bey, came up to help them. According to reports, there were around fifteen hundred horsemen. The soldiers had bullets that were longer ranging, and they killed some of the Druze, while remaining out of range of their bullets. Khaṭṭār Bey was wounded in the neck and died several days later, and the soldiers were victorious. Bashīr Bey Nakad returned to his home and took up a post with the government.

THE CONSUL GENERAL MR. WOOD COMES TO DAMASCUS FROM TUNIS.

Mr. Wood, the consul general of England and representative of Her Majesty the Queen of England in Tunis, was sent by his government to Damascus because he was an expert on Syrian affairs. During one of his meetings with Fu'ād Pasha, who had just received an imperial decree promoting him to the rank of minister, [the pasha] was heard to say, "The south Lebanon has been taken care of; there remains only the north for us to deal with." Now who can hear such words emanating from the mouth of the greatest man of the Empire and still doubt that what happened to the Christians of the Lebanon was by order of [the government]? I verified these words with the consul general himself, that he said to Fu'ād Pasha, "Your land is drenched in the blood of

Christians." [379] As for Fu'ād Pasha's words, his principles of implementation became clear later when he sent troops against Yūsuf Bey Karam, although they were not successful in battling him because the roads were so difficult and hundreds of people in that region had readied themselves against thousands of soldiers. They drove them off, killing many of them, and the affair ended with Yūsuf Bey's submission with amnesty to the French consul, after which he went to Paris.

THE DECISION OF THE INTERNATIONAL COMMISSION.

The international commission in Beirut ended in a joint decision on the part of the great powers and the Ottoman Empire that the Lebanon would be ruled by a Christian vizier from outside the Lebanon, to be appointed by the Ottoman Empire with the approval of the five Great Powers, Russia, Austria, Great Britain, France and Prussia. The annual tax imposed on the mountain by the Empire would be 7,000 purses, not subject to increase; the troops necessary for maintaining order would be natives, and no foreign soldier would enter unless called in temporarily by the ruling vizier for an emergency. The vizier, soldiers, government employees and council members' salaries were to be paid by the Empire from—even if it was more than—the tax assessed to the mountain. The mountain was to be divided into districts and subdivided into administrative directorates. Over districts were to be placed district officers drawn from the religion of the majority, Muslim, Maronite, Orthodox, Catholic or Druze. So also were the administrative directors to be taken from the religion of the majority.

The independent rule of chieftains over their clans was ended, [380] and to rule the mountain the Empire sent a ruler known as the Governor General of the Lebanon, with the rank of vizier. He was Dāūd Pasha, an Armenian Catholic; his rule was honest, and he remained for years before being dismissed. After him Franco Pasha was sent; he was Aleppan by origin, Latin by rite, and conducted himself well. He died in 1873, and Rustum Pasha was sent as Governor General of the Lebanon. He is Latin by rite, Italian by origin, and his conduct is praiseworthy.

In 1873 I end my discussion of the events in Syria. Let the reader know that by what I have written I intend no blame of the Empire for what it brought upon its subjects, be they Muslim, Christian or Druze, for everything it did was its right to do. The basis of its power over all its subjects was to lead them to conduct themselves in obedience to those who were made shepherds over them by the Creator, for all power derives from God, and without total obedience to authority it is possible neither to implement justice among subjects nor to protect them from enemy attacks. My sole intention was to illustrate the results of disobedience to the orders of one's overlords and to explain the causes for what happened to the subjects and their leaders, for we have never yet seen a state wreak vengeance on obedient subjects. What I have written is sufficient to warn those who deny the necessity of obeying their overlords, who alone are authorized by their statutory monarch to punish, not clan chieftains unless they are carrying out the monarch's orders. A rational person will be convinced by the results of opposition, which have been clearly set forth, [381] that it is incumbent upon subjects to have no allegiance save to their rightful monarch, whose every order they should obey explicitly and implicitly. If they are harmed by anything, they should complain to no one but him. A shepherd is the only person with the authority to chastize his flock.

THE MALES OF THE MISHĀQA FAMILY IN SYRIA.

Inasmuch as the desire of the person who requested this [work] was for the particulars of my family, I have mentioned in the proper places what happened to it. Now I will end with a report of [my family] to the present date and the names of its male individuals.

Ever since I realized in 1870 that I was getting too old to work, I have stayed at home. I retired from my post as vice-consul of the United States of America, and my eldest son was appointed in my place.

The members of the Mishāqa family in Syria, the sons of Jirjis Mishāqa and their sons, are:

(1) Mikhāyil Mishāqa and his offspring:

(a) Nāṣīf, vice-consul of America, aged 35; his son Mikhāyil, aged three;

(b) Salīm, dragoman of the British consulate; aged 29;

(c) Ibrāhīm, physician, student at the American College in Beirut, aged 23;

(d) Iskandar, still at school, aged 16;

(2) Jibrā'īl Mishāqa, judge of the city of Zaḥle; his son Sulaymān is still in school;

(3) Rūfā'īl Mishāqa, Catholic member in the ruling council of the Lebanon; his sons: Yūsuf is in the capital, and Dāūd is in school;

Cavass and cancelliere.

(4) sons of the late Khalīl, Ibrāhīm and Salīm, still in school, and

(5) son of the late Ibrāhīm, Iskandar, still in school.

I hope the reader will disregard slips and infelicitous expressions he finds in what I have written, for a man is subject to mistake, especially when he is as old, advanced in years and ridden with disease (no less than seven) as I am. I wrote down only what I knew to be true, without exaggeration; what I did not know myself to be true I mentioned, but the guarantee of veracity is up to the person who told it.

The draft of this work was completed by the writer on Saturday, the twenty-second of October, 1873, in Damascus, Syria.

Appendices

Appendix A

Terms and Titles

(Turkish given in parentheses in modern spelling)

Āghā (*ağa*): generally a title of military rank, for officers up to approximately the level of captain.

Amīn al-fatwā (*fetva emini*): commissioner of the *fetvahane*, which dealt with applications to the Shaykh al-Islām for privately sought opinions (official governmental applications went through a separate office, the *telhîsçi*[1]).

Amīn al-surra (*surra emini*): commissioner of purse, who was in charge of the presents sent annually by the Ottoman Sultan to the Sharīfs of Mecca.

Amīn kilar al-hajj (*hac kıları emini*): commissioner of supplies for the pilgrimage.

'*Amūd* rial: the standard against which currency was evaluated.

Bey: civilian title of rank.

Bimbāshī (*binbaşı*): commander of a battalion, major.

Bulūkbāshī (*bölük başı*): captain of a company.

Bustānjī bāshī (*bostanci başı*): originally the head of the Garden Corps, the guards of the imperial precincts; later the title simply indicated high rank.

Cancelliere (It.): an official in the chancellery of a consulate or legation.

Chāwish (*çavuş*): sergeant-at-arms.

Daftardār (*defterdar*): financial commissary-general of a province.

Dhikr: a Sufi meditative session. Among the permissive orders, musical accompaniment and dancing are common practice; in certain, predominantly lower-class orders the *dhikr* can be fairly unbridled.

Dhimma: the largely theoretical "covenant" between *dhimmī*s and Muslims; see *dhimmī* below.

Dhimmī: Christians, Jews and Mazdaeans (Zoroastrians), the "protected" peoples allowed to live in Muslim territory, retain their own religion and a certain degree of autonomy in internal affairs and be exempt from military conscription. In theory (and Ottoman practice) *dhimmī*s paid the poll-tax (*jizya*) for the privilege of protected status.

Dragoman (Ar. *tarjumān*): literally "translator," dragomans were consular officials who often had considerable authority.

Efendī: a civilian title of rank, generally for members of the ulema and high-ranking government secretaries. The soubriquet "our efendi" (Ar. *afandīnā*, Tk. *efendimiz*) was used for reference to one's liege lord.

Emir (Ar. *amīr*): the highest hereditary title of nobility in the Lebanon.

Falaq: the instrument used to administer the bastinado.

Fatwā: a legal opinion issued by a consultative jurist (*muftī*) in response to a question on legality.

Firmān (*ferman*): imperial decree or letter patent.

Funduqlī (*fındıklı*): a coin.

Ḥākhām: a title of learning and respect among Oriental Jews, similar to Rabbi.

Ḥākim (*hâkim*): civilian ruler of a district.

Ḥukmdār (*hükümdar*): military governor.

Kākhya (*kâhya*): steward of an emir or provincial governor.

Kavass (Ar. *qawwās*): native guard of a foreign consulate.

Khān: a khan, or caravanserai, a large edifice, usually vaulted, in which are grouped practitioners of a like trade.

Khawāja (*hoca*): In Ottoman usage the title *hoca* (from the Persian *khwāja*) was applied particularly to officials who served in master secretarial capacities, as well as to members of the ulema who functioned as teachers. In the Levant, where it was given the pronunciation *khawāja*, the title was applied to Christian merchants, the Arabic *m'allim* ("master") being used for master clerks and secretaries.

Khazīna-kātibī (*hazine kâtibi*): treasury clerk.

Liwā' (*liva*): an administrative district, same as a *sanjaq*, q.v.

Mālikāna (*mâlikâne*): a life-interest land lease.

M'allim: master clerk or secretary. See *khawāja*.

Mamlūk: a military slave, generally of Turkish or Circassian origin.

Mīr-ālāy (*mîralay*): commandant of a regiment, colonel.

Mīrī taxes: taxes that were paid to the Ottoman "operational" treasury for the expenses of the central administration; the term has been translated throughout as "state tax."

Mīr-liwā' (*mīrliva*): "lord of a standard"; in early Ottoman usage the title was applied to provincial governors; later it was chiefly a military title approximately equivalent to brigadier general or commandant of a brigade.

Mīrmīrān (*mīrmīrân*) equivalent to *beylerbeyi*, a title generally awarded provincial governors, pashas of the second class.

Muftī: consultative jurist.

Muhrdār (*mühürdar*): seal-keeper.

Mujtahid: the highest degree of the Shi'ite ulemá; a *mujtahid* is licensed to exercise *ijtihād*, personal initiative, to make decisions on legal questions.

Muqaddam: a hereditary title of noble rank, between emir and shaykh.

Mutasallim (*mütesellim*): the ruler of an administrative district (*sanjaq*) appointed by a pasha who was the de jure governor but whose principal territory was too far away to be effective. Such districts were given to pashas whose income from their provinces was insufficient for their needs.[2]

Mutaṣarrif (*mütesarrif*): governor of a *sanjaq*, or *liwā';* also administrator of a land lease (*taṣarruf*).

Mutawālī pl. *matāwila:* Shi'ite Muslim, generally applied to the indigenous Shi'ites of the Lebanon and Palestine. This term is not used to refer to Shi'ites in general.

Mutawallī (*mütevelli*): holder of certain fiefs in the Lebanon; also the intendant of endowed (*waqf*) land.

Oke (Ar. *ūqiyya*): a weight of varying magnitude; in Beirut it was a little less than half a pound.

Qāḍī (*kadı*): judge of the judiciary, cf. *muftī*.

Qapūjī (*kapıcı*): originally gatekeeper, but later simply a title of rank.

Qapūkatkhudā (*kapikâhya*): agent of a regional ruler at the imperial court.

Qāymaqām, qāyim-maqām (*kaymakam*): governor of a town or district under a *mutasarrif.*

Qintār: a weight of approximately 120 lbs.

Sagbānbāshī (*seğmenbaşı*): originally chief keeper of the hounds; the *sagbān*s were incorporated as a division of the Janissaries.

Sanjaq (*sancak*): an administrative district, also in Egypt the Mameluk who ruled such a district.

Sar'askar (*serasker*): commander-in-chief.

Sharīf: a descendant of the Hashimite nobility of Mecca.

Shaykh (pl. *mashāyikh*): in the Levant, a hereditary title of nobility, ranking below *muqaddam* (q.v.); also a Muslim title of learning.

Shaykh al-Islām (*şeyhülislâm*): title of the Mufti of Constantinople, the official head of the body of learned Muslims in the Ottoman Empire.

Shaykh al-Khalwa: a Druze title of distinction.

Shūshe (or *abū-shūshe*): an old silver coin with the effigy of Maria Theresa.

Silāhdār: bearer of arms.

Silāḥshūr (*silahşur*): a title of high rank in the Ottoman imperial service.

Tufangjī (*tüfekçi*): musketeer; the *tufangjī bāshī* (*tüfekçibaşı*), chief of the musketeers, served as chief of police under a pasha.

Tūgh (*tuğ*): the crest or pennant of horse-hair attached to the helmet or staff as ensign of rank, especially for pashas of provincial gubernatorial status, who ranked three *tuğs*.

Vâli (Ar. *wālī*): governor of a province (*eyâlet*).

Yūzbāshī (*yüzbaşı*): centurion, captain in the army.

Appendix B

Genealogical Chart of the Emirs of Mount Lebanon
of the House of Shihab
(Only those mentioned in Mikhayil Mishaqa's memoirs are shown;
ruling emirs shown in heavy outline.)

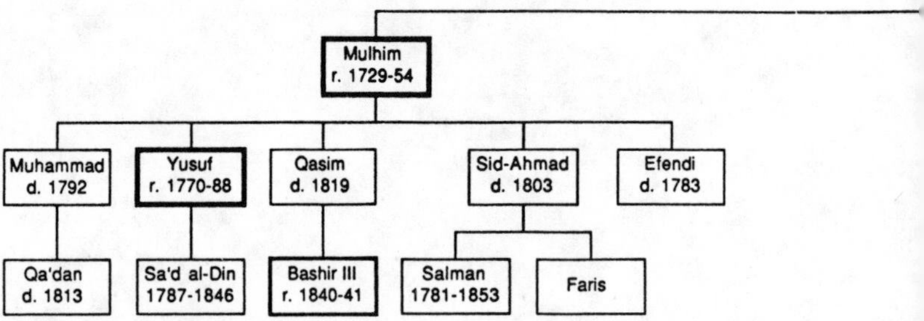

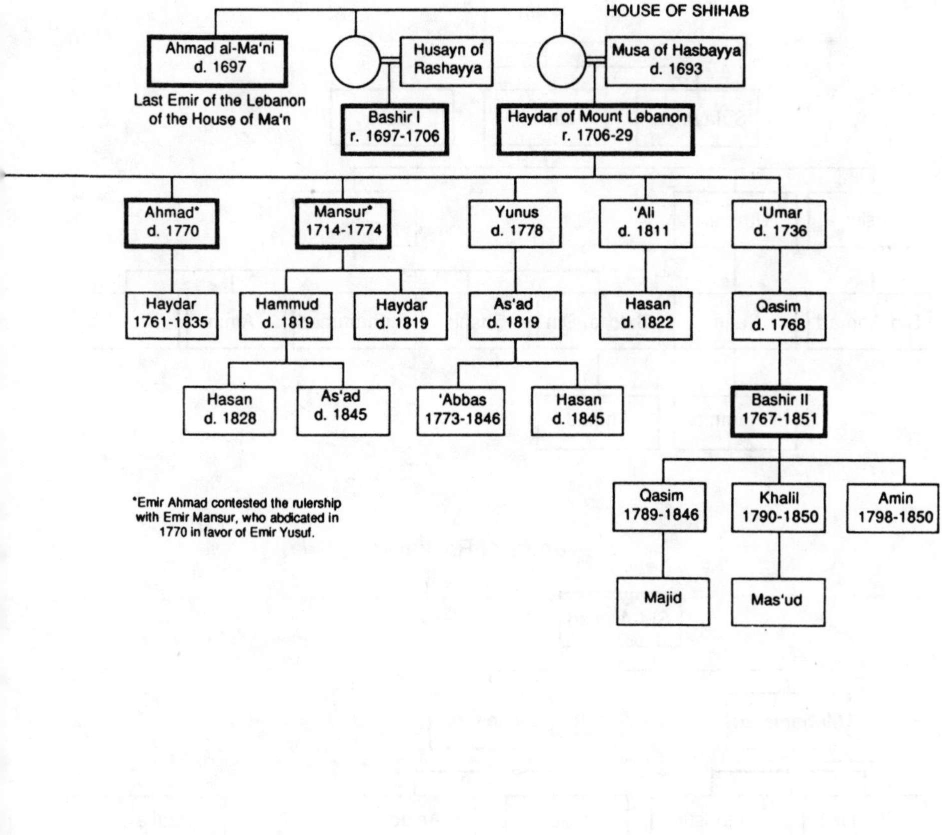
HOUSE OF SHIHAB
Ahmad al-Ma'ni d. 1697
Husayn of Rashayya
Musa of Hasbayya d. 1693
Last Emir of the Lebanon of the House of Ma'n
Bashir I r. 1697-1706
Haydar of Mount Lebanon r. 1706-29
Ahmad* d. 1770
Mansur* 1714-1774
Yunus d. 1778
'Ali d. 1811
'Umar d. 1736
Haydar 1761-1835
Hammud d. 1819
Haydar d. 1819
As'ad d. 1819
Hasan d. 1822
Qasim d. 1768
Hasan d. 1828
As'ad d. 1845
'Abbas 1773-1846
Hasan d. 1845
Bashir II 1767-1851
Qasim 1789-1846
Khalil 1790-1850
Amin 1798-1850
Majid
Mas'ud
*Emir Ahmad contested the rulership with Emir Mansur, who abdicated in 1770 in favor of Emir Yusuf.

Appendix C

Emirs of Hasbayya

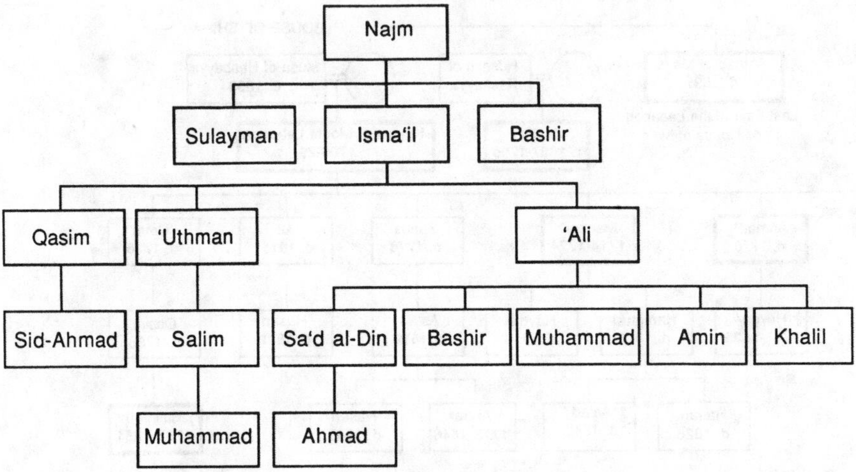

Emirs of Rashayya

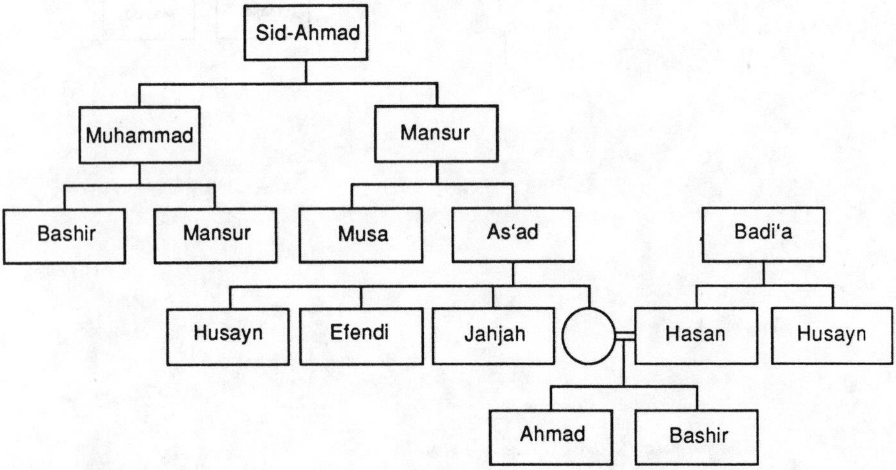

Shaykhs of the House of Jumblat

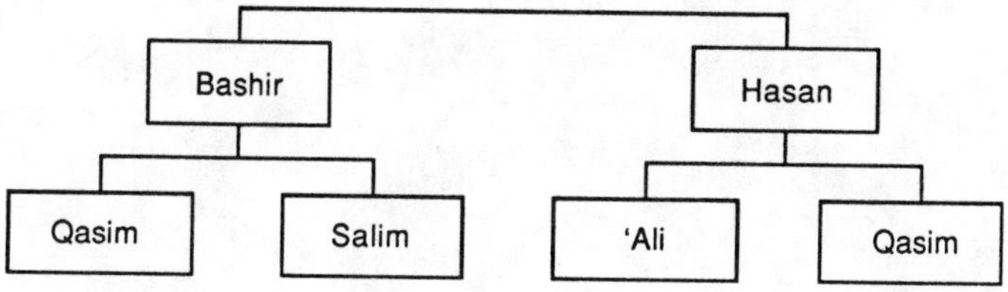

The Mishaqa Family

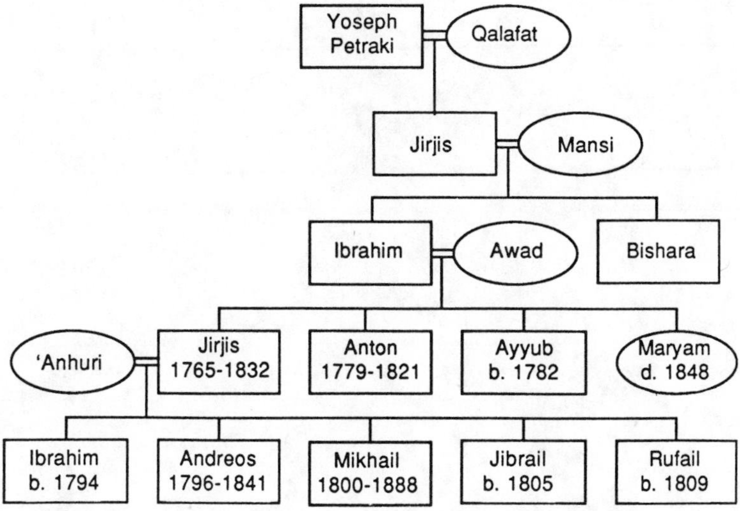

Notes

PREFACE

1. A thorough search for this manuscript was undertaken at the Greek Orthodox Patriarchate in Damascus, but unfortunately it could not be located for use in this translation.

2. There is a slight difficulty here. The editors of the printed version claim that the handwriting in the patriarchate manuscript is quite similar to Mishāqa's hand as evidenced by letters then in the possession of Mr. Rustom and known to have been written by him. However, Mishāqa himself says on page 110 of the Arabic text (p. 166 of the translation) that he was writing with his left hand because his right side was paralyzed, presumably by a stroke. The AUB manuscript, on the other hand, is copied in a peculiar, back-slanted hand that might very well be that of a right-handed person forced to write with his left.

INTRODUCTION

1. Jurjī Zaydān, *Tarājim mashāhīr al-sharq fī 'l-qarn al-tāsi' 'ashar* (Beirut: Maktabat al-Khayyāṭ, n.d.), p. 213.

2. Aḥmad al-Budayrī al-Ḥallāq. *Ḥawādith Dimashq al-yawmiyya: 1154-1175h/1741-1762m*, recension by Muḥammad Sa'īd al-Qāsimī, edited by Aḥmad 'Izzat 'Abd al-Karīm (Cairo: Maṭba'at Lajnat al-Bayān al-'Arabī, 1959); Mīkhā'īl Burayk al-Dimashqī, *Tārīkh al-Shām: 1720-1782*, edited by Aḥmad Ghassān Sbāno (Damascus: Dār Qutayba, 1402/1982); Ḥaydar Aḥmad al-Shihābī, *al-Ghurar al-ḥisān fī tawārīkh ḥawādith al-azmān*, edited by Asad Rustum and Fu'ād E. Bustānī as *Lubnān fī 'ahd al-umarā' al-shihābiyyīn* (Beirut: al-Jāmi'a al-Lubnāniyya, 1969).

3. The point has been well made that until the nineteenth century local histories in Arabic are concerned exclusively with the writer's own community.

A reader of Mīkhā'īl Burayk's history of Damascus would scarcely know that there were Muslims in the city, while Aḥmad al-Budayrī's history leaves the reader with the impression that at the same time and in the same city there were no Christians. See Thomas Philipp, "Class, Community, and Arab Historiography in the early Nineteenth Century—The Dawn of a New Era," *International Journal of Middle East Studies* 16 (1984), p. 170.

4. Of this extraordinarily successful community Muḥammad Rafīq Bey and Muḥammad Bahjat Bey, the authors of a detailed Ottoman handbook on the Vilâyet of Beirut, say: "Among all the Christians of Asia, these Uniate Orthodox are known for their intelligence, good character, discrimination and property, and more especially are the sciences and arts widespread among these Arab Christians . . . Their personal enterprise and acumen in commercial transactions are amazing" (*Bayrūt Vilāyati* [Vilāyat Maṭba'asī, 1335-36] I, 21). For the origins of Greek Catholicism see below, p. 10 and note 9.

5. Such as Mīkhā'īl al-Ṣabbāgh (1775-1818), who wrote a history of Shaykh Ẓāhir al-'Umar; Niqūlā al-Turk (1763-1828), author of a report on Napoleon's invasion of Egypt; and Ibrāhīm al-'Awra (1797-1863), author of a history of Sulaymān Pasha.

6. Thomas Philipp, "Class, Community," p. 170.

7. Kamal S. Salibi, *The Modern History of Lebanon* (London: Weidenfeld and Nicolson, 1965), p. 5.

8. Ḥaydar Aḥmad, *al-Ghurar al-ḥisān*, iii, 641f.

9. See translation, p. 51.

10. See translation, p. 88.

11. See translation, p. 76.

12. See translation, p. 21.

13. Of the many confessional groups that were, and are, in the Lebanon: the Maronites, a uniate branch of Roman Catholicism, were located primarily in the northern range of Mount Lebanon between Nahr al-Kalb and Nahr al-Bārid, although, during the eighteenth century, they moved in large numbers into regions that had formerly been almost totally Druze; Greek Catholics, large influxes of whom from Syria, primarily from Aleppo and Damascus, occurred from the latter half of the eighteenth century on, were employed extensively in Ottoman administration throughout the provinces; Greek Orthodox, from whom the Greek Catholics split, were the major representatives of Christianity in the entire area; Druze, followers of an offshoot of Isma'ili Islam propagated in the 11th century, centered in the Shūf and in Wādī al-Taym (whatever the actual legal standing of the Druze was vis-à-vis Islam, they were popularly perceived as apostate from the body of Islam, see p. 44); Shi'ites, largely concentrated in Jabal al-'Āmil in the south, B'albak, the Biqā' Valley and northern Palestine; and Sunni Muslims, practically limited to the large towns and Syria. There were also substantial populations of indigenous Jews who lived in towns and cities.

14. On the other hand, the Shihābs kept their conversions as secret as possible from the Ottomans. The personal reactions of members of a family to such conversions were another matter altogether: Emir Ḥasan Ḥammūd "al-Istānbūlī" murdered his own father and uncle in cold blood when they converted

to Christianity (see trs. p. 102).

15. The first, Emir Ma'n b. Rabī'a al-Ayyūbī, settled in B'aqlīn in the Shūf in 1120 after battling King Baldwin of the Latin Kingdom of Jerusalem.

16. Ṭannūs al-Shidyāq, *Akhbār al-a'yān* (Beirut: Librairie Orientale, 1970), i, 238.

17. Ḥaydar Aḥmad al-Shihābī, *Tārīkh al-Amīr Ḥaydar*, ed. N. Mughabghab (Cairo: Maṭba'at al-Salām, 1900), ii, 750.

18. Translation, p. 183.

19. It is probably for this reason that no Abullam' is mentioned in Mishāqa's history.

20. Translation, p. 46.

21. Ḥaydar Aḥmad, *al-Ghurar*, i, 7f.

PART ONE: 1750-1804

1. Throughout this work, "the Lebanon" refers to Mount Lebanon only, also referred to simply as "the mountain." In Mishāqa's time Mount Lebanon included neither the coast nor the south of present-day Lebanon. "Syria" refers to the entire region known as Greater Syria, which includes the later states of Syria, Lebanon, Palestine, Jordan and some of eastern Turkey. Politically the area comprised the Ottoman provinces (*eyâlet*) of Damascus, Tripoli, Ṣaydā (Sidon, which held the *sanjaq* of Beirut and the rulership [*ḥukūma*] of Mount Lebanon in suzerainty), and Acre (which included the *sanjaq* of Jerusalem and the coast down to Gaza).

2. *Mushāqa* is the word for the remains of natural fibers after they have been combed and drawn through a *mimshaqa*, a carding comb, the impurities removed and the floss and husks are left behind. The family name should properly be "Mushāqa," but the colloquial pronunciation "Mishāqa" has been retained throughout.

3. For this and all other titles, see Appendix A.

4. Leaf tobacco used in waterpipes, from the Turkish *tütün*, "tobacco".

5. *Shaykh* (pl. *mashāyikh*) is a hereditary title of nobility for some of the clan chieftains of the area. *Mutawālī* (pl. *matāwila*) is the term for the Twelver Shi'ites, particularly those of southern Lebanon and northern Palestine, where they formed clans. Since Mishāqa refers to Shi'ites in general as *shī'a* but always refers to the Shi'ite clans of the south as *mutawālī*s, the two terms will be distinguished in the translation.

6. The modern town of Ṣūr is the ancient Tyre.

7. Vizier (Ottoman *vezīr*) was a title of rank bestowed on provincial governors. It is used throughout this work synonymously with "governor" (*vâli*). "The Empire" is used to translate *al-dawla* (Turkish *devlet*), the term that encompassed the ruling machinery and power elite of the Ottoman Empire, which is also referred to as "The Sublime Empire" (*al-dawla al-'aliyya, devleti aliye*), not to be confused with the "Sublime Porte" (*al-bāb al-'ālī, bab-i âli*), the office of the Grand Vizier.

8. In 1705, when Bashīr Pasha became the governor of Ṣaydā, Ṣafad and

Jabal 'Āmil were detached from the Shūf of Mount Lebanon. Ṣafad and Acre were given to Shaykh Ẓāhir al-'Umar al-Zaydānī, who gave the Shawmar and Tuffāḥ regions to the Munkir clan and Shqīf to the Ṣa'b clan. Mushrif b. 'Alī al-Ṣaghīr petitioned Bashīr Pasha and received Bshāra. See Ḥaydar Aḥmad, *al-Ghurar al-ḥisān*, i, 7f.

9. Mishāqa's statement is not quite accurate. There is no one date to which one can point as the founding of uniate Greek Catholicism. Throughout the late 17th and early 18th centuries various Orthodox metropolitans and patriarchs in Syria recognized the supremacy of Rome. It was the Antiochan patriarch Cyril V al-Za'īm (1672-1720) who formally submitted to the papal see in 1718. At the death of the Patriarch Athanasius al-Dabbās in 1724, two patriarchs of the See of Antioch were proclaimed within a week of each other: in Damascus a nephew of the Metropolitan of Sidon and Tyre Euthymius al-Ṣayfī, the pro-Latin Seraphim Ṭānās (not al-Ṣayfī), was invested on September 20, 1724, confirmed by the Ottoman governor, and took the name Cyril, while in Constantinople the candidate of Mount Athos, Silvester the Cypriot, was consecrated patriarch by the oecumenical synod on September 27, 1724. Armed with an imperial decree, Silvester had Cyril deposed from the patriarchal seat in Damascus, and Cyril fled, taking refuge with Emir Ḥaydar in the Lebanon, later settling in the monastery near Ṣaydā that his uncle the Metropolitan Euthymius had built in 1710 (not 1725 as Mishāqa writes). The legal battles between the Orthodox and Uniates for control of local churches and church property continued well into the nineteenth century. The uniate Greek Catholics, or Melkites, were not recognized as a separate *millet* by the Ottomans until 1839. See Mīkhā'īl Burayk, *Tārīkh al-Shām* (Damascus: Dār Qutayba, 1982), pp. 19ff. and Robert M. Haddad, "The Orthodox Patriarchate of Antioch and the Origins of the Melkite Schism," Harvard University Ph.D. dissertation, 1965.

10. Psalm 5:7.

11. As a youth Aḥmad Pasha came from Bosnia to Constantinople and was taken into the service of the *ma'jūn āghāsī*, one of the commissioners of the Royal Kitchen. When the vizier Ḥakīmzāda 'Alī Pasha went to Egypt, he was accompanied by the young Aḥmad, who there joined the service of 'Abdullāh Bey, the Custodian of the Cairo Citadel. After killing one of the custodian's *mamlūks*, he took refuge with Ṣāliḥ Bey, who held most of Egypt at that time. Aḥmad Pasha's soubriquet, *al-Jazzār* ("the Butcher"), was earned for his rigor in exacting revenge on the Hanādī bedouins for their murder of his old master when he served as *mutasallim* in the Buḥayra region in Egypt under Zulfiqār Kāshif. See Ḥaydar Aḥmad, *al-Ghurar*, i, 74, 96; Muḥammad Thurayyā, *Sijill-i 'Uthmānī*, I, 277.

12. A good deal of legend has accumulated on Aḥmad Pasha's early years. According to some sources, "a Christian Bosnian by birth, Aḥmad committed a sex crime when a boy, fled to Constantinople [and] sold himself to a Jewish slave dealer" (Hitti, *History of Syria*, p. 689).

13. The Mameluks of Egypt are referred to by Mishāqa as "the Ghuzz," i.e., the Oghuz tribe, a historical misnomer. Ḥaydar Aḥmad gives the following as a short sketch of the history of Ottoman Egypt: "When His Majesty our lord Sultan Selim conquered Egypt [in 1517] and ended the reign of the Circassian

Mameluks, killing their sultan Qānṣawh al-Ghūrī and his offspring, he left to protect the region seven bands of the imperial troops called Janissaries. Over each group he set a leader called *katkhudā*, and Egypt was divided among these seven groups . . . The *katkhudā*s ruled Egypt from father to son until there appeared Ibrāhīm Katkhudā, who held precedence over the others, and he acquired mameluks until he had many of them. When it was time to collect imperial taxes, he gave his mameluks banners and sent them out into the Egyptian countryside to gather taxes. A banner is called *sanjaq* in Turkish, and in Egypt a person before whom a banner is carried is called a *sanjaq* . . . After [Ibrāhīm's] death [the mameluks] took over, gained control of Egypt, banished the Janissary bands, seized the reigns of power district by district and province by province and divided the region amongst themselves and 14 *sanjaq*s. Outstanding among them was Ṣāliḥ Bey, who gained ascendency over them and ruled alone . . . After Ṣāliḥ Bey, his mameluk 'Alī Bey took over and gained great fame" (Ḥaydar Aḥmad, *al-Ghurar*, i, 81f).

14. Attributed by Ḥaydar Aḥmad to Ilyās Adda (*al-Ghurar*, ii, 409).

15. Attributed by Ḥaydar Aḥmad to Niqūlā al-Turk (*al-Ghurar*, ii, 410).

16. Ḥaydar Aḥmad makes no mention of this incident. He says that Aḥmad Bey al-Jazzār fled Egypt after having seen Ṣāliḥ Bey struck down in cold blood by Muḥammad Bey Abū'l-Dhahab and realizing that his turn was soon to come. The Mameluk Emir 'Alī Bey is said to have killed many *sanjaq*s, emirs and military men after Aḥmad Bey had fled; the incident may have been misattributed to al-Jazzār. See Ḥaydar Aḥmad, *al-Ghurar*, i, 75f.

17. According to Ḥaydar Aḥmad (*al-Ghurar*, i, 92, 96), he arrived in A.H. 1185 (1771-72) and was accompanied only by his mameluk Salīm and his slave Abū'l-Mawt.

18. *Kākhya* (Turkish *kâhya* and *kethuda*, from the Persian *kadkhudā*), steward and manager of affairs.

19. Crimean Tatars were generally used as couriers. The Qapūjī Bāshī (*kapıcıbaşı*) was chief guard of the Harem; the Silāḥshūr [not "shilaḥshūr" as in text] was a title, given in the early Ottoman period to the Household Guard, that later became honorary; the Bustānjī Bāshī (*bostancıbaşı*) was head of the Garden Guard; see Gibb & Bowen, *Islamic Society and the West*, I, i, 87.

20. The "seraglio" (*sarāy*, also familiar in the French spelling, serail) was the provincial seat of imperial government and residence of the governor.

21. The physician was a Christian: the expression is a euphemism for alcohol, which is not permitted to Muslims, i.e., other than Christians.

22. See Appendix A.

23. The officer in charge of a North African troop in Shaykh Ẓāhir's service was Aḥmad Āghā al-Dangizlī (Denizli). When the Ottoman admiral Ḥasan Pasha brought the Ottoman fleet to drive Shaykh Ẓāhir from Acre, Denizli bribed the admiral to use his influence to obtain a pardon for Shaykh Ẓāhir. However, Ibrāhīm al-Ṣabbāgh persuded Shaykh Ẓāhir to fight, and Denizli withdrew his men from the defense because his arrangement with Ḥasan Pasha had been violated. According to Ḥaydar Aḥmad (*al-Ghurar*, i, 111ff.), it was Denizli's North Africans who killed Shaykh Ẓāhir in 1189/1775.

24. Reading *bak* with the MS.

25. Muḥammad Bey Abū'l-Dhahab had driven his old master 'Alī Bey from Egypt, and 'Alī Bey had taken refuge with Shaykh Ẓāhir al-'Umar in Acre. Abū'l-Dhahab managed to trick 'Alī Bey into crossing the border of Egypt at al-'Arīsh, where Abū'l-Dhahab was waiting for him and took him prisoner, shortly after which 'Alī Bey died. To punish Shaykh Ẓāhir for his support of 'Alī Bey, Abū'l-Dhahab got permission to invade Palestine from the Sublime Porte, which was worried over Shaykh Ẓāhir's alliance with the Muscovite fleet at Cyprus. After taking Jaffa, he advanced on Acre, and Shaykh Ẓāhir fled to Jabal al-Rīḥān for safety. Abū'l-Dhahab seems to have died of an apoplectic fit, which was attributed to his destruction of the monasteries of Ḥannā and Mār Ilyās in Ṣafad. After Abū'l-Dhahab's death, Shaykh Ẓāhir returned to Acre, whence he was driven out by the Qāpūdhān Bāshī Ḥasan Pasha and killed, as related previously. See Ḥaydar Aḥmad, *al-Ghurar*, i, 108ff.

26. *Arbāb al-qalam*, the traditional name for the clerical class. Military people were classed as *arbāb al-sayf*, "masters of the sword."

27. Tersâne (or "Tarskhāna" as spelled by Mishāqa), the section of Istanbul on the Golden Horn where the admiralty was located.

28. The chronogram (*wa-aḍḥā bihi Ismā'īl masjūnā*) yields 1203; Ḥaydar Aḥmad (*al-Ghurar*, ii, 426) gives the poem with the correct reading, *biki* instead of *bihi*, totaling 1219.

29. According to Muḥammad Thurayyā (*Sijill-i 'Uthmānī*, I, 277) he was appointed *muḥāfiẓ* of the Beirut coast with the rank of *mīrmīrān* in 1187/1773-4, was awarded the rank of *beylerbeyi* in 1189/1775 and, with the defeat of Shaykh Ẓāhir al-'Umar, was made *vâli* of Ṣaydā in Dhū'l-Ḥijja of that same year (December 1775). In 1199/1785 he was appointed *vâli* of Damascus, and in Jum. II 1201 (March 1787) he was reappointed *vâli* of Ṣaydā. According to Ḥaydar Aḥmad (*al-Ghurar*, i, 98f., 115f.), some time elapsed between the time Aḥmad Āghā was in Beirut under Emir Yūsuf and the time he was made governor of Ṣaydā. After fortifying Beirut, he was asked by Emir Yūsuf to abandon his post but refused; Emir Yūsuf was forced to ask Shaykh Ẓāhir al-'Umar to summon a Muscovite fleet from Cyprus to get Aḥmad Āghā out of Beirut. Finally, after four months of siege, Aḥmad Āghā sought quarter from Shaykh Ẓāhir and left Beirut for Acre, where he was employed as a tax collector by Shaykh Ẓāhir. After gathering the taxes of the region, he absconded with the revenues to Damascus, where he was gladly received by the governor, 'Uthmān Pasha al-Miṣrī, who despised Shaykh Ẓāhir. Thereafter Aḥmad Āghā went to Constantinople, became an Ottoman and was made governor of Afyūn in Qarāḥiṣār. At the beginning of Sultan 'Abdul-Ḥamīd I's reign (1774-89) he was appointed governor of Ṣaydā [i.e., in 1775].

30. Reading, with MS, *li-i'rāḍ*.

31. The Kharrūb region, as it is generally spelled and pronounced today, is consistently given its classical spelling by Mishāqa as "Kharnūb." See Anīs Frayḥa, *Mu'jam asmā' al-mudun wa'l-qurā al-lubnāniyya* (Beirut: Maktabat Lubnān, 1972), p. 64.

32. Emir Ḥaydar, son of Emir Mūsā of Ḥāṣbayyā, was chosen Emir of Mount Lebanon after the death of his cousin, Emir Bashīr I, who ruled from 1697 to 1705. Bashīr of the House of Shihāb had been elected emir after the

death of his maternal uncle, Emir Aḥmad of the House of Ma'n, who died in 1697 without issue, ending the line of Ma'n emirs who had long ruled the mountain.

33. Damascus surrendered to Khālid in September 635. See Philip K. Hitti, *History of Syria* (London: Macmillan, 1951), p. 414.

34. This was Emir Bashīr son of Emir Najm of Ḥāṣbayyā and brother of Emir Ismā'īl, then ruling emir of Hāṣbayyā. See Appendix C.

35. The gradual conversion of the Shihābī emirs to Maronite Christianity began with the sons of Emir Mulḥim. Emir Bashīr II was born Christian, but he concealed his religion so effectively that during his rule Ottoman officialdom never actually knew what he was, though they suspected him of being Christian. Various branches of the family had remained Sunni Muslim, while others either had become Druze or were so closely identified with the Druze that they were assumed to have adopted the religion.

36. *'Uqqāl* (sing. *'āqil*), Druze presbyters who have reached a certain stage of initiation into the Druze religion.

37. I.e., a liegeman of the House of 'Abdul-Malik.

38. The French invasion of Egypt actually occurred in 1798. Mishāqa may have miscalculated from the Islamic year.

39. Reading, with MS, *fī makhālib* for the *bi-jānib* of the text.

40. Reading, with MS, *fa-na'rifuh.*

41. Portion between asterisks is from MS for lacuna in the text.

42. Text and MS have *LYDR'W'*: read *li-yudārū.*

43. Portion between asterisks is from the MS for lacuna in the text.

44. Jarjūra is a diminutive of Jirjis.

45. Reading, with the MS, *ukhtahumā.*

46. *Laylan* added in margin of the MS.

47. *Jizya*, the poll-tax paid by non-Muslims.

48. Koran 2:14.

49. Portion between asterisks taken from the MS.

50. Such address by the ruling emir entitles the recipient to the hereditary title of shaykh.

51. The Jumblāṭ clan originated with Jān-Pūlād, an Ayyubid Kurd who was made ruler of Killis, north of Aleppo, in 1572. The name Jān-Pūlād was corrupted to Janbulāṭ, then Jumblāṭ, the form in which it is familiar today. The first Jumblāṭ in the Lebanon was Jān-Pūlād b. Sa'īd, a descendant of the original Jān-Pūlād who came to Beirut in 1630 and served the Ma'n emir Fakhr al-Dīn II. His son 'Alī married the daughter of Shaykh Qablān al-Qāḍī al-Tanūkhī, the headman of the Shūf. When the shaykh died in 1712 without an heir, 'Alī was elected to succeed him in his fiefs. It was he who granted the land for the Greek Catholic Dayr al-Mukhalliṣ. See Ṭannūs al-Shidyāq, *Akhbār al-a'yān*, pp. 136f., 141f.

52. The 'Imād clan originated with 'Imād and his brothers, Sirḥāl (or variously, Sirḥān) and Abū-'Adhrā, who came to the Lebanon in the 16th century from al-'Imādiyya near Mosul. At the end of the 18th century, a quarrel between Qāsim 'Abdul-Salām al-'Imād and Shaykh 'Alī Jumblāṭ led to the division of the Druze into Jumblāṭī and Yazbakī factions. The Yazbakī faction, led by the 'Imād clan, included the Talḥūq and 'Abdul-Malik clans. See Ṭannūs

al-Shidyāq, *Akhbār al-a'yān*, pp. 158ff.

53. The Abū-Nakad shaykhs trace their ancestry to an Arab tribe that left the Arabian Peninsula at the time of the conquest of Egypt and North Africa. They lived in Morocco for many centuries, where they became known as the Banū-Nakad. In 1120, when Emir Ma'n al-Ayyūbī came to the Shūf, they joined him and served the House of Ma'n until its demise, after which they gave their allegiance to the House of Shihāb. See Ṭannūs al-Shidyāq, *Akhbār al-a'yān*, pp. 166ff.

54. Reading with MS. *yuḥāribunā* for the *nuḥāribuhā* of the text.

55. MS has *al-qurbān* ("the mass") for the *al-qur'ān* of the printed text.

56. MS has *dīniyya* ("religious"); printed text and margin of MS have *daqīqa* ("precise").

57. *Kharāj*, normally the land tax, is used loosely here for the poll-tax.

58. According to Ḥaydar Aḥmad (*al-Ghurar al-hisān*, p. 183), the massacre took place in February 1797, and there were not six but five Abū-Nakads killed, Shaykh Bashīr, Shaykh Wākid, Shaykh Sīd-Aḥmad, Shaykh Qāsim and Shaykh Murād. Afterwards the Nakad seat at 'Abayh was attacked and plundered. The remaining members of the family fled to Wādī Maghdalā, where they were apprehended and thrown into prison at Dayr al-Qamar, only to be murdered by 'Imāds. The women and a few small children escaped to Damascus with Shaykh Salmān Abī-Nakad, and thus, says Emir Ḥaydar, "the name of the House of Abū-Nakad was effaced."

59. The *jawālī* was a head tax imposed on Christians and Jews; the *farīda* was a head tax imposed on all adult males.

60. The *mālikāna* lease, introduced at the end of the seventeenth century, gave a contractor a life interest in the revenue he could realize from the land he leased. This type of lease was originally intended to eliminate some of the abuses of year-by-year tax-farming, when tax-farmers, having only a limited interest in the holding, would make every effort to squeeze as much as possible from a lease in one year. See Gibb & Bowen, *Islamic Society and the West*, I, ii, 22f.

61. Reading *ṣūratī* from the MS for the *khilqatī* of the text.

PART TWO: 1804-1820

1. The governorship of Damascus carried with it the prestigious title and office of Mīr al-Ḥajj (superintendent of the pilgrimage), who was charged with making all necessary preparations for and escorting the annual pilgrim caravan from Damascus to Mecca.

2. Portion between asterisks taken from the MS for the lacuna of the text.

3. The standard gesture of acceptance of written orders from a superior.

4. The local pronunciation and spelling of Bayt al-Dīn.

5. A large curved knife.

6. Joseph Jérôme le Français de Lalande (1732-1807). His *Astronomie* was published in Paris in 1764.

7. Psalm 19:1.

8. *'Askar muntaẓam*, i.e. troops trained and drilled in the European manner,

unlike the older Ottoman troops organized like the Janissaries.

9. Chasseboeuf, Comte de Volney, author of *Les ruins, ou Méditations sur les révolutions des empires*; Tadmur is the site of Palmyra.

10. An instrument like a dulcimer, played with picks.

11. The two traditional divisions of the sciences, *naqlī* (traditional, or accepted by tradition) and *'aqlī* (rational, or accepted by demonstrative proof). The *naqlī*, or "Arabic", sciences include grammar, philology, exegesis, prosody, etc.; the *'aqlī*, or "Greek", sciences include mathematics, physics, astronomy, philosophy, etc.

12. The shaykh is using the language of Sufism. He means those who have been initiated into the inner (*bāṭin*) meaning that lies behind the external manifestation of a phenomenon.

13. A reference to the story of Moses and Khiḍr (Koran 18:60-82), in which the figure universally identified as Khiḍr performs three seemingly outrageous acts, to each of which Moses objects violently. In the end Khiḍr explains his actions, the esoteric significance of which Moses had been unaware.

14. Portion between asterisks taken from MS for lacuna in text.

PART THREE: 1820-1830

1. Proverbs 9:8.

2. "Christ is risen," the customary greeting during Eastertide.

3. The reforms, known as the Tanẓīmāt, were first promulgated by Sultan 'Abdul-Majīd in 1839.

4. Portion between asterisks taken from MS for lacuna in the text.

5. Koran 9:29.

6. Matthew 10:33.

7. Matthew 10:28, Luke 12:4. Portion between asterisks taken from MS for lacuna in the text.

8. *Ṭābiyya*, a turban that formed part of the Maronite priestly garb.

9. Bahā' al-Dīn al-'Āmilī (1546-1622) was a great polymath of the Safavid period in Iran. A Shi'ite scholar who came from Jabal al-'Āmil in the south of Lebanon, he was celebrated principally as a theologian and jurist, though he was also learned in mathematics and medicine. His compendium on mathematics, *Khulāṣat al-ḥisāb*, became a standard work in the late medieval period.

10. From the MS.

11. The Yazīdīs are a highly syncretistic sect in Kurdistan whose doctrines have been so misunderstood by others that they are generally considered to worship the devil. When applied by Muslims and Christians to others, the term "Yazīdī" is highly derogatory.

12. Portion between asterisks taken from MS. for lacuna in text.

13. Apparently "Abū-Ibrāhīm" is Jirjis Mishāqa. In the text he is referred to as *wālid Ibrāhīm* until the end of the section, where he is called Abū-Ibrāhīm, the normal form.

14. From MS for lacuna in text.

15. Text has 1826, clearly a misprint. The year A.H. 1240 began in

August 1824.

16. This attack took place in January 1825. See Ḥaydar Aḥmad, *al-Ghurar*, p. 766.

17. Emirs Ḥasan and Ḥusayn were killed by their cousins in Rajab 1240 (Feb. 1825). See Ḥaydar Aḥmad, *al-Ghurar*, p. 776.

18. I.e., *kākhya*, see part i, note 18.

19. See part i, note 60.

PART FOUR: 1831-1840

1. The Egyptian siege of Acre began on November 23, 1831.

2. Ḥaydar Aḥmad gives the text of Ibrāhīm Pasha's address, which is dated the 22nd of Dhū'l-Ḥijja (*al-Ghurar*, p. 850).

3. The 27th of Dhū'l-Ḥijja is given by Ḥaydar Aḥmad as the date of the fall of Acre (*al-Ghurar*, p. 851). Other sources give May 27, 1832; see Kamal S. Salibi, *The Modern History of Lebanon* (London: Weidenfeld and Nicolson, 1965), p. 29.

4. Text has *wa'l-Ḥabasha* ("and Ethiopia"). Ḥaydar Aḥmad (*al-Ghurar*, p. 853) gives the texts of Ibrāhīm Pasha's reports, which are signed "Vāli of Jidda and the Hejaz," which he was.

5. Also known as 'Alī Pasha.

6. Arabic style, hours are counted from sunrise.

7. Colonel Sèves, a Napoleonic officer who organized Muḥammad-'Alī Pasha's army and was given the title Sulaymān Pasha.

8. The Lijāh, known to the ancient world as Trachon, is a vast lava stream south of Damascus.

9. *Jāhil* (lit. "ignorant"), an ordinary Druze who has not undergone the necessary instruction to become *'āqil* (lit. "rational," an initiate).

10. In the text Mishāqa explains the transformation of the Arabic word *kharā* ("shit") into *ḥazā* by moving the dot from the first letter to the second. *Qurūn* ("horns") and *qiṭṭ* ("cat") are vulgarisms for male and female genitalia.

11. By Islamic law a divorced wife may be remarried to the same man, either immediately or after an intermediate marriage to someone else, depending upon the circumstances of the divorce. By "more than one wife," Mishāqa probably means more than one wife at a time, in contradistinction to Islamic law, which allows up to four legal wives at one time.

12. In Islamic law property may not be alienated from the heirs, whose shares are stipulated by Koranic legislation.

13. Apparently a diminutive of Yasū', Jesus.

14. Sir Moses Montefiore, 1784-1885, a wealthy British stockbroker who received a baronetcy in 1846 for humanitarian efforts on behalf of his fellow Jews overseas (*Encyclopedia Judaica*, vol. 12, pp. 270-75).

15. Sir Richard Wood, 1806-1900, was a dragoman to the British Embassy in Constantinople in 1834, employed in Syria in 1832-33 and 1835-36, appointed British consul in Damascus in May 1841, and agent and consul general in Tunis in 1833-79. Obituary in the *Times*, August 8, 1900, p. 3.

16. The Convention of London by Great Britain, Austria, Prussia, Russia

and Turkey for the pacification of the Levant was signed on July 15, 1840.

17. Having a light complexion and hair (*ashqar*) is commonly thought to indicate bad temper.

18. Text has Baḥrī Bey, an obvious error.

PART FIVE: 1840-1873

1. Safranbolu (Za'farānbūl) is directly north of Ankara in Anatolia, not far from the Black Sea coast.

2. In 1946 Emir Bashīr's remains were removed from Istanbul and deposited in the family vault in Bayt al-Dīn.

3. From here to next asterisk deleted from printed text.

4. From context, the text has been emended to read: *nādā aḥaduhum 'alā Ibrāhīm.*

5. More properly "ossuary"; as in Greece and other rocky mountainous regions, desiccated bones are removed from the ground and placed in ossuaries, called *khashkhāshe* pl. *khshākhīsh.*

6. The plan for the administration of the Lebanon, suggested by the Austrian Prince Metternich and implemented at the beginning of 1843, is known as the double kaymakamate: the northern district was administered by a Maronite district governor, or *qāymaqām*, and the southern district by a Druze. The first *qāymaqām*s were Ḥaydar Abū'l-Lam' for the north and Aḥmad Arslān for the south. See Salibi, *Lebanon*, p. 63.

7. From here to end omitted from the printed text. Page numbers in brackets refer to pages in the Beirut MS.

8. In a letter to Mr. [Eli] Smith, an American missionary, dated October 1844, in the possession of Dr. Assad Rustom, Mishāqa says the following: "It is not unknown to you that my means of livelihood were from three sources: first, 7000 piastres paid to me annually by His Excellency Emir Sa'd al-Dīn; second, a few feddans of cattle in the Ḥūle region, exempt from taxation by the above-mentioned emirs; and third, from the practice of medicine. Now, in view of the present situation in Ḥāṣbayyā, I have given up hope altogether of the emirs, and the practice of medicine is not sufficient for my livelihood in this city, so I shall have to abandon that and find some other type of work. What I have found to be most suitable is the commerce of buying and selling and accepting deposits, but I do not possess enough capital to enable to me to live from the profits alone. Therefore, I have gone into partnership with one of my brethren, Khawāja Ilyās Abū-Qāsim, who is extremely honest and experienced in this line. We have written to our brethren in Beirut and elsewhere in this regard through our brother Ibrāhīm, and we hope for great success, with God's help and that of our brethren, along with the assistance of our exalted consul in this regard . . . " (introduction to Beirut edition of *Muntakhabāt min al-Jawāb &c.*, p. viii). Mishāqa continues, asking Mr. Smith to assist him with recommendations for commissions among the European community.

9. Alexander Keith's book appeared under various titles (*Evidence of the Truth &c.* and *The Evidence of Prophecy*) in various editions, beginning in 1833.

10. This treatise was translated by Eli Smith and published in the *Journal of the American Oriental Society*, 1 (1847): pp. 171-217.

11. Emir 'Abdul-Qādir of Algeria (1808-83) was proclaimed Sultan of the Arabs in Algeria in 1832. In 1837 he obtained the province of Oran and part of Algiers by treaty with the French, against whom he led a resistance until 1847, when he surrendered to the Duc d'Aumale and was taken to France. In 1852 he was released by Louis-Napoleon and settled in Damascus in 1855, where he lived the rest of his life.

12. Number in the MS is illegible; according to the dates given on MS p. 351, Monday should have been the 10th.

13. *Sarākī*, sing. *sarkī*, from the Turkish *sergi*, a type of voucher redeemable against taxes.

14. *Awrāq konsuliyya* (?); MS is not clear.

APPENDIX A: TERMS AND TITLES

1. See Gibb & Bowen, *Islamic Society and the West*, I, ii, 86.
2. See Gibb & Bowen, *Islamic Society and the West*, I, i, 198.

Bibliography

Aḥmad al-Budayrī al-Ḥallāq. *Ḥawādith Dimashq al-yawmiyya: 1154-1175h 1741-1762m.* Recension by Muḥammad Sa'īd al-Qāsimī. Edited by Aḥmad 'Izzat 'Abd al-Karīm. Cairo: Maṭba'at Lajnat al-Bayān al-'Arabī, 1959.

Aḥmad Rāsim. *Rasmlī va kharīṭalī 'uthmānlī tārīkhī.* 4 vols. Constantinople: Maṭba'a-i Abū'l-Ḍiyā, 1326-28.

Anonymous. *Ḥurūb Ibrāhīm Bāshā al-miṣrī fī Sūriyya wa'l-Anāḍol.* Edited by Asad Rustum. Heliopolis: al-Maṭba'a al-Sūriyya, 1927.

Baedeker, Karl. *Konstantinopel, Balkanstaaten, Kleinasien, Archipel, Cypern.* Leipzig: Karl Baedeker, 1914.

———. *Palestine and Syria.* New York: Charles Scribner's Sons, 1912.

Barbir, Karl K. *Ottoman Rule in Damascus, 1708-1758.* Princeton: Princeton University Press, 1980.

Barthélemy, Adrien. *Dictionnaire arabe-français: Dialectes de Syrie: Alep, Damas, Liban, Jérusalem.* Paris: Paul Geuthner, 1935-69.

Çağatay, Neş'et. "Osmanlı Ímparatorluğunda reayadan alınan vergi ve resimler." *Ankara Üniversitesi Dil ve Tarih-Coğrafya Fakültesi Dergisi* 5 (1947): 483-511.

Crawford, Mary B. "Dr. Meshaka." *The Women's Missionary Magazine of the United Presbyterian Church* 3, no. 5 (Dec. 1889): 1-5.

Fleischer, H. O. "Über das syrische Fürstenhaus der Benû-Schihâb." *Zeitschrift der Deutschen Morgenländischen Gesellschaft* 5 (1851): 46-59.

Frayḥa, Anīs. *Mu'jam asmā' al-mudun wa'l-qurā al-lubnāniyya.* Beirut: Maktabat Lubnān, 1972.

Gibb, H. A. R., and Harold Bowen. *Islamic Society and the West.* Volume One. 2 parts. London: Oxford University Press, 1963-65.

Haddad, Robert M. "The Orthodox Patriarchate of Antioch and the Origins of the Melkite Schism." Ph.D. dissertation, Harvard University, 1965.

———. *Syrian Christians in Muslim Society: An Interpretation.* Princeton: Princeton University Press, 1970.

Harik, Iliya F. *Politics and Change in a Traditional Society: Lebanon, 1711-1845.* Princeton: Princeton Unviersity Press, 1968.

Ḥasan Āghā al-'Abd. *Tārīkh Ḥasan Āghā al-'Abd.* Edited by Yūsuf Nu'aysa. Damascus: Wizārat al-Thaqāfa, 1979.

Ḥaydar Aḥmad al-Shihābī. *al-Ghurar al-ḥisān fī tawārīkh ḥawādith al-azmān.* Edited by Asad Rustum and Fouad E. Boustany as *Lubnān fī 'ahd al-umarā' al-shihābiyyīn.* 3 parts. Beirut: Imprimerie Catholique, 1933. Reprint. Beirut: al-Jāmi'a al-Lubnāniyya, 1969.

———. *Tārīkh al-Amīr Ḥaydar Aḥmad al-Shihābī.* Edited by Na'ūm Mughabghab. Cairo: Maṭba'at al-Salām, 1900.

Hitti, Philip K. *History of Syria.* London: Macmillan & Co., 1951.

Hourani, Albert. *Political Society in Lebanon: A Historical Introduction.* Cambridge: Center for International Studies, Massachusetts Institute of Technology, 1986.

Jessup, Henry Harris. *Fifty-Three Years in Syria.* London and Edinburgh: Fleming H. Revell Co., n.d.

Lockroy, Édouard. *Ahmed le Boucher: La Syrie et l'Égypte au XVIIIe siècle.* Paris: Paul Ollendorff, 1888.

Mīkhā'īl Burayk al-Dimashqī. *Tārīkh al-Shām: 1720-1782.* Edited by Aḥmad Ghassān Sbāno. Damascus: Dār Qutayba, 1402/1982.

Mishāqa, Mīkhā'īl. "A Treatise on Arab Music, Chiefly from a Work by Mikhāil Meshāḳah, of Damascus." Translated by Eli Smith. *Journal of the American Oriental Society* 1 (1849): 171-217.

———. "al-Jawāb 'alā iqtirāḥ al-aḥbāb." Beirut. Jafet Library, American University of Beirut. MS 956.9 M39jA.

———. *Muntakhabāt min al-jawāb 'alā iqtirāḥ al-aḥbāb.* Edited by Assad Rustom and Soubhi Abou Chacra. Ministère de l'Éducation Nationale et des Beaux-Arts, Direction des Antiquités, Textes et Documents Historiques, 2. Beirut: Catholic Press, 1955.

Muḥammad Rafīq and Muḥammad Bahjat. *Bayrūt vilāyatī.* 2 vols. N.p: Vilāyat Maṭba'asī, 1335-36.

Muḥammad Thurayyā. *Sijill-i 'uthmānī, yākhūd tadhkira-i mashāhīr-i 'uthmāniyya.* 4 vols. Istanbul: Maṭba'a-i Āmira, 1308-11.

Philipp, Thomas. "Class, Community, and Arab Historiography in the Early Nineteenth Century—The Dawn of a New Era." *International Journal of Middle East Studies* 16 (1984): 161-175.

———. *The Syrians in Egypt, 1725-1975.* Stuttgart: Franz Steiner, 1985.

Polk, W. R. *The Opening of South Lebanon, 1788-1840.* Cambridge: Harvard University Press, 1963.

Redhouse, Sir James W. *A Turkish and English Lexicon.* Istanbul: Çağrı Yayınları, 1978.

Rustum, Asad Jibrā'īl. *Al-Maḥfūẓāt al-malikiyya al-miṣriyya: bayān bi-wathā'iq al-Shām wa-mā yusā'id 'ala fahmihā wa-yūḍiḥ maqāṣid Muḥammad 'Alī al-kabīr.* Beirut: al-Maṭba'a al-Amerikiyya, 1940-43.

———. *al-Uṣūl al-'arabiyya li-tārīkh Sūriyya fī 'ahd Muḥammad-'Alī Bāshā.* Beirut: al-Maṭba'a al-Amerikiyya, 1930-34.

Salibi, Kamal S. *The Modern History of Lebanon.* London: Weidenfeld and Nicolson, 1965.

Shidyāq, Ṭannūs al-. *Akhbār al-a'yān fī jabal lubnān.* Edited by Fouad E. Boustany. Publications de l'Université Libanaise. Section des Études Historiques, 19. Beirut: Librairie Orientale, 1970.

Waldmeier, Theophilus. *Ten Years Life in Abyssinia and Sixteen Years in Syria.* London: S. W. Partridge & Co., n.d.

Wild, Stefan. *Libanesische Ortsnamen: Typologie und Deutung.* Beiruter Texte und Studien, 9. Beirut, 1973.

Zaydān, Jurjī. *Tarājim mashāhīr al-sharq fī 'l-qarn al-tāsi' 'ashar.* Beirut: Maktabat al-Khayyāṭ, n.d.

Index